Digital Imagery and Informational Graphics in E-Learning:
Maximizing Visual Technologies

Shalin Hai-Jew
Kansas State University, USA

INFORMATION SCIENCE REFERENCE

Hershey · New York

Director of Editorial Content: Kristin Klinger
Senior Managing Editor: Jamie Snavely
Assistant Managing Editor: Michael Brehm
Publishing Assistant: Sean Woznicki
Typesetter: Kurt Smith, Sean Woznicki
Cover Design: Lisa Tosheff
Printed at: Yurchak Printing Inc.

Published in the United States of America by
      Information Science Reference (an imprint of IGI Global)
      701 E. Chocolate Avenue
      Hershey PA 17033
      Tel: 717-533-8845
      Fax: 717-533-8661
      E-mail: cust@igi-global.com
      Web site: http://www.igi-global.com/reference

Library of Congress Cataloging-in-Publication Data

Hai-Jew, Shalin.
  Digital imagery and informational graphics in E-learning : maximizing visual technologies / by Shalin Hai-Jew.
    p. cm.

  Includes bibliographical references and index.
  Summary: "The information contained within this book will show that although the development and selection of instructional materials is generally done towards the end of the instructional design process, it must be viewed in a more inclusive way in that the visuals themselves may affect many other components of the educational design"--Provided by publisher.

  ISBN 978-1-60566-972-4 (hardcover) -- ISBN 978-1-60566-973-1 (ebook) 1.
Instructional systems--Design. 2. Image processing--Digital techniques. 3.
Computer-assisted instruction. 4. Educational technology. I. Title.
  LB1028.38.H35 2010
  371.33'466--dc22
                2009021596

British Cataloguing in Publication Data
A Cataloguing in Publication record for this book is available from the British Library.

Table of Contents

Section 1
Laying the Groundwork for Digital Imagery

Section 4
Guiding Values in Digital Imagery

Chapter 12
Designing Informational Graphics for a Global Multi-Cultural Context

Chapter 13
Applied Ethics for Digital Imagery

Section 5
Looking Ahead to a Shimmering Digital Future

Foreword

The deeper one gets into educational theory and pedagogical techniques the more one needs to remember the importance of the simple statement "a picture is worth a thousand words." The power of this saying isn't just that in many situations a picture is actually worth a thousand words of explanation, it's that in many situations a picture (or a visual) is worth way more than thousands of words could ever be. In many cases, the graphic conveys and explains things in a way that words simply cannot fully express. Sometimes it is an emotional description, but in the educational world, many times it is the ability to explain a complex concept or process that remains abstract until, via pictures, animation, video, etc., the student can better mentally represent it.

Aside from various notions of learning styles or teaching styles, visuals can add to the whole experience of the learning event by making the subject matter more realistic and exciting, which leads to improved motivation to learn in general. Visuals with respect to e-learning are of particular importance in that instruction and learning is accomplished via means other than personal or physical interaction. With constantly improving technology and connectivity, the use of visuals should be continually re-evaluated so as to maximize their capability to enhance instruction and learning whenever possible.

The famous Chinese proverb (Confucius 551-479 BC) "I hear and I forget; I see and I remember; I do and I understand," really brings the importance of visuals to light. Modern research continues to move beyond the understanding that relevant images presented with text does produce an illustrative effect that generally enhances comprehension and learning. Current research is now focusing more on what types of visuals work best and in what circumstances. Many other considerations must also be looked at such as the student's ability to comprehend the visuals, prior learning (knowledge base), the ability to acquire or create the visuals, how the visuals will be accessed and used by the student, as well as the subject matter itself. With carefully selected and utilized visuals in place, the facilitation of higher order processing and connections occurs so that the information learned moves beyond short term memory or "learning for now," into long term memory and true understanding.

Newer visual technologies are allowing the student to actually be part of the process in a more active and dynamic use of visuals. Immersive environments and choice-directed videos are allowing students to explore more possibilities dealing with the subject matter. Technologies such as Linden Lab's Second Life™ (SL) and other virtual reality engines are taking the concept of visuals to a completely new level. "I do and I understand," is now actually being accomplished with visuals, through the use of avatars and virtual worlds with unlimited educational possibilities.

As an electronic media coordinator, I have personally worked with the author in the digitization, creation and manipulation of many types of visuals to be used by professors. I have personally observed that many times a professor has a sense that it is important to have the same visuals as used in on-campus courses but doesn't understand how to best translate it into an e-learning environment. One answer isn't always the best answer in that different situations call for different solutions. Sometimes a high-resolution photograph is better than video; sometimes, it isn't. Sometimes a video is better than a Flash simulation, sometimes it isn't. Sometimes, a fully immersive virtual environment would be overkill when a simple diagram would do. Additionally, as an instructor in the military, I have seen how sometimes concepts are not understood by soldiers until a step back is taken, so that soldiers can visualize the whole picture instead of just one specific component. Digital graphics such as those explained in this book were used to improve understanding and performance. Knowing that the use of visuals is of great benefit is only part of fully understanding the concept of the proper use of visuals in education as a whole.

This book brings to light many important aspects of visuals. Vital answers to the questions of why, how and where to use visuals will be presented so that the true value of different types of graphics can be utilized. The information contained within this book will show that although the development and selection of instructional materials is generally done towards the end of the instructional design process, it must be viewed in a more inclusive way in that the visuals themselves may affect many other components of the educational design. The type, quality and degree of visuals used can affect everything from how the course will be conducted to how the assessments will be done. This informative book will guide you in understanding visuals and properly incorporating them within your educational presentations and endeavors.

Brent A. Anders
Kansas State University, USA
Sergeant First Class, Senior Instructor, Army National Guard

Preface

THE ORIGIN OF THIS BOOK

The idea for *Digital Imagery and Informational Graphics in E-Learning: Maximizing Visual Technologies* originated with my work as an instructional designer. On a daily basis, I work with faculty members striving to create effective online learning experiences. These professors hail from a range of fields. While they bring intense expertise to their own respective areas of expertise, many also bring with them traditions in higher education. It is said that higher education is often a verbal environment—both oral and textual, and it's less visual. This tendency has carried over to e-learning. Yet, the contemporary installed-base generations of learners were raised on multimedia, digital immersiveness, and high-tech. These are people who connect through sophisticated wifi mobile communications devices. Visual thinking has become second nature for many; textual readings have receded in popularity. Digital imagery is a nexus for information, aesthetics, technology, and pedagogical design; it is ubiquitous. Its language may not be so clear to those teaching via e-learning. Words may be imagistic in a semantic way, but digital imagery embodies and communicates visual concepts directly.

Recent research includes rich findings about the human mind and visual cognition and learning—in relation to multimedia. Cognitive research has surfaced deep insights about how people perceive and use visual imagery. This research combined with pedagogical research enables visuals to more effectively introduce concepts, combine complex data streams into coherent information, and convey mental models and simulations. In situations of real-time decision-making which integrate large flows of information, dynamic digital visuals far surpass traditional images in capturing and conveying information and meaning.

E-learning deploys designed imagery for content, display, organization, interaction, branding, and navigation. Imagery allows for multiple ways of conveying information and telling a story. There are ways to create learning that has stronger retention. Informational visualization strengthens information extraction through "visual data mining" and exploratory data analysis. Images can be highly nuanced, information-full, and culturally bound; they may bridge cultural differences and maintain valuable understandings through time.

The educational technologies enabling e-learning have made it much simpler to integrate visuals and digital graphics into the learning flow. Using these technologies appropriately will involve a larger awareness of the image context for learning and also the techniques behind the uses of such technologies. While many superb graphic artists design various visuals, many non-experts have long had their hand in creating effective visuals for learning, regardless of their métier. "Those who discover an explanation are often those who construct its representation," observes Edward R. Tufte in *Visual Explanations: Images and Quantities, Evidence and Narrative*.

At the same time, the technologists in the field have enabled sophistication in creating and deploying digital imagery, which may be singular-dimensional all the way to 3D and 4D. Higher Net bandwidth has delivered ever more complex imagery, including live-rendered and multi-stream visuals. Authoring tools enable technologists and designers to actualize images for electronic and Web delivery. These artifacts are more expressive and more usable. Hardware and software advancements enable the capture, editing and publishing of rich-sensory visual data.

Digital imagery rarely exists independent of multimedia—with integrated sound and text. In higher education, it is usually integrated into an overall e-learning path. That said, there are still benefits in analyzing digital imagery as one part of the e-learning experience and as a separate facet of instructional building and design. Educators and trainers would do well to know about these changes in order to enhance their teaching and learning work.

THE COMPOSITION OF THIS BOOK

Digital Imagery and Informational Graphics in E-Learning consists of 14 chapters. The early chapters lay the groundwork for an exploration of digital imagery in e-learning. Section 1, "Laying the Groundwork for Digital Imagery," consists of two chapters. Chapter 1, "Pedagogical Theories and Research: Re: Imagery in E-Learning," explores some of the educational theories that affect the use of digital visuals in

Figure 1. The contextual focus of digital imagery and informational graphics in e-learning

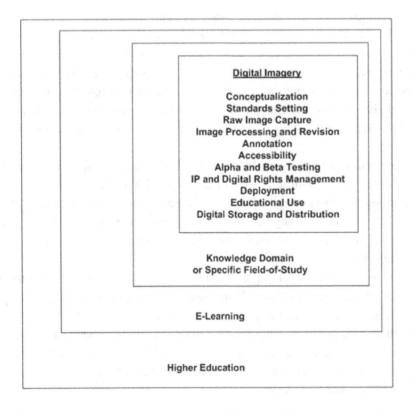

e-learning. Chapter 2, "Visual Literacy in E-Learning Instructional Design," engages concepts of visual literacy in this Digital Age, in order to help viewers understand visual information and intended (and unintended) effects. This chapter also shows the importance of accessibility in visual literacy.

The next section, "Digital Graphics in E-Learning," examines the practical application of graphics in online learning with the following chapters: Chapter 3, "The Applied Role of Graphics in E-Learning," and Chapter 4, "Types of Graphics in E-Learning." Chapter 3 deals with how graphics are currently used in e-learning. Chapter 4 introduces the wide range of digital graphics types.

The heart of this text involves the section "Designing Graphics for E-Learning." Within this are chapters that address visual design. Chapter 5, "Information and Visualization Imagery," addresses the way information and imagery are created, including those with live data streams and sophisticated user builds. Chapter 6, "Capturing and Authoring Tools for Graphics in E-Learning," highlights the functions that authoring tools enable for image captures and manipulations. Chapter 7, "Procedures for Creating Quality Imagery for E-Learning," defines quality in digital imagery in pedagogical contexts and then offers practical ways to achieve this. Chapter 8, "Building Interactive and Immersive Imagery," focuses on the creation of discovery learning, game and simulation spaces through digital imagery design. Chapter 9, "Collaborative Image Creation," describes the work of both co-located and virtual teams in creating educational images through collaborations. Chapter 10, "Effectively Integrating Graphics into E-Learning," examines strategies for integrating images—whether self-generated or inherited—into various learning situations for learning efficacy. Chapter 11, "The Storage and Access of E-Learning Visuals," looks at the repositories and digital libraries of graphical images and multimedia resources. This chapter explores the ways these storehouses are populated with contents, how they are catalogued, searched, retrieved and deployed.

The next section is "Guiding Values in Digital Imagery," and consists of two chapters. Chapter 12, "Designing Informational Graphics for a Global Multi-Cultural Context," takes a globalist view of imagery and the nuanced meanings that may be extrapolated from various images and dynamic visual interactions. Chapter 13, "Applied Ethics for Digital Imagery," provides a rich overview of ethical concerns and issues in the creation and deployment of digital imagery. This chapter offers some practical approaches to handling various ethical concerns.

The last section, "Looking Ahead to a Shimmering Digital Future," projects the changes in technologies and pedagogical approaches for the uses of digital imagery in e-learning. Chapter 14, "Future Digital Imagery," will coalesce the current research and practices in the educational and training uses of digital imagery and focus on the near-term future.

READERS OF THIS WORK

The readers of this work may be faculty and staff supporting e-learning. Technologists and instructional designers may find the text helpful, in their anticipation of the functionalities that are in research and development currently and also in maximizing existing digital imagery authoring tools and resources. Graduate students may also find this text informative for their work and studies. Knowing how to engage the e-learning technologies may enhance the creation of teaching and learning experiences online.

THE RESEARCH AND WRITING APPROACH

This text is presented as a part-handbook part-survey text, within the framework of building contents for higher educational e-learning. This was written in a general way so as to bridge many knowledge domains. The emphasis has been on practical approaches to enhance online learning and training, with the pedagogical theories as a backdrop. An assumption is that faculty and staff (technologists and instructional designers, in particular) work in a do-it-yourself (DIY) sphere as a daily reality. Continuing economic pressures have encouraged universities, colleges, departments, and programs to build their own in-house capacity to create and use digital imagery strategically for learning.

There are other texts that engage issues of multimedia design theories, specific applications of digital mediums for education, how-to books on various capturing devices and authoring tools, and theoretical works on e-learning. This book will not pursue these various lines of inquiry to the utmost. Rather, this will provide a primer approach to the complex issues of digital imagery use in e-learning with a practical and applied approach.

Purposive design effects are preferable to accidental ones, and this knowledge may empower educational practitioners. It is hoped that this text will help start more widespread academic discussions and experimentation in this area. While discussions in this area and field can get fairly complex fairly quickly, the focus here was to keep the discussions simple albeit without misrepresenting the larger complexities. A special effort was made to avoid citing software products and entities by name. Also, unique terminology from special domain fields relating to digital visuals was avoided, and a conscious effort was made to use the most widely used terminology in the most understandable way. That was in part due to the fast-changing resources in this field. Another reason is to protect the text's longevity.

Many websites could be cited as exemplars for this text. However, with the widespread flux of sites and ever-changing technologies, readers would be better served with a more solid information foundation and the encouragement to seek resources that have relevance to their particular interests and work. The affordances of the Internet and World Wide Web (WWW) are growing exponentially, and I trust that users will have the savvy to explore their interests and fulfill their digital graphics needs.

Another related caveat refers to the digital imagery in this text. The images here are necessarily 2D and 3D delivered via a 2D black-and-white paper surface, given the limited affordances of a paper book (even though it does have an electronic doppelganger). Intellectual property constraints also limited the showing of various imageries to those available by copyright release or in the public domain. I bring up these limits to encourage readers to go online to experience the digital imageries described in this text.

It is hoped that this text will be helpful to users who work in a complex and dynamic instructional design and digital e-learning environment. Suffice it to say that one doesn't know what one doesn't know about a topic at the beginning of writing a book, and now, a year later, I am a little better informed. However, it would be incautious to suggest that this is anything more than an opening salvo in this field.

Shalin Hai-Jew
Author

Acknowledgment

I'd like to thank my students through the years, who have constantly supported and challenged me to work smarter and harder. My supervisors have all encouraged intellectual adventurism and reaching beyond my then-current abilities—to good ends. Of special note are the following: Virgilio Enriquez, Connie Broughton, Guo Tao, Helen Perlo, Dr. Norma Goldstein, and Scott Finkeldei. My editors have also shaped my work through the years. I appreciate the support of John G. Fox, II, Carrie Janssen, Alan Chong Lau, Dr. Edward H. Perry, Dr. Michele L. Pilati, Paula Smith, and Nancy Hays. My faculty and administrator clients have introduced me to many worlds of knowledge and so many opportunities for learning and growth. Thanks to Tyler Heath, Rebecca Beistline, and all the others at IGI Global who made this book possible. Their responsiveness and support have made this a very adventuresome and pleasant process.

I have deep gratitude to the researchers and writers, whose works are cited here for a more holistic view, and I hope that I have accurately reflected their ideas. I am thankful to those who've contributed to this book directly: Brent A. Anders, Dr. Ramesh C. Sharma, Dr. Jason Caudill, Diana Marrs, Jason Maseberg-Tomlinson, Julia Morse, and Hattie Williams. Those who've worked long know how valuable it is to work with ethical people who have fine follow-through. Thanks also to Dr. Carol Stockdale, for her encouragement of risk-taking and change at a critical moment.

For R. Max.

Section 1
Laying the Groundwork for Digital Imagery

Chapter 1
Pedagogical Theories and Research:
Re: Imagery in E-Learning

ABSTRACT

Some pedagogical theories and research have direct application to the use of digital imagery in electronic learning (e-learning). Applied perceptional research forms a foundational understanding of how humans see through their eyes. Cognitive theories address how the mind handles visual information. Pedagogical theories provide understandings of how individuals process information and learn effectively. These concepts lead to applied uses of digital imagery in e-learning contexts. These principles and practices will be introduced, analyzed, and evaluated in the context of the creation and use of digital imageries in e-learning. Then, strategies for how to apply theory to the selection, creation, and deployment of digital imagery in e-learning will be proposed.

CHAPTER OBJECTIVES

- Provide an overview of the relevant perceptual theories
- Present an overview of the relevant pedagogical theories
- Summarize the applied research and findings related to visual imagery in e-learning
- Identify some areas for further theory development and research

INTRODUCTION

This short chapter addresses the uses of digital imagery in electronic learning (e-learning). Digital imagery is multi-dimensional, information-rich and purposive. They are designed for particular aims in particular learning domains and contexts, and for defined learners.

DOI: 10.4018/978-1-60566-972-4.ch001

A foundational understanding of applied pedagogical theories may inform the planning, creation, development, handling, use and storage of digital imageries. These theories focus on human perception at a foundational level; this is critical because imagery is sensory—and understanding the underlying sensory mechanisms will enhance strategies to develop visuals. The psycho-physical phenomena of how reflected frequencies translate into a meaningful visual image is not fully understood ("Electromagnetic spectrum," Dec. 2008, n.p.), but what is known should be employed. Human cognition, particularly visual learning, visual working memory and visual long-term memory, will enhance understandings of how the mind processes learning that involves visuals.

Various learning principles and conceptualizations that provide strategic direction for digital imagery creation follows. The diversity of these ideas results because of the juncture of visuals, e-learning, technologies, and the human learner in this topic. These include ideas of the importance of an imagistic learning context or environment, based on situated cognition, adult learning theory, and constructivism. From these concepts, there are spinoffs to applied uses of digital imagery in self discovery learning, problem-based learning, case studies, and co-created emergent curriculums. This is not a comprehensive conceptualization, but rather an attempt to capture some of the most salient ideas in practice currently.

AN OVERVIEW OF RELEVANT PERCEPTIONAL AND PEDAGOGICAL THEORIES

A simple visualization of the approach in this chapter follows in "Applicable Pedagogical Theories and Research related to Digital Imagery in E-Learning." The foundational structure is built on applied perceptional research, which draws from human perception, visual cognition, and visual memory. Built on the perception is cognition, or how the human behind handles information. Pedagogical theories comprise the next layer up, and at the top are the applied uses of digital imagery in e-learning contexts.

More pedagogical theories and research factors may be added, but Figure 1 is an early diagram to provide an approach to conceptualizing how theories and research relate to digital imagery in e-learning. Applied research with live learners has contributed further insights into professional uses of digital imagery in e-learning. These findings will also be addressed briefly.

This section will begin with the foundational level of the perceptional and pedagogical theories related to the use of digital imagery in e-learning and then progress to build further understandings of these concepts. The importance of starting out with visual perception is based on the fact that cognition relies on the senses for information: "As Hutchins (1995) so effectively pointed out, thinking is not something that goes on entirely, or even mostly, inside people's heads. Little intellectual work is accomplished with our eyes and ears closed. Most cognition is done as a kind of interaction with cognitive tools, pencils and paper, calculators, and increasingly, computer-based intellectual supports and information systems" (Ware, 2004, p. 2).

Applied Perceptional Research

Human eyes are complex organs. This visual system senses electromagnetic radiation (photons) by photo-receptors, which capture this wave-and-particle information as light (Beckhaus & Kruijff, 2004). An image is focused on through the lens and is captured via the retina. (Figure 2)

Figure 1. Applicable pedagogical theories and research related to digital imagery in e-learning

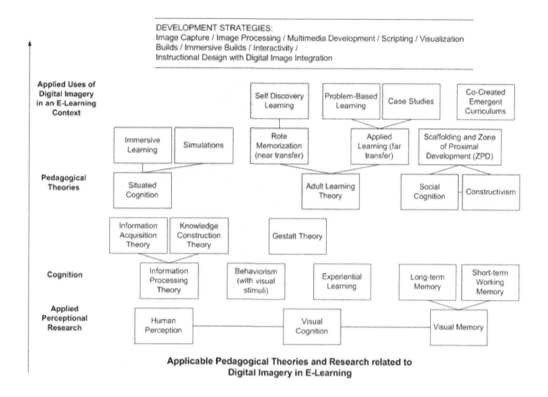

The main sensing mechanism, the retina, contains light-sensitive photoreceptor cells, rods and cones. Rods capture low-light black-and-white vision. There are rods distributed throughout the retina, but none in the fovea or the blind spot. Cones capture color in long-wavelength, medium-wavelength, and short-wavelength (or red, green and blue / RGB); these require brighter light. The human perception of color then comes from these three types of cone cells, as combinations of RGB color. Cones concentrate in and near the fovea, with a few "present at the sides of the retina." Objects in the fovea are seen most clearly and sharply. The photons of light are changed to neural impulses by the eyes. Visual information goes through the rods and cone cells through intermediate cells in the retina to the optic nerve fibers, which then send this information to the brain ("Eyes," 2008).

Different parts of the eyes capture different information. "As the angle from the center of the gaze increases, acuity is reduced, but sensitivity to movement and flicker increases" (Poynton & Mooney, 1997, p. 162). The eye-point in approaching a scene affects not only how it is perceived but the quality of the visual information. The ease of focus and the mobility of the eyes' focus therefore expand the capability of image capture. People, who have approximately 120 million visual sensory cells, have a depth perception of up to approximately six meters. Human eyes may focus, with accommodation, from 20 centimeters to infinity. The maximum field of view is 210 degrees (Beckhaus & Kruijff, 2004, p. 54).

Figure 2. Schematic diagram of the human eye

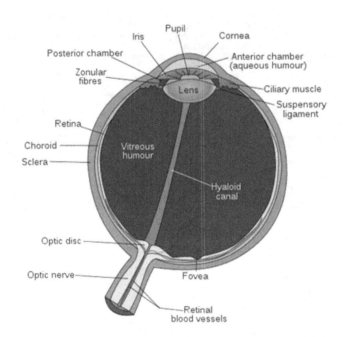

Cognition

The human mind directs the eyes' focus to salient visual features. People tend to focus on movement and on bright colors, which draw their attention. "The density of the receptors (and with it the visual acuity as well) decreases exponentially from the fovea towards the periphery. To make up for any potential loss of information incurred by the decrease in resolution in the periphery, the eyes are rapidly re-oriented via very fast (up to 900°/ s), ballistic motions called *saccades. Fixations* are the periods between saccades during which the eyes remain relatively fixed, the visual information is processed and the location of the next fixation point is selected" (Minut & Mahadevan, 2001, p. 457). Human eyes are capable of surprising perception: "In the study of perception, *just noticeable differences* measure the very limits of human abilities to detect the faintest of differences between, say, two adjacent colors almost exactly alike in a continuous spectrum of 100,000 colors" (Tufte, 1997, *Visual Explanations,* p. 73).

Interestingly, the human mind tends to process information using a kind of "bilateral symmetry." In these phenomena, people will view half of a symmetrical object, check to see that the other half is symmetrical, and then cease visual exploration. This sort of visual shorthand has implications on the intake of information. "Half-faces carry the same information as full faces. Halves may be easier to sort (by matching the right half of an unsorted face to the left half of a sorted face) than full faces. Or else an asymmetrical full face can be used to report additional variables" (Tufte, 2001, *The Visual Display...,* p. 97).

"Persistence of vision" refers to the residual image that is left after the disappearance of the initial visual stimulus. The persistence of sensory phenomena even when viewers know that they are illusions are likely hard-wired into people's brains and are resistant to change (Ware, 2004, p. 14). Understanding such hard-wiring is critical to the design of effective visuals.

The "Gestalt theory" of visual perception suggests that the human mind tends to perceive individual components as organized patterns. Patterns may reveal relationships between data sets and phenomena. Visual pattern recognition of familiar patterns may be captured in a tenth of a second or less. For novel and unlearned patterns, those may be apprehendable fairly quickly but usually only involve approximately three feature components (Ware, 2008, p. 55).

Vision may also be understood to be perceivable on various levels of abstraction—from general to figurative to detailed levels. Alesandrini offers a different set of categories based on the realism of imagery as representational, analogical (similar to symbolic) and arbitrary. "A representational graphic, such as a photograph, looks similar physically to the object to which it refers…An analogical graphic refers to similarity. As the name implies, this type of graphic uses analogy or metaphor to communicate…An arbitrary graphic, on the other hand, is one that does not resemble an object but uses graphs, charts, diagrams, and the like to show the organization of an object or the relationship of an object to other objects" (Lohr, 2003, p. 29).

The capturing of a visual sensation results in a brief preservation of that information in a kind of buffer that lasts from a sub-second to a second, with the decay rate influenced by "intensity, contrast, and duration of the stimulus" and whether or not there is a second exposure (Reed, 2004, p. 32). Visual perception and visual memory do not only involve a mechanistic sense of seeing, but requires focused attention and the encoding of that information into memory. Human selectivity of perception ("the allocation of capacity"), concentration, and purposive memory affects what is captured (Reed, 2004, p. 53).

First, the learner must focus on key graphics and words in the lesson to select what will be processed. Second, the learner must rehearse this information in working memory to organize and integrate it with existing knowledge in long-term memory. Third, in order to do the integration work, limited working memory capacity must not be overloaded. Lessons should apply cognitive load reduction techniques, especially when learners are novices to the new knowledge and skills (Clark & Mayer, 2008, p. 41).

Information in short-term memory may be lost within 20-30 seconds unless it is rehearsed (Reed, 2004, p. 70). Practice or reviewing may increase human retrieval frequency, recall speed, and potential accuracy. "Maintenance rehearsal" may be practiced to protect the long-term memory. Memories do inevitably fade, even if they were vivid at the moment of intake (Reed, 2004). Visual images have to be retrievable from the long-term memory, with practiced recall critical to strengthening the synaptic paths. Long-term memory has been conceptualized as not one system but as multiple ones (Reed, 2004, p. 118). "Unattended" sensory channels tend to capture information in piecemeal and attenuated ways. Even with full human attention, there are limits to human perception.

Visual information is considered to be enhanced by inferences to fill in gaps left by generally poor visual perception: "Helmholtz examined the human eye and concluded that it was, optically, rather poor. The poor quality information gathered via the eye seemed to him to make vision impossible. He therefore concluded that vision could only be the result of some form of unconscious inferences: a matter of making assumptions and conclusions from incomplete data, based on previous experiences" ("Eye," 2008, n.p.).

The information processing theory suggests that the human mind has a limited capacity to engage information. Here, there's a short-term, working memory of concepts being perceived and considered in the temporal now. And there's a long-term memory that stores information from the past and may be accessed for use by surfacing the visual information in the working memory. Visual working memory has a limited capacity to hold information—to about three to five simple objects or patterns (Ware, 2004, pp. 352 – 353).

Paivio's dual-coding theory (1990) suggests that there are different memory systems for different information types, one for verbal and one for imagistic: "Paivio broadly defines verbal and imaginal memory. Verbal memory includes activity related to language systems (auditory and speech), while imaginal memory includes pictures, sounds, tastes, and nonverbal thoughts (imagination)" (Lohr, 2003, p. 37). These two types of memory systems very different in this schema, with different processor types for verbal and image memory. However, information in either processor may activate information in the other processor, so images may evoke words, and words evoke images. This conceptualization explains why abstract ideas and emotions may have less of a long-term impact. "Words that are abstract (emotions, ideas) are less likely to stimulate nonverbal memory and are less likely to be remembered, since the chance of learning is much greater when two, rather than one, memories are involved" (Lohr, 2003, p. 37). This concept supports the multimedia principle of multiple channels of information delivery to learners.

Eye tracking is an important research tool for virtual environments in order to enhance the design of what learners see. Haffegee, Alexandrov and Barrow note:

Human vision is arguably our most powerful sense, with our eyes constantly darting around in an almost subconscious manner to create a complete picture of the visual scene around us. These movements can unveil information about the way the brain is processing the incoming visual data into its mental image of our surroundings (Nov. 2007, pp. 225 – 226).

Recent findings in cognitive neuroscience suggest that while there are physical brain structure locations where visual processing occurs. The occipital lobe of the brain handles vision; the temporal lobe deals with advanced visual processing (Reed, 2004). Various parts of the brain help an individual respond to the visual cues with the proper sensory-motor responses, to perceive direction and speed, to perceive whole objects, and to properly sense depth (Bechtel, 2008). This researcher notes:

For many researchers, one sign of the lack of differentiated function beyond striate cortex was the lack of evidence that these areas were topologically organized in the manner of striate cortex. The very lack of a topological organization suggested that these areas operated holistically to integrate sensory information... (Bechtel, 2008, p. 106).

Visual memory's intactness in the long-term memory may even be affected by "retroactive interference" or post-event, post-observation experiences. Memory may be conceptualized as a malleable capability.

Maintaining organizational structures for information, with deeper understanding of relationships between elements, may enhance long-term memory, too. Imagery may be visualized as both static and dynamic or kinematic. Interestingly, visuals may also spring from the imagination, with people sometimes confusing internal and external sources of their realities.

Pedagogical Theories

The literature on education references visual learners. These are learners who prefer receiving information in visual depictions, along with other methods of informational conveyance. Levin (1981) suggests that there are five general instructional functions of graphics:

1.   decoration (low informational value, not clear association with instructional content, may be eye-catching for viewers)
2.   representation (concretize concepts)
3.   organization (structure and hierarchy of information)
4.   interpretation (to understand ambiguous content)
5.   transformation (to make information more memorable) (Lohr, 2003, pp. 29 – 33).

Before analyzing the applications of digital imagery, this section will offer some foundational instructional principles surrounding the use of visuals and imageries.

Behaviorism and Visual Hard Wiring

Foundational concepts of behaviorism apply to the use of human visual hard-wiring to produce particular perceptual, cognitive and behavioral effects from visuals. The operant concepts of behaviorism include those of positive reinforcement, negative reinforcement, positive punishment, and negative punishment. Positive reinforcement involves the presentation of a stimulus to reward a behavior in order to increase that action. Negative reinforcement involves the removal of a stimulus following a behavior to increase that behavior (such as removing a "demerit" to negatively reinforce the behavior). Positive punishment refers to the presentation of a stimulus following a behavior that decreases that behavior (such as posting a visual label to punish a particular behavior). Negative punishment refers to the removal of a stimulus following a behavior that decreases that action.

Some Learning Theories in E-Learning

E-learning has drawn a number of learning theories. Having a sense of which theories and principles are in use will allow those designing and using digital imagery to better plan strategies for the image capture, use, and deployment for electronic learning.

J. Piaget's ideas contribute to the importance of offering learning on a developmental track, suited to the learner's particular readiness to learn and developmental stage. B. Bloom's Taxonomy of Educational Objectives is often cited for the three types of learning: cognitive (knowledge), affective (attitudes) and psychomotor (physical skills) and the levels of learning: knowledge, comprehension, application, analysis, synthesis, and evaluation. Some would suggest creativity or innovation would be at the top of that hierarchy of learning. H. Gardner's multiple intelligences theory affects the multimedia delivery of learning.

A neo-behaviorist school focuses on the importance of a social context for learning (R. Gagné). Here, experts and novices interact in a zone of proximal development (L. Vygotsky) and support each other's learning. The concept of "scaffolding" learning for the various levels of co-learners also stems from his ideas. D. Laurillard's ideas evoke the importance of dialogue around learning. J. Lave and E.

Wenger focus on the development of communities of practice around particular knowledge domains. Researchers have shown how avatars in immersive virtual spaces may create a sense of co-presence and situatedness of the communications and experience (Nowak & Biocca, 2003; Prasolova-Forland, 2002, as cited in Bente, Rüggenberg, Krämer, & Eschenburg, 2008, p. 293).

Other theories focus on the applied effects of education. W.G. Perry focuses on the ethical development of learners. P. Freire's ideas evoke social liberation (and change) through learning. M. Knowles' andragogy conceptualizations emphasize the unique needs of adult learners for practical, hands-on and applied learning.

More recent applications of e-learning involve emergent curriculums with shared co-creation of learning between faculty and learners. Adaptive learning is not pre-defined but "inherently a creative, generative and reflective process." This is used for more complex learning and higher cognitive processing for greater deep learning and far-transfer within the discipline (Roach et al., 2000, as cited in Dempster, 2003, p. 132). Adaptive learning may include "student-centered, resource-based, discussion-led and collaborative learning" types of curriculum (Dempster, 2003, p. 135). Problem-based learning and project-based learning have also become more widely used for real-world applicability.

Mixing cognition and multimedia development are various researchers. R.C. Clark and R. E. Mayer's (2008) principles involve practical concepts. The "multimedia principle" suggests that using both words and pictures vs. words alone is more helpful for learners. The "spatial contiguity principle" suggests that words should be placed corresponding to images, not separated from the visuals, for more efficacy. The "modality principle" suggests that words should be delivered as audio narration than on-screen text. The "temporal contiguity principle" proposes a synchronicity between the use of imagery and audio. The "redundancy principle" suggests that explanations should be in audio or text, not both. The "coherence principle" suggests that adding extraneous information may harm the learning (pp. 3 – 4). In other words, extraneous "words, pictures, and sounds when giving a multimedia explanation" should be minimized (Mayer, 2000, pp. 372 – 373). Working memory has limited capacity, so builders of e-learning have to compensate for that with downloadables and decision-making systems (Clark & Mayer, 2008, pp. 38 – 39). Learners should not be flooded with excessive visual information but focused selected images that support the learning and are not merely decorative.

In more unique applications, there has been research in immersive digital spaces and simulations, based on the findings of experiential learning (such as D.A. Kolb's experiential learning cycle, based on K. Lewin, J. Dewey and J. Piaget).

Kolb (1984, p. 38) defines learning 'as the process whereby knowledge is created through the transformation of experience.' According to his model 'learning begins with a concrete experience followed by collection of data and reflective observations about that experience. On the abstract conceptualization stage a learner makes generalizations, draws conclusions, and forms hypotheses about the experience. In the final stage, the learner tests these hypotheses and ideas through active experimentation in new circumstances (Kiili, 2005, p. 17, as cited in Schönwald, Euler, Angehrn, & Seufert, 2006, p. 17).

This work has led to experiential computing.

The idea behind experiential computing (Jain 2003; Jain et al. 2003) is that decision makers routinely need insights that come purely from their own experience and experimentation with media and applications. These insights come from multiple perspectives and exploration (Gong et al. 2004). Instead of analyzing an experience, experiential environments provide support for naturally understanding events. In the context of MIR (multimedia information retrieval), experiential environments provide interfaces for creatively exploring sets of data, giving multiple perspectives, and allowing the user to follow his insights (Lew, Sebe, Djeraba, & Jain, 2006, p. 4).

The conventions of multiverse game play must consider the motives of game players. Bartle suggests that people go online into immersive spaces to explore, socialize, achieve and control others (Castronova, 2005, p. 72). Digital gaming research has involved economics explorations (Castronova) and explorations into "gameplay" or what makes playing fun and engaging (Prensky, 2002, p. 4). Players seem to like a sense of discovery, and they like new sensations and experiences. "Hard fun" involves engaging learning: "When we enjoy learning, we learn better" (Rose & Nicholl, 1998, as cited in Prensky, 2002, p. 6).

Visual Priming

Priming refers to preparation of the human mind to accept, focus on, or "see" particular information. Priming often happens on a subconscious level. A subset of e-learning involves visuals that are used for the subconscious priming of learners. Such visual elements may direct learner attention to a particular part of an image. Some used in psychological and cognitive research involve the use of sub-second flashes of images to prime learners' minds towards future learning or to promote particular attitudes or behaviors. In some immersive 3D spaces, the pacing of particular sequences or visuals may set expectations for the speed of the simulations or the interactivity that follows.

Priming effects can occur even if information is not consciously perceived. Bar and Biederman (1998) showed pictorial images to subjects, so briefly that it was impossible for them to identify the objects. They used what is called a masking technique, a random pattern shown immediately after the target stimulus to remove the target from the iconic store, and they rigorously tested to show that the subjects performed at chance levels when reporting what they had seen. Nevertheless, 15 minutes later, this unperceived exposure substantially increased the chance of recognition on subsequent presentation (Ware, 2004, p. 230).

Exposure to the image features primed the visual memory to ease subsequent recognition. Most priming occurs in educational research, and plenty of cognitive research and user testing would enhance the effectiveness of subconscious image effects on learners. Priming may also be used in the creation of antecedents for learning, to prepare learners' minds.

People can be quite sensitive to the appearance of avatars, including their blink rates in terms of evaluating such factors as like or dislike, pleasant or unpleasant, good or bad, friendly or unfriendly, reliability or unreliability, courageousness or timidity, strength or weakness, not nervousness or nervousness, active or not active, intelligent or not intelligent, careful or careless, or relaxed or tense (Takashima, Omori, Yoshimoto, Itoh, Kitamura, & Kishino, 2008, pp. 169 – 176).

"Affect" or emotion that may be evoked with a flashed image (not even captured on the conscious level) may affect people's perceptions and resulting behaviors.

An image doesn't have to be as awful as a car hitting a child to have this effect, however. A face with a fearful expression will do. Neuroscientist Paul Whelan even found that flashing an image of a fearful face for such a short time that people aren't consciously aware that the face is fearful—they report that it looks expressionless—will trigger the amygdale. And that makes the memory more vivid, lasting, and recallable (Gardner, 2008, p. 49).

Visualizations support human cognition or thinking in a number of ways:

first, by supporting visual queries on information graphics, and second, by extending memory. For visual queries to be useful, the problem must first be cast in the form of a query pattern that, if seen, helps solve part of the problem" (Ware, 2004, p. 352). Once learners know what is salient in the particular image, they may identify and track these in the visuals for problem solving. Memory extension, suggests Ware, occurs via "a display symbol, image, or pattern can rapidly evoke nonvisual information and cause it to be loaded from long-term, memory into verbal-propositional processing centers (2004, p. 352).

There's a need for deeper semantic coding (for learner sense-making) to place information into long-term memory.

Applied Research and Findings

Various researches have gone into the efficacy of visual imagery in e-learning, based on eye-tracking technologies, user responses, and performance. People will use informational visuals to help them in problem solving, according to eye-tracking research (Yoon & Narayanan, 2004). Video has been found to work better when learners need to do exploratory work, but this preference does not appear with basic fact-finding assignments (Christel & Frisch, 2008). Well designed visuals are beneficial for less experienced learners (or "novices") in the lesson contents (Clark & Mayer, 2008).

Some imagery and simulation situations involve risks of negative learning, inferences that may be suggested by the visuals and the interactions but which are often unintentional and misleading. The fidelity of various images may or may not be important to the learning, based on the particular learning domain and context. In a situation where the imagery should be analyzed for decision-making, the imagery should be high-fidelity and photo-realistic. In a situation where the imagery has to evoke a fictional place, the fidelity may be more analogical or symbolic or abstract. Some even argue for subtlety in design. "In designing information, then, the idea is to use *just notable differences,* visual elements that make a clear difference but no more—contrasts that are definite, effective, *and* minimal" (Tufte, 1997, *Visual Explanations,* p. 73).

Some Areas for Further Theory Development and Research

More theory development would be helpful in understanding what is and is not effective in terms of e-learning contexts. More understandings of networks and communities of practice would be helpful. The roles of the global publics in e-learning spaces may enhance this work—particularly in reference to ideas of creativity, culture, and quality interchanges.

While the foundation of pedagogical theories is fairly solid, the implications of the theories have not been explored, and their efficacy or inefficacy has not been backed up by much research. Newer theories may address different demographic groups' learning in e-learning and in immersive spaces. Domain-specific theories may be evolved. There need to be clearer theories of the learning occurring (or not) in ambient intelligent and augmented reality spaces. More findings are needed in mobile learning, immersive learning in 3D social spaces, and augmented virtuality.

Research should probe user experiences in the various incarnations of e-learning. Different types and applications of digital visuals in learning contexts would develop this field. Technological affordances should be probed, particularly those that combine extant technologies for a range of captures, visual effects, live information streams, and so on. User-generated contents should be explored. Currently, most of this field seems to be researched from the technology side in terms of new functionalities and improvements.

CONCLUSION

Imageries in e-learning are used in many ways. They offer "visual memorization" ways to memorize facts. They set up case studies authentically. They offer ways for people to understand signs and symptoms of diseases. They immerse learners into simulations and immersive learning contexts that are three-dimensional and four-dimensional (3D with the inclusion of time). Imageries enrich discovery learning spaces, where there are virtual kiosks, slideshows, videos, and interactive games, for rich learning. They are co-created or solely created by learners, who may contribute to the richness of a learning domain.

This first chapter aimed to give a general overview of some applied theories in the use of digital imagery in e-learning and to set the e-learning context. The application of these ideas to live learning contexts will become clearer in the following chapters.

REFERENCES

Bagdanov, A. D., del Bimbo, A., Nunziati, W., & Pernici, F. (2006). A reinforcement learning approach to active camera foveation. In *Proceedings of the VSSN '06*, Santa Barbara, CA (pp. 180).

Ball, R. & North, C. (2008). The effects of peripheral vision and physical navigation on large scale visualization. CHCCS/SCDHM: Windsor, Ontario, Canada. ACM. 9 - 16.

Bechtel, W. (2008). *Mental mechanisms: Philosophical perspectives on cognitive neuroscience*. New York: Routledge, Taylor & Francis Group.

Beckhaus, S., & Kruijff, E. (2004). Unconventional human computer interfaces. In *Proceedings of the SIGGRAPH 2004*.

Bente, G., Rüggenberg, S., Krämer, N. C., & Eschenburg, F. (2007). Avatar-mediated networking: Increasing social presence and interpersonal trust in Net-based collaborations. *Human Communication Research, 34*, 293.

Castronova, E. (2005). The right to play. In J. M. Balkin & B. S. Noveck (Eds.), *The state of play: Law, games, and virtual worlds* (pp. 68-85). New York: New York University Press.

Castronova, E. (2005). *Synthetic worlds*. Chicago: The University of Chicago Press.

Christel, M. G., & Frisch, M. H. (2008). Evaluating the contributions of video representation for a life oral history collection. In *Proceedings of the JCDL '08* (pp. 241-250). New York: ACM.

Clark, R. C., & Mayer, R. E. (2003). *E-learning and the science of instruction.* San Francisco: Pfeiffer, John Wiley & Sons.

Clark, R. C., & Mayer, R. E. (2008). *E-learning and the science of instruction: Proven guidelines for consumers and designers of multimedia learning* (2nd ed.). San Francisco: John Wiley & Sons.

Dempster, J. (2003). Developing and supporting research-based learning and teaching through technology. In C. Ghaoui (Ed.), *Usability evaluation of online learning programs* (pp. 28-258). Hershey, PA: Information Science Publishing.

Dovey, J., & Kennedy, H. W. (2006). *Game cultures: Computer games as new media.* Maidenhead, UK: Open University Press.

Electromagnetic spectrum. (2008). *Wikipedia.* Retrieved September 13, 2008, from http://en.wikipedia.org/wiki/Electromagnetic_spectrum

Eye. (2008). *Wikipedia.* Retrieved December 6, 2008, from http://en.wikipedia.org/wiki/Eye

Gardner, D. (2008). *The science of fear.* New York: Dutton.

Haffegee, A., Alexandrov, V., & Barrow, R. (2007). Eye tracking and gaze vector calculation within immersive virtual environments. In *Proceedings of the VRST 2007*, Newport Beach, CA (pp. 225-226). New York: ACM.

Lew, M. S., Sebe, N., Djeraba, C., & Jain, R. (2006). Content-based multimedia information retrieval: State of the art and challenges. *ACM Transactions on Multimedia Computing . Communications and Applications, 2*(1), 1–19.

Lohr, L. L. (2003). *Creating graphics for learning and performance.* Upper Saddle River, NJ: Merrill Prentice Hall.

Mayer, R. E. (2000). The challenge of multimedia literacy. In A. W. Pailliotet & P. B. Mosenthal (Eds.), *Reconceptualizing literacy in the media age.* Stamford, CT: JAI Press, Inc.

Minut, S., & Mahadevan, S. (2001). A reinforcement learning model of selective visual attention. In *Proceedings of the AGENTS '01*, Montréal, Quebec.

Po, B.A., Fisher, B.D., & Booth, K.S. (2004). Mouse and touchscreen selection in the upper and lower visual fields. CHI 2004: Vienna, Austria. ACM: 359 - 366.

Poynton, C. A., & Mooney, M. A. (1997). Tutorial—color and type in information design. In *Proceedings of the CHI 97.*

Prensky, M. (2002). The motivation of gameplay or, the REAL 21st century learning revolution. *Horizon, 10*(1), 8.

Reed, S. K. (2004). *Cognition: Theory and applications* (6th ed.). Australia: Thomson Wadsworth.

Reyes, R., Hodges, W., & Gaither, K. (2004). Visualizing the evolution of horned lizards using 3D morphing techniques. In *Proceedings of the Conference on Visualization '04*. Washington, DC: IEEE.

Schematic diagram of the human eye. (n.d.) *Eye. Wikipedia*. Retrieved December 7, 2008, from http://en.wikipedia.org/wiki/Image:Schematic_diagram_of_the_human_eye_en.svg

Schönwald, I., Euler, D., Angehrn, A., & Seufert, S. (2006, January). *EduChallenge learning scenarios: Designing and evaluating learning scenarios with a team-based simulation on change management in higher education* (SCIL Report 8). Swiss Center for Innovations in Learning.

Takashima, K., Omori, Y., Yoshimoto, Y., Itoh, Y., Kitamura, Y., & Kishino, F. (2008). Effects of avatar's blinking animation on person impressions. In *Proceedings of the Graphics Interface Conference 2008*, Windsor, Ontario, Canada (pp. 169-176).

Tufte, E. R. (1997). *Visual explanations: Images and quantities, evidence and narrative*. Cheshire, CT: Graphics Press.

Tufte, E. R. (2001). *The visual display of quantitative information* (2nd ed.). Cheshire, CT: Graphics Press.

Ware, C. (2004). Foundation for a science of data visualization. In *Information visualization: Perception for design* (2nd ed.). San Francisco: Morgan Kaufmann Publishers.

Ware, C. (2008). *Visual thinking for design*. San Francisco: Morgan Kaufmann Publishers.

Yoon, D., & Narayanan, N. H. (2004). Mental imagery in problem solving: An eye tracking study. In *Proceedings of the 2004 Symposium on Eye Tracking Research and Applications* (pp. 77-84). New York: Association for Computing Machinery, Inc.

KEY TERMS AND DEFINITIONS

Cognition (n): Human thought and awareness, perception, knowing dual coding theory (n): A cognitive theory that suggests the mind processes information on two tracks: visually and verbally

Foveated Vision (n): The centering of an image on the center of the retina or the "fovea"; the centering of a region of interest (ROI) in a live or recorded image using foveated computer imaging

Gestalt Theory (n): The concept that understanding involves looking at something in a holistic way, as a larger pattern

Information Processing Theory (n): The idea that the human mind (like a computer) applies logical rules and strategies in the interpretation of information

Long-Term Memory (n): The stable part of the human memory that maintains information over time, into decades

Multimedia Theory (n): A number of concepts about how to best script and create multimedia to enhance learning; these include the multimedia, modality, redundancy, spatial contiguity, temporal contiguity, coherence, and individual differences principles

Saccade (n): A series of jerky movements of the eyes when changing focus from one aspect to another

Salient (adj): Relevant, important, noticeable

Selective Visual Attention (n): The phenomena of viewers paying more attention and focus to specific regions of interest (ROI)

Sensory Memory (n): A foundational level of memory of sensory impressions (long after the sensation has passed)

Short-Term Memory (n): The active working memory that holds a small amount of information for a brief time for real-time access and use

Situated Cognition (n): The concept and phenomena of how people learn within a social context and informational context

Verbal Memory (n): The storage of textual and auditory language in human memory

Visual Perception (n): The ability to capture and interpret information from visual light through the eyes

Visual Perception Theory (n): An explanation of why people "mentally" see what they do, which comes not only from visual stimuli

Visual Working Memory (n): The short-term retention of visual information

Working Memory (n): Also known as short-term or "active" memory

Chapter 2
Visual Literacy in E-Learning Instructional Design

ABSTRACT

Visual literacy refers to a deeper knowledge of what images convey, where the visual data comes from, how it is captured, how it may be manipulated, and how it may be deployed for the most effective conveyance of information. It may clarify nuanced messages embedded in imagery. This chapter addresses the principles of visual literacy in the context of e-learning. It will introduce some foundational terminology and visual phenomena. This will help readers evaluate the veracity of digital images and have a better understanding of digital visual effects. A sidebar by Jason Maseberg-Tomlinson shows the need for accessibility and how building this feature into an image is a part of visual literacy.

CHAPTER OBJECTIVES

- Explain some basic concepts and values of visual literacy
- Define visual literacy
- Explain the various angles of visual literacy related to digital imagery
- Introduce the importance of accessibility in visual literacy

INTRODUCTION

Over the years, there have been digital captures mythical monsters, spaceships, and missing persons. Cell phones were lined up to "pop" kernels of corn. Public figures have used plenty of airbrushing of their

DOI: 10.4018/978-1-60566-972-4.ch002

images for publications and movies. Images with political implications have been launched to change people's minds about one political candidate, scenario, or policy. There are "animated documentaries," "edutainment," and various mash-ups of different forms that confuse fact and fiction through visuals. Web information quality "ranges from very high to wrong to intentionally fraudulent" (Albers, 2007, p. 84).

People live and work in a "digital enclosure" of imagery of various qualities and provenance. Without some media savvy and visual literacy, people will continue to fall for illusions and digital sleight-of-hand. Even with the protections of visual literacy, given the sophistication of digital imagery creation and editing, and the massive floods of digital data (with less and less attention paid to their analysis), there may always be a degree of uncertainty as to the origins of an image and various interpretations of its meanings.

While there are some working definitions of information and media literacy, there's not one widely accepted working one for visual literacy. Multiple disciplines, art history, education, rhetoric, philosophy, and graphic design, use this term. While visual literacy is not independent of a cultural context, there are some universals in the understanding of this term.

The rationale for having a working definition is to create an awareness of where visual images come from, how they may be manipulated, how to "question" the images, and how they are used in the world. This awareness may lead to a metacognition beyond the experiential.

This visual literacy may enhance an individual's ability to engage the world of visual information with more savvy. Visual literacy relates to larger literacies needed for functioning in modern societies. "Anthropologists have found that literate human societies have evolved a wide range of literacies, each a complex set of practices and beliefs about communication and knowledge associated with particular educational, linguistic, and social contexts" (Walton & Vukovic, 2003, p. 65). These literacies involve awareness of visual conventions: "To be a 'literate' citizen one must increasingly be able to critically evaluate digital visual materials, make decisions using digital visual representations of data and ideas, and use computers to create effective visual communications" (Spalter & Tenneson, 2006, para. 1). It is important to realize that the media isn't the only message, but the content is important (Franco, da Cruz & de Deus Lopes, 2006, para. 11). Ware quips: "We are all cognitive cyborgs in this Internet age in the sense that we rely heavily on cognitive tools to amplify our mental abilities" (2008, p. ix).

There have been some inroads made towards a definition, with one author illuminating some of the dimensions. "Visual literacy, like visual culture, is complex, multidimensional, and embedded within a range of visual, cognitive, aesthetic, and nonvisual (emotional, ethical) dimensions. The notion of the *visual complex*, that is, a relational or situational concept of visual studies, can arguably serve as a multidimensional and embedded working model, useful in providing the practical coherence for *visual studies*," suggests P. Dallow (2008, p. 101).

Visual literacy involves plenty of background knowledge: what the visual capture, editing, and deployment technologies can do; the messages that images convey—both on a conscious level and a subconscious level; a "reverse engineering" awareness of how images were created; where the raw or originating imagery came from (if possible), and some ways to properly handle imagery. Visual literacy involves knowledge of relevant terminology. It also involves awareness of the legal information framework within which such images are used, with a role for ethics. Ideally, visual literacy would involve the ability to take part in this discourse, as a producer of imagery for others' consumption.

Similarly, multimedia literacy involves both content and process literacy. The first involves understanding instructional messages from words, images, sounds, and actions. The process of literacy involves an ability to make sense of messages and to create messages that make sense to others in the multimedia milieu (Mayer, 2000, p. 365). There are technological systems created to enhance youth's graphical literacy, as through the multi-user video capture and editing system that "invites young users to create, explore, manipulate and share video content with others" (Vaucelle, Africano, Davenport, Wiberg & Fjellstrom, 2005). Clearly, the addition of multimedia potentially adds more information as well as more "noise" to the message, which means more complexity in unraveling the various effects on the viewers.

Current generations of learners tend to be more "visually stimulated" than prior generations. As the so-called "visualizers generation," they are conversant in some aspects of visuals. "Indeed, we live in an era of visual information processing, which means that researchers and academics are competing for students' attention against Pods, camera phones, and graphic-intensive video games. Without graphics it is difficult to keep this generation of students engaged" (Lewis, Dishon, Johnson, & Firtion, 2008, pp. 34 - 35). Youth culture emphasizes imagery over text literacy. With diminishing levels of reading in academia, the role of digital imagery may be on the rise.

Basic Concepts and Values of Visual Literacy

Visual literacy ("visuacy"), credited to John Debes (1969) is defined as the competency to draw meaning from an image. Debes wrote:

Visual Literacy refers to a group of vision-competencies a human being can develop by seeing and at the same time having and integrating other sensory experiences. The development of these competencies is fundamental to normal human learning. When developed, they enable a visually literate person to discriminate and interpret the visible actions, objects, and symbols, natural or man-made, that he encounters in his environment. Through the creative use of these competencies, he is able to communicate with others. Through the appreciative use of these competencies, he is able to comprehend and enjoy the masterworks of visual communication (p. 27, as cited in Branch, 2000, pp. 381 – 382).

A more modern definition reads as follows: "Definition: Visual literacy is the understanding of messages communicated through frames of space that utilize objects, images, and time, and their juxtaposition. The principles, rules, and form that characterize a visual grammar are based on communicating perception and the ecology of symbol systems" (Branch, 2000, p. 383).

Six visual literacy goals have been identified for students of all ages and include becoming "more creative and critical thinkers by identifying, analyzing, interpreting, and evaluating what they see"; producers of visuals for visual communications; perceptive individuals "by recognizing and appreciating aesthetics of visual imagery and by understanding, accepting, and valuing personal, cultural, and historical differences in image creation"; responsible citizens by reflecting on the roles that visuals play "in reflecting and influencing society"; discriminating consumers that understand "the motives, methods, and emotional appeal of advertising visuals in a modern society," and lifelong learners "with a positive attitude about learning how to learn about visual images" (Lacy, 1987, as cited in Branch, 2000, pp. 380 - 381).

Visual learning generally has been approached in an integrationist way, without pulling out digital visuals as stand-alone entities. Considering the digital element is helpful in considering other parts of literacy that add to visual literacy.

The concept of visual literacy rests on information literacy, or the ability to "locate, evaluate and use effectively the needed information" accurately, efficiently, competently, and creatively (Presidential Committee on Information Literacy. 1989, p. 1). The Association of College and Research Libraries (2000), in their *Information Literacy Competency Standards for Higher Education*, identified five performance indicator standards used to assess information literacy programs:

> **Standard One:** The information literate student determines the nature and extent of the information needed.
>
> **Standard Two:** The information literate student accesses needed information effectively and efficiently.
>
> **Standard Three:** The information literate student evaluates information and its sources critically and incorporates selected information into his or her knowledge base and value system.
>
> **Standard Four:** The information literate student, individually or as a member of a group, uses information effectively to accomplish a specific purpose.
>
> **Standard Five:** The information literate student understands many of the economic, legal, and social issues surrounding the use of information and accesses and uses information ethically and legally (*Information Literacy Competency Standards for Higher Education*).

"Visual literacy" also rests on the tradition of multimedia or electronic media literacy, with text, audio, graphics, video, animation, and interactivity part of the canon of e-learning and communications.

Mayer suggests that five basic cognitive skills are needed for multimedia mixes. "In particular, when multimedia messages consist of words and graphics, students need skill in five basic cognitive processes: selecting relevant words, selecting relevant images, organizing words into a coherent representation, organizing images into a coherent representation, and integrating verbally based and visually based representations with one another and with prior knowledge" (Mayer, 2000, p. 370).

The Digital Visual Environment

The digital visual environment for e-learning is pervasive; visuals are a part of most online courses and trainings. Also, these visuals are able to be manipulated by users, who also may contribute to the visual information-rich repositories and sites with portable images. This environment is also constantly changing in terms of the types of information that may be captured and shared. Plenty of visuals that may have been considered private are now available online.

Those who are visually literate need to be able to step out of the sensory moment and cognitively analyze the digital imagery—to understand embedded visual messages, possible interpretations, and maybe what information has not been shown in the image. Another important awareness is to realize how digital imagery amplifies information. It focuses on selective information; it directs viewer attention. Most websites and online sources integrate visuals as a matter of course.

Figure 1 "The University Life Café and User Produced Multimedia" is a screenshot of a mental wellness site for college students. The photos, arts imagery, and videos are created by site users to express their various mental states and to provide support for their peers through sharing.

Figure 1. The University Life Café and user produced multimedia

Digital Visual Literacy

Six main areas of competencies have been defined in relation to digital visual literacy. They include the following:

1. Content and Resources
2. Techno for Capture, Creation, Editing, Deployment, and Storage
3. Meaning Making
4. Related Laws and Ethics
5. Human and Visual Perception
6. Roles in E-Learning

In Figure 2, "Some Angles for Digital Visual Literacy," these six competency areas are further elaborated on in the outer orbit.

1. Content and Resources

One of the most accessible parts of visual literacy relates to the knowledge and savvy needed to find and use digital visuals. This involves knowledge of the types of visual resources available, from discrete images to video to immersive spaces. Awareness of digital imagery forms should also include clarity

Figure 2. Some angles of digital visual literacy (Hai-Jew, 2009)

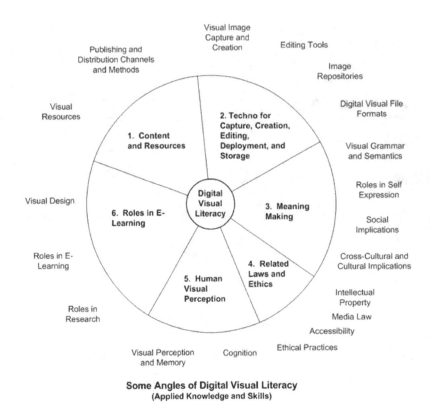

Some Angles of Digital Visual Literacy
(Applied Knowledge and Skills)

about how they are used—in a symbolic way or a sensory way, and then for what learning purposes. This also involves the awareness of the publishing and distribution channels and methods for accessing these resources for particular teaching and learning needs.

The location and selection of relevant content involves the understanding of the standards needed for the resources.

- What visual contents must be depicted?
- What richness of metadata and information provenance needs to be shown?
- What fidelity is needed in representing a particular facet of the learning?
- What sorts of technologies must the images interact with? Learning management systems? Repositories? Tangible digital storage devices?
- How may the images gain credibility within a particular learning domain?
- How may the images work together for cumulative learning and a sense of harmony?
- How will the images be integrated with textual information?
- Should the images be static or dynamic?
- What are the accessibility standards of the particular imagery?

2. Techno for Capture, Creation, Editing, Deployment, and Storage

The technologies for visual image capture and creation have become more sophisticated over time. Visual literacy should involve a general awareness of cameras, scanners, and remote sensors. It should also include awareness of the software tools used for editing and authoring imagery. How to access and effectively use image repositories would be important. How to create and output digital imagery that may be portable and interchangeable would be important on a digital visual literacy résumé.

Viewers of digital imagery should be aware that all of these are approximations. The current technologies only capture a portion of the visual data available. Many types of images cannot reproduce the "range of colors and degrees of illumination of the real world" (Messaris, 1994, p. 10). The greater sophistication of digital imagery comes from the multi-camera captures for stereo illustrations and 3D illustrations. Fused images create new visual effects. Holograms, fractals, and machine art offer yet other visuals.

3. Meaning Making

One of the most important parts of visual literacy involves making meaning from digital imagery. Visuals have their own grammar and semantics. Ware calls the ability to focus on particular layers or aspects of an image "feature level tuning," and suggests that this helps people extract informational value (2008, p. 52). Imagery has personal and social meanings; practical and aesthetic values. Visuals contain self-expression as well as team expression. There are cultural implications as well as cross-cultural ones. Images evoke different meanings for different users.

Critical literacy offers some insights on interpreting mediated realities: Visual literates "(1) scrutinize their initial understandings of textual and media representations; (2) engage in a critique of their own ideologically mediated perceptions of the situation described or inscribed in the text in question; and (3) sort out 'truths' from half-truths, accuracies from inaccuracies, facts from fiction, reality from myth, and objectivity from bias" (Semali, 2000, p. 277).

While there are standards for the interpretability of still aerial images, many are calling for standards for moving images as well (Irvine, Fenimore, Cannon, Roberts, Israel, Simon, Watts, Miller, Brennan, Avilés, Tighe & Behrens, 2004, n.p.). Field-specific metrics and other quantitative elements may help define the quality standards of various types of captured images and visuals.

Meanings are made not only in the general senses but also in the unique aspects of various domain fields with their original conventions. Even various types of images have their own grammar—from node-link diagrams to maps to satellite imagery to video to 3D immersive visuals. A visually literate individual should be able to analyze digital imagery used in a domain field to learn about standards for imagery use to a degree. He or she should be able to work with subject matter experts to understand analytical frameworks for analyzing and using such images. An individual should also understand the unique image capture approaches in different fields.

For much visual content available to the public, teams of people may affect the contents of visual imagery. These may be people with various types of background knowledge from subject matter experts to photographers to photo editors to multimedia specialists to graphic artists. There may be archivists or digital repository curators. There may be gatekeepers who vet the images before anything is made available to the public. The more highly processed an image is and the more versioning an image goes through, often, the less of the original intent remains. These are possible considerations in analyzing digital imagery.

The Perception of Movement

Ware describes how visual movement may be created though having a static foreground frame vs. the moving background (Howard & Childerson, 1994). Vection is the illusory impression of self-motion.

Foreground / background: Much stronger vection is perceived if the moving part of the visual field is perceived as background more distant from the observer than foreground objects (Howard and Heckman, 1989). In fact, vection can be perceived even with quite a small moving field, if that field is perceived to be relatively distant. The classic example occurs when someone is sitting in a train at a station and the movement of an adjacent vehicle (seen through a window) causes the person to feel he or she is moving even though this is not the case (Ware, 2004, p. 291)

Image Veracity and Forensics

Image competence at its core must involve identifying the image, drawing inferential meaning from it, and identifying artifice or manipulations. Given the different modes of understanding from one image, it will be critical to view that visual from different angles. Images, which are all necessarily finite, have a limited capacity to contain information. Differing interpretations still have to ultimately refer back to the original image and the capturing devices used. Image acquisition forensics may track an image's creation back to its originating device via device's "color interpolation coefficients and noise statistics" (McKay, Swaminathan, Gou & Wu, 2008, pp. 1657 – 1660). Other methods use algorithms to detect further processing beyond the direct output of images from a digital camera (Swaminathan, Wu, & Liu, 2006).

Meaning-making from digital imagery implies determining the veracity of captured photo-realistic images. With the sophistication of image editing technologies, some argue that evaluating digital imagery for veracity may be difficult if just viewing the images alone. In that context, people would look for signs of image editing, untrue light affecting different parts of the image, or other visual inconsistencies. If a larger context is available, then the provenance of the image should be probed and the context of the image capture.

The connected metadata and provenance of the image will add another layer of information to help source the imagery. Where an image has been and how it has been handled has effects on the concept of information security. An image that has gone through many hands may have picked up various manipulations and edits, for example. Those involved in image forensics may draw out more information than is described here.

The social and political implications of the image need to be explored to understand if there is possibly a propagandist's hand behind an image. The credibility of the source then matters. If the source is a computing machine or sensor, that can also be probed for unusual effects and potential manipulations.

Visual Aesthetics

Another aspect of meaning making from imagery involves aesthetics, or the appreciation of beauty in its various forms. This involves having the proper language to discuss the visuals and their effects. It may also include having historical points of reference in terms of schools of thought on art. Visually literate individuals need to be able to appreciate the visuals and articulate their sensibilities.

Points-of-View

Video has a long history of different conventions to convey information. Camera angles may convey power or weakness—not arbitrarily—but because video angles reflect real-life situations. "In other words, this visual device is based on perceptual habits a viewer can be expected to have developed in everyday, real-world experience, even without any previous exposure to visual media" (Messaris, 1994, p. 9).

Digital visuals are no longer in the "flatlands" of 2D (to borrow a term from Edward R. Tufte). Researchers have explored how events should be timed for dramatic effects. More recent digital visuals have brought in the concept of different points-of-view in an immersive 3D scene: the God's eye view, the over-the-shoulder-view, the aerial view, the multiplayer views, the wingman view and the map view. The paraproxemic principle (Meyrowitz, 1986) involves a sense of created intimacy with the viewers because of point-of-view and video capture perspective (Messaris, 1994). At the same time, researchers have also probed how users navigate such virtual spaces based on points of interest. They use multiple windows and information streams to convey synchronous information.

Points-of-view refer to both egocentric and exocentric views of the world. A first-person character-based point-of-view is an egocentric or subjective world view:

The egocentric frame of reference is, roughly speaking, our subjective view of the world. It is anchored to the head or torso, not the direction of gaze (Bremmer et al., 2001). Our sense of what is ahead, left, and right does not change as we rapidly move our eyes around the scene, but it does change with body and head orientation (Ware, 2004, p. 333).

A map represents an exocentric view—or the use of a perspective outside an individual. Another term for this may be "floating player view" for high-level action summaries (Hoobler, Humphreys & Agrawala, 2004, p. 163). This view is considered external to a character and therefore more objective.

3D involves depth. The way the brain sees is that it extracts "an outline representation of the retinal image" and then starts parsing the depth and distances. It uses "binocular disparity" to understand the differences between the images formed in each eye. The mind also uses "motion parallax" to look at the amount of change in the retinal image by a change of the viewer's position in relation to the object.

The brain uses "texture gradients" or changes in the retinal image of the density of a pattern. Messaris explains: "When we look at a pattern of straight, parallel lines stretching away from us, the visual image we receive is one of increasing density as distance increases until all the lines appear to converge in a single 'vanishing point.' The same general principle is also in evidence, although perhaps less obviously, when we look at any surface bearing a regular pattern: tiles, pebbles, grass, and so on." And the last element is occlusion, the partial blockage of one object by another, to get a sense of which is closer to the viewer (Messaris, 1994, p. 11 - 12).

Digital Artifice and Effects

A variety of digital imagery manipulations are possible to create certain impressions that may affect human perceptions and behaviors. For example, "false continuity" involves the linking of an unrelated image to a prior one that may suggest false relationships or causations (Messaris, 1994, p. 35). Associational juxtapositions create that sense of relatedness artificially.

Overlaying one image over another is yet another manipulation. Revealing some information but not others is another. "Photo-shopping" an image by factually changing information around is also another example of artifice.

Some human observations effects may occur in a subconscious way, in an effect known as "priming".

Bar and Biederman (1998) showed pictorial images to subjects, so briefly that it was impossible for them to identify the objects. They used what is called a masking technique, a random pattern shown immediately after the target stimulus to remove the target from the iconic store, and they rigorously tested to show that the subjects performed at chance levels when reporting what they had seen. Nevertheless, 15 minutes later, this unperceived exposure substantially increased the chance of recognition on subsequent presentation (Ware, 2004, p. 230).

Deictic Gestures

A gesture that links the subject of a spoken sentence with a visual reference is a "deictic gesture" or "deixis" (see Figure 3). Understanding such gestures is an important culturally-based aspect of visual literacy. "Deixis has its own rich vocabulary of identity, space or time. For example, an encircling gesture can indicate an entire group of objects or a region of space" (Levelt, et al., 1985; Oviatt, et al., 1997, as cited in Ware, 2004, p. 309). Deictic gestures strengthen the sense of visual context.

4. Related Laws and Ethics

The main laws related to visual imagery involve intellectual property rights, trademark, patents, and trade secrets laws. Media law touches on privacy, non-defamation, non-libel, and non-slander, in addition to the IP described earlier. Accessibility defines the guidelines for clear labeling of imagery and animations for access by those with visual acuity and cognitive processing issues. Ethical practices in the uses of digital visuals vary depending on the culture and the context. Some common universals involve issues of accuracy, proper crediting (and pay for used images), and clear provenance.

5. Human Visual Perception

Understanding human visual perception is an important part of visual literacy because imagery is made for perception. Computer graphics are designed to deliver "the best perceived image in the least amount of time" (Cater, Chalmers, & Ward, 2003, p. 270). The nuances of visual perception and visual memory are critical areas of learning, along with cognition. While the human eye may process a spectral range from 400 nm to 800 nm (nanometer or one billionth of a meter), vision may be trained using neural feedback to extend vision into "both the ultraviolet and near infrared" (Williams, Maraviglia, & Moran, 2002, n.p.). Technologies themselves may capture invisible light and make these visible to human vision.

There is no widely accepted unifying theory of space perception. Ware observes that how depth cues interact has been addressed in research:

Figure 3. An avatar (Sjalin Rajal) in a deictic gesture (indicating "over here")

For example, the weighted-average model assumes that depth perception is a weighted linear sum of the depth cues available in a display (Bruno and Cutting,1988). Alternatively, depth cues may combine in a geometric sum (Dosher et al., 1986). Young et al. (1993) proposed that depth cues are combined additively, but are weighted according to their apparent reliability in the context of other cues and relevant information. However, there is also evidence that some depth cues—in particular, occlusion,--work in a logical binary fashion rather than contributing to an arithmetic or geometric sum. For example, if one object overlaps another in the visual image, it is perceived as closer to the observer (Ware, 2004, p. 281).

Plenty of work has already been done in how people perceive the foreground and the background in imagery; open and closed shapes; textures, and lines. Color theory has been researched extensively since Sir Isaac Newton's discovery of color relationships on a spectrum of natural order and the complementary colors' vibration effects. Various works have been written about color tone (the lightness or darkness of color); tint (the lightness of the color created by the addition of white); shade (the darkness of a color by the addition of black), and hue (when the color is referred to rather than the tone). Light affects the perception of the intensity of color. Reflectance refers to the amount of light bounced off a surface such as metals or water.

Saccadic Eye Movements

While images resonate in the brain often as smooth imagery, the eyes actually move in jerky movements or "saccades" on "scanpaths" (Josephson & Holmes, 2002, p. 43) to collect information—with 2 to 5 saccades per second. Information comes into the visual system as a series of discrete snapshots (Ware, 2004, pp. 364 – 365). The eyes move from fixation to fixation, moving with convergence as objects approach and then with divergence as objects move away.

Illusion Creation

Human visual perception knowledge may be used in the creation of illusions. Human inattention to details may be used for the inferring of 3D in a visual. "The crucial point, as far as the perception of pictures is concerned, is that 'inattention' to details of shading and color is part of every human being's standard mental apparatus for inferring three-dimensionality and object identity in a visual scene. Therefore, we should not be surprised to find that lack of shading and color in the specific case of pictures does not pose significant interpretational obstacles to uninitiated viewers" (Messaris, 1994, p. 11).

For example, some researchers observe the following in the creation of self-motion: "Field size: In general, the larger the area of the visual field that is moving, the stronger the experience of self-motion" (Howard & Heckman, 1989, as cited in Ware, 2004, p. 291).

There are ways to optimize the viewer's ability to see patterns. "Experimental work by Biederman and Cooper (1992) suggests that the optimal size for recognizing a visual object is about 4 to 6 degrees of visual angle. This gives a useful rule of thumb for the optimal size for rapid presentation of visual images so that we can best see the visual patterns contained in them" (Ware, 2004, pp. 228 – 229). Similar research is also used to avoid unintended patterning, like moiré effects.

Attention-getting has become more challenging because of the competition of various media (often entertainment and communications-based) for human attention. The human eye tends to go to certain colors, to size, to the center of the screen, and to movements.

Low Working Visual Memory

People have low short-term visual working memory, in a phenomena labeled "change blindness" by Rensink (2000). People tend to remember so little visually that people generally will not notice changes, particularly those made mid-blink. "Iconic memory information in retinal coordinates decays within about 2300 msec (Phillips, 1974). By the time 400 msec have elapsed, what little remains is in visual working memory" (Ware, 2004, p. 357).

Given the poor visual working memory, some have asked why then the world seems so rich and detailed? "The answer to this dilemma is that the world 'is its own memory' (O'Regan, 1992). We perceive the world to be rich and detailed, not because we have an internal detailed model, but simply because whenever we wish to see detail we can get it, either by focusing attention on some aspect of the a visual image at the current fixation or by moving our eyes to see the detail in some other part of the visual field" (Ware, 2004, p. 357).

6. Roles in E-Learning

Lastly, visual literacy involves awareness of and skills in creating and using digital imagery in research and e-learning; it includes strategies for visual design. This aspect of literacy involves role awareness in terms of functions along the digital visual production and deployment chain.

Research and E-Learning

Work scenarios require deeper levels of visual literacy:

In many workplaces, advanced digital video technology is not only a means of communication via video conference, but is also used for collaborative video analyses, e.g. in the area of professional sports, teacher education or in the life sciences. Such advanced technologies may include tools for the selection of single video scenes from existing video information and for the direct integration of video scenes with e-communication facilities. Thus, we are confronted with a situation where we need to establish new components of visual literacy and digital literacy that relate to such work scenarios. Literary concepts cannot be restricted to static and text-based media anymore, but have to integrate the understanding, analysis and active use of non-linear and audiovisual media as well including the use of digital video technology (Pea, 1991; Pea & Gomez, 1992, as cited in Zahn, Hesse, Finke, Pea, Mills & Rosen, 2004, p. 737).

A common argument is that there is a large hunger for digital imagery in e-learning for today's generation of college learners. On the research front, there's pressure to document phenomena in objective and creative ways. In e-learning, imagery may be used for a variety of learning endeavors for learning, project design, mental modeling, and other purposes.

There are numerous nuances to how to effectively design a visual solution to a teaching or learning challenge. The design of imagery for "pre-attentive processing" will differ than designing imagery that will be thoroughly analyzed and vetted. Another example is that of changing a visualization from a presentation tool to a discovery one (Ma, 2007, p. 6). Designing for e-learning not only involves designing for reusability and portability between various technological systems used contemporaneously but also future-proofing the imagery for longer shelf-life.

Visual Design

It may be that the principles of information design are universal (Tufte, 1990, *Envisioning Information*) in some aspects, but they are also unique and culturally sensitive and localized in others.

The effective design of visuals for e-learning means a changing of so-called "screen pixels to brain pixels" (Ware, 2004, p. 53). These involve the design of shared virtual spaces for learning. These involve the capturing of interaction metaphors for human-computer interface design. This involves designing embedded ideas for interactivity and "wayfinding" in immersive spaces. This involves the design of frames of reference as well. There should be a range of ways to express the same information albeit with different images.

Visual design involves the juncture of high technology, pedagogy, and digital visuals and imagery. This must involve rich and original strategies to capture, build and deploy such visuals. Future digerati will have to determine what a full visual literacy knowledge- and skill-set involves.

CONCLUSION

Visual literacy essentially means greater awareness of the digital information environment in which people live, work, exchange ideas, and share their senses of the world. It involves sophisticated use of knowledge and skills to evaluate information in a complex and competitive global world. It also involves the ability to participate fully, as creators of contents. And finally, it involves engagement with the visual and larger real world with a sense of ethics and legal strictures. Being visually literate for instructors, instructional designers, and multimedia developers should enhance the work they do in e-learning.

REFERENCES

Adobe. (n.d.). *Adobe Flash accessibility design guidelines*. Retrieved December 15, 2008, from http://www.adobe.com/accessibility/products/flash/best_practices.html

Albers, M. J. (2007). Information salience and interpreting information. In *Proceedings of the SIGDOC '07*, El Paso, Texas, USA. New York: ACM.

Branch, R. M. (2000). A taxonomy of visual literacy. In A. W. Pailliotet & P. B. Mosenthal (Eds.), *Reconceptualizing literacy in the media age*. Stamford, CT: JAI Press, Inc

Caldwell, B., Cooper, M., Reid, L. G., & Vanderheiden, G. (2008). *W3C Web content accessibility guidelines (WCAG) 2.0*. Retrieved December 15, 2008, from http://www.w3.org/TR/2008/REC- sW-CAG20-20081211/

Cater, K., Chalmers, A., & Ward, G. (2003). Detail to attention: Exploiting visual tasks for selective rendering. In *Proceedings of the Eurographics Symposium on Rendering 2003*. New York: ACM.

Dallow, P. (2008). The visual complex: Mapping some interdisciplinary dimensions of visual literacy. In J. Elkins (Ed.), *Visual literacy*. New York: Routledge.

Franco, J. F., da Cruz, S. R., & de Deus Lopes, R. (2006). Computer graphics, interactive technologies and collaborative learning synergy supporting individuals' skills development. In *Proceedings of the International Conference on Computer Graphics and Interactive Techniques*. New York: ACM.

Hoobler, N., Humphreys, G., & Agrawala, M. (2004). Visualizing competitive behaviors in multi-user virtual environments. In *Proceedings of the IEEE Visualization 2004*, Austin, TX (pp. 163-170). Washington, DC: IEEE.

Information Literacy Competency Standards for Higher Education. (2000). *The Association of College and Research Libraries*. Retrieved November 23, 2008, from http://www.ala.org/ala/acrl/acrlstandards/informationliteracycompetency.cfm

Irvine, J. M., Fenimore, C., Cannon, D., Roberts, J., Israel, S. A., Simon, L., et al. (2004). Feasibility study for the development of a motion imagery quality metric. In *Proceedings of the 33rd Applied Imagery Pattern Recognition Workshop (AIPR '04)*. Washington, DC: IEEE.

Josephson, S., & Holmes, M. E. (2002). Visual attention to repeated Internet images: Testing the scanpath theory on the World Wide Web. In *Proceedings of the ETRA '02*, New Orleans, LA. New York: ACM.

Lewis, T. L., Dishon, N., Johnson, K. T., & Firtion, M. (2008). Creating surveys for the visualizers generation: The use of affective imagery to capture perceptions of the computing discipline. *Journal of Computing Sciences in Colleges, 23*(5), 34–43.

Ma, K.-L. (2007). Machine learning to boost the next generation of visualization technology. *IEEE Computer Graphics and Applications, 27*(5), 6–9. doi:10.1109/MCG.2007.129

Mayer, R. E. (2000). The challenge of multimedia literacy. In A. W. Pailliotet & P. B. Mosenthal (Eds.), *Reconceptualizing literacy in the media age.* Stamford, CT: JAI Press, Inc.

McKay, C., Swaminathan, A., Gou, H., & Wu, M. (2008). Image acquisition forensics: Forensic analysis to identify imaging source. In [Washington, DC: IEEE.]. *Proceedings of the ICASSP, 2008,* 1657–1660.

Messaris, P. (1994). *Visual 'literacy': Image, mind, and reality.* Boulder, CO: Westview Press.

Presidential Committee on Information Literacy. *Final Report.* (1989). Retrieved November 23, 2008, from http://www.ala.org/ala/mgrps/divs/acrl/publications/whitepapers/presidential.cfm

Semali, L. (2000). Implementing critical media literacy in school curriculum. In A. W. Pailliotet & P. B. Mosenthal (Eds.), *Reconceptualizing literacy in the media age.* Stamford, CT: JAI Press Inc.

Spalter, A. M., & Tenneson, D. K. (2006). The graphics teaching tool. In *Proceedings of the International Conference on Computer Graphics and Interactive Techniques.* New York: ACM.

Swaminathan, A., Wu, M., & Liu, K. J. R. (2006). Image tampering identification using blind deconvolution. In [Washington, DC: IEEE.]. *Proceedings of the ICIP, 2006,* 2309–2312.

Tufte, E. R. (1990). *Envisioning information.* Cheshire, CT: Graphics Press.

Vaucelle, C., Africano, D., Davenport, G., Wiberg, M., & Fjellstrom, O. (2005). Moving pictures: Looking out / looking in. In *Proceedings of the International Conference on Computer Graphics and Interactive Techniques.* New York: ACM.

Walton, M., & Vukovic, V. (2003, March-April). Cultures, literacy, and the Web: Dimensions of information "scent". *Interaction, 10*(2), 64–71. doi:10.1145/637848.637864

Ware, C. (2004). Foundation for a science of data visualization. In *Information visualization: Perception for design* (2nd ed.). San Francisco: Morgan Kaufmann Publishers.

Ware, C. (2008). *Visual thinking for design.* San Francisco: Morgan Kaufmann Publishers.

WebAIM. (n.d.). *Creating accessible flash content.* Retrieved December 9, 2008, from http://webaim.org/techniques/flash

WebAIM. (n.d.). *Creating accessible images.* Retrieved December 18, 2008, from http://webaim.org/techniques/images

Williams, E., Maraviglia, C., & Moran, A. M. M. (2002). From x-rays to radar: Using color to understand imagery. In *Proceedings of the 31st Applied Imagery Pattern Recognition Workshop (AIPR '02).* Washington, DC: IEEE.

Zahn, C., Hesse, F., Finke, M., Pea, R., Mills, M., & Rosen, J. (2004). Advanced digital video technologies to support collaborative learning in school education and beyond. In *Proceedings of the 2005 Conference on Computer Support for Collaborative Learning: Learning 2005: The Next 10 Years*, Taipei, Taiwan (pp. 737- 742).

KEY TERMS AND DEFINITIONS

Brightness (n): The luminance of an object, separate from its hue or separation (with pure white as having maximum brightness)

Field of View (n): The breadth of a visible angle or expanse

Forensics (n): The use of investigative techniques, technology and science to establish facts

Graphical Literacy (n): A deep knowledge of graphics, where they come from, how they're made, and the messages within each

Interaction Metaphor (n): A cognitive model for virtual interaction, in which one thing is set as representing another

Lightness (n): The amount of illumination or pale coloration of an object; a shade of color

Luminance (n): The quality of reflecting light; the intensity of light

nm (n): A nanometer or one billionth of a meter, used to measure light wavelengths

Semantics (n): The study of meaning, significance

Stereography (n): The technique of portraying solid bodies on a planar surface

Stereoscopy (n): A three-dimensional (3D) image capture

Tunnel Vision (n): A narrowed field of vision; severe constriction of the visual field

Vection (n): The illusory impression or visual sensation of self-motion

SIDEBAR

Accessibility and Visual Content: No Longer Contradicting Forces

Jason Maseberg-Tomlinson
Kansas State University, USA

One of the many things web designers and web accessibility specialists have in common is the knowledge that graphics can be of value to many learners. It cannot be denied that users with many disabilities need graphics to truly understand new concepts and ideas. Someone with a learning disability, for instance, may have to read text many times over to begin to understand a concept. Once that concept is understood it still may not make it to the memory and a day later the comprehension is gone. We know that people who have trouble with words tend to think and learn in other ways. Pictures provide new levels of understanding; add the ability to manipulate pictures or information and one is able to commit those actions to kinetic, or muscle, memory as well as visual memory and sometimes even auditory memory. Such a large percentage of the population benefits from graphics and dynamic environments, it would be a waste of time to write all web pages as text. On the other hand, using only these methods comes at an accessibility cost to other learners.

Over the last ten years it has not been simple to write dynamic graphic content and still communicate with people who cannot access such visuals, someone who is blind for instance; however, innovation moves forward and the times are changing. In the past, the World Wide Web Consortium's (W3C) Web Content Accessibility Guidelines (WCAG) spoke of using HTML and CSS to make accessibility pages. Many people learned new tricks and found that CSS could be used for many magical designs (check out the CSS Zen Garden for examples: www.csszengarden.com/), but there were still limitations against using many new technologies.

The 2008 release of the WCAG 2.0 changes this. WCAG 2.0 is no longer technology specific (Caldwell, Cooper, Reid, & Vanderheiden, 2008). Rather, it is focused on ideas and concepts that make pages accessible. Pages cannot be designed without limitations, but use of accessibility controls and parameters allow for a much larger playing field that is still considered accessible by the WCAG. This playing field is new, but the pieces have been a long time coming. In the past couple years Flash has become more and more accessible thanks to a couple of key players.

Adobe Flash is one of the most widely available technologies on the web according to WebAIM. org (Creating Accessible Flash) and it is only logical that both Adobe and Freedom Scientific (makers of JAWS, one of the most popular screen readers for people who are blind) have both been working on methods of making the technology accessible. Flash has been working with increased accessibility options since the release of Macromedia Flash MX (Creating Accessible Flash). Controlling reading order of Flash objects is one of the more simple additions in the past couple years. Adding keyboard accessibility through the addition of programmable key commands have opened even more doors; this allows people who do not use the mouse to manipulate objects and for navigation to step through content at their own pace with their own controls. Self-voicing allows content designers to create their own audio content and instruction negating the need for screen readers. Recent changes in captioning allows new interfaces to be built with the buttons or key commands to turn on and off closed captions in a number of languages.

For users, the latest versions of JAWS (Job Access With Speech: a screen reader developed by Freedom Scientific) take advantage of the new changes in Flash. JAWS has many keyboard commands that are active in order for users to navigate a computer and common software; they turn off and focus on Flash keyboard commands given by the content while in the Flash environment. JAWS also has the ability to turn off its voice (the program speaks to the user to guide them) to allow for Flash audio commands to be heard loud and clear. JAWS will also read text equivalents from Flash and also interact with Flash created buttons much like it uses alternative text or "alt=" tags for graphics in HTML.

It has become easier to create accessible Flash objects and with WCAG 2.0 designers will be able to achieve Level AAA accessibility on a page written entirely of Flash. Nevertheless, the topics and guidelines of WCAG 1.0 still stand. Pages must be written in an accessible format using not only the aforementioned tools, but also the following guidelines.

First, alternatives to Flash still need to be made available. Not everyone has the latest software. Even if that were the case, it is truly hard to make a page that will be accessible to everyone. Disabilities affect people in a number of ways (visuals, audio cues, timing, motor control, flicker rates, etc.) and you should consider making your content accessible to the widest range of users.

Second, content must follow logical order. Web interaction has become very dynamic and adaptive technology is very linear, like reading this sidebar. Much of the web content we use changes the instant we make a choice on a form. If new information is created on the server, the page changes instantly no matter where we are reading on the page, without our need to refresh the browser. These pages affect visual impairments most; whether someone is using a screen reader or a magnification program, someone focused on the bottom of the page is not seeing the top information change. This can lead to very confused users. If information changes there should be cues to let readers know they need to start over.

For any Flash objects, tab and reading order must be programmed correctly. Although it may appear on the screen from top to bottom and left to right in a browser, the text may not appear in the same order in the page code. Screen readers read through the code, not the page, from top to bottom. Add Tab order text, such as ".tabIndex=1" to guide users through forms, and correct the order of text in your code that is out of place when read from top to bottom. For many pages, it helps to read the code yourself or try using one of the many Firefox Add-ons or Opera to view the page as text only, without tables, or in another linear format.

Flicker rate must also be taken into consideration. Flash content moves at various paces and any strobe or flashing content should flicker slower than 1 time per second, or faster than 55. Photo epilepsy is common and quite possible with some of the content being used on fast moving sites with heavy animation, although we do not commonly think about it while designing pages.

Lastly, the same standards and requirements that accessibility specialists have been talking about for years are still significant today. Information has to be presented in many formats and with the following in mind:

- Videos with spoken text need captions.
- Written text has to be accessible for screen readers to synthesize.
- Graphics need to have alternative text and descriptions.
- Content needs to be easily controlled by the keyboard.
- Timed events or constraints need to be reasonable so that someone has time to read, respond or take as much time as needed to progress.

- Color should not be the sole means of communicating information and it should never interfere with contrast.
- Refer to the WebAIM.org site on Flash and images for more great tips.

The purpose of a site should drive site design. If a site is driven by information and content, use of accessible formats is vital. Using HTML for navigation is ideal. Many designers choose to start with a site that is 100% accessible and built on a base of HTML and CSS. Graphics, Flash, and PHP are added as mental or visual seasoning. Think of visuals enhancing, rather than replacing, textual information or distracting from content. Kinetic interaction and dynamic graphics are a powerful new option in web design and very helpful as enhancements. Accessible sites are able to reach wider audiences and people who benefit from either text or graphics on the same page.

Web content and accessibility are evolving together, allowing for new trends in content design to be used more and more every year. Pages with graphics and dynamic content are an obvious help to many users, but it has been a struggle to use certain types of images deemed inaccessible by various content standards. These times are fading and the possibilities are endless in regards to accessible yet dynamic and visual content. WCAG 2.0 allows for freedom of technologies but the ideals of version 1.0 still hold true and the same basic accessibility needs exist. Do yourself a favor and learn about using Flash accessibly. Visit webaim.org or adobe.com for articles and tips.

Section 2
Digital Graphics in E-Learning

Chapter 3
The Applied Roles of Graphics in E-Learning

ABSTRACT

In today's modern and networked generation, sophisticated graphics are expected for learning. These digital graphics fulfill a number of learning purposes: to direct attention, to provide examples, to offer evidentiary proofs, to set a context, to introduce a personage or character, to offer an affective jolt to increase memory retention, to entertain, and others. Digital graphics work on both subconscious and conscious levels, and these effects will be examined. This chapter will enhance reader awareness of these rich and varied roles and potentially evoke a variety of creative graphical solutions.

CHAPTER OBJECTIVES

- Consider the applied roles of graphics in e-learning
- Introduce graphical user interface; visual branding; documentation and verification; human identity and social presence; explanations, exemplification, categorization, comparison and contrast; relationships, cause and effect, and causal analysis; processes; downloads and enablements; argumentation and persuasion; complex information visualizations over time; decision-making and problem-solving; the creation of an immersive virtual context; extension of the human imagination; augmented reality, mobile applications, and ambient intelligence, and user-generated imagery
- Enhance reader awareness of potential creative graphical solutions based on the roles of digital graphics in e-learning

DOI: 10.4018/978-1-60566-972-4.ch003

INTRODUCTION

Graphics and visuals fulfill numerous roles in e-learning, for both academic and work-place training purposes. In a general sense, these enhance the e-learning and keep it from being purely textual reading and writing. Images may supplement a curriculum. Still and dynamic images contribute to a full-sensory multi-media learning experience, enhanced by sound and interactivity. Visuals may make online learning more engaging and memorable. Visuals may be a centerpiece of the learning—the analysis, problem-solving and decision-making. Images may convey complex information.

A majority of visuals in e-learning work on the conscious levels but often go unnoticed by users who may be inattentive or untrained in looking at the graphics analytically. Digital images also promote different types of literacy: "statistical, graphic, cartographic and domain" literacy for youth (MacEachren, Harrower, Li, Howard, Downs & Gahegan, 2002). Visuals can enhance human imagination, and they can promote more accurate visualizations of particular phenomena.

This chapter will explore the various functions of digital imagery in e-learning and will offer examples of each type. One assumption is that there may be overlapping functions of the images, but that there are likely central guiding purposes. These will be organized in the order of the more simplistic, stand-alone images and then move to the more complex, immersive visuals. The organizing concept will be based around that of the main learning purposes of the images and their uses in the particular e-learning contexts. This involves consideration both of the motivations of the creators of the visual, the uses by the instructors, and the uses by the learners. Examples of each and some design implications for each will be considered.

Designing a Graphical User Interface

Graphical user interfaces (GUIs) create a context for users to interact with a computer. The GUI not only offers a context but particular depictions of functionalities that may be actualized via the interface. "The user interface is one of the most important parts as all interaction is done using it, and therefore it must be intuitive, understandable, easy to use, and all functionality needed by the user must be accessible with it" (Kamsin, 2007, para. 20). These design structures help users navigate visually cluttered Web pages for easier accessibility (Lee, 2004). Interfaces may be tangible ones such as touch-screen (van den Hoven, Frens, Aliakseyeu, Martens, Overbeeke, & Peters, 2007).

Types of Devices

Visuals may enhance user understandings of how to use a particular online tool. These include cyber dashboards that emulate equipment or machines, such as cockpit software support systems (Williams, 1988) and biofeedback systems. User interfaces may include those for tabletop groupware systems, which integrate computing with real-world work surfaces. A whole body of research tracks how to design such interfaces for illiterate and semi-literate computer users (Medhi, Prasad, & Toyama, 2007).

These may be user interface designs for software programs like learning / course management systems (L/CMSes). GUIs are designed also as portals to data repositories. For smaller hand-held mobile devices, the user interfaces have to be even more creative for effective use given the small screen displays, limited available colors, relatively limited resolutions and limited processing power (Paekle, Reimann & Rosenbach, 2003).

Design Considerations

Such design brings together a range of fields of learning and high-tech devices. Marcus explains, "User interface design requires good visual design of metaphors, mental models, navigation, appearance, and interaction to represent data, functions, tasks, roles, organizations, and people. Techniques of simplicity, clarity, and consistency can improve the communication effectiveness of user interfaces for the Web, mobile devices and information appliances, and performance (productivity) tools. In particular, the use of appropriate typography, layout, color, animation, and symbolism can assist developers to achieve more efficient, effective communication to more diverse user communities" (Marcus, 2001, p. 221).

Depending on the unique user needs, the user interfaces may have to consider a wide assortment of factors.

Mobile devices could be used to provide essential IT services like internet access, communication, information, education and banking in areas where no fully developed infrastructures like the electric grid and wire-based net connections are available. Highly usable interfaces will be a critical factor in the development of successful mobile devices and applications. This is especially true if such IT services should become accessible to illiterate or semi-literate users and users without any previous computer experience where the interface will have to rely largely on graphics and speech as interaction mechanisms (Paelke, Reimann & Rosenbach, 2003, p. 57).

An array of sophistication needs to be considered in terms of users. Visualizations also need to be aesthetically pleasing as well as useful (Skog, Ljungblad & Holmquist, 2003). On a more dynamic level, the user interface may involve affective builds to influence users, and at the same time, may involve technologies to capture user affective signals for higher usability in human-computer interactions. While such technologies are still some years away in terms of the state of the art, there has been progress in this area (Pantic, Sebe, Cohn & Huang, 2005).

Examples

GUIs are used in small-screen mobile devices, Web-based interfaces for websites, user interfaces with simulations, portals to data repositories, interfaces with learning / course management systems, and others.

Design Implications

An interface needs to be directive without intrusiveness. Intuitive interfaces need to guide users regarding their respective uses. Often, an overarching design uses a visual metaphor to describe the interactivity, such as with a scenario or equipment simulation. Programs that build "wireframes" are used to demonstrate the designs with an interactive build albeit without fully built-out contents. (Figure 1)

Branding the Learning

Digital visuals may "brand" the e-learning. As a business strategy, branding refers to the connecting of emotions and values to a company or product line—through logos, language, advertising and market-

Figure 1. An instructor view of the Axio™ Learning / Course Management System (L/CMS) © 2009. Axio Learning. Used with permission.

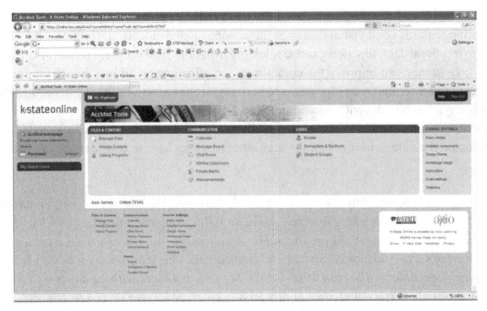

ing campaigns, products and services, and press coverage, with the ambition of supporting consumer good will and loyalty. Branding in higher education helps differentiate and identify one course or online series of courses from another. This endeavor may involve the use of logos (often with taglines), icons or symbols; trademarks or registered marks; a designed look-and-feel, and consistent imagery. The "brand equity" of a university refers to the value of its reputation and name in the larger society and world, based on its brand—built through strategy and quality service. A course or program-of-study brand should be aligned and unified around the core values of the knowledge domain. Learner loyalty means higher learner retention and less student "churn" or turnover. Branding may lower the cost of capturing new students.

With the short attention spans of modern day learners, brand creation needs to be focused and succinct. On the back end, information about learners is data-mined from various sources (including "data marts" about learner demographics), and with collaborative filtering, learner needs may be assessed and addressed within a course or program of study. Various feedback loops (as a kind of dialogue-based marketing) are a critical part of the branding, to keep the brand fresh and relevant to learners.

The branding may be applied to tangibles like CDs and DVDs, learning / course management systems, video elements, websites, and other aspects of e-learning. This branding may enhance the reputation of the module, training or course. It may use aesthetic touches to set an overall sense of tone, professionalism, and quality. This may enhance the marketing and sales efforts as well.

Digital visuals play a large role in setting the tone of an e-learning space or experience. Graphic design unifies the disparate elements of ideas, iconography, sound, textual content, interactivity, imagery, and navigational structures / user interfaces, in an aesthetically pleasing way to convey an over-arching mood. Tone relates closely to the purpose of the e-learning, whether the tone is humorous or serious, concrete or abstract, joyful or somber. They may contribute to a mix of tones over time for learning effect.

Figure 2. A small sampling of academic logos

Digital visuals also enhance the attraction and "enchantment" of human-computer interactions (McCarthy, Wright, Wallace, & Dearden, 2006). These authors cite sensuality; full human engagements (desires, feelings and anxieties); "being-in-play"; "paradox, openness, and ambiguity," and the unfinalisability and transformational character of some online experiences as enchanting (p. 373).

Examples

Logos (see Figure 2), icons, look-and-feel designs, interactivity, and avatar designs, may all be a part of the branding of e-learning materials and experiences. These help create and magnify reputations across the Internet and WWW.

Design Implications

Branded learning needs to be aesthetically aligned within the learning domain and consistent. The brand should help that particular module or series stand out memorably in a global field of learning contents.

Documentation and Verification

Various types of digital images may be used for documentation and verification. Digital scans of court documents are commonly used to bolster historical, political and legal assertions. Photorealistic images are used to portray different types of realities. Visuals captured via satellite photos, sonic visual captures, microscopic digital image capture, telescopic digital visual capture, and others, may establish facts. Such images often require both an effective way of measuring the size of the objects in the viewfinder and also a white setting as a way to adjust the baseline color for accuracy.

Data extraction is a critical element in some raw image captures. For example, some may want to detect and quantify individual persons in a crowd (Green, Blumenstein, Browne & Tomlinson, 2005, n.p.). Others may want to extract roads or structures from aerial imagery (Agouris, Doucette, & Stefanidis, 2001).

There are a number of endeavors to preserve cultural heritage through digital archival (Addison, 2002), even though such endeavors may be painstaking (Gladney, Mintzer, Schiattarella, Bescós, & Treu, 1998), and adding value to the captures by placing secondary information with the object for contextualization. The high resolution 3D models to capture cultural heritage offers a separate artifact than the original (Koller & Levoy, 2005). For example, 3D captures are used to preserve context around historically valuable vases (Shiaw, Jacob & Crane, 2004) from archaeological sites.

Objects from various archaeological digs have been captured for virtual reality depictions:

The immersive VR (virtual reality) visualization of the recovered information gave them the opportunity to explore it in a new and dynamic way and, in several cases, enabled them to make discoveries that opened new lines of investigation about the excavation. This helps users understand the complex spatial relationships between "the artifacts, the architecture, and the stratigraphy from the site (Acevedo, Vote, Laidlaw & Joukowsky, 2001, p. 493).

"Archival documents" refer to "the paper trails of individuals living their lives, or corporate bodies carrying out their functions" (Fachry, Kamps & Zhang, 2008, p. 102). These are digital byproducts of regular life and work processes.

Examples

These include any image captures via the many means possible, within a number of fields—meteorology, medical sciences, astronomy, geology, journalism, history, archaeology, art, literature, political science, and others. Preservation endeavors capture digital "equivalents" of their physical counterparts for "world heritage" (Addison, 2002, pp. 343 – 354, and 380). Damaged manuscripts may be restored digitally using UV light captures for badly damaged texts for more informational value, and 3D captures to represent crinkled or curled documents, with digital flattening for readability (Brown & Seales, 2001). Visuals may be raw data or processed, analyzed data.

Born-digital information may also be "grabbed" through screenshots, video grabs, *machinima-* videography, and other information captures. For video, this sense of control slows the transience of images and makes the experience infinitely repeatable. Live information captures—through sensors or web cams—may add an element of live surveillance to the documentation. Documentary video may be archived for research and later reference.

Design Implications

Images used for documentation and verification need to have a clear "chain of custody" in terms of their acquisition. There should be ways to adjust for accurate color and size, as well as time-of-day of the capture. The more information available about the image capture, the better.

Conveying Human Identity (Telepresence) and Social Presence

Digital visuals are often used in social networking sites to convey individual human identities and telepresences, particularly in "distributed" and "disembodied" situations of interaction. Visuals, for example, are used in e-learning to humanize the members of a course and to create communities-of-practice (and networks-of-practice). These telepresences create a sense of co-location and connection. They may also create a sense of motivation for learning, with a sense of shared camaraderie and mutual support.

These digitally-enabled telepresences may include photo-realistic or modified head shots used as digital avatars in chat rooms and online communities. These avatars may include imaginary created avatars that evoke aspects of human personality or non-human (animal) or inanimate sorts. These may be photo-realistic, 2D drawings, 3D whole-body characters, fictionalized *manga* characters evolved from photos, or other designs. "Perfect video avatars" are being created for collaborative, augmented real-time virtually mediated conferencing (Prince, Cheok, Farbiz, Williamson, Johnson, Billinghurst,

& Kato, 2002, p. 364). 3D "depth streams" of live "tele-immersion" conferencing is yet another model for live and rich interactivity (Yang, Yu, Nahrstedt, & Bajscy, 2006, n.p.).

Trade characters (that embody corporations) may be humans, giants, talking animals, or other entities and objects. Some telepresences are automated robots, which use artificial intelligence and natural language to interact with human users. A pedagogical agent, designed to enhance the learning, may be portrayed as a person or some other life-form or entity.

The role of emotion is fairly critical in defining a character. Some computers with perceptual intelligence are emotion-aware machines and may offer a level of synchronous interactivity with human users (Rheingold, 2003, p. 90). More recent interactive robots may have full back-story builds with unique beliefs, motivations, histories and values to guide their behaviors in the immersive spaces.

Some telepresences may involve invisibility or near-invisibility, which enables lurking and unobtrusive observations.

In some immersive social spaces, people may identify closely with their respective avatars (Raab, 2003, p. 3). Some instructors ask students to make their avatars as close to an official head-shot of themselves as possible in order to further this likeness. In IP multicasts, people use their live "talking head" images to convey a sense of themselves to the other participants.

Visuals may convey group identities as well, by communicating their self-chosen symbols and colors and adding visual representations of their levels of activity or popularity. Group telepresence may involve any number of informational facades to the outside world as well as communications to those in-group.

Telepresences—whether individual or group—evolve with interaction or the communications that occur between the "disembodied" individuals inhabiting the avatars and other expressions of human presence. Some suggest that the work that is created by the individuals may be interpreted as residuals of presence. This is no static identity but one that is being built with the accrual of interactions and artifacts. Such builds of characters and presences promote social and emotional intelligence development. They support trust-building and collaboration.

Examples

Human telepresences are conveyed in profiles and avatars; group telepresences are conveyed through various information streams. The live and asynchronous participation of the people behind the avatars and group telepresences continue to evolve telepresence. Video may convey telepresences powerfully—through video captures of presentations and lectures, customized video feedback to learners or groups of learners, narrated cases, and live "stimulated recall" or interactive teacher and learner thinking (Tochon, 2007, pp. 53 – 65).

Design Implications

Social cognitive theory suggests that people benefit from the co-construction of knowledge through communications and interactivity, and the digital representations of their "being" in digital space will play a critical part in some types of learning that involve teamwork, innovations, far-transfer learning, and collaboration. (Figure 3)

Figure 3. Social presences expressed through avatars on Help Island in SL

Explanations and Exemplifications / Illustrations / Categorization, Grouping and Typology / Comparison and Contrast

One of the most common uses of imagery in e-learning is to explain and to provide examples. These digital images may be photo-realistic image captures of *realia*. These may be dramatizations or re-enactments, as in digital drawings, models or video captures. These may involve video-taped demonstrations. There may be detailed cutaways of particular aspects of an image for deeper explanations. There may be special effects such as the ghosting of the highlighted part of the object to maintain its sense of location.

Images are often integrated directly into computer training tools:

The use of computer training tools where the student can interact with a computer model can give good feedbacks. 3D analytical approach is especially useful in determining the fundamental molecular events using a web-based, visually-oriented system that allows efficient querying of gene expression (Kamsin, 2007, para. 1).

A further step in explaining is providing a more macro view through categorization. Categorizing items into different groupings may be enhanced with the use of imagery as these allow points of color and size comparison. Various typologies may be represented as parts of ontologies or data models or structures. These define objects and their interrelationships with other entities, in a particular domain field (or in a cross-domain situation).

Volumetric information may also be a point of comparison. 3D images may be manipulated for viewing from various angles. Digital imagery files are often used for comparison and contrast. Timelines, charts and tables may show changes over time between particular factors. Photo-realistic images may show before and after visuals, in a tsunami or hurricane situation. Images may be placed side-by-side for visual identification and differentiation. Facial recognition software may be used to differentiate individuals. Different immersive atmospheres and contexts may be compared and contrasted to evoke moods.

One type of explanation may be a reproduction—of a projected scenario or event. These may be used for training and planning for catastrophic events, or these may be used as part of a presentation in a court case to show a potential interpretive sequence of events.

Examples

Learners may identify different tissue types using magnetic resonance imaging (MRI) (Wünsche & Lobb, 2004). Coastal mapping integrating satellite imagery with orthoimagistic overlays may promote "safe navigation, coastal resource management, coastal environmental protection, and sustainable coastal development and planning" (Di, Ma, Wang, & Li, 2003). High-resolution sensor data applications involve "precision agriculture, forest resource management, and environment assessments of transportation systems" (King, 2000, pp. 2602 – 2604). Simulated imagery may allow the control of multiple parameters to lead to a fuller understanding of targeted phenomena (Blake & Brown, 2003). A 3D model and simulation of a kelp forest enhanced an aquarium exhibit (Brutzman, 2002).

Design Implications

Explanations should be comprehensive and detailed; the examples offered should include a number of possibilities for the best accuracy in terms of identifying the different entities. If examples may be shown from a variety of angles and at different levels of focus, that would be helpful, too. Categories should be comprehensive (all-inclusive of the various types) and mutually exclusive (so the categories are not overlapping or confusing). Comparisons and contrasts should define the exact points-of-comparison and the standards used in those comparisons.

Showing Relationships / Cause and Effect / Causal Analysis

Fractals, geometrical shapes generated by computers through formulas and machine-inspiration, may show complex relationships, such as crystalline shapes or epidemiological infection trails through a society. Simulations with live data feeds or sensors may create real-time interactive scenarios that show relationships between various entities. Common ones here involve real-time weather simulations (Treinish, 2002, "Case study…", p. 549), and their effects on various aspects of the environment or human experience. Learners may group around visual models and engage in observational inquiry and more easily detect patterns—by decomposing complex processes, comparing elements, identifying relevant factors, and model "causal" understandings (Smith & Blankinship, 1999, n.p.).

Examples

Images that show relationships involve much back-end complexity in terms of supporting details and analysis. In a complex world, relationships between factors and entities may be nuanced or complex. A variety of sims tools exist for eLearning applications in finance. These involve financial portfolio tracking, mapping portfolios in relation to others, sector tracking, asset allocator, mutual funds map, fund analyzers, buy or rent mortgage calculator, home buying worksheet, home buying worksheet, retirement worksheets and others (Gold, 2001, p. 78). Interactive spreadsheets are also very common, particularly for popular use. Simulations have played an important role in business applications:

Business simulations play a major role in industry and higher education for more than 40 years. They preserve the knowledge of complex dynamic systems by modeling the cohesions and dependencies between the simulations' objects and transfer the modeled information by simulating its dynamic aspect on computer systems. In that way the knowledge about the behavior of the dynamic system is transferred to the specific target group. Depending on what knowledge should be preserved, the cohesions of the system for the audience the simulation may differ (Hampel & Bernroider, 2004, n.p.).

Immersive displays have been used for applications in computer science, automotive engineering, and chemical exploration (Pape & Anstey, 2002, p. 55).

Design Implications

Viewers of the imagery should be able to discern where the images have come from and the underlying logic behind the assertions of causal relationships, the degree of causation, and possible confounding factors. The more contextual information for users, the better.

Processes and Procedures: "How-to" Directional and Fresh Designs

Informational processes and directional ("how-to") procedures may be depicted to show steps in a process and over time. Time-lapse captures by digital cameras may be shown to illuminate gradual changes or evolution. The power of sequencing is that this may be done in live capture mode, or it may be recorded and replayed for critical moments of change. Nuanced changes may be powerfully captured. Learners who want to review the steps to a process may be able to control the focus on particular digital slides or images, which are enhanced with textual and / or auditory explanations.

In terms of performance art, dance is mixed with science, math and computer science in live performances, with dance moves choreographed by a collaboration with computers (Burg & Lüttringhaus, 2006). An adaptation combining "gesture, scenography, and space" was used to "question the distinctions between theater, installation, and ritual" in a performance of Fleury's Massacre (Dolinsky & Nelson, 2007, pp. 249 – 250). Other digital affordances create so-called event spaces for interactions to capture creativity and open-ended exploration among dancers and performers (Thomsen, 2008, pp. 383 – 390).

Images may be captured as individual brainstormings, sketching, and the abstracting of designs; these may also be collaborative works, aided with various authoring and communications technologies. Some software programs enhance storytelling with digital pictures, with tools to help novices (Landry & Guzdial, 2006, pp. 160 – 168).

Examples

Common processes depicted digitally include both the commonplace and the more complex. Commonplace processes may include how to cook a particular dish, set up a particular piece of equipment, or conduct an effective digital image capture. More complex processes may involve how to analyze a biosecurity situation, develop a combat plan, create a business plan, or design a complex solution for land-use. One augmented reality simulation with a haptics glove reviews virtual assembly operations (Zhao & Madhavan, 2006). Others use data gloves to manipulate digital objects in a 3D environment

(Qi, Martens, van Liere, & Kok, 2005). Yet another endeavor uses 3D virtuality for upper extremity rehabilitation (Galego & Simone, 2007).

Design Implications

Processes need to be depicted accurately at all critical junctures. The image captures need to be detailed and real-world. Because this learning often involves action and "doing," there should be plenty of downloadables for easier learning and transfer of the actions into the lived environment.

Reaching In-World: Downloadables and Enablements

The cliché "out of sight, out of mind" may apply to various visual understandings. For that reason, various downloadables may be created for use in print form in the physical world. Digital designs, blueprints, overlays, maps, and other "downloadables" may be created for accurate printable form. Reference images and models may also be helpful as physical referents. Photos of individuals may also be downloaded for wallet shots for identification or recognition. Some references may be downloaded to mobile devices or global positioning systems (GPS) devices for further user enhancements.

These may be used for the creation of other objects, like projected digital "paper" with foldlines for origami. Designed computerized experiences offer ways to reach in-world and to enable greater skill functions. One project uses multimodal interaction strategies—projected video clips, projected animations onto paper, electric field sensing of touch inputs on a desk surface, and "swept-frequency sensors to detect paper folds"—to convey the folding of origami shapes.

More importantly, the Origami Desk project incorporated numerous aspects of design—hardware design, installation design, interface design, graphic design, sensor design, software design, content design—into an interactive experience aimed at making the user forget about the technology altogether (Ju, Bonanni, Fletcher, Hurwitz, Jidd, Post, Reynolds & Yoon, 2002, 399).

Examples

Any number of digital image objects may be designed for easy printability and download use. These may be downloaded digitally to mobile devices, too, for portable reference. These downloadables may include design documents, maps, photos, and models—for direct in-world reference.

Design Implications

Most digital images will be versioned in various ways for deployment via repositories, LMSes, mobile devices, and printers. Conceptualizing the various outputs will enhance the planning and execution of digital image creation and deployment in the learning environment.

Argumentation and Persuasion, Call to Action, and User Behavioral Roles

Digital imagery may be used for a behavioral effect on viewers, to encourage particular behaviors—whether for political, marketing and sales, or other aims. Action-motivating images may be still or dynamic. The critical aspect here is to spark appetite or some kind of behavioral action. Appeals to action may be logical and cognitive, and these may stand up under rigorous analysis over time. Other appeals may appeal to emotions or quick decision-making, and these appeals to instinct or emotions may hold up less well. Visual information may set expectations for work situations as well.

Illustrations in particular help meld ideas in often clearly artificial non-photorealistic ways. For example, these may use mixed scales to convey a message about size: a squirrel holding an air-conditioning unit in its paws. Or an illustration may humanize a health issue by overlaying images of models' faces over red blood cells.

Examples

Political ad campaigns, marketing campaigns, advertising endeavors, and some non-profit organizational appeals may all involve some call to action. In higher education, some examples would include a meditation that combined nature images and music; demonstrated exercise techniques; lab demonstrations (with the understanding that students would emulate the analyses and processes), and field trip captures that may suggest a particular course of travel and learning actions. Other types of actions evoked by images may involve their use as prompts for discussion, analysis and self-awareness, as in a diabetes education endeavor (Frost & Smith, 2003).

Design Implications

Appeals to action using images should follow ethical standards of not misrepresenting information and not manipulating decision-makers.

Portraying Complex Information (Over Time)

One of the most important affordances of digital imagery involves the portrayal of complex information streams and the inter-relationships between different data streams. Univariate and multivariate data may be captured through a range of means (remote sensors, digital cameras, web cams, scanners, satellite, and others) in real-time, collated, computer-analyzed (particularly for interdependence) and re-deployed for human use for observation, analysis and learning. Most live captures may be reconstructed for later analysis and comparisons.

The control of time may be one aspect of the portrayal of the information. Or the depiction of the data may be time dependent. Time may be portrayed in discrete pre-determined intervals, or it may be displayed continuously and in a linear way. Current data may be contrasted with past information based on established cycles. Or time may be captured in an ordinal way (such as before / after a particular event). Time itself may be shown branching off depending on events captured (Müller & Schumann, 2003). Controlling live time may be done through time-lapse, slow motion, fast motion, or others.

There are rich ways used to show time-varying data, which may often be volatile.

Müller and Schumann offer some helpful questions in considering the time aspect.

- Does a data element exist at a specific time? (Existence of a data element)
- When does a data element exist on time? Is there any cyclic behavior? (Temporal location)
- How long is the time span from beginning to end of the data element? (Temporal interval)

- How often does a data element occur? (Temporal texture)
- How fast is a data element changing or how much difference is there from data element to data element over time? (Rate of change)
- In what order do data elements appear? (Sequence)
- Do data elements exist together? (Synchronization) (2003, p. 737).

Glyphs encode information through visuals, with multiple values encoded in the icon parameters. "The shape, color. transparency, orientation. etc., of the glyph can be used to visualize data values. Glyph rendering is an extension to the use of glyphs and icons in numerous fields, including cartography. logic. semiotics, and pictorial information systems" (Ebert, Shaw, Zwa, & Starr, 1996, p. 205). Various lines may connect time and feature values. One example of a glyph depicting time involves a circular image with the months listed in clockwise order, and various values are depicted as extensions outwards along the various splines around the circle. Maps overlaid with satellite renderings of storm systems and winds are common multi-variate visualizations.

Designing an effective glyph requires sophisticated planning for effective use of the screen real-estate. "Multivariate data visualization requires the development of effective techniques for simultaneously conveying multiple different data distributions over a common domain. Although it is easy to successfully use color to represent the value of a single variable at a given location, effectively using color to represent the values of multiple variables at the same point at the same time is a trickier business." Some combine color with texture to "co-locate variables" to communicate ever-richer ways to portray information (Shenas & Interrante, 2005, p. 443).

Visuals may also change based on behaviors by the user. Inputs by users may have effects on the environment.

Programmed "chance factors" may also have effects. For example, the simulation of dispersive contaminants in an urban environment for security planning (Qiu, Zhao, Fan, Wei, Lorenz, Wang, Yoakum-Stover, Kaufman, & Mueller, 2004) *may be visualized and depicted based on different scenarios. Network traffic may be monitored and represented using 2D and 3D visualizations* (Le Malécot, Kohara, Hori & Sakurai, 2006).

Medical interventions, such as simulated surgery using haptic devices, may capture time-based effects based on the users' inputs via the touch devices. These include augmented reality systems such as ultrasound-guided needle biopsies (State, Livingston, Garrett, Hirota, Whitton, Pisano & Fuchs, 1996). High-resolution medical images may be used for regular and mobile diagnosis for improved care, with a focus on unique cases (McLoughlin, O'Sullivan, Bertolotto, & Wilson, 2006). There are endeavors to maintain parts of medical images in lossless formats while the rest of the image is compressed in more lossy forms (for easier digital size manageability); the high resolution preservation enhances legal and clinical uses of the images in this hybrid compression approach (Bai, Jin, & Feng, 2004).

Information technologies have enabled complex visualizations, such as a project to look at the interactions between "population growth, economic activity, and environmental effects" in an econometric model (Wegenkittl, Gröller, & Purgathofer, 1997, pp. 71 – 79). Others included the fusion of multiple wind tunnel experiments into one visualization (Severance, Brewster, Lazos, & Keefe, 2001).

Time-series data has critical implications for a number of fields.

The analysis of time-series data is one of the most widely appearing problems in science, engineering, and business. In the last years this problem gained increasing importance due to the fact that more sensitive sensors in science and engineering and the widespread use of computers in corporations have increased the amount of time-series data collected by many magnitudes (Müller & Schumann, 2003, p. 737).

The real-time aspects must include an ability to engage complexity.

Visualization can be an important tool for displaying, categorizing and digesting large quantities of inter-related information during laboratory and simulation experiments. Summary visualizations that compare and represent data sets in the context of a collection are particularly valuable. Applicable visualizations used in these settings must be fast (near real time) and should allow the addition of data sets as they are acquired without requiring re-rendering of the visualization (Robbins & Gorman, 2000).

Such images play a critical role in supporting analytics data interpretation and sense-making of larger systems phenomena. Screen design is used to reduce information complexity and enhance emergency procedure responses (Jones, Ma, Starkey, & Ma, 2007). Complex images that are poorly designed may quickly result in incoherence.

Live situations involve unpredictability; they are evolving. Live imagery may offer real-time, situational awareness. The use of complex rugged sensors enables the capturing of information from the ocean bottom, outer space, active volcanoes, and even nano-level miniaturized depictions. Making the information useful may require de-noising the data (removing irrelevant information). It may mean offering white-color balancing and ways to measure or understand the size of the object depicted. For example, measurement tools are needed to measure distances, angles and volumes in 3D visualizations (Preim, Tietjen, Spindler, & Peitgen, 2002, pp. 21 – 28). This type of imagery needs to exist on the accurate planes of depth as contrasted to 2D, which is more forgiving and less precisely defined. Some measures are fixed while others are dynamic, depending on how close in to an image that a user has zoomed.

High-resolution displays sometimes involve the use of scalable display walls with projected images (Jeong, Renambot, Jagodic, Singh, Aguilera, Johnson, & Leigh, 2006, para. 3). Large-scale imagery may often have to be broken down into tiles or segments for easier rendering and analysis. High dynamic range images contain plenty of visual information with different lighting exposures to capture a range of lighting experiences. Some of these effects may be created synthetically with renderers.

The depiction of volumetric flow or movement of materials (gases, liquids, and solids) is used in "space science, numerical analysis, biomedical applications, robotics" (Li, 1992, p. 44). These depictions capture turbulence.

Some kinds of machine art depict "alive painting"—or a machine-based creativity. Various fractals may be purely machine-generated and highly variant.

Other images involve the evolution of artificial life (a-life) based on complex algorithms that mimic various life forms and biology-based environments. Here, there are individual robot creature life cycles and environmental interactions. While early forms of a-life were built on geometric models, or simple visuals, since then, kinematic, physical, behavioral, cognitive and evolutionary elements have been built into such creations (Terzopoulos, 1999).

Examples

There are many examples of 3D visualizations. Artificial life captures microcosms of digital flora and fauna interacting in a digital environment. For example, a 3D scene visualization and data organization shows corn growing cycle that integrates remote sensing information (Hu, Xie, & Du, 2004). Other programs show human avatars as they interact with each other socially in immersive 3D spaces.

Design Implications

The underlying simulation model behind a time-based complex scenario must be accurate to the world for the visuals to be considered valid (see Figure 4). There need to be clear points of references for an understanding of size, time, color, and other issues of scale. There should also be clear relevance of the information for understanding, analysis and decision-making. If users are to navigate through this construct or immersive space, there should be clear way-finding ideas for navigation. There must be ways to make meaning.

Figure 4. The National Oceanic and Atmospheric Administration's National Weather Service and Multiple Information Streams Delivered via the WWW (NOAA, 2009)

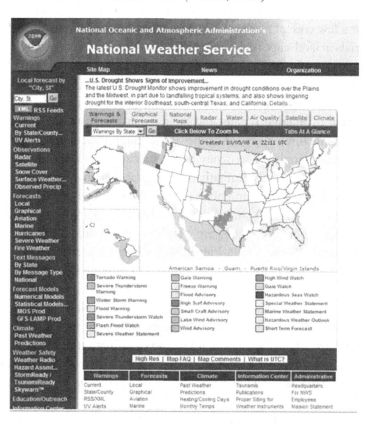

Decision-Making and Problem-Solving

A further step after considering data for analysis involves real-world decision-making and problem-solving. Some researchers suggest that problems previously believed to be unsolvable may now be addressable with the huge deposits of information on the Web (Liu, Wang, Li, Li, Ma, Lu, & Ma, 2007). Virtual problem-solving environments (PSEs) set up scenarios in which users may consider relevant information and make decisions, with some systems simulating effects from those decisions.

These environments bring together rich expertise.

PSEs (problem solving environments) also provide infrastructure for vertical integration of computational knowledge. Specific elements that may be incorporated into a comprehensive PSE include knowledge of the relevant discipline(s); the best computational techniques, algorithms and data structures; the associated programming techniques; the relevant user interface and human-computer interface design principles; the applicable visualization and imaging techniques; and methods for mapping the computations to various computer architectures (Bramley 2000). A PSE can consolidate knowledge from a range of experts in these disparate areas into a system that offers the end user a powerful set of computational tools (Johnson & Weinstein, 2006, n.p.).

Visuals enhance case studies, too, which also combine decision-making and problem-solving. These may include group discussions and work, which contribute to possible solutions.

Some problem-solving environments offer close-ended solutions where the learning artifacts channel responses to one or a few correct responses. Others offer content for a variety of possible solutions, such as learning materials in landscape architecture that allow a multitudinous choice of possible design responses of varying quality—based on a range of considerations and standards. Here, the visuals—topological maps, climate studies, and on-ground photos—create a sense of realism.

In healthcare, there are plenty of text and images to create analytical situations; visuals here may involve stereo digitization of internal organs and their reconstructions. CT (computer tomography), MRI (magnetic resonance imaging), x-rays and other visual capture methods provide images of internal organs. There are virtual endoscopies. There may be screen captures or photos of machine readings to enhance the reality of the medical analytical situation. Digital imaging is used medical education and therapy planning in exploring vascular structures (Hahn, Preim, Selle & Peitgen, 2001, para. 2). 3D surgical simulations (Linney, 1991), 3D ultrasounds based on echo data (Fattal & Lischinski, 2001, pp. 403 – 410), and other types of image captures are widely used in medical training. Holographic video displays convey medical data (Plesniak, Halle, Pieper, Wells, Jakab, Meier, Benton, Guttmann, & Kikinis, 2003, pp. 589 – 596). Digital medical imagery is archived to provide teaching resources; aid medical professionals with difficult cases; support epidemiological studies, and contribute to the development of technologies that support human health (Power, Politou, Slaymaker, Harris & Simpson, 2004, p. 273).

Bioinformatic visualizations provide biologically relevant insight into data (such as gene expression microarrays in the life sciences), and these allow the examination of thousands of variables from large data sets simultaneously (Saraiya, North, & Duca, 2005). Such visualizations may help facilitate diagnoses, plan surgeries, understand human physiology, and discover new clinical treatments (Johnson & Weinstein, 2006, para.1).

In business courses, business strategy and problem solving are applied through computerized visualization (Gresh & Kelton, 2003). High dimensional marketing data for financial asset management is available through another visualization (Smuelders & Heijs, 2005). Interactive algebra software, with visual formulas and symbols, enhance computer science learning (Tran, 2006).

Some decision-making is aided by automation. The work of dispatchers and air traffic controllers who have to consider a large number of data variables over a wide geographic region to ensure secure operations is supported by user interrupt signals to alert operators or to pass along warnings (Anderson, Pottinger, Schroeder, & Adapa, 1993).

Immersive virtual multiverses involve all sorts of complex decision-making and cooperative behaviors to solve shared in-universe challenges, such as the need to gather resources, to plan and execute attacks, and build up town defenses.

Examples

A simple visual used to test for the ability to cope with visual complexity and visual planning would be mazes. Others involve scenarios that place learners in a simulation—for business, military, ethics, sales, and other types of learning. Case studies may set up problem-solving scenarios based on a set of facts and limited information. Live telemedicine and evidence-based medicine (EBM) may enhance medical care and diagnostic surety in collaboration over distances.

Design Implications

There must be clear design of the problem-solutions that learners will experience and a clear tie-in to learning values. The visual information that learners have need to clearly relate to the problem-based learning.

Creating an Immersive Virtual Context

3D images play a critical role in creating multi-sensory immersive imagery. They create a sense of context and orient users to the space—even those who've just entered the virtual space for the first time. Immersive visuals convey character; provide clues for way-finding through the immersive virtual reality, and create excitement for user engagement. These objects are guided in part by built-in physics engines in the online multiverse, and their behaviors contribute to the sense of virtual realism. The images may be used to move the narrative forward and to offer smooth experiential segues. The images may communicate information about a particular game state.

Immersive virtual environments offer interactivity with live, human participants. Landscapes change as they move through different parts of the immersive virtual spaces. As they engage with the various "bots," they are able to wield equipment, communicate with others, and make changes to the world around them and to themselves. The input devices may be touch screens, data gloves, keyboards, game devices, or other objects.

Automated characters may also provide interactivity. They may be emo-agents, with full emotional range.

Recently a new breed of agents has begun to surface in everyday applications: these agents appear on screen as embodied entities—whether humans, or anthropomorphized objects and animals—facilitating our interactions with software applications, navigating menus and web-pages, offering tips and cus-

tomizing our online purchases. These embodied agents converse and interact with humans through text bubbles, sometimes accompanied by sound clips of their utterances, often expressing colorful personalities through animated gestures (Maldonado, Lee, Brave, Nass, Nakajima, Yamada, Iwamura & Morishima, 2005, p. 408).

They may have natural and communicative gestures:

In human communication theory, a gesture that links the subject of a spoken sentence with a visual reference is known as a deictic gesture, or simply deixis. When people engage in conversation, they sometimes indicate the subject or object in a sentence by pointing with a finger, glancing, or nodding in a particular direction. For example, a shopper might say, 'Give me that one,'; while pointing at a particular wedge of cheese at a delicatessen counter. The deictic gesture is considered to be the most element of linguistic acts...Deixis has its own rich vocabulary (Levelt, et al., 1985; Oviatt, et al., 1997, as cited in Ware, 2004, p. 309).

Others may be non-player characters whose digital presences add richness to the surroundings but which do not interact as directly with human participants.

Cognitive models may change how a certain immersive scene is portrayed. "*Cognitive models go beyond behavioral models in that they govern what a character knows, how that knowledge is acquired, and how it can be used to plan physical and sensing actions. Cognitive models can also play subsidiary roles in controlling cinematography and lighting for computer games and animation*" (Funge, 2000, p. 42). *Live interactions may result in live collaborations and performances in the arts, with the power of improvisation* (Mueller, 2007).

Examples

Currently, immersive spaces include those portraying artificial life (based on evolutionary and biological principles), human social interactions (for business administration, anthropology, education, military science, and other fields), and focused situations of interactivity (as in foreign language study).

Design Implications

Visualization technologies must engage users. "Our thesis is that *visualization technology, no matter how well it is designed, is of little educational value unless it engages learners in an active learning activity.* If this is true, then the key question to consider is what, if any, forms of active engagement with visualization technology can have a positive impact on how much a learner learns" (Naps, Fleischer, McNally, Rößling, Hundhausen, Rodger, Almstrum, Korhonen, Velázquez-Iturbide, Dann, & Malmi, 2002).

Extending the Human Imagination: Invisible World Realities, Abstractions, Illusions and Special Effects

Visualizations may engage real data and data analysis, or it may involve hypothetical or imaginary concepts, or "thought experiments" that may be impractical to actualize but with concepts that are critical to consider. Invisible worlds of microbial agents, nano-level creations, atoms, and even postulated realities may be depicted through digital imagery. Synthetic images provide a greater range of potentiality in terms of what may be imaged. Expert programmers may build "multidimensional structures which they manipulate or traverse in order to specify, predict, and simulate program behavior" (Petre & Blackwell, 1997, p. 109).

The core rationale for a visualization is to create insight, defined as the true nature of a situation. Insight must generally meet the following criteria:

Complex. Insight is complex, involving all or large amounts of the given data in a synergistic way, not simply individual data values.

Deep. Insight builds up over time, accumulating and building on itself to create depth. Insight often generates further questions and, hence, further insight.

Qualitative. Insight is not exact, can be uncertain and subjective, and can have multiple levels of resolution.

Unexpected. Insight is often unpredictable, serendipitous, and creative.

Relevant. Insight is deeply embedded in the data domain, connecting the data to existing domain knowledge and giving it relevant meaning. It goes beyond dry data analysis, to relevant domain impact (North, May – June 2006, p. 6).

Insight is especially critical to achieve in situations where meanings are elusive. Digital imagery may extend human imagination by making abstract concepts more tangible. For example, large mesoscale weather models may be deployed (Treinish, 2000,"Multi-resolution visualization…") or visualizations of ocean currents at a global scale (Crocker, Matthews, Emery, & Baldwin, 2007). Large-scale aerodynamic calculations (Ma & Crockett, 1999) may enhance user conceptualizations. Another visualization involves the gathering of large amounts of airflow data to help helicopter pilots in simulated hazardous conditions (Aragon & Hearst, Apr. 2005). Algorithms may be visualized (Blumenkrants, Starovisky & Shamir, 2006) with both high-tech and low-tech methods, like hand-drawing (Hundhausen & Douglas, 2000, p. 21). Line illustrations themselves are complex to effectively create and use because they are "so highly abstracted from the full-color, continuous-tone real world" (Andrews, 2006, p. 1). Cosmology and astrophysics phenomena may be digitally depicted (Weiskopf, Borchers, Ertl, Falk, Fechtig, Frank, Grave, King, Kraus, Müller, Nollert, Mendez, Ruder, Schafhitzel, Schär, Zahn, & Zatloukal, 2006).

Digital artists may create myths and illusions with non-photorealistic images. These allow for more abstract and symbolic representations (Gal, Sorkine, Popa, Sheffer, & Cohen-Or, 2007). Photos may be turned into *manga* characters, replete with animations. These creations may enhance storylines. These may offer visions of fictional futures.

Synthetic non-playable characters may be introduced into immersive games. Synthetic speech animations may be built over a photo-realistic video of a speaker, and a computer-created voice may channeled through this videorealistic image of this human actor (Ezzat, Geiger, & Poggio, 2002). This multidimensional morphable model (MMM) is only one of a number of integrations of the photorealistic with the digital synthetic.

Overlays of special effects may be created in digital space, such as relighting structures and artifacts. Stylized shadows with highlights for designer influences may be applied to digital objects and characters (Aniyo, Wemler & Baxter, 2006). Sprinkles of digital glitter may be overlaid on a scene. Computer art, which is dated back to 1956 by the Digital Art Museum, may evoke rich visual sensations. Kaleidoscopic effects, fractals, holography, and other types of digital image arts are popular and used for a variety of situations.

Some digital images have been set up as memorials—to celebrate or remember some event, phenomena, persons, or values. Others are created for bragging rights. Electronic kudos are posted online for a kind of digital posterity.

Extreme size depictions may be commonly created. Extreme-scale studies involve those from astronomy, atmospheric sciences, geology, biology, chemistry, nano-technology, and others. Cross-sections of seeds, organs, buildings, and other elements may offer fresh insights.

Examples

Fictional effects may involve special effects such as created imaginary creatures and fictional multi-verses. Simulations of potential disaster or accident scenarios may be portrayed in these digital scenarios, too, as ways to plan for potential trouble. A new, creative software meshes disparate images into a photo-realistic virtual tour using geometric scene matching, so people may segue between various locales as they navigate the 3D terrain created from 2D images (Sivic, Kaneva, Torralba, Avidan & Freeman, 2008).

Design Implications

Such visualizations and simulations need to be planned thoroughly to promote multiple complex lessons and to avoid negative learning (see Figure 5).

Augmented Reality, Mobile Applications, and Ambient Intelligence

Digital visuals enhance real-world real-time experiences in real-spaces through augmented reality. Such digitally enhanced installations may make a museum experience more immersive and interactive (Garzotto & Rizzo, 2007). Location sensing through "sentient chips" have created new generations of aware devices (Rheingold, 2003, p. 85), which allows for location-sensitive delivery of visual information. Scenes are modeled for specific learning outcomes. Augmented reality allows for maximizing embodied learning, in real-space and real-time, with physical presences—and the ability to enhance physical practice and muscle-memory learning (with the benefit of digital imagery, voice, and informational overlays). Augmented reality supports the physical embodiment of the learner in real space for a "body sense."

Some reality augmentations extend human capabilities, such as their visual acuity with see-through (and semi-opaque) head-mounted displays and the intermediation of cameras and technologies (Rheingold, 2003, pp. 89 – 90). There may be synchronized 3D overlays of the natural world (p. 92) based on spatial coordinates. There may even be live foreign language translation of text for users in a real space (p. 94), with the visualization and aural augmentations operationalizing information in a live situation. Augmented reality *machinima* involves the mixing of physical with virtual contents for digitized machine-cinema (Lang, MacIntyre, & Zugaza, 2008).

In one case, designers built virtual representations of buildings in the past to be viewable on mobile devices, once those were pointed at a particular building.

In addition, the user can view the building at different times in its past and literally see it morphing into its current state. Another interesting aspect of our prototype is that as the user moves the device the view they see on their mobile interface moves with them, thus allowing the user to experience the real and the virtual world at the same time (Baillie, Kunczier, & Anegg, 2005, p. 283).

Visuals may be brought in to enhance navigation by users—with audio directions to augment the visuals—in mobile device guides (Chittaro & Burigat, 2005, p. 107).

Ambient intelligence may often be seen as an interactive installation with information helpful in everyday life, like bus schedule information (Skog, Ljungblad & Holmquist, 2003). Library displays, student commons areas, and other such locales also may offer time-critical and localized information.

By ambient information visualization, we mean information visualization applications that do not reside on the screen of a desktop computer, but in the environment or periphery of the user. Using ambient information visualization, dynamically updated data sources can be presented in new environments, where a traditional computer display may not be suitable (Skog, Ljungblad & Holmquist, 2003, n.p.).

Here, people may interact with the machines with tablet PCs, mobile hand-helds, gestures, clothing, or even without any particular device of their own.

There are a range of creative in-world experiences that are enhanced by virtual technologies. For example, ping-pong involves digitally augmented cooperative play with an athletic-tangible interface, with full body motion in physical spaces, at a reactive ping-pong table. This project uses sound-based

Figure 5. A screenshot of an immersive 3D art gallery

ball tracking technology and is sensitive to the rhythm and style of play. Multi-sensory add-ons change the experience of ping-pong play between two players (Ishii, Wisneski, Orbanes, Chun & Paradiso, 1999, pp. 394 – 401).

Physical art informs some types of ambient information delivery: Virtual paintings, aesthetic informational collages, and digital family portraits have all been transplanted into ambient intelligent displays (Skog, Ljungblad & Holmquist, 2003, n.p.). Such installations are built into physical spaces, where there are other competing visuals, sounds and attention-getters, so ambient intelligent spaces need to offer valuable information in an eye-catching way. Often, the information needs to be updated regularly as well. "Ambient visualization" refers to informative displays communicating information on the periphery of attention.

Spatial hypermedia enhances reality with digital annotations. These technologies may enhance collaborative virtual environments with spatial layouts to capitalize on human spatial memory. These may also be used to develop conceptual work spaces. GPS receivers may offer digital compass guidance for indirect navigation and enhance in-field collaborations in augmented spaces (Grønbæk, Vestergaard, & Ørbæk, 2002, pp. 117 – 126).

Geocoding connects an address to geographic coordinates, and these are often portrayed as satellite maps with an overlay of addresses. Geospatial data may enhance real-time collaborations in real spaces. These may enhance situational awareness and the responsiveness of first responders in emergencies and soldiers in military situations. These may be used for urban planning and understanding neighborhoods. Geospatial data has applications in "scientific, civil, military and industrial" realms and so need federated systems that are heterogeneous, secure, and efficient (Aloisio, Cafaro, Flore, & Quarta, 2005, pp. 701 – 705).

Examples

Augmented reality, mobile applications and ambient intelligence not only develop cognitive and affective learning but also focus on muscle memory—through embodied learning. The benefits of using real-time and real-spaces, with overlays of digital information, offers enhanced experiential learning. These involve in-world treasure-hunt gaming, museum installations, military exercises, dance, digital art, and others.

Design Implications

Designing digital imagery for augmented reality will involve plenty of considerations for the physical space, the technologies, and the learner experiences. There are challenges to designing for the small-screen limitations of mobile devices, given their limited size, color and contrast, affordances. Ambient intelligence installations involve using physical spaces and people's presences and multi-leveled communications (through actions, movements, vocalizations, and input into computers) for rich interactivity and learning.

User-Generated Contents

One pedagogical strategy for learning involves the creation of user-generated contents—to represent their depth of learning, build electronic portfolios for training and professional development, support their personal expression and articulate emotions, and use the various related tools. Consumers of a multimedia who also produce contents have been dubbed "prosumers," and some of their works have entered the mainstream as part of open-source collaborations and even for-profit company endeavors.

User-created imagery may enhance the learning (Franco, da Cruz, & de Deus Lopes, 2006). In undergraduate biology, students may create their own graphics as digital frame grabs of microscopic slides.

These graphics allow the undergraduate students to dramatically improve their learning opportunities and to visualize biological microstructures. Analytical study, dimensional reconstructions, presentation graphics for laboratory practical exams, multimedia presented term projects and "digital legacies" are now a part of these students' cognitive armamentarium (Blystone, 1994, p. 198).

They may take relevant photos and describe what each shows or exemplifies. The way they "frame" an image capture informationally may enhance the value of the student thinking work and their legwork.

User-created work may be a basis for deeper course analysis and discussions. Nuanced effects of various images may be discussed. Learners may probe collections of digital photos and write up summaries and analysis of these. Images may be captured from outside the academic realm in order to enhance academic studies. Digital visuals may be created from fieldwork projects, apprenticeships, work-study opportunities, or other work-related circumstances.

This use of user created work is especially helpful in ill-structured domains that are highly complex and variable in terms of applications and outcomes. User contributions may enhance multi-dimensional knowledge networks that build on cutting-edge knowledge.

Some user-generated work may involve automated creation by computers (such as mazes created from images) (Pedersen & Singh, 2006), but that may detract from individual human creativity (Gal, Sorkine, Popa, Sheffer, & Cohen-Or, 2007). Other systems involve new "collage" creations assembled from pre-made 3D shapes to make the build smoother and less difficult than building from scratch.

Examples

User-generated contents are common in a variety of fields, particularly those that emphasize creativity and design: filmmaking, game design, website design, architecture, fashion, and art.

Design Implications

Learners will need clear general guidelines but also room to express their creativity; they will need access to the technologies needed from beginning to end for their projects. And finally, there should be showcasing of their work in digital repositories.

CONCLUSION

This chapter has shown some of the applied uses of digital imagery—static and dynamic, freestanding and integrated-immersive—in presenting information and supporting human understanding, analysis, decision-making and problem-solving. These show only some of the common uses of digital imagery in e-learning. As this field continues to evolve, it's likely that these uses will become more complex and richer.

REFERENCES

Acevedo, D., Vote, E., Laidlaw, D. H., & Joukowsky, M. S. (2001). Archaeological data visualization in VR: Analysis of lamp finds at the Great Temple of Petra, a case study. In *Proceedings of the IEEE Visualization 2001*. Washington, DC: IEEE.

Addison, A. C. (2004). Virtual heritage—technology in the service of culture. In *Proceedings of the 2001 conference on Virtual reality, archeology, and cultural heritage* (pp. 343-354). New York: Association of Computing Machinery, Inc.

Agouris, P., Doucette, P., & Stefanidis, A. (2001). Spatiospectral cluster analysis of elongated regions in aerial imagery. In *Proceedings of the 2001 International Conference on Image Processing* (pp. 789-792). Washington, DC: IEEE.

Aloisio, G., Cafaro, M., Flore, S., & Quarta, G. (2005). A Grid-based architecture for earth observation data access. In *Proceedings of the SAC 05,* Santa Fe, NM, (pp. 701-705). New York: ACM.

Anderson, M. D., Pottinger, H. J., Schroeder, C. M., & Adapa, R. (1993). Advanced graphics zoom in on operations. *IEEE Computer Applications in Power, 6*(2), 25–28. doi:10.1109/67.207468

Andrews, B. (2006). Introduction to perceptual principles in medical illustration. In *Proceedings of the International Conference on Computer Graphics and Interactive Techniques*. New York: ACM.

Aniyo, K., Wemler, S., & Baxter, W. (2006). Tweakable light and shade for cartoon animation. In *Proceedings of the 4th international symposium on Non-photorealistic animation and rendering* (pp. 133-139). New York: ACM.

Aragon, C. R., & Hearst, M. A. (2005). Improving aviation safety with information visualization: A flight simulation study. In *Proceedings of the CHI 2005* (pp. 41-450). New York: ACM.

Bai, X., Jin, J. S., & Feng, D. (2004). Segmentation-based multiplayer diagnosis lossless medical image compression. In M. Piccardi, T. Hitz, S. He, M. L. Huang, & D. D. Feng (Eds.), *Proceedings of the 2003 Pan-Sydney Area Workshop on Visual Information Processing, VIP2003,* Sydney, Australia (pp. 9-14). Australian Computer Society, Inc

Baillie, L., Kunczier, H., & Anegg, H. (2005). Rolling, rotating and imagining in a virtual mobile world. In [New York: ACM.]. *Proceedings of the Mobile HCI, 05,* 283–286.

Blake, P. L., & Brown, T. W. (2003). Quantitative fusion of performance results from actual and simulated image data. In *Proceedings of the 32nd Applied Imagery Pattern Recognition Workshop (AIPR '03)* (pp. 1-4). Washington, DC: IEEE.

Blumenkrants, M., Starovisky, H., & Shamir, A. (2006). Narrative algorithm visualization. In [New York: Association of Computing Machinery, Inc.]. *Proceedings of the SOFTVIS, 2006,* 17–26. doi:10.1145/1148493.1148496

Blystone, R. V. (1994, August). Computer graphics in the undergraduate biology laboratory. *Computer Graphics, 28*(3), 198–200. doi:10.1145/186376.186394

Brown, M. S., & Seales, W. B. (2001). The digital Atheneum: New approaches for preserving, restoring, and analyzing damaged manuscripts. In *Proceedings of the JCDL '01* (pp. 437-443). New York: ACM.

Brutzman, D. (2002). Teaching 3D modeling and simulation: Virtual kelp forest case study. In *Proceedings of the WEB 3D '02*, Tempe, AZ (pp. 93-101). New York: ACM.

Burg, J., & Lüttringhaus, K. (2006). Entertaining with science, educating with dance. *ACM Computers in Entertainment, 4*(2), 1–15. doi:10.1145/1129006.1129008

Chittaro, L., & Burigat, S. (2005). Augmenting audio messages with visual directions in mobile guides: An evaluation of three approaches. In [New York: ACM.]. *Proceedings of the Mobile HCI, 05*, 107–114.

Crocker, R. I., Matthews, D. K., Emery, W. J., & Baldwin, D. G. (2007). Computing coastal ocean surface currents from infrared and ocean color satellite imagery. *IEEE Transactions on Geoscience and Remote Sensing, 45*(2), 435–447. doi:10.1109/TGRS.2006.883461

Di, K., Ma, R., Wang, J., & Li, R. (2003). Coastal mapping and change detection using high-resolution IKONOS satellite imagery. In *Proceedings of the 2003 annual national conference on Digital government research* (pp. 1-4). New York: ACM.

Dolinsky, M., & Nelson, T. (2007). Interfectio Puerorum: Digital projections and the 12th century Fleury's Massacre. In *Proceedings of the C&C '07*. New York: ACM.

Ebert, D. S., Shaw, C. D., Zwa, A., & Starr, C. (1996). Two-handed interactive stereoscopic visualization. In *Proceedings of the Seventh IEEE Visualization 1996 (VIS '96)*. Washtington, DC: IEEE.

Ezzat, T., Geiger, G., & Poggio, T. (2002). Trainable videorealistic speech animation. In *Proceedings of the 29th annual conference on Computer graphics and interactive techniques* (pp. 388-398). New York: ACM.

Fachry, K. N., Kamps, J., & Zhang, J. (2008). Access to archival material in context. In *Proceedings of the IIiX '08, Information Interaction in Context*, London, UK. New York: ACM.

Fattal, R., & Lischinski, D. (2001). Variational classification for visualization of 3D ultrasound data. In [Washington, DC: IEEE.]. *Proceedings of the IEEE Visualization, 2001*, 403–410.

Franco, J. F., da Cruz, S. R., & de Deus Lopes, R. (2006). Computer graphics, interactive technologies and collaborative learning synergy supporting individuals' skills development. In *Proceedings of the International Conference on Computer Graphics and Interactive Techniques*. New York: ACM.

Frost, J., & Smith, B. K. (2003). Visualizing health: Imagery in diabetes education. In *Proceedings of the 2003 conference on Designing for user experiences* (pp. 1-14). New York: ACM.

Funge, J. (2000). Cognitive modeling for games and animation. *Communications of the ACM, 43*(7), 42–48. doi:10.1145/341852.341862

Gal, R., Sorkine, O., Popa, T., Sheffer, A., & Cohen-Or, D. (2007). 3D collage: Expressive non-realistic modeling. In *Proceedings of the 5th international symposium on Non-photorealistic animation and rendering* (pp. 7-14). New York: ACM.

Galego, B., & Simone, L. (2007). Leveraging online virtual worlds for upper extremity rehabilitation. In *Proceedings of the IEEE 33ʳᵈ Annual Northeast Bioengineering Conference, 2007, NEBC '07* (pp. 267-268). Washington, DC: IEEE.

Garzotto, F., & Rizzo, F. (2007). Interaction paradigms in technology-enhanced social spaces: A case study in museums. In *Designing Pleasurable Products and Interfaces, Proceedings of the 2007 conference on Designing pleasurable products and interfaces*, Helsinki, Finland (pp. 343-356). New York: ACM.

Gladney, H. M., Mintzer, F., Schiattarella, F., Bescós, J., & Treu, M. (1998). Digital access to antiquities. *Communications of the ACM, 41*(4), 56. doi:10.1145/273035.273048

Gold, S. (2001). E-learning: The next wave of experiential learning. *Developments in Business Simulation and Experiential Learning, 28*, 76–79.

Green, S., Blumenstein, M., Browne, M., & Tomlinson, R. (2005). The detection and quantification of persons in cluttered beach scenes using neural network-based classification. In *Proceedings of the Sixth International Conference on Computational Intelligence and Multimedia Applications (ICCIMA '05)*.

Gresh, D. L., & Kelton, E. I. (2003). Visualization, optimization, and business strategy: A case study. In [Washington, DC: IEEE.]. *Proceedings of the IEEE Visualization, 2003*, 531–538.

Grønbæk, K., Vestergaard, P. P., & Ørbæk, P. (2002). Towards geo-spatial hypermedia: Concepts and prototype implementation. In . *Proceedings of the HT, 02*, 117–126.

Hahn, H. K., Preim, B., Selle, D., & Peitgen, H.-O. (2004). Visualization and interaction techniques for the exploration of vascular structures. In *Proceedings of the IEEE Visualization 2001*. Washington, DC: IEEE.

Hampel, A., & Bernroider, E. W. N. (2004). A component-based framework for distributed business simulations in e-business environments. In [Academic Publishers.]. *Proceedings of the ICEB, 2004*, 370–375.

Hu, N., Xie, D., & Du, K. (2004). Data structure of corn scene visualization. In *Proceedings of the 2004 IEEE International Geoscience and Remote Sensing Symposium, IGARSS '04* (pp. 4846-4849). Washington, DC: IEEE.

Hundhausen, C., & Douglas, S. (2000). Using visualizations to learn algorithms: Should students construct their own or view an expert's? In *Proceedings of the 2000 IEEE International Symposium on Visual Languages (VL'00)* (pp. 21-28). Washington, DC: IEEE.

Ishii, H., Wisneski, C., Orbanes, J., Chun, B., & Paradiso, J. (1999). PingPongPlus: Design of an athletic-tangible interface for computer-supported cooperative play. In *Proceedings of the CHI 99* (pp. 394-401). New York: ACM.

Jeong, B., Renambot, L., Jagodic, R., Singh, R., Aguilera, J., Johnson, A., & Leigh, J. (2006). High-performance dynamic graphics streaming for scalable adaptive graphics environment. In *Proceedings of the 2006 ACM / IEEE SC /06 Conference (SC '06)*.

Johnson, C. R., & Weinstein, D. M. (2006). Biomedical computing and visualization. In *Proceedings of the 12th International Conference on Parallel Architectures and Compilation Techniques (PACT'03)*. Australian Computer Society, Inc.

Jones, J. M., Ma, R., Starkey, R. L., & Ma, Z. (2007). Information complexity and appropriate interface design in nuclear power plant control rooms. In *Proceedings of the Joint 8th IEEE HFPP / 13th HPRCT* (pp. 45-49).

Ju, W., Bonanni, L., Fletcher, R., Hurwitz, R., Judd, T., & Post, R. (2002). Origami desk: Integrating technological innovation and human-centric design. In [New York: ACM.]. *Proceedings of the DIS, 2002*, 399–405.

Kamsin, A. (2007). Integrated 3D multimedia Web based application in biology: A prototype. In *Proceedings of the Computer Graphics, Imaging and Visualisation (CGIV 2007)*. Washington, DC: IEEE.

King, R. L. (2000). A challenge for high spatial, spectral, and temporal resolution data fusion. In *Proceedings of the 2000 IEEE International Geoscience and Remote Sensing Symposium, IGARSS '00* (pp. 2602-2604). Washington, DC: IEEE.

Koller, D., & Levoy, M. (2005). Protecting 3D graphics content. *Communications of the ACM, 48*(6), 74. doi:10.1145/1064830.1064861

Landry, B. M., & Guzdial, M. (2006). iTell: Supporting retrospective storytelling with digital photos. In [New York: ACM.]. *Proceedings of the DIS, 2006*, 160–168.

Lang, T., MacIntyre, B., & Zugaza, I. J. (2008). Massively multiplayer online worlds as a platform for augmented reality experiences. In *Proceedings of the IEEE Virtual Reality 2008*, Reno, NV (pp. 67-70). Washington, DC: IEEE.

Le Malécot, E., Kohara, M., Hori, Y., & Sakurai, K. (2006). Interactively combining 2D and 3D visualization for network traffic monitoring. In [New York: ACM.]. *Proceedings of the VizSEC, 06*, 123–127. doi:10.1145/1179576.1179600

Lee, A. (2004). Scaffolding visually cluttered Web pages to facilitate accessibility. In Proceedings of the AVI '04, Gallipoli, Italy (pp. 90-93). New York: ACM.

Li, H. (1992). Three-dimensional computer graphics using EGA or VGA card. *IEEE Transactions on Education, 35*(1), 44–49. doi:10.1109/13.123416

Linney, A. D. (1991). 3D graphics in surgical simulation. In *Proceedings of the IEEE Colloquium on 3-D Imaging Techniques for Medicine* (pp. 211-213). Washington, DC: IEEE.

Liu, J., Wang, B., Li, M., Li, Z., Ma, W.-Y., Lu, H., & Ma, S. (2007, September). Dual cross-media reference model for image annotation. In *Proceedings of the MM '07*. New York: ACM.

Ma, K.-L., & Crockett, T. W. (1999). *Parallel visualization of large-scale aerodynamics calculations: A case study on the Cray T3E* (Tech. Rep. TR-99-41). Institute for Computer Applications in Science and Engineering (ICASE).

MacEachren, A. M., Harrower, M., Li, B., Howard, D., Downs, R., & Gahegan, M. (2002). Supporting statistical, graphic/cartographic, and domain literacy through online learning activities: MapStats for kids. In *Proceedings of the 2002 annual national conference on Digital government research* (pp. 1-5). Digital Government Society of North America.

Maldonado, H., & Lee, J.-E. R., Brave, S., Nass, C., Nakajima, H., Yamada, R., Iwamura, K., & Morishima, Y. (2005). We learn better together: Enhance eLearning with emotional characters. In *Proceedings of the Computer Supported Collaborative Learning 2005: The Next Ten Years!* (pp. 408-417).

Marcus, A. (2001). Cross-cultural user-interface design for work, home, play, and on the way. In *Proceedings of the SIGDOC '01*, Santa Fe, NM, USA. New York: ACM.

McCarthy, J., Wright, P., Wallace, J., & Dearden, A. (2006). The experience of enchantment in human-computer interaction. *Personal and Ubiquitous Computing, 10*, 369–378. doi:10.1007/s00779-005-0055-2

McLoughlin, E., O'Sullivan, D., Bertolotto, M., & Wilson, D. C. (2006). MEDIC-MobilE diagnosis for improved care. In *Proceedings of the SAC '06* (pp. 204-208). New York: ACM.

Medhi, I., Prasad, A., & Toyama, K. (2007). Optimal audio-visual representations for illiterate users of computers. In *Proceedings of the WWW 2007: Technology for developing regions. Session: Communication in Developing Regions. International World Wide Web Conference Committee*, Banff, Alberta, Canada (pp. 873-882). New York: ACM.

Mueller, P. (2007). Part III: Live visuals tutorial. Annotated slideshow. In *Proceedings of the SIGGRAPH 2007* (pp. 127-151).

Müller, W., & Schumann, H. (2003). Visualization methods for time-dependent data – an overview. In *Proceedings of the 2003 Winter Simulation Conference* (pp. 737-745).

Naps, T. L., Fleischer, R., McNally, M., Rößling, G., Hundhausen, C., Rodger, S., et al. Velázquez-Iturbide, J.A., Dann, W., & Malmi, L. (2002). Exploring the role of visualization and engagement in computer science education. In *Proceedings of the Annual Joint Conference Integrating Technology into Computer Science Education, Working group reports from ITiCSE on Innovation and technology in computer science education* (pp. 131-152). New York: ACM.

North, C. (2006). Toward measuring visualization insight. *IEEE Computer Graphics and Applications, 26*(3), 6–9. doi:10.1109/MCG.2006.70

Paelke, V., Reimann, C., & Rosenbach, W. (2003). A visualization design repository for mobile devices. In *Proceedings of the 2nd international conference on Computer graphics, virtual Reality, visualisation and interaction in Africa* (pp. 57-62). New York: ACM.

Pantic, M., Sebe, N., Cohn, J. F., & Huang, T. (2005). Affective multimodal human-computer interaction. In [New York: ACM.]. *Proceedings of the MM, 05*, 669–676.

Pape, D., & Anstey, J. (2002) Workshop: Building an affordable projective, immersive display. In *Proceedings of the International Conference on Computer Graphics and Interactive Techniques* (pp. 55). New York: ACM.

Pedersen, H., & Singh, K. (2006). Organic labyrinths and mazes. In *Proceedings of the NPAR 2006*, Annecy, France. New York: ACM.

Petre, M., & Blackwell, A. F. (1997). A glimpse of expert programmers' mental imagery. In *Proceedings of the Seventh Workshop on Empirical Studies of Programmers*. New York: ACM. Retrieved November 24, 2008, from http://portal.acm.org/citation.cfm?id=266409

Plesniak, W., Halle, M., Pieper, S. D., Wells, W., III, Jakab, M., Meier, D. S., et al. (2003, October). Holographic video display of time-series volumetric medical data. In *Proceedings of the 14th IEEE Visualization Conference 2003* (pp. 589-596).

Power, D., Politou, E., Slaymaker, M., Harris, S., & Simpson, A. (2004). A relational approach to the capture of DICOM files for grid-enabled medical imaging databases. In *Proceedings of the SAC '04* (pp. 272-279). New York: ACM.

Preim, B., Tietjen, C., Spindler, W., & Peitgen, H.-O. (2002). Integration of measurement tools in medical 3D visualizations. In . *Proceedings of the IEEE Visualization, 2002*, 21–28.

Prince, S., Cheok, A. D., Farbiz, F., Williamson, T., Johnson, N., Billinghurst, M., & Kato, H. (2002). 3-D Live: Real time interaction for mixed reality. In *Proceedings of the CSCW '02*, New Orleans, LA (pp. 364-371). New York: ACM.

Qi, W., Martens, J.-B., van Liere, R., & Kok, A. (2005). Reach the virtual environment—3D tangible interaction with scientific data. In *Proceedings of OZCHI 2005*, Canberra, Australia, (pp. 1-10).

Qiu, F., Zhao, Y., Fan, Z., Wei, X., Lorenz, H., & Wang, J. (2004). Dispersion simulation and visualization for urban security. In [Washington, DC: IEEE.]. *Proceedings of the IEEE Visualization, 2004*, 553–560.

Raab, M. (2003). *Games and eLearning: Attempt to identify reasons why games are popular and how they can be applied to make eLearning more popular.* Unpublished master's thesis, Trinity College, Dublin, Ireland.

Rheingold, H. (2003). *Smart mobs: The next social revolution.* Cambridge, UK: Perseus Publishing.

Robbins, K. A., & Gorman, M. (2000). Fast visualization methods for comparing dynamics: A case study in combustion. In *Proceedings of the 11th IEEE Visualizatoin 2000* (pp. 433-437).

Saraiya, P., North, C., & Duca, K. (2005). An insight-based methodology for evaluating bioinformatics visualizations. *IEEE Transactions on Visualization and Computer Graphics, 11*(4), 443–456. doi:10.1109/TVCG.2005.53

Severance, K., Brewster, P., Lazos, B., & Keefe, D. (2001). Wind tunnel data fusion and immersive visualization: A case study. In . *Proceedings of the IEEE Visualization, 2001*, 505–600.

Shenas, H. H., & Interrante, V. (2005). Compositing color with texture for multivariate visualization. In *Proceedings of the 3rd international conference on Computer graphics and interactive techniques in Australasia and South East Asia.* New York: ACM.

Shiaw, H.-Y., Jacob, R. J. K., & Crane, G. R. (2004). The 3D vase museum: A new approach to context in a digital library. In *Proceedings of the JCDL '04* (pp. 125-134). New York: ACM.

Sivic, J., Kaneva, B., Torralba, A., Avidan, S., & Freeman, W. T. (2008). Creating and exploring a large photorealistic virtual space. In *Proceedings of the IEEE Computer Vision and Pattern Recognition Workshops*. Washington, DC: IEEE.

Skog, T., Ljungblad, S., & Holmquist, L. E. (2003). Between aesthetics and utility: Designing ambient information visualizations. In *Proceedings of the IEEE Symposium on Information Visualization 2003*. Washington, DC: IEEE.

Smith, B. K., & Blankinship, E. (1999). Imagery as data: Structures for visual model building. In *Computer Support for Collaborative Learning. Proceedings of the 1999 Conference on Computer Support for Collaborative Learning.*

Smuelders, R., & Heijs, A. (2005). Interactive visualization of high dimensional marketing data in the financial industry. In *Proceedings of the Ninth International Conference on Information Visualization (IV '05).*

State, A., Livingston, M. A., Garrett, W. F., Hirota, G., Whitton, M. C., Pisano, E. D., & Fuchs, H. (1996). Technologies for augmented reality systems: Realizing ultrasound-guided needle biopsies. In *Proceedings of the 23rd annual conference on Computer graphics and interactive techniques* (pp. 439-446). New York: ACM.

Terzopoulos, D. (1999). Artificial life for computer graphics. *Communications of the ACM, 42*(8), 33–42. doi:10.1145/310930.310966

Thomsen, M. R. (2008). Sites of flux: Imagining space in the dance-architectures of the changing room and sea unsea. *Personal and Ubiquitous Computing, 12*, 383–390. doi:10.1007/s00779-007-0160-5

Tochon, F. V. (2007). From video cases to video pedagogy: A framework for video feedback and reflection in pedagogical research praxis. In R. Goldman, R. Pea, B. Barron, & S. J. Denny (Eds.), *Video research in the learning sciences.* Mahwah, NJ: Lawrence Erlbaum Associates, Publishers.

Tran, Q.-N. (2006). Interactive computer algebra software for teaching and helping students to study foundations of computer science. In *Proceedings of the Consortium for Computing Sciences in Colleges* (pp. 131-143).

Treinish, L. A. (2000). Multi-resolution visualization techniques for nested weather models. In *Proceedings of the conference on Visualization '00* (pp. 513-517).

Treinish, L. A. (2002). Case study on the adaptation of interactive visualization applications to web-based production for operational mesoscale weather models. In . *Proceedings of the IEEE Visualization, 2002*, 549–552.

Van den Hoven, E., Frens, J., Aliakseyeu, D., Martens, J.-B., Overbeeke, K., & Peters, P. (2007). Design research & tangible interaction. In *Proceedings of the TEI '07,* Baton Rouge, LA, USA.

Ware, C. (2004). Foundation for a science of data visualization. In *Information Visualization: Perception for Design* (2nd ed.). San Francisco: Morgan Kaufmann Publishers.

Wegenkittl, R., Gröller, E., & Purgahofer, W. (1997). Visualizing the dynamical behavior of Wonderland. In *Proceedings of the IEEE Computer Graphics and Applications* (pp. 71-79).

Weiskopf, D., Borchers, M., Ertl, T., Falk, M., Fechtig, O., & Frank, R. (2006, July-August). Explanatory and illustrative visualization of special and general relativity. *IEEE Transactions on Visualization and Computer Graphics, 12*(4), 522–534. doi:10.1109/TVCG.2006.69

Williams, D. A. (1988). A conceptual discussion for an airborne graphics software support system. In *Proceedings of the IEEE 1988 National Aerospace and Electronics Conference* (pp. 748-753). Washington, DC: IEEE.

Wünsche, B. C., & Lobb, R. (2004). The 3D visualization of brain anatomy from diffusion-weighted magnetic resonance imaging data. In *Proceedings of the 2nd international conference on Computer graphics and interactive techniques in Australasia and South East Asia* (pp. 74-83). New York: ACM.

Yang, Z., Yu, B., Nahrstedt, K., & Bajscy, R. (2006). A multi-stream adaptation framework for bandwidth management in 3D tele-immersion. In *Proceedings of the NOSSDAV '06*, Newport, RI. New York: ACM.

Zhao, W., & Madhavan, V. (2006). Virtual assembly operations with grasp and verbal interaction. In *Proceedings of the VRCIA 2006*, Hong Kong, PRC (pp. 245-254). New York: ACM.

KEY TERMS AND DEFINITIONS

Ambient Visualization (n): Informative displays communicating information in the periphery of attention

Archival Documentation (n): Digital or paper documents that are a normal by product of work flows or living

Branding (n): The creation of a course, program, department, or university's unified image through its values, services, vision, public messages, and designed look-and-feel; public identity management

Data Glove (n): An input device into a 3D scene

Dynamic (adj): Moving, energetic, changing over time, active

Geospatial Hypermedia (n): Technologies that support spatial information visualization for enhancing collaborative virtual environments online and in real-space (in augmented reality)

Head-Mounted Displays (HMD) (n): A device worn on the head that conveys synthetic information in visual overlays on real view-dependent environments

High Dynamic Range (adj): The capturing of real scenes using a number of exposures

IP Multicast (n): The use of the Internet Protocol infrastructure to connect various participants in a collaborative session involving interactive communications, audio, video, text, and shared imagery

Mesoscale (adj): Middle scale; 1-100 km. in horizontal extent in terms of scale of phenomena (in meteorology); intermediate between small and synoptic scales

Multivariate (adj): Consisting of several or more variables or factors

Orthoimage (n): A satellite or aerial image that has been orthorectified into a map-accurate form, with the removal of distortions; also known as "orthomaps"

Pedagogical Agent (n): A digital entity created to support learning by offering learning tips

Photorealistic (adj): Resembling the fidelity of a photographic image, in structure, color, lighting, and other features

Simulation (n): An enactment, an imitation

Static (adj): Not moving, showing no change (or little change), stable

Stratigraphy (n): The classification and interpretation of stratified rocks, as a branch of geology

Video-Realistic (adj): Resembling the fidelity of a video-capture, in movement, structure, color, lighting, motion dynamics, and others

Visual Analytics (n): Strategies to measure the efficacy of visuals and visualizations

Visualization (n): A created image that mimics the real; a mental image

X-Ray (n): A radiograph made by electromagnetic radiation (which is capable of penetrating solids) for medical or scientific examination and diagnosis

Chapter 4
Types of Graphics in E-Learning

ABSTRACT

Digital graphics commonly used in e-learning come in various image types and dimensions, each of which enables different types of information communications. The concept of dimensionality builds on how images work on the x, y, and z axes. This also builds on the affordances of digital imagery with live updates, movements, interactivity, emotionality, and other features that may be overlaid or imbued into visuals. This chapter addresses still images to dynamic ones. Considering the types of graphics and the informational value of each category should enhance their development and use in e-learning.

CHAPTER OBJECTIVES

- Introduce dimensionality in digital graphics
- Discuss the uses of 1D lines or vectors
- Examine the uses of 2D shapes and texts (including icons, diagrams, glyphs, graphemes, drawings or illustrations, image maps, photographs, and visualizations
- Describe 2D graphics that simulate three dimensions
- Analyze three dimensional graphics (including bas relief, photogravure, digital rubbings or frottage)
- Introduce 3 ½ D graphics that simulate or imply movement
- Highlight 4D or moving or animated graphics (including sprites, modeling for film or game work, and flowfields)
- Explore 5D graphics with psychological or emotional content (including avatar depth, emotional flocking, emo contents and characters)

DOI: 10.4018/978-1-60566-972-4.ch004

- Showcase 6D graphics combined with other media, especially sound or speech
- Introduce 7D graphics that interact with humans or computer systems
- Consider 8D for digital augmentation to reality (including haptics, personal computing devices, surfacing computing)
- Introduce the concept of "mixed dimensionality" in digital imagery in e-learning

INTRODUCTION

Graphics have long played an important role in higher education and workplace-based trainings. The use of digital graphics have extended the value of one, two and three-dimensional visuals to the fourth dimension and beyond. Combined with high tech data captures, databases, and multimedia design, digital graphics enable interactivity and real-time live updating. These graphics may be more full-sensory and immersive. They may be real-time expressive. Many of the effects now pseudo-possible in non-digital (often illusion-based) form are enhanced, magnified and amplified with digital and computer-mediated means at higher visual quality. Digital images are usually Web-deliverable through desk-top computers, with some requiring more computing power.

Such digital graphics may be stand-alone, self-explanatory, and usable as an individual learning object, with informational value. They may be integrated into a larger context for sense-making and exploration. Digital images may be stand-alone visuals, or they may be integrated with other multimedia and text. They may be illustrations in e-books; live video captures, or slides in a simulated laboratory; digital avatars in an immersive space. Various image types offer different affordances. They help clarify complex information and relationships: "Users cannot understand the raw data, which is normally plain text specifying the position of each atom or the height of each location. Visualizing such data in a 3D environment allows us to understand how the data should be interpreted" (Itoh & Tanaka, 2006, n.p.).

Digital imagery, even simple line drawings, involves complexity. There may be a sense of focus by how objects are ordered in the foreground or background. There may be perceptions of depth. Various real-world images may be overlaid with synthetic overlays and artificial effects, or images may be mixed (aerial photographs and maps) for deeper informational value.

At the most basic level, these consist of bits and bytes. Digital images echo the world of matter in that small bits make up an illusion of wholeness (Negroponte, 1995). N. Negroponte of MIT's Media Lab writes:

A bit has no color, size or weight, and it can travel at the speed of light. It is the smallest atomic element in the DNA of information. It is a state of being: on or off, true or false, up or down, in or out, black or white. For practical purposes we consider a bit to be a 1 or a 0. The meaning of the 1 or the 0 is a separate matter. In the early days of computing, a string of bits most commonly represented numerical information (1995, p. 14).

One way of thinking of digital visual contents borrows from Clark's five-types of contents model (2007): fact, concept, process, procedure, and principle. Facts are discrete pieces of information. Concepts involve "groups of objects, events, or symbols designated by a single name." Processes point to how something works. Procedures are series of steps resulting in the completion of particular tasks. Principles are guidelines that result in the completion of a task; these may show cause-and-effect relationships (Clark & Mayer, 2008, pp. 60 – 61).

DIMENSIONALITY

As a simple organizing structure, this chapter will be arranged around the idea of spatial dimensions. The widely accepted 1-dimensional to 3-dimensional forms will be used along with the 4th dimension (with the addition of time). Also, based on Dowhal's definitions, this will include considerations of digital images through the 7th dimension. The following then are Dowhal's 0 to 7 dimensions:

0D: pixel or point
1D: line or vector
2D: shapes
2 ½ D: 2D graphics that simulate three-dimensionality
3D: true three-dimensional graphics using geometrical models
3 1/2 D: 2D or 3D graphics that simulate or imply movement
4D: Moving or animated graphics
5D: Graphics with added psychological or emotional content
6D: Graphics combined with other media, especially sound or speech
7D: Graphics that interact with humans or computer systems (Dowhal, 1996, pp. 149 – 160).

As categories, these will not all be mutually exclusive. There may be multi-dimensional graphics that include various types of psychological content but also include sound and interactivity. Digital images will be presented in each category if they meet the minimum requirements, but they may include other features as well.

Images are not infinitely malleable. They all have limitations based on form, and those confines must be clear because they constrain information communications. For example, there are limitations to the illusions that a 2D image may evoke for 3D or 4D realities. Visualizations may convey a limited amount of live information coherently for decision-making without flooding the senses with excessive information. Photo-realistic images can convey a finite set of meanings, and that is also true for non-photo-realistic imagery (which may carry moods better and focus on ideas more clearly with an elision of extraneous details but which may lack the immersive detail of photo-realism) (Klein, Li, Kazhdan, Corrêa, Finkelstein, & Funkhouser, 2000).

Figure 1 offers a simplistic way of visualizing the seven dimensions.

0D: Pixel or Point

Rarely are single pixels or points (whether gray-tone or color) used as stand-alone images. These are the minimum lowest levels of digital images. When considering the most basic unit of a digital image, that would be a pixel or point. While digital images may represent atom-level and even sub-atomic level images, those are usually depicted through the use of many pixels to magnify the microscopic images. Some images use pointillism which highlight the pixels or points, but again, those miniature elements all work collectively to evoke images.

Figure 1. Visualizing seven dimensions (Hai-Jew, 2010)

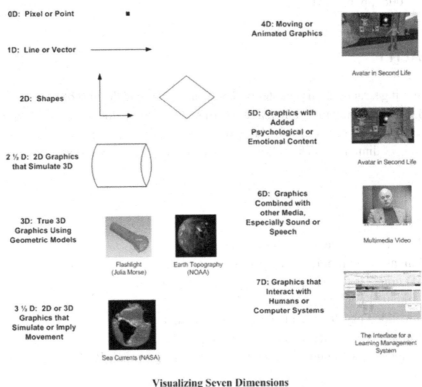

Visualizing Seven Dimensions

(an interpretation per Dowhal, 1996, pp. 149 – 160)

1D: Lines or Vectors

A one-dimensional image usually exists only along the x-axis or the y-axis. A simple timeline may be a one-dimensional image because it moves along one linear chronology (on the x-axis). A vector is a quantity which contains both magnitude and direction, sometimes indicated by an arrow. Lines or vectors often show directionality and magnitude, usually in a measureable quantitative way.

2D: Shapes (and Texts)

Still, two-dimensional shapes are some of the most common used in e-learning. These exist on both the x- and the y-axes. While these are flat (without the z-axis), plenty of information may be conveyed through two dimensions. The following then are some common 2D shapes used in e-learning, organized in the most simple to the more complex 2D images. In addition to shapes, some assert that historically "the act of writing has always been considered as an activity producing *visual* results, namely text" (Haralambous & Bella, 2005, p. 134). Technologies have been improving for the increased readability of text in e-texts and Web-delivery systems, to match text readability. Informal image objects like sketches, notes, and whiteboard images are also captured for e-learning (Saund, Fleet, Larner, & Mahoney, 2003). Digital images often will include embedded text.

Icons

Icons are some of the most basic 2D shapes. These discrete graphical elements are used to indicate functions, file types, and other labeling information in user interfaces and online spaces. These are often used consistently. Icons may also be small graphical avatars to represent individuals' presence and style. It usually denotes a single entity of interest but "does not qualify or describe the entity it signifies; it only denotes it, carrying little or nothing semantic" (Thomas-Meyers & Whitaker, 2006, p. 1206). An icon is highly functional and stripped down in its evocation of meaning.

Diagrams

2D diagrams offer information-rich visuals about how systems work. These may include flowcharts, computer networks, matrices, schedules, maps, organizational charts, spatial brainstorming depictions, charts, web site maps, and graphs. These often include text, labels, measures (of distance, size, volume, inputs and outputs), and explanatory details.

Glyphs

Glyphs represent multivariate data, with the various values represented by certain visual and sometimes textual features of objects used. Glyphs may represent "both simple relations and interactions between variables" (Chernoff, 1973, as cited in Lee, Reilly, & Butavicius, 2003, n.p.). Different diagrams—scatterplots, whisker plots, bar graphs, distributed curves—are all examples of glyphs. Meanings may be embedded in glyph visualizations, which also evoke figurative forms, such as Chernoff Faces, which display data in cartoon faces via different facial features. Researchers have suggested that embedding information this way may capitalize on the human tendency to perceive real facial features, and working with such hard-wired human tendencies may engage viewers more (Lee, Reilly, & Butavicius, 2003).

In a sense, knowledge glyphs serve as a "micro-interface" between the viewer and the information portrayed:

A knowledge glyph is distinguished from a glyph by virtue of affording users additional leverage on the semantics of the entity being depicted. The semantic support afforded by a knowledge glyph lies in its ability to interrelate the denoted entity's projection or occurrence within multiple referential contexts (Thomas-Meyers & Whitaker, 2006, p. 1205).

Predictive knowledge glyphs are used for decision-making (Thomas-Meyers & Whitaker, 2006).

Graphemes

A grapheme is a primitive visual (the visual equivalent of a phoneme to speech recognition), such as a letter of an alphabet or a minimal unit of a writing system. Text is a visual representation of meaning and sound. Some visualizations may be of "dancing symbols" and strings of code assembling and transforming "like luminous characters suspended behind my eyelids," in the words of one expert programmer (Petre & Blackwell, 1997, p. 115).

Drawings or Illustrations

Drawings or illustrations—as scanned images or drawn on tablets—may be some of the most creative and original visuals. Cutaways may provide interior imagery or close-up views of a particular depicted object. These may convey more of a freehand style and demonstrate the originality of classically trained artists. Cartoons are drawings that follow a particular format and conventions of humor and political wit. These may involve 2D caricatures (Gal, Sorkine, Popa, Sheffer, & Cohen-Or, 2007).

Image Maps

Image maps are a type of illustration that involves some interactivity, where rollovers or mouse-overs or clicks on certain parts of the image will lead to other parts of a website, or sound effects, or information delivery (via text, sound or imagery). Other types may involve activities like drag-and-drops (see Figure 2), spatial matching, "jigsaw" puzzle solving, and mixes and matches.

Photographs

Photographs provide a large bulk of the visual imagery in e-learning, as these are often easy to capture and prepare for uploading and use. Photos often are information-rich and useful for analysis and learning as well. Photos taken in sequence with different light exposures may offer high dynamic range, with more

Figure 2. A sample drag-and-drop image map

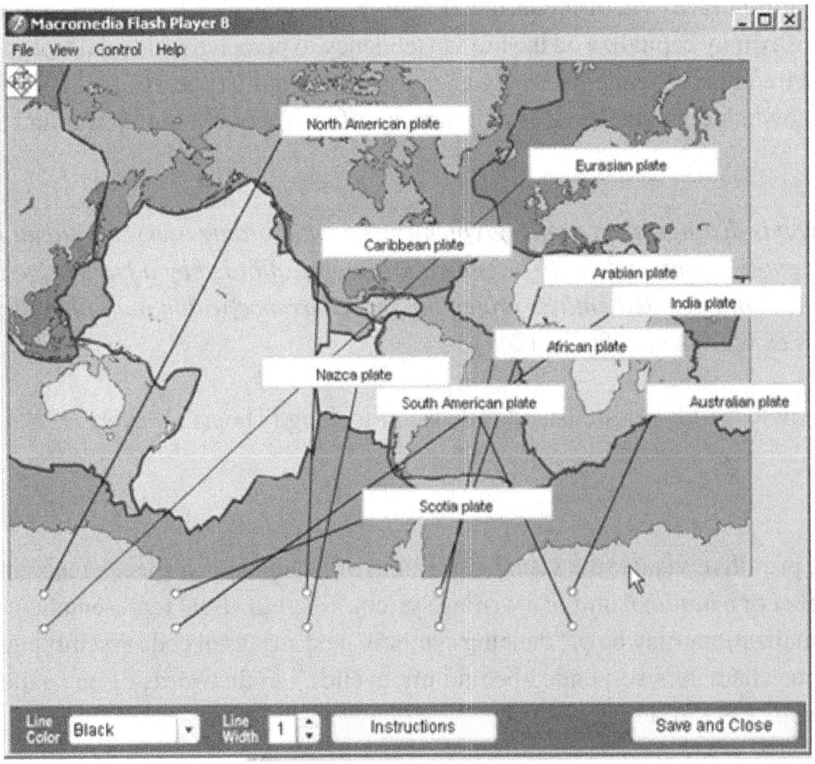

vivid color range and channels (beyond the eight bits per color channel) (Debevec, Reinhard, Ward, & Pattanaik, 2004). Photomontages may provide a sense of summary or a collection of images organized into a composite in an aesthetic or informative way. These medleys of images are often used to evoke a sense of history or context. Photo collages may provide "event summaries" (Diakopoulos & Essa, 2005, p. 183). Visuals capture the sense of a textured universe, from the microscopic to the macro.

Visualizations

Spatial visualizations represent objects in 2D spaces to show the organization of information. In these, similar objects are located closer to each other; relationships between objects are defined. "The algorithms that generate spatial representations, generically known as multidimensional scaling algorithms (Kruskal 1964, Shepard 1980), have also been applied to data visualization, exploration and analysis" (Lowe & Tipping 1996, Mao & Jain 1995, as cited in Lee, Reilly, & Butavicius, 2003, n.p.).

2D images may help users visualize something elusive or abstract by conveying it as a type of physical form:

Software is a huge industry producing the most complicated data-driven systems ever created. Developing large software systems is an extremely complex, team-oriented, engineering activity. One aspect that makes software production particularly difficult is that software is invisible. It has no physical shape or form. By making software visible we can help software engineers cope with the inherent complexity, help managers better understand the software process, and thereby improve productivity of the production process. The fundamental research problem in displaying software, as in Information Visualization, involves inventing visual metaphors for representing abstract data (Chuah & Eick, 1997, p. 183).

In 2D, there are creative ways to express different types of information. For example, time may be expressed as a shape: "wedges, rings and time slices" to represent temporal data in a single view. There may be coloration of geographical spaces in 2D (Shanbhag, Rheingans, & desJardins, 2005, pp. 211 – 218). Texturing, line size, and other factors may be brought into play to convey information, based on the conventions of the particular knowledge domain. The fine details of a visualization may support human comprehension and analysis of complex data sets:

Data visualization has the potential to assist humans in analyzing and comprehending large volumes of data, and to detect patterns, clusters and outliers that are not obvious using non-graphical forms of presentation. For this reason, data visualizations have an important role to play in a diverse range of applied problems, including data exploration and mining, information retrieval, and intelligence analysis (Lee, Reilly, & Butavicius, 2003, para. 1).

These also offer opportunities to analyze 3D volumetric structures (Zsaki, 2008, p. 167). The greater the human understandings, the better the decision-making that may come from the information.

This suggests that visualizations need to be well labeled and clearly and accurately rendered:

One of the goals of scientific visualization is to display measurements of physical quantities so the underlying physical phenomena can be interpreted accurately, quickly, and without bias. Great care is taken in choosing where such measurements will be made so that inferences about the underlying phenomena will be correct. How important is it to craft visualizations analogously, carefully placing arrows, curves, or other visual icons that display the data? What are the best ways to craft visualizations? (Laidlaw, Kirby, Jackson, Davidson, Miller, da Silva, Warren, & Tarr, 2005, p. 59).

Often, the surface meaning of digital imagery only shows one small aspect of the informational value of the object. For example, digital means may be used to annotate images that are captured with global positioning system data and audio information (Dias, Jesus, Frias & Correia, 2007); the automated metadata adds a level of value.

Various learning / course management systems (L/CMSes) that deliver e-learning also have embedded visuals for branding and context-building. These involve color themes, images, and logos (that may indicate function) to create a unified look-and-feel.

2 ½ D: 2D Graphics that Simulate Three-Dimensionality

Dowhal suggests two-and-a-half dimensions as those images that simulate 3D. By the use of illusions, a 2D image may create the sensation of three dimensions: length, width *and* depth. Here, objects may be drafted by isometric drawing with the horizontal edges drawn at a 30-degree angle and verticals projected perpendicularly (at a 90-degree angle) from a horizontal base. The lines all have to be drawn to scale for accuracy of representation.

Common 2 ½ D images are geometric shapes like cubes, cones, and spheres, created with lines and shading. Back shadows may be used to create the sense of depth. The sensations of depth may be created with lines leading up to a horizon and the conscious use of foreground and background placement of objects.

So-called 2 ½ D graphics are more common than actual 3D images in many types of e-learning simply because of the ease of creating such images for use. Actual 3D engines are less commonly used. Those in engineering and architecture may draw on computer-aided design (CAD) and computer-aided three-dimensional interactive application (CATIA)-types of software programs to design and present their models.

There are some technologies now that create 3D visualizations from a series of 2D images. Also, there are visualization tools that may create 3D buildings from the footprint data of buildings (Laycock & Day, 2003).

3D: True Three-Dimensional Graphics using Geometrical Models

Three-dimensional images (3D) involve length, width and depth; they include a sense of volume. These have come to the fore with the popularization of immersive game and communications spaces for education and training. The inclusion of 3D has diminished physical boundaries in modeling and planning for uses of physical spaces in design—in architecture, engineering, logistics, interior design, and numerous fields. 3D images may be reproductions from the real world, or they may be pure imaginary creations.

3D in immersive spaces require a rigorous 3D geometry and appropriate surface textures, which often requires an "expensive and tedious" process of development (Sormann, Bauer, Zach, Klaus, & Kanrer, 2004, p. 148). These include more full-dimensional information for viewers. Perspectives of 3D spaces will change as viewers change their locations in relation to various objects in the 3D spaces. Objects have volumetric depth. 3D experiences are more in-depth and immersive. Here, still 3D images will be addressed; those that include animation and movement will be addressed in the next half-category of Dowhal's 7 dimensions.

An example of 3D is shown in Figure 3, with an isometric view of a flashlight.

3D images require more of a sense of orientation and situating of the graphics. "In the absence of prior knowledge, 3D models have arbitrary scale, orientation and position in the 3D space. Because not all dissimilarity measures are invariant under rotation and translation, it may be necessary to place the 3D models into a canonical coordinate system. This should be the same for a translated, rotated or scaled copy of the model" (Tangelder & Veltkamp, 2004, n.p.).

New media art involve "digitality, interactivity, hypertextuality, dispersal, and virtuality (Lister, Dovey, Giddings, Grant, & Kelly, 2003, as cited in Liao, 2008, p. 87).

Bas Relief

Computer software gives users access to creative visual creation skills of the past. Bas relief or low-relief image captures involve sculptures in which the figures project slightly from the background. "Bas-relief (or low relief) presents the unique challenge of squeezing shapes into a nearly-flat surface while maintaining as much as possible the perception of the full 3D scene" (Weyrich, Deng, Barnes, Rusinkiewicz, & Finkelstein, 2007, pp. 32-1 to 32-7). Color engraving may be done digitally "with both fine lines and also wide areas of uniformly colored regions (high-frequency and low-frequency)" (Misic, Buckley, & Parker, 2002, pp. III – 773 to III – 776).

Photogravure

Digital photogravure emulates the intaglio (incised carving for "counsersunk die," using a design sunk below the surface) process of photo-mechanical printing or the use of etched metal or wood plates or

Figure 3. Flashlight—isometric view (Morse, 2008)

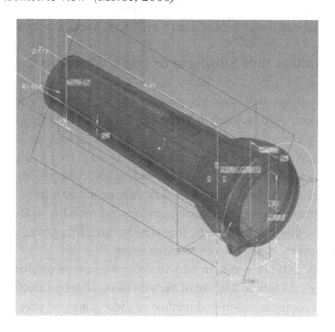

cylinders to create images. In this process, a plate is etched or engraved. Then ink is applied on the plate, and the plate is then wiped clean. The remaining ink in the recesses is used to make the print. In digital photogravure, images may be changed to emulate facial engraving. There may be emulations of copperplate engraving visual effects. Ostromoukhov explains:

The engraving style helps to port the look and feel of one engraving to another. Once different libraries of pre-defined mappable engraving styles and an appropriate user interface are added to the basic system, producing a decent gravure starting from a simple digital photo will be a matter of seconds (1999, p. 417).

Digital Rubbings or Frottage

Digital rubbings or frottage effects may also be created, with the emulation of the visual effects of rubbing a media like chalk or lead over a relief-like surface. This digital "rubbing" serves as a form of information capture (Lee, Pak, Kim, Kim & Lee, 2007). It opens the way for creating digital stencils, with the creation of imagery by brushing color over a perforated pattern onto a digital image using digital pens and pads.

Other Digital Formations

Other common 3D digital formations include crystals, fractals; spaces; characters and avatars, and physical objects. Three-dimensional images more often capture a sense of the four-walls real-world. They immerse individuals in full-sensory digital spaces. They create memorable visual sensations. Kinetic depth is an important aspect of immersiveness, which needs to combine visual accuracy with combined stereo and kinetic depth cues (Ware, 2006, p. 105). They may evoke imaginary worlds with reality that may keep people immersed and engaged for a long time. Well designed spaces do not convey an "empty of life" feeling found in some virtual immersive spaces (Ibañez, Delgado-Mata & Gómez-Caballero, 2007, p. 241). 3D images may be delivered via some mobile devices for learning value although most mobile terminals still have poor image processing (Sohn, Park, Yoon, Woo, Park & Yoo, 2005).

3 ½ D: 2D or 3D Graphics that Simulate or Imply Movement

3 ½ D digital imagery may shape-shift; they may simulate or imply movement. Various tools may convey dynamism—color (Ware, 2000, as cited in Weiskopf, 2004); texture; image sequencing and speed, and illusions.

Background changes may imply movement. 2D stills may be played in a kind of order to simulate action. Movement may be choreographed as in avatars and digital creatures, where purposive movement evokes particular effects. Crowds, herds or flocks may engage in apparently independent movements which still show group patterning. Various walking engines and mobility models exist for avatar walking. Movement may be the dispersion of mists, fog, clouds, dust, fire, gases, or liquids. There may be time-series animations showing changes to a particular scene.

Video (most commonly 2D) is a common way to show movement or change in time-space; these are often considered images in motion. The use of digital video—from production to post-production to mastering—has become a common end-to-end method of videography to save on costs (Swartz, 2005).

Holograms depict the interference pattern of superimposed beams of coherent light with one directly from a source and other reflected or scattered from a physical object (Kasper & Feller, 1987, p. v, as cited in Layng, 1996). Some digital holograms may be experienced with physical "markers" that interact with the computer's webcam. The marker activates a "smart grid" on the computer screen which creates an interactive 3D hologram experience (Rao, Mar. 20, 2009).

Graphics that show movement may imply changes over time; communicate avatar character or purpose, and offer aesthetically pleasing choreographed details. Elegant design here must show natural dynamic motion.

4D: Moving or Animated Graphics

The fourth dimension involves the addition of time to the third dimension. This addition may show actions and changes over time. The movement of 3D avatars in immersive spaces may be a 4D object. 3D video may show immersive changes over time or interactivity with 3D objects. These may show changes over time. These may be photo-realistic captures, or they may be non-photorealistic *machinima* and synthetic, dramatized depictions.

Sprites

3D "sprites" or animated objects may help draw viewers' attention to a particular fact, as eyes follow movement. 3D digital creatures may be designed following in-depth planning processes: "Assuming that the original conceptual creature designs and camera work are provocative, derivative execution of the computer graphics work is often the result of using the tool at hand rather than allowing the creature and shot design to determine the tools. Though there is no failsafe way to avoid creating derivative work, a way to safeguard against it is by first dissecting the design concepts without respect to the technology. Adherence to this process of analysis will create an environment in which the performance requirements drive the application of technology rather than the other way around" (McLaughlin, n.d., n.p.). Animation pipeline processing may result in realistic character movements.

Modeling for Film or Game Work

Digital film and game design work are considered the very high-end in digital imagery creation because of the complex work required and the need for quality builds.

For film work, designers of digital creatures may build off of physical models and objects, and digitally augment these. They may use live human actors to capture facial details of emoting or verbal communications (using facial motion tracking and markers placed on the human face) (Thalmann, Kalra & Escher, 1998). Claymation (clay + animation) effects require plenty of attention to details and painstaking work but offer visual effects that are not easily imitated through other means. They may use reference materials to build the context and background. Early story reels, filmed versions of a series of storyboards for dramatic timing, may be filmed to capture the director's intentions for the camera work.

Time-lapse imagery may capture changes that occur over a season, over years, or even possibly over millennia. One simulated 4D widely available on the WWW shows a house decomposing and returning to nature over 200 years, for example.

Information streams may be depicted over time for trend-lines and the meta-perspective. This may be used to show large-level changes to a region in regards to population growth, urban-rural evolution, or climate, for example. Geological shifts over time may be captured, with geospatial data captures and depictions. Epidemiological effects may be modeled into the future based on various interventions, using 3D fractals as they evolve.

Flowfields

Flowfields may show how liquids and gasses may disperse over time and space. Volume rendering may provide visualizations of dense 3D volumetric datasets—by representing this information as color, direction, and opaqueness.

Often, these time-based visualizations may be manipulable by users in terms of setting input parameters. They may speed up time or change aspects of the scenario in order to see effects, in a time warp, through slider bars or different parameter inputs or specific queries. Some visualizations may combine information from different data sets for the purposes of analysis, contrast, and presentation.

3D imagery may be captured in 3D form with high-end cameras or multiple cameras, or they may be extrapolated from some software programs that may turn 2D (sequential) images into 3D ones.

5D: Graphics with Added Psychological or Emotional Content

Graphics may create a sense of mood and emotion. 5D graphics are those with added psychological or emotional content. Abstractions like Rorshach ink blots may contain 5D meanings along with more specific imagery.

The role of psychological and emotional motivations behind avatars has been evolving for years. Many also are designed with histories, personalities, and values.

Avatar Depth

These additional factors of avatar cognition, knowledge, history, values, and emotional states affect avatar's actions and add richness to the interactions with live people. Some complex systems integrate visual captures of human user emotions in their interactions with digital avatars for complex, and pseudo-realistic interactions.

Emotional Flocking

Designers even address how emotions are conveyed through flocks or groups of digital beings. "Emotions are represented in terms of the arousal and valence dimensions and they are visually expressed in a simple way through the behavior and appearance of the individuals in the flock. In particular, the arousal value parameterizes the Reynolds' flocking algorithm, and the valence value determines the number of different colors in the flock" (Ibáñez, Delgado-Mata, & Gómez-Caballero, 2007, p. 241). Autonomous pedestrians may portrayed in various interior and exterior public spaces for large-scale simulations (Shao & Terzopoulos, 2005, pp. 19 – 39).

Often, such creatures may sense static and mobile objects and behave accordingly, sometimes reactively and sometimes proactively.

Figure 4. A human avatar in Second Life (Williams, 2008)

Emo Contents and Characters

Emotional contents and characters have been designed to bring in the affective element to e-learning. Some learning strives to simulate high stress and high risk. Other types of e-learning evoke business meetings or workplace settings with a range of different emotions that may be expressed throughout the day. Some online trainings help learners read complex intercultural situations.

6D: Graphics Combined with other Media, Especially Sound or Speech

Graphics are often mixed with other media for "multimedia." Slideshows may involve sound or speech. Video is often accompanied by speech, music, and sound effects. Screencasts are often narrated. Avatars (see Figure 4) — whether human-embodied or automated — tend to speak with natural language. "Media are always mixtures of sensory and semiotic elements, and all the so-called visual media are *mixed* or hybrid formations, combining sound and sight, text and image. Even vision itself is not purely optical, requiring for its operations a coordination of optical and tactile impressions" (Mitchell, 2008, p. 15). The opposite is true as well. Indeed, visuals have been used to express sound, as in the use of Morse code, and letters and symbols to express pronunciations and sound, and symbols to convey musical notes.

7D: Graphics that Interact with Humans or Computer Systems

On the simple end of digital images that interact with human or computer systems are the automated types of interactivity: image maps that lead to further information or effects, simple interfaces that offer choices for the users. More complex images are user interface designs, which enable people to work with databases, repositories, and learning / course management systems, among others.

Visualizations may be adjusted for re-visualization as well, in 7D graphics. Visualizations have to answer meaningful questions for the users, in terms of information value and analysis (Lee, Reilly, & Butavicius, 2003, n.p.). Some visualization systems involve continuous data capture and delivery.

Figure 5. "Mystery in a Feedlot" (A Public Health Mystery) (Hai-Jew, 2009) **Note:** *Learners may interact with pieces of this public health mystery.*

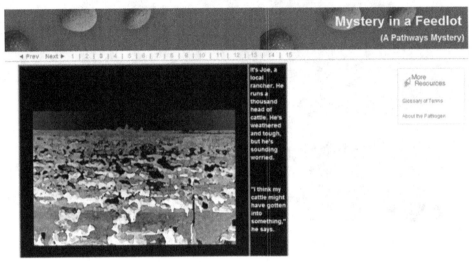

The role of human visual perception a core design feature in terms of conveying information with clarity. For example, convey 3D flowfields perceptually poses technological and communications challenges: "It is hypothesized that perception of the orientations of streamlines in space can greatly benefit from stereoscopic depth cues and motion parallax. In addition, because stereoscopic depth perception is a super-acuity and relies on such factors as small-scale stereoscopic disparity gradient based on texture, stereoscopic depth judgments will be exceptionally sensitive to display quality. In conventional displays, the aliasing of pixels gives completely spurious texture information to the mechanisms of stereoscopic depth perception. The result showed that stereo and motion cues are essential to perceiving the orientation of 3D lines. If, however, the contours are rendered as shaded tubes, good orientation information is available even without stereo or motion depth cues" (Ware, 2006, p. 101)

In immersive spaces, the graphics there allow people to "embody" their avatars and interact in 3D and 2D (less commonly now) immersive spaces (see Figure 5).

8D? For Augmented Reality?

An 8th dimension may involve digitally augmented physical spaces or "augmented reality," which may use various props and tactile objects (with physical "graspable user interfaces"), along with physical space. A range of combined digital and analog / physical spaces may be considered 8D.

There may be a physical rendition of digital spaces: One system *"integrates the benefits of two major interaction paradigms: graphical and physical user interfaces. Tagged transparent tiles are used as modular construction units. These tiles are augmented by dynamic graphical information when they are placed on a sensor-enhanced flat panel display. They can be used independently or can be combined into more complex configurations, similar to the way language can express complex concepts through a sequence of simple words"* (Rekimoto, Ullmer, & Oba, 2001, p. 269). These tiles then represent real-world objects and may be used for communications with a computerized system.

Many professions involve a majority of work in fields—"surveyors, archaeologists, medical practitioners in the outback, farmers"—so mobile handhelds will be important (Pham & Wong, 2004, p. 123) for information sharing, learning, decision-making and other applications. 3D virtual environments for mobile spaces do require much in terms of "computation, communication and memory" (Pham & Wong, 2004, p. 123). Context-aware (location-aware) mobile devices are also being designed for tourist applications such as tourist guides (Norrie, Signer, Grossniklaus, Belotti, Decurtins, & Weibel, 2007, pp. 855 – 870) as well as mobile device users in particular wifi-enabled locales (Matsubara, Mizukubo, Morita, Tarumi, & Kusunoki, 2005, pp. 475 – 480).

Haptics

Haptics or touch play an important role in immersive virtual reality. *"Most of the VR (virtual reality) systems include visual and auditive experiences, as they are easily reproduced through popular devices like screens and speakers. In order to increase immersion and interaction, advanced VR (virtual reality) systems includes also haptic devices to simulate the sense of touch and proprioception. This could not be achieved by using the classic keyboard and mouse interface"* (Ott, De Perrot, Thalmann, & Vexo, 2007, p. 338). Haptic devices have been brought into play such as through physical Braille readers that interface with computers. They also may have whimsical twists as in the use of a haptic neck-band to simulate virtual "kisses" (Saleh, Rahman, Eid & El Saddik, 2008, n.p.).

Personal Computing Devices

Accessorized personal devices with embedded computing may be used for more real-world immersiveness into the virtual. Here, "bracelets, buttons, (and) jackets" may capture, share and store information. "…a futuristic UI (user interface) for a mobile environment might no longer rely totally on hands and fingers (handheld), but instead might take advantage of different body parts for performing specific tasks" (Pham & Wong, 2004, p. 128).

Surface Computing

Surface computing involves the embedding of computing into everyday human spaces like floors, walls and ceilings. These may involve computerizing various artifacts like physical robots, furniture, clothes, artworks, and multifaceted new creations. "Most make heavy use of physical metaphors as the basis for interaction, the increased size of display surfaces making it possible to represent virtual objects in a life-size way. Most also recognize the power of both bimanual (and even multi-touch) input to support gesture in order to perform integrated natural actions on digital objects. And many combine the manipulation of physical artefacts (sic) with digital interaction, as seen in many of the 'tangible computing' ideas that have emerged over the years" (Terrenghi, Kirk, Sellen & Izadi, 2007, p. 1157).

Designers often draw from how people actually use physical spaces and objects in designing their digital equivalents in surface computing. They "ask how we can employ perhaps different methods to attain those same ends digitally" (Terrenghi, Kirk, Sellen & Izadi, 2007, p. 1165). Indeed, there are fundamental differences between the manipulation of physical vs. digital media. This allows for multi-modal feedback using both digital and physical sensory channels. This design requires interdisciplinary understandings—socially, psychologically, physically, and technologically.

"8 D" may enable more complex immersive practices that may involve physical skill sets and muscle memory. These may include both real-time information gathering through sensors and helpful decision-making outputs and augmentations for users.

Mixed Dimensionality

While the concept of dimensionality offers a frame for this discussion, many digital works cross boundaries and really have a "mixed dimensionality." Various visualizations mix the second and third dimensions: "2D and 3D views are used together in many visualization domains, such as medical imaging, flow visualization, oceanographic visualization, and computer aided design (CAD)" (Tory, 2003, p. 371).

CONCLUSION

Different types of digital graphics are used for different learning purposes and competencies in e-learning. The digital aspects of these offer rich affordances for instructors who may exploit the various dimensionalities for visualizations and learning effects. As the technologies evolve further, these will require continuing assessment to evaluate the best way to capture, create and design these for learning.

REFERENCES

Cai, K.-Y., Zhao, L., & Wang, F. (2006). A dynamic partitioning approach for GUI testing. In *Proceedings of the 30th Annual International Computer Software and Applications Conference (COMPSAC '06)*.

Chuah, M. C., & Eick, S. G. (1997). Glyphs for software visualization. In *Proceedings of the 5th International Workshop on Program Comprehension (WPC '97)* (pp. 183-191). Washington, DC: IEEE.

Clark, R. C., & Mayer, R. E. (2008). *E-Learning and the Science of Instruction: Proven Guidelines for Consumers and Designers of Multimedia Learning* (2nd ed.). San Francisco: John Wiley & Sons.

Debevec, P., Reinhard, E., Ward, G., & Pattanaik, S. (2004) High dynamic range imaging. In *Proceedings of the SIGGRAPH 2004*.

Diakopoulos, N., & Essa, I. (2005). Mediating photo collage authoring. In *Proceedings of the UIST '05*. New York: ACM.

Dias, R., Jesus, R., Frias, R., & Correia, N. (2007). Mobile interface of the MEMORIA project. In *Proceedings of the SIGIR '07,* Amsterdam, The Netherlands.

Dovey, J., & Kennedy, H. W. (2006). *Game Cultures: Computer Games as New Media.* New York: Open University Press.

Downhal, D. (1996). A seven-dimensional approach to graphics. In [New York: ACM.]. *Proceedings of the SIGDOC, 96,* 149–160.

Franco, J. F., da Cruz, S. R., & Lopes, R. deD. (n.d.). Computer graphics, interactive technologies and collaborative learning synergy supporting individuals' skills development. In *Proceedings of the International Conference on Computer Graphics and Interactive Techniques*. New York: ACM.

Gal, R., Sorkine, O., Popa, T., Sheffer, A., & Cohen-Or, D. (2007). 3D collage: Expressive non-realistic modeling. In *Proceedings of the 5th international symposium on Non-photorealistic animation and rendering* (pp. 7-14). New York: ACM.

Geigel, J., & Musgrave, F. K. (1997). A model for simulating the photographic development process on digital images. In *Proceedings of the 24th annual conference on Computer graphics and interactive techniques*.

Haralambous, Y., & Bella, G. (2005). Injecting information into atomic units of text. In *Proceedings of the Doc Eng. '05*, Bristol, UK (pp. 134-142). New York: ACM. Ibáñez, J., Delgado-Mata, C., & Gómez-Caballero, F. (2007). A novel approach to express emotions through a flock of virtual beings. In *Proceedings of the 2007 International Conference on Cyberworlds* (pp. 241-248). Washington, DC: IEEE.

Itoh, M., & Tanaka, Y. (2006). 3D component-based visualization framework for generating simple 3D applications using Web services. In *Proceedings of the 2006 IEEE/ WIC / ACM International Conference*.

Jardosh, A., Belding-Royer, E. M., Almeroth, K. C., & Suri, S. (2003). Towards realistic mobility models for mobile ad hoc networks. In [New York: ACM.]. *Proceedings of the MobiCom, 03*, 217–229.

Jayant, C., Renzelmann, M., Wen, D., Krisnandi, S., Ladner, R., & Comden, D. (2007). Automated tactile graphics translation: In the field. In . *Proceedings of the ASSETS, 07*, 75–82. doi:10.1145/1296843.1296858

Kahlouche, S., Achour, K., & Djekoune, O. (2003). A genetic algorithm for geometric primitives extraction. In *Proceedings of the Seventh International Symposium on Signal Processing and its Applications* (pp. 509-512). Washington, DC: IEEE.

Kittler, J., Hilton, A., Hamouz, M., & Illingworth, J. (2005). 3D assisted face recognition: A survey of 3D imaging, modelling and recognition approaches. In *Proceedings of the 2005 IEEE Computer Society Conference on Computer Vision and Pattern Recognition*.

Klein, A. W., Li, W., Kazhdan, M. M., Corrêa, W. T., Finkelstein, A., & Funkhouser, T. A. (2000). Non-photorealistic virtual environments. In *Proceedings of the SIGGRAPH 2000*. New York: ACM.

Kwon, Y.-M., Kim, I.-J., Ahn, S. C., Ko, H., & Kim, H.-G. (2001). Virtual heritage system: Modeling, database & presentation. In *Proceedings of the Seventh International Conference on Virtual Systems and Multimedia*. Washington, DC: IEEE.

Laidlaw, D. H., Kirby, R. M., Jackson, C. D., Davidson, J. S., Miller, T. S., & da Silva, M. (2005). Comparing 2D vector field visualization methods: A user study. *IEEE Transactions on Visualization and Computer Graphics, 11*(1), 59–70. doi:10.1109/TVCG.2005.4

Layng, J. M. (1996). The creation and varied applications of educational holograms. In R.E. Griffin, D.G. Beauchamp, J.M. Hunter, & C.B. Schiffman (Eds.), *Eyes on the Future: Converging images, ideas and instruction.* University Park, PA: Penn State Press.

Lee, K. (2007). 3D urban modeling and rendering with high resolution remote sensing imagery on mobile 3D and web 3D environments: System architecture and prototype implementation. In *Proceedings of the Urban Remote Sensing Joint Event.* Washington, DC: IEEE.

Lee, M. D., Reilly, R. E., & Butavicius, M. A. (2003). An empirical evaluation of Chernoff faces, star glyphs, and spatial visualizations for binary data. In *Proceedings of the Conferences in Research and Practice in Information Technology.* Australian Computer Society, Inc.

Lee, W., Pak, J., Kim, S., Kim, H., & Lee, G. (2007). TransPen & MimeoPad: A playful interface for transferring a graphic image to paper by digital rubbing. In *Proceedings of the International Conference on Computer Graphics and Interactive Techniques.* New York: ACM.

Liao, C. L. (2008, March). Avatars, Second Life®, and new media art: The challenge for contemporary art education. *Art Education, 61*(2), 87.

Lin, W.-M., Tsay, M.-T., & Wu, S.-W. (1996). Application of geographic information system to distribution information support. *IEEE Transactions on Power Systems, 11*(1), 190–197. doi:10.1109/59.486095

Masui, T. (1992). Graphic object layout with interactive genetic algorithms. In *Proceedings of the IEE Workshop on Visual Languages* (pp. 74-80). Washington, DC: IEEE.

Matsubara, K., Mizukubo, Y., Morita, T., Tarumi, H., & Kusunoki, F. (2005). An agent control mechanism in virtual worlds for mobile users. In [Washington, DC: IEEE.]. *Proceedings of the International Conference on Active Media Technology, 2005,* 475–480. doi:10.1109/AMT.2005.1505401

Matsuyama, T., & Takai, T. (2002). Generation, visualization, and editing of 3D video. In *Proceedings of the First International Symposium on 3D Data Processing Visualization and Transmission (3DPVT'02).* Washington, DC: IEEE.

Misic, V., Buckley, R. R., & Parker, K. J. (2003). Encoding and processing of color engravings (using MRC). In *Proceedings of the IEEE ICIP 2002.*

Mitchell, W. J. T. (2008). Visual literacy or literary visualcy. In J. Elkins (Ed.), *Visual Literacy.* New York: Routledge.

Mochocki, B., Lahiri, K., & Cadambi, S. (2006). Power analysis of mobile 3D graphics. In *Proceedings of the conference on Design, automation and test in Europe.*

Moreau, N., Leclère, M., Chein, M., & Gutierrez, A. (2007). Formal and graphical annotations for digital objects. In [New York: ACM.]. *Proceedings of the SADPI, 07,* 69–78.

Negroponte, N. (1995). *Being Digital.* New York: Alfred A. Knopf.

Norrie, M. C., Signer, B., Grossniklaus, M., Belotti, R., Decurtins, C., & Weibel, N. (2007). Context-aware platform for mobile data management. *Wireless Networks, 13,* 855–870. doi:10.1007/s11276-006-9858-y

Ostromoukhov, V. (1999). Digital facial engraving. In [New York: ACM.]. *Proceedings of the SIG-GRAPH, 99,* 417–424.

Ott, R., De Perrot, V., Thalmann, D., & Vexo, F. (2007). MHaptic: A haptic manipulation library for generic virtual environments. In *Proceedings of the 2007 International Conference on Cyberworlds* (pp. 338-345). Washington, DC: IEEE.

Petre, M., & Blackwell, A. F. (1997). A glimpse of expert programmers' mental imagery. In *Proceedings of the Seventh Workshop on Empirical Studies of Programmers*. Retrieved November 24, 2008, from http://portal.acm.org/citation.cfm?id=266409

Pham, B., & Wong, O. (2004). Handheld devices for applications using dynamic multimedia data. In *Proceedings of the 2nd international conference on Computer graphics and interactive techniques in Australasia and South East Asia.* New York: ACM.

Rao, L. (2009, March 20). *GE uses digital hologram to advertize (sic) windmills.* Retrieved May 8, 2009, from http://www.techcrunch.com/2009/03/20/ge-uses-digital-hologram-to-advertize-windmills/

Rekimoto, J., Ullmer, B., & Oba, H. (2001). DataTiles: A modular platform for mixed physical and graphical interactions. *Letters Chi, 3*(1), 269–276.

Saleh, A., Rahman, M., Eid, M., & El Saddik, A. (2008). KissMe: Bringing virtual events to the real world. In *Proceedings of the VECIMS 2008, IEEE International Conference on Virtual Environments, Human-Computer Interfaces, and Measurement Systems,* Istanbul, Turkey. Washington, DC: IEEE.

Saund, E., Fleet, D., Larner, D., & Mahoney, J. (2003). Perceptually-supported image editing of text and graphics. In *Proceedings of the UIST 2003,* Vancouver, BC, Canada (pp. 183-192).

Schwarte, R. (2001). Dynamic 3D-vision. In *Proceedings EDMO 2001* (pp. 241-248). Washginton, DC: IEEE.

Shanbhag, P., Rheingans, P., & desJardins, M. (2005). Temporal visualization of planning polygons for efficient partitioning of geo-spatial data. In . *Proceedings of the IEEE Symposium on Information Visualization, 2005,* 211–218. doi:10.1109/INFVIS.2005.1532149

Shao, W., & Terzopoulos, D. (2005). Autonomous pedestrians. In *Proceedings of the Eurographics / ACM SIGGRAPH Symposium on Computer Animation* (pp. 19-21).

Sohn, J.-H., Park, Y.-H., Yoon, C.-W., Woo, R., Park, S.-J., & Yoo, H.-J. (2005). Low-power 3D graphics processors mobile terminals. *IEEE Communications Magazine,* 90. doi:10.1109/MCOM.2005.1561925

Sormann, M., Bauer, J., Zach, C., Klaus, A., & Karner, K. (2004). VR modeler: From image sequences to 3D models. In *Proceedings of the 20th spring conference on Computer graphics.* New York: ACM.

Sribunruangrit, N., Marque, C., Lenay, C., & Gapenne, O. (2004). Graphic-user-interface system for people with severely impaired vision in mathematics class. In *Proceedings of the 26ᵗʰ Annual International Conference of the IEEE EMBS* (pp. 5145-5148). Washington, DC: IEEE.

Swartz, C. S. (2005). Understanding digital cinema: Introduction. *ACM Computers in Entertainment, 3*(2), 1–9. doi:10.1145/1063723.1063725

Tangelder, J. W. H., & Veltkamp, R. C. (2004). A survey of content based 3D shape retrieval methods. In *Proceedings of the Shape Modeling International 2004, (SMI'04).*

Terrenghi, L., Kirk, D., Sellen, A., & Izadi, S. (2007). Affordances for manipulation of physical versus digital media on interactive surfaces. In *Proceedings of the CHI 2007* (pp. 1157-1166).

Thalmann, N. D., Kalra, P., & Escher, M. (1998). Face to virtual face. *Proceedings of the IEEE, 86*(5), 870–883. doi:10.1109/5.664277

Thomas-Meyers, G., & Whitaker, R. (2006). Knowledge glyphs as a tactic for multi-planar visualization of simulation products. In Proceedings of the 2006 Winter Simulation Conference (1203-1209). Washington, DC: IEEE.

Tory, M. (2003). Mental registration of 2D and 3D visualizations (an empirical study). In . *Proceedings of the IEEE Visualization, 2003,* 371–378.

Ware, C. (2006). 3D contour perception for flow visualization. In *Proceedings of the 3rd symposium on Applied perception in graphics and visualization* (pp. 101-106). New York: ACM.

Warnock, J. E. (2000). The changing landscape of graphic arts. *IEEE Computer Graphics and Applications, 20*(1), 32–33. doi:10.1109/38.814547

Weiskopf, D. (2004). On the role of color in the perception of motion in animated visualizations. In *IEEE Visualization.*

Weyrich, T., Deng, J., Barnes, C., Rusinkiewicz, S., & Finkelstein, A. (2007). Digital bas-relief from 3D scenes. *ACM Transactions on Graphics, 26*(43), 32-1-32-7.

Williams, H. (2008). *A human avatar in Second Life.*

Zhang, Y., Xie, P., & Li, H. (2007). Multi-scale colour 3D satellite imagery and global 3D Web mapping. In *Proceedings of the Urban Remote Sensing Joint Event.* Washington, DC: IEEE.

Zsaki, A. M. (2008). cuttingIPlane: An interactive tool for exploration of 3D datasets via slicing. In *Proceedings of the C3S2E-08,* Montreal, QC, Canada. New York: ACM.

KEY TERMS AND DEFINITIONS

1D (adj): Existing along one axis, usually the y axis (usually length or width, or a one-dimensional measure)

2D (adj): Existing along two axes: x and y axes (usually length and width, for shapes; two-dimensional measures)

3D (adj): Existing along three axes, x, y and z axes, with x depicted in red, y in green and z in blue (traditionally), inclusive of length, width and depth (and volume)

4D (adj): Existing on the x, y and z axes, and with a time or temporal dimension (time variance)

Bas Relief (low relief) (n): A flat digital image that depicts a sculpture in which the figures project slightly from the background and may be viewable from various angles

Density (n): The compactness of a substance

Flocking (n): The congregating of a group of digital birds

Granularity (n): The size of a digital object (level of detail)

High Dynamic Range (HDR): Digital images through the melding of three exposures of the same shot

Informational Graphic (n): Non-pictorial graphics that depict entities and the relationships among those entities

Maquette (n): Three dimensional sculptures usually rendered in clay for character development

Resolution (n): The level of detail portrayed via the dots per linear inch or number of pixels, the sharpness of a digital image, the distinguishing between adjacent objects or sources of light

Pixellation (n): The dissolving of an image into fuzziness and the appearance of the pixels within the image

Spatial Hypermedia (n): Technologies that enhance the perception of real-space and dimensionality in relation to geographical systems, conceptual workspaces, indirect navigation, and in-field collaborations

Spectral (adj): Resembling or suggesting a spectrum or array of colors (arranged in order of magnitudes of a common physical property)

Stencil (n): A device used for applying a pattern or design to a surface, with a coloring substance rubbed over the stencil and the color passing through cut-out sections to the surface

Surface Computing (n): The use of physical spaces, physical artifacts, digital technologies and techniques to create interactive spaces for computing

Synthetic Images (n): Images generated by computer and not captured from a real-world situation

Tensor Field (n): A digital depiction of the stresses and strains in materials, used in the physical sciences and engineering

Tessellation (n): The fitting together of like forms (like squares or triangles) in a checker or mosaic pattern

Time Series Animation (n): A depiction of changes over time, which involves visual changes

Volume (volumetric) Rendering (n): The visualization of dense 3D volumetric datasets, often using form, color, texture, size, and other elements

Section 3
Designing Graphics
for E–Learning

Chapter 5
Information and Visualization Imagery

ABSTRACT

Information and visualization imagery conveys data for more effective learning and comprehension, memory retention; analytic tractability; decision-making and information aesthetics. These types of visualization imagery may be built both in simple and complex ways. Complex and live data streams may be collated and delivered via interactive tools delivered via the Web, with some bolstering simulation learning. This chapter addresses the types of visualizations used in e-learning, strategies for creating these, and the ways to avoid unintended and negative learning.

CHAPTER OBJECTIVES

- Define information and visualization imagery and their uses in e-learning
- Explore the types of visualizations used in e-learning (in terms of dimensions, delivery devices, and extreme visualizations)
- Investigate the processing spectrum of digital imagery for information and visualization
- Describe some core components of complex, multi-stream visualizations
- Explain the main reasons to visualize information
- Contrast static with dynamic information visualizations
- Study the value-added extraction of information from visualizations
- Consider live data streams and complex multi-stream visual information
- Address strategies for creating effective information imagery and visualization imagery
- Describe how to design a full mental model

DOI: 10.4018/978-1-60566-972-4.ch005

- Explore how to avoid misconceptions or negative learning
- Provide a method for evaluating information and visualization imagery

INTRODUCTION

Epidemiologists use these to track the spread of a disease through a population and to track how it is spread. Chemists view these to predict complex molecular interactions. Scientists use these (in part) to decide whether a spaceship should be launched into orbit. Architects use these to discuss a building's floor plan. Economists examine various scenarios depicted by these. Environmentalists view these to plan how to go about protecting a forest habitat. Meteorologists use these to predict the general landfall of a hurricane. Archaeologists go to a website to check out the stratigraphy of an archaeological dig half a world away. Deep sea divers study these to get a sense of the particular environments that they'll be entering. What these professionals refer to are information and visualization imagery.

Visualizations are a powerful affordance of digital and Web technologies. Foremost, these enable the communication of complex and information-rich details via imagery. They enable fresh ways of modeling information, particularly those with spatio-temporal aspects or large quantitative datasets. Designing visualization languages is "grounded in human conceptualization" (Douglas, Hundhausen & McKeown, 1995, p. 342). This field draws on typography, graphics, psychology and computer science. In recent decades, these have been designed to operate in computer and virtual environments.

These depictions, if designed around learning theory and instructional design, may increase the "learnability" of some course contents (Duchastel, 2003, pp. 310 – 311).

Ware defines visualization as 'a graphical representation of data or concepts,' which is either an 'internal construct of the mind' or an 'external artifact supporting decision making.' In other words, visualizations assist humans with data analysis by representing informational visually. This assistance may be called cognitive support (Tory & Möller, Jan. – Feb. 2004, p. 72).

Information imagery and visualizations enhance complex analysis and decision-making by engaging large datasets in manageable ways. These approaches to handling information have integrated technologies like cameras and sensors to create live situational awareness. Robots may be sent to capture a 3D view of an indicated position (Kemp, Anderson, Nguyen, Trevor, & Xu, 2008). Visualizations may involve the use live datafeeds. These enable the monitoring of situations, and the inspection and exploration of difficult environments using sensors. These enable high-risk or hostile environment simulations. Visualizations may be employed to develop schemas or mental models. Extremely large and extremely small (mesoscale to nano-scale) may be depicted. Even elusive works of the imagination may be captured as through gyrokinetic simulations (Crawford, Ma, Huang, Klasky, & Ethier, 2004) and particle-level interactions (Ma, Schussman, Wilson, Ko, Qiang & Ryne, 2002). Various futures may be projected on trend lines using visualizations.

Experiential situated cognition may be employed to model the real world, with plenty of modeling of natural physics and phenomena: flora and fauna, oceans, clouds, fire, landscaping, and the earth and sky (The elements of nature: Interactive and realistic techniques, 2004, n.p.). Ultimately, information imagery and visualizations promote "information aesthetics," the elegant delivery of high artistry and high information value through digital interfacing (Lau & Moere, 2007, n.p.).

INFORMATIONAL AND VISUALIZATION IMAGERY IN E-LEARNING

At the most basic level, informational and visualization imagery need to portray information in a visible way to users. The depictions need to capture user attention, and the images need to convey the information accurately. Designers of visualizations have plenty of research on human visual perceptions: how they respond to colors (with warm colors "advancing" and cooler colors "receding"); the hardwired illusions that may be created; the persistence-of-vision and after-image phenomena; how people's eyes and attention follow motion (Weiskopf, 2004, p. 305); how images are interpreted in the foreground and background of an image; how depth perception is viewed, and how much information may be perceived simultaneously (before sensory overload or flooding) through visual and lingual (particularly audio) channels.

Information and visualization imagery are data-hungry models, with plenty of requirements for information that exists below the imagery surfaces. On the surface, the informational and visualization imagery may come in a range of forms. Image maps may convey spatial relationships with embedded interactive access. Glyphs (visual objects that contain one or more data variables) may deliver static contents with plenty of visual and textual annotation. Meaning is coded into the shapes, colors, transparencies, orientations, and other aspects. Icons are often used in cartography (map-making), logic, semiotics (the study of signs and symbols) and pictorial information systems (Ebert, Shaw, Zwa & Starr, 1996).

Photomosaics are arrangements of photos that form a composite image. These may be aerial captures or seabed photos, with the close-ups used for forensic analysis. The screen real estate may be extended through the use of semi-transparency:

Semi-transparency increases the amount of information that interfaces can expose in a given screen space by allowing content from a window to remain partially visible while other windows overlap it (Gyllstrom, Miller & Stotts, 2007, p. 425).

Screen captures or screen shots are realistic captures of what's on the computer screen. These are annotatable. They may be non-motion or motion. And these are often used with voice and audio overlays. These may create visualizations of technological systems or involve the capture of *machinima* (machine + cinema) in immersive spaces. These are often used for process-oriented or sequential tasks.

Fractals are 3D and 4D geometric (and non-geometric) shapes that may express formulas visually. These may also be a result of machine art. Mathematical models may be expressed in fractals to show system relationships—such as the human and machine activity on a website, the epidemiological disease paths in a society, or others. These forms tend towards irregularity, but are meaningful at both macro and micro levels. Plenoptic images (3D and 4D ones) may be viewed from multiple angles, and various software programs have enabled their editing for particular visualizations and effects (Seitz & Kutulakos, 1998).

Photo-realistic images may be captured by digital cameras, sensors, scanners, and other input devices. These devices may be microscope-enhanced (with resulting photomicrographs) or telescope-enhanced (with photo-telescopes). These may originate from satellite, acoustical image capture machines, sonograms, x-rays, and CAT scans. To maintain their informational value, these images have to be captured with a proper sense of size and measure, and correct white-balance in the lighting; these may need post-capture editing adjustments for correctness.

Digital video adds the power of movement and sound. These may involve realistic or synthetic imagery. These may be sequential or non-sequential depictions. These may capture storytelling effectively as well as the passage of time; these may also show narrative interactions between peoples and entities with clarity.

Photo-realistic images may be rendered to appear synthetic. Manga-style face captures are enabled from photographs through composite sketching (Chen, Liu, Rose, Xu, Shum & Salesin, 2004, pp. 95 – 102, and 153). Videorealistic captures may now be turned into a "spatiotemporally coherent cartoon animation through video 'tooning" (Wang, Xu, Shum & Cohen, 2004, pp. 574 – 583).

Synthetic digital images—such as image morphing; photo-mosaicing; cartoon rendering from photo images; computerized drawing; photogravure effects, intaglio printmaking effects, and etching simulations; machine art; acoustic-synched imagery; digital sculpting—may be used for other visual effects. Such images may simulate laboratories, locations, and interactive experiences. Digital avatars, particularly those powered with artificial intelligence and animations, may communicate a sense of a lively or living presence and individuality. Machine art, which results from so-called "chaos tools" or "morphogenesis" for artificial life creations, may evoke a techno aesthetic.

Knowledge Structures

Some digital contents may be displayed as ontologies, taxonomies or data models or structures (Angles & Gutierrez, Feb. 2008, pp. 1:1-1:2). A hypothetical knowledge structure "integrates the ideas, assumptions, relationships, insights, facts, and misconceptions that together shape the way an individual views and interacts with reality" (Steiger & Steiger, 2007, p. 1), and is an embodiment of domain knowledge in order to abstractly reason about the domain (objects, grouping, interrelationships, sequences, processes, and behaviors).

Metaphoric Mapping

Clearly, visualizations must go beyond fidelity to have instructional value. The mapping of data to visual metaphors for cognitive support and coherence is a critical aspect of visualization design. Such extended comparisons should not conflate factors unintentionally, and they should not suggest relationships that may not exist. A selected metaphor needs both "expressiveness" and "effectiveness" (MacKinlay, 1986, as cited in Marcus, Feng & Maletic, 2003, p. 28). "Expressiveness" refers to the metaphor's ability to visually represent the information fully; "effectiveness" refers to how clearly the information is "visually perceived," the aesthetic value, and the optimization of the metaphor in terms of polygons needed to render. There need to be sufficient visual parameters in the metaphor for displaying the relevant information. The authors elaborate:

The relationship between data values and visual parameters has to be a univocal relationship; otherwise, if more than one data value is mapped onto the same visual parameter than it will be impossible to distinguish one value's influence from the other. On the other hand, there can always be visual parameters that are not used to map information, as long as there is no need for them to be utilized (Marcus, Feng & Maletic, 2003, p. 28).

Baecker, et al.'s Metaphor Theory begins with a source domain to the left. This domain is "tangible, concrete and recognizable." The target domain involves concepts and processes. Bridging the source and the domain is the metaphoric mapping, which serves as a bridge of understanding, in order to best define the source and the concepts and processes which affect that source (as cited in Wells and Fuerst, 2000, p. 1).

Time-based visualizations need to have clear time progressions with identified changes over time. 3D imagery should involve clear size, shape and color measures –for the optimal accuracy—and these should allow changes of perspectives and angles. Emotional or "affective computing" aspects of visualizations need to be designed with care, so as to avoid unintended effects.

TYPES OF VISUALIZATIONS

Visualizations are generally categorized into two types: scientific visualizations involve hard science data with an inherent physical component, and informational visualizations involve abstract, non-spatial data (Tory & Möller, Jan. – Feb., 2004, p. 72), often quantitative. There are also more large simulated data sets created by super computers, which enable real-world data exploration and benefits from visual support (Nocke, Böhm, & Flechsig, 2003).

Visualization Dimensionality

Visualizations may be depicted in various ways. Static two-dimensional ones may be still images, with value-added overlays. An example would be a map overlaid with street information, satellite views, terrain views, or other data. Static 3D may consist of still images reflecting z-axis spatiality, volume, depth, and rich perspective. Dynamic 2D may involve movement in video, animations, *machinima*, and animated tutorials. Dynamic 3D may involve three-dimensional volumetric flows, dispersions, and immersive movement Wössner, Schulze, Walz, & Lang, 2002). The other dimensions may involve the visualization of movement or animation (4D), the integration of psychological or emotional contents (5D), graphics combined with sound or speech (6D), graphics that interact with humans or computer systems (7D), or even more complex reality augmentations (8D). Visualizations may involve a variety of dimensionality from 1D through 8D, as described in the prior chapter.

Visualizations may be interactive, which means that users may be able to change input parameters or different effects related to the visual experience. Non-interactive ones involve those that display the information but do not accept inputs from users.

Delivery Devices

Visualizations may be delivered through different devices: electronic kiosks, multi-screen wall displays, desktop computers, mobile devices, head-mounted displays, augmented reality installations, augmented virtuality computer displays, and others. Augmented reality has enabled the integration of the virtual with the real, "seamlessly with a fantasy virtual playground by capitalizing on infrastructure provided by wearable computer, mixed reality, and ubiquitous computing research" (Cheok, Goh, Farbiz, Liu, Li, Fong, Yang, & Teo, 2004, pp. 779 – 780). These may involved mixed reality outdoor gaming arenas, tactile (touch or haptic) interfaces, live kinesthetic or movement-based learning (muscle memory), and interactive smart rooms. Ambient visualizations occur in digital installations and displays in real spaces.

Much work has gone into the creation of methods for offering "visualization interfaces that offer multiple coordinated views on a particular set of data items…designed for navigating and exploring complex information spaces" (Becks & Seeling, 2004, p. 193).

Wearable computers have to be designed for rugged real-space uses. "Using a wearable computer is in many aspects different from using a stationary desktop computer. The operating conditions may vary considerably and are not known beforehand. The use may also be restricted by some external factors (e.g. traffic or weather). The user should be able to operate the computer while walking, without losing focus on the current primary task (user's attention may be divided between primary and secondary tasks; in our case, the selection is considered secondary task). Hence, the interaction technique should allow easy, natural, intuitive, and forgiving input" (Lehikoinen & Röykkee, 2003, p. 45).

Extreme Visualizations

Extreme visualizations involve depictions of extremely small-scale to large-scale imagery. Registering large-scale geographic information system imagery will require lossiness of information, when delivered to a desktop machine. To access close-up details, there may have to be the "tiling" of an image for up-close fine-grained views; this is especially useful in wide area surveillance (Crisp, Perry & Redding, 2003, n.p.). In archaeology, there are endeavors to digitally capture the complex information of an archaeological dig, with the various artifacts and their locations in the soil, represented through statigraphy, which involves 3D mapping of a live site. Archaeologists are offering this information in a federated database with visualizations that are accurate and informative (Pettersen, Bordes, Ulm, Gwynne, Simmich & Pailthorpe, 2008, n.p.).

Digital geographic data accounts for a lot of the large-size digital artifacts and visualizations. "The increasing volume and diversity of digital geographic data easily overwhelm traditional spatial analysis techniques that handle only limited and homogeneous data sets with high-computational burden. To discover new and unexpected patterns, trends, and relationships embedded within large and diverse geographic data sets, several recent studies of geospatial data mining have developed a number of sophisticated and scalable spatial clustering algorithms, outlier analysis techniques, spatial classification and association analysis methods, and spatial data-cleaning and integration tools" (Han, Altman, Kumar, Mannila & Pregibon, 2002, p. 57).

Some visualizations include imagery inside the human body. Others are theoretical ones about micro-level realities. Others feign forms of nature, such as cellular morphogenesis. Other "extreme" visualizations may involve "medical imaging, fluid flow simulation, and geographic information systems (GIS)" (Tory & Möller, 2004, p. 72).

There are dispersion models of gases and particles, such as air flow and contaminant transport (Qiu, Zhao, Fan, Wei, Lorenz, Wang, Yoakum-Stover, Kaufman, & Mueller, 2004, pp. 553 – 560); the directionality of a cloud or gas or particles may be depicted with streamlines to show the paths of flow with clarity. Other depictions use directional texturing. The modeling of fluids and gases involving motion and flows involve technological complexity (Laramee, Weiskopf, Schneider, & Hauser, 2004, pp. 51 – 58). The visual grammar of capturing turbulence in flows—of air, water and liquid materials—now may also include "color weaving" and "texture stitching" (Urness, Interrante, Marusic, Longmire, &

Figure 1. The processing spectrum of digital imagery for information and visualization (Hai-Jew, 2009)

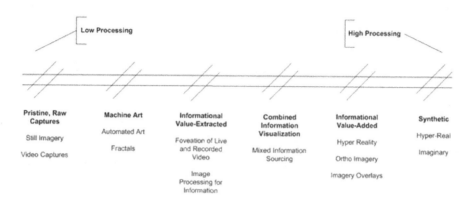

The Processing Spectrum of Digital Imagery for Information and Visualization

Ganapathisubramani, 2003, pp .115 – 121). The modeling of kinetics—reaction, diffusion—is an important aspect to the research.

Schema-level visualizations are also complex. These include plenty of researched information and information streams. These may assert complex interrelationships, all of which are based on known information and possibly some degree of interpretation. The "transparency" of a visualization will be important to help users vet the validity of the data.

The sizes of visualizations and their complexity mean that more computing power is required. This means that desktop systems may not be up for some tasks.

Scientists are faced with a problem that as their simulations grow to sizes where interesting features and structures can be resolved, the features themselves become too small (relative to the size of the data) to find, and the structures too large to visualize. Interactive navigation and exploration of these datasets is essential, and small features can only be properly understood if shown in the context of larger structures, showing both large scale structures and small scale features in the same visualization is essential. However, the data size prevents efficient rendering of even single frames, let alone multiple frames per second that is required for interactive exploration (LaMar & Pascucci, 2003, p. 61).

Information-rich visualizations may range from those requiring low processing to more high-end and complex ones. Figure 1, "The Processing Spectrum of Digital Imagery for Information and Visualization," shows a rough continuum of different types of visualization outputs.

Complex and multi-stream visualization imagery are more than simple visuals. These may take many forms, but many are expressed as virtual "dashboards" with discrete information flows. Others may be 3D depictions or immersive spaces. They may be aerial photos overlaid with various types of value-added information.

Figure 2, "Some Core Components of a Complex Multi-Stream Visualization," addresses core components of digital visualization. A visualization is only as good as its originating information streams, which should be multi-sourced for accuracy. That information needs to be vetted and de-noised. Then

Figure 2. Some core components of a complex, multi-stream visualization (Hai-Jew, 2009)

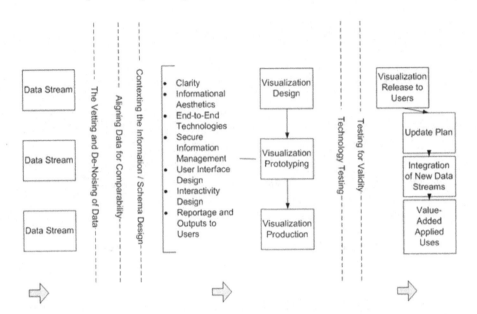

the data should be aligned for comparability (Han, Altman, Kumar, Mannila, & Pregibon, 2002) and data dimensionality (Fahnestock & Read, 2000). This data alignment opens up potentially significant errors of assumptions, or the incorrect interpolation of data. Effective information integration requires plenty of analytical attention (Bakshi, Knoblock & Thakkar, 2004). That information also needs to be contextualized or organized into a schema that matches with the real-world that the visualization is depicting.

The visualization design, prototyping and production follows—with a focus on informational clarity, informational aesthetics, technology choices, secure information handling, user interface design, interactivity design, and outputs. The technologies have to be tested, and the validity of the visualization needs to be assessed. After this passes muster, it may then be released to users. Even at the time of release, there should be some planning for updating the visualization, integrating new data streams (as needed), and pursuing value-added applied uses of that tool. One example of such complex modeling involves the creation of "human terrain data" which brings together "sociocultural, anthropologic, and ethnographic data and other non-geophysical information about the human population and society" for use in intelligence, military, and diplomatic endeavors (Silerman, 2007, p. 260). Another involves the fusion of multi-sensor data by "aligning multiple image modalities into the same coordinate system" (Vasile, Waugh, Greisokh, & Heinrichs, 2006, n.p.).

A visualization's power comes from the quality of the underlying information as well as the design of the visualization itself. The design of the learning, the transparency of the visualization, the information sharing, and the user interactivity also affect the quality.

WHY VISUALIZE?

Visualizations may be low or high-value ones depending on the magnitude of the decision that will follow based (in part or in whole) on that visualization. In a complex world, the implications of decisions may not be that apparent early on, and the law of unintended consequences may always be a factor. Visualizations may be used for a variety of purposes and with audiences with different aims and levels of sophistication.

People may choose to visualize information for a number of objectives.

- Offer new ways of seeing, understanding spatial concepts and exploring data for research and academic pursuits
- Support awareness and learning of complex and information-rich datasets; entities and their inter-relationships through "exploratory data analysis" (Nakakoji, Takashima, & Yamamoto, 2001, p. 77).
- Communicate spatial or graphical information (without other efficient ways to communicate this)
- Depict spatio-temporal contexts, phenomena, experiments, and projections
- Enhance complex analysis
- Support complex decision-making
- Create live situational awareness, high-risk or hostile environment simulation
- Develop a conceptual model or schema
- Conceptualize large systems for a broad "panoptic" view
- Simulate and model predictively, into the future
- Enable experiential, immersive, persistent and multi-sensory situated cognition
- Model real-world, real-time situations
- Embody the imagination, elusive ideas, and innovations
- Promote discoveries and new learning
- Promote information aesthetics

In a business workflow, visualizations may be created for any part of the project: the research phase, the proposal, the work planning, the presentation to stakeholders, the presentation to customers, and the actual design and delivery. E-learning instructors and content providers may create visualizations to enhance learning. In academia, visualizations may be created in any part of the research grant cycle.

In some problem-solving situations, visualizations used for synchronous remote collaboration need to promote communications and sharing among the participants to be effective. The researchers assert: All visualization conditions improved remote collaborators' performance over the control condition. Full access to a shared visualization best facilitated remote collaboration by encouraging tool use and fostering discussion between the partners" (Balakrishnan, Fussell & Kiesler, 2008, p. 1227).

Visualizations may enhance complex workflows. Figure 3, "The Academic Research Flow," is an informational graphic that describes the complex work that goes into research. At various phases, digital imagery may be used to describe the work and to communicate learning points.

STATIC VS. DYNAMIC, CONTINUOUS INFORMATION AND VISUALIZATION IMAGERY

"Static" visualizations may generally be described as those that do not involve fresh or changing streams of information. The information is already defined. There are no built-in animations, but there may be

Figure 3. The academic research flow

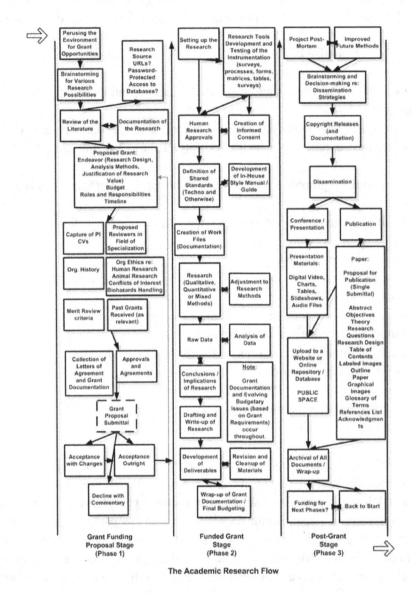

The Academic Research Flow

interactivity. Visualizations that are non-animated 2D and 3D images may often contain plenty of helpful information.

Most tend to be multivariate data displays, with multiple information strands. The high data density, if designed well, may reduce cognitive demands on human memory. They may aid in the perceptual monitoring of complex information and aid in pattern recognition (Tory & Möller, 2004, p. 73).

More dynamic visualization of imagery may embody richer complexity. These may be continuous or discrete model visualizations. Continuous modeling suggests continuity in time. Discrete models suggest more stasis.

Continuous model visualization encompasses all visualization algorithms that use a continuous model of the data (i.e., the algorithm assumes that the phenomenon being studied is continuous, even if the data values are discrete) and is roughly analogous to "scientific visualization." Discrete model visualization includes visualization algorithms that use discrete data models and roughly corresponds to "information visualization (Tory & Möller, 2004, p. 72).

Some visualizations combine the work of people from cross-functional domains.

Landscape design and engineering, by definition, occurs over large areas and requires the input of a great number of specialists. These include experts in earth engineering, water management, agrarian management, land economy, legal policy and transport infrastructure to name just a few. Furthermore, landscape interventions inevitably affect large numbers of people living perhaps on or near a particular site. It is often critical for the designers of a landscape project to communicate their vision to the local inhabitants. It is therefore necessary that the tool of the landscape designer and engineer allow various specialists and lay members to participate in a collaborative design process (Piper, Ratti, & Ishii, 2002, p. 356).

Building Conceptual Models from Naïve Mental Models

A critical affordance of digital imagery involves the ability to help learners create mental models of phenomena in the world—equipment, systems, and human groups. Information and visualization imagery offer some of the most complex mental modeling possible and often the most complex integration of information in imagery. Well made visualizations offer analytic tractability and stronger grounds for sense-making, decision-making and problem-solving. Understanding informational imagery will strengthen the work of "architecting visualizations."

A mental model is a learner's internal conceptualization of a system or paradigm, a situation, a personage, a phenomena or equipment. A mental model is created to enhance a learner's sense-making. This is balanced against an expert's conceptual model (Alexander & Judy, 1988), on which the designed learning is based. A conceptual model establishes a context for the task and classifies problems based on underlying principles and concepts). These may be known as substructures, an analogue of the world, or an operationalized mental template for "meaning and form" (Riggins & Slaughter, 2006, p. 4). There may be discrepancies between theories-in-use (what people believe and which inform their actions) and espoused theories (what people say they believe). A mental model may be a schema, an underlying organizational framework or pattern.

Mental models may involve both implicit and explicit knowledge, what a learner assumes below the surface of consciousness as well as conscious knowledge. Parts of a mental model may be internal while other parts may be external or surfaced. Part of effective learner involves the surfacing of internal mental modeling and conceptualizing. Even naïve mental models have a value because these give faculty a basis from which to help a learner evolve to a more sophisticated mental model, and ultimately, a conceptual model acceptable from an expert view.

Mental modeling with imagery draws from the theories of cognitivism, constructivism, and situated cognition. Broadly speaking, constructivism asserts that learners make meanings in their own minds and in communications interactions with others. Cognitivism involves the study of the human mind, their awareness, perceptions, and mental functions. Multimedia theories and dual channel theory (auditory –

verbal and visual – pictorial also enter to the design of visualizations to manage cognitive load (Mayer & Moreno, 1998, pp. 99 - 113).

Different types of mental models may be created:

Representation: describes, articulates, renders coherent, illustrates and defines
Predictive: anticipates, proposes trend lines, predicts, and projects / forecasts
Proscriptive: defines how something should be ideally
Speculative: proposes an un-testable thesis, purely theoretical (may be mental models at extreme scales, beyond sight, sound, and human perception)
Live Info-Heavy Modeling: collates live, dynamic, and multi-variate information (from remote sensors, monitoring devices, cameras, people, and other sources) into a semi-coherent larger view / visualization; may be user-interactive and user-manipulatable for analysis and decision-making (Hai-Jew, 2008, Slides 6 - 7)

Effective visualizations to build mental models involve the identification of threshold concepts that once-understood provide a broad base for comprehension of more advanced concepts. The visualization should foment cognitive dissonance based on beliefs, perceptions, attitudes and behaviors, to help learners adjust their internal mental models to be closer to the expert conceptual models. There should be a defined learning approach, context, clear terminology, defined learning objectives, specific learning objects, clear relationships between the learning objects, interactivity, and designed learning opportunities.

Contrary to some assumptions, naïve mental models have pedagogical relevance. These need to be surfaced to learners in a visualization, so learners may develop a sense of metacognition and may avoid negative transfer. Learners may define relationships between informational objects in a domain-specific database as compared to an expert-based domain competency model (Ahmad, de la Chica, Butcher, Tumner, & Martin., 2007, pp. 452 – 461). Naïve mental models tend to be elusive, poorly developed, incomplete, poorly structured, difficult to articulate, illogical, overly general and invalid (Nardi & Zarmer, 1991, p. 487). To be effective, visualizations then need feedback loops to address learner misconceptions.

Interactivity with Static Visualizations

Sometimes, interactivity will enhance the effectiveness of a visualization. This allows user control of some parameters in order to make changes to the outputs. This may make a visualization more customizable.

Ware describes three classes of interactivity in visualizations: data manipulation, exploration and navigation, and problem solving.

At the lowest level is the data manipulation loop, through which objects are selected and moved using the basic skills of eye-hand coordination. Delays of even a fraction of a second in this interaction cycle can seriously disrupt the performance of higher-level tasks. At an intermediate level is an exploration and navigation loop, through which an analyst finds his or her way in a large visual data space. As people explore a new town, they build a cognitive spatial model using key landmarks and paths between them; something similar occurs when they explore data spaces…At the highest level is a problem-solving loop through which the analyst forms hypotheses about the data and refines them through an augmented visualization process. The process may be repeated through multiple visualization cycles as new data is added, the problem is reformulated, possible solutions are identified, and the visualization is revised or replaced (Ware, 2004, pp. 317 - 318).

Some researchers describe some functions of user interactivity in their 3D software visualization: getting an overview of the collection, zooming in on issues of interest, filtering out less relevant contents, requesting details-on-demand, viewing relationships among items, keeping a history of actions "to support undo, replay, and progressive refinement" of searches, and extracting of sub-collections and query parameters (Marcus, Feng & Maletic, 2003, pp. 28 - 29). Another visualization system allows users to pan and zoom, display image metadata, download an image copy, control the size of the image table, or even choose three styles of imagery (shaded relief, topographic map and photograph—aerial or satellite) (Barclay, Gray & Slutz, 2000).

Evaluating Visualizations

As perceptual models of information, visualizations must communicate to the various users to be effective.

The effectiveness of a visualization depends on perception, cognition, and the users' specific tasks and goals. How a viewer perceives an item in a visualization display depends on many factors, including lighting conditions, visual acuity, surrounding items, color scales, culture, and previous experience (Ware, 2000, as cited in Tory & Möller, 2004, p. 73).

To evaluate the efficacy of visualizations, there exist a variety of methods.

A variety of visualization evaluation methods exist, including empirical methods such as controlled experiments, usability testing, longitudinal studies, and analytical methods such as heuristic evaluation and cognitive walkthroughs (North, May – June 2006, p. 6).

VALUE-ADDED INFORMATION EXTRACTIONS

Some visualizations are used for culling or extracting new data and understandings. These visualizations may be photo-realistic or synthetic. ("Realistic" image captures do not necessarily imply that the event captured wasn't a dramatization or a manipulated reality capture. This means that the image capture is at the level of detail of video-realism or photo-realism). The added value may come from machine intelligence, from user annotations of image contents (Newsam & Yang, 2007, pp. 1 – 8), innovative experiments, pattern recognition (Han, Altman, Kumar, Mannila, Pregibon, 2002, p. 58) and referring to historical data. A core element of information extraction involves "change detection" between multi-temporal image sequences at a particular location. Other systems have been developed to automatically discover objects and cut out the backgrounds (Liu & Chen, 2007, pp. IV-345 – IV -348).

Other manipulations may involve grayscaling an image and then adding color inversely to stretch the meaning or dynamic range of the image. People may highlight information with value, such as adding false color to change focal points or colorizing aspects of an image to make parts less noticeable or distracting (Williams, Maraviglia, & Moran, 2002, n.p.).

Photorealistic Extractions

Live video captures may use automated means to "foveate" on particular faces for identification (facial recognition) value. Imagers may capture visible light information in non-invasive ways for study (Hyman, Graham, & Hansen, 2007, pp. 25 – 30). Video captures and still images may be "de-noised" for clearer visual semantics; remotely sensed images may be cleaned up at the pixel level (Qian, Zhang & Qiu, 2005, pp. 524 – 528). Remotely sensed images may be enhanced with the addition of "land-use classification, similarity retrieval and spatial data mining" for new applications (Newsam & Yang, 2007, n.p.). Eyeglasses may be automatically removed from facial images (Wu, Liu, Shum, Xu, & Zhang, 2004, pp. 322 – 336).

Satellite or aerial imagery may provide information about roads, land use compliance, geological land-mass shifts, machine-enabled human counting (as in crowds), and changes to building structures. Computers may extract specific information from an image, such as the recognition of motor vehicles from aerial imagery orthophotos (Leberl, Bischof, Grabner & Kluckner, 2007). From the technology side, there are continuous endeavors to improve true orthoimage generation (Zhou & Xie, 2006) and orthoimagery and street map conflation (Chen, Knoblock, Shahabi, Chiang, & Thakkar, 2004) (see Figure 4).

Researchers may set up a photo-realistic situation to learn new information. For example, the real-world physical properties of clay are used in a 3D tangible interface for landscape analysis, which involves simulated floods and structures captured digitally for real-world planning (Piper, Ratti, & Ishii, 2002). The topography of a clay landscape model, with its changing geometry, is captured via a ceiling-mounted laser scanner to capture a depth image of the model.

Virtually all geographical information systems (GIS) information is an approximation because of the infinite complexity of the earth's surface ("Toward Improved Geographic Information Services within a Digital Government," 1999, p. 4). Aerial imagery often requires orthorectification to correct the image capture for map-accurate scale and form—to account for topographic diversity, lens distortion, camera tilt, and other image distorting factors. On-ground images may need orthocorrection, too, to address incomplete boundaries, edge blurring, or other distortions. Informational overlays to geographic imagery may include linework, buildings, roads, geographic symbols, and boundaries.

Computers are brought in to enhance human decision-making from real images. One example is the work of optimal traversal planning via existing road networks (Kazemi, Shahabi, Vincent, & Sharifzadeh, 2007). This functionality is common in the planning of road trips.

For the security and entertainment industries, meaningful information may be extracted from video sequences via video visualizations. These functionalities may pull videos from video conferencing systems, video emails, security and traffic cameras, and the entertainment industry to help identify the places in the video that might warrant more direct human attention (Daniel & Chen, Oct. 2003). Another system uses visual attention to extract regions of interest (ROI) in image retrieval (Marques, Mayron, Borba & Gamba, 2006). Automated diagnostics magnify the value of human time spent in analyzing digital imagery. Particular textures may be used to pull out specific images from large databases (Pothos, Theoharatos, Economou, & Ifantis, 2007, pp. 502 – 509). Machine intelligence may classify "what is rock, urban, forest, lakes and rivers, green vegetation and dry vegetation" from satellite imagery and identify these through image overlays (Suter & Nüesch, 1995, p. 88).

Computers may also enhance design. One program captures a range of physical human motions from data sets to understand real-world motion parameters (Kovar & Gleicher, 2004). The affordances

Figure 4. Aerial photograph vs. digital orthophoto (US Geological Survey)

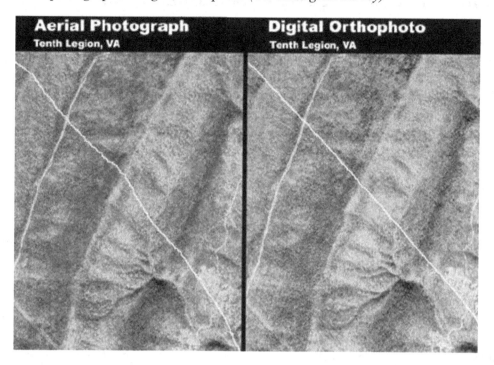

of computers allow the making of "explosive" mediated experiences, such as the "rapid serial" visual presentations that "explode" for viewers (Wittenburg, Forlines, Lanning, Esenther, Harada & Miyachi, 2003, pp. 115 – 124). This then is a form of hyper-reality.

Synthetic

Digital reconstructions of events (battles, terrorist attacks, crowd behaviors, weather events, geological occurrences, and disasters) may be used to analyze the interventions and to brainstorm more efficient ones. Potential events (forest fires, poisonous gas dispersion) may be simulated in a visualization to plan for effective interventions. Materials may be analyzed through special technologies that emulate the softness and "deformability" of real-world objects (Huang, Liu, Bao, & Guo, 2005, pp. 221 – 226). Various materials may be captured and visualized digitally through their "spectral, directional and spatial" representations (Dorsey, Rushmeier, & Sillion, 2008, p. 9).

Wireframes are design tools used to model the development of a prototyped site which enables viewers to partially experience the navigational structure, interactivity and design elements. This is often used in the proposal stages of a project.

Augmented reality involves efforts to "embed the natural physical world seamlessly with a fantasy virtual playground by capitalizing on infrastructure provided by wearable computer, mixed reality, and ubiquitous computing research" (Cheok, et al., 2004, pp. 779 – 780). Digital visual and sound overlays may transform a physical training site into the scene of a hostage stand-off, a mock battle, or a cityscape with digital buildings from the 1920s.

LIVE DATA STREAMS AND COMPLEX MULTI-STREAM VISUAL INFORMATION

Visualizations may be fed with live data streams in augmented virtuality (live information fed into a simulated virtual space; haptic devices that may reach into 3D immersive spaces) or in informational "dashboards." Complex multi-stream information is used for security, disaster preparedness, and other work that may require situational awareness. Continuous model visualization may involve live data that is being captured through remote sensors, cameras, or other devices. Computer intelligence may be brought in to "register" or mark particular scenes of interest to human users. For accuracy, visual information is often triangulated with other sources of data for proper decision-making.

Mobile Internet Visualizations

Some conceptual work spaces are built for use in augmented reality via the wifi "mobile Internet". One actualization of this has participants using tablet laptops integrated with high-tech tools that make the device context-aware. "In our experiments with geo-spatial hypermedia, the application domain of architecture and landscape architecture has had a number of implications on our work with the actual physical interface. We envision a tablet computer like device, which is integrated with GPS, digital compass, mobile Internet, and a camera for taking pictures and placing them on absolute coordinates in the literal geo-spatial workspace. Information may be retrieved on the tablet computer and annotations may be entered relative to the actual location of the user in the space" (Grønbæk, Vestergaard, & Ørbæk, 2002, p. 124). This enables the individuals to visualize their shared work, shared processes and interrelationships, with real-time synchronized updates of information on a shared project. This is a key functionality—the reflection of shared changes for co-visualization in a synchronous circumstance in shared visual workspaces (Hsieh & Shipman III, 2002, pp. 217–226). Shared visualizations may promote virtual teaming along the lines of shared mental models (Thomas & Bostrom, 2007, pp. 1 – 8).

CREATING EFFECTIVE INFORMATION AND VISUALIZATION IMAGERY

The creation of visualizations is a nontrivial task. There is high variance between the effectiveness of visualizations in one field and another. "Information visualization encounters a wide variety of different data domains. The visualization community has developed representation methods and interactive techniques. As a community, we have realized that the requirements in each domain are often dramatically different" (Chi & Riedl, 1998).

The design of visualizations assumes an understanding of human perception. Building visualizations will require a basic understanding of the pedagogical theories behind this as well as the research on human visual perception. The hard-wiring of the human brain results in certain predictable aspects to perception, which have implications for the perception of dimensionality, colors, distances, movement, shapes, axes and planes.

The field offers insights on ways to design information effectively. "When we reason about quantitative evidence, certain methods for displaying and analyzing data are better than others. Superior methods are more likely to produce truthful, credible, and precise findings. The difference between an excellent analysis and a faulty one can sometimes have momentous consequences" (Tufte, 1997, p. 27). There are "Gestalt Laws" of pattern perception, which offer some evocative insights on proximity, similarity, connectedness, continuity, symmetry, closure, relative size, figure and ground (Westheimer, Koffka, & Kohler, 1912, 1935, as cited in Ware, 2004, pp. 189 – 197) in 2D design. There are findings on how to manage human attention through close-ups, call-outs; text annotations; sizing and bolding; sequencing, and interactions with audio and other aspects of multimedia.

The nuances of motion detection offer a research interest.

The perception of dynamic patterns is less well understood than the perception of static patterns. But we are very sensitive to patterns in motion and, if we can learn to use motion effectively, it may be a very good way of displaying certain aspects of data (Ware, n.d., as cited in Weiskopf, 2004, p. 305).

At the same time, technologies have been improving in terms of what may be visually depicted. Progressively variant textures (vs. homogeneous ones) are captured with more nuance by "scale, orientation, color, and shape variations of texture elements" (Zhang, Zhou, Velho, Guo, & Shum, 2003, pp. 295 – 302). There's even more accurate modeling of hair geometry (Wei, Ofek, Quan & Shum, 2005).

Designing a Mental Model

Some basic steps to designing a mental model follow:

1. Identify a learning domain. Select a portion (or the whole) to model.
2. Define the foundational realities.
3. Define the learning objectives and outcomes.
4. Define the relevant terminology and nomenclature.
5. Define the range of possible variables and measures.
6. Define relevant processes within the model.
7. Prototype and build the mental model while considering and adhering to mental modeling standards.
8. Build learning scenarios.
9. Build test scenarios, and test with novices, amateurs, and experts. (Note: Novices are considered those who may be naïve initial learners but who are on track to be an expert-in-the-making. Amateurs, on the contrary, are seen as those who will "remain a quite unsophisticated user" and who are not on an expertise track in the particular field) (Davis & Moar, 2005, p. 159).

Six core principles of multimedia design offer helpful direction for the building of digital visualizations.

The multimedia principle suggests that relevant and informative (not decorative) imagery should be integrated with text for fuller learning and memory retention.

The contiguity principle suggests that related text and graphics should be placed in close proximity to each other (Clark & Mayer, 2003).

The modality principle suggests that audio narration is preferable to onscreen text delivery, to maximize the audiovisual channels of learning (Clark & Mayer, 2003).

The redundancy principle suggests that audio alone with graphics may work more effectively than "audio and redundant onscreen text" for learning. Such text may overload the visual channel of cognition. (Clark & Mayer, 2003, p. 102) Redundant onscreen text may be helpful, however, when there are no pictorial presentations; when there is plenty of opportunity to process the pictorial presentation, and "when the learning must exert greater cognitive effort to comprehend spoken text than printed text" (p. 105). Text redundancy may be effective if it is interspersed between the multimedia images as stand-alone words on a screen.

The coherence principle suggests that all embellishments to the learning should be omitted, with a clear focus on what needs to be learned only. Extra background sounds or entertaining stories may distract learners from the relevant learning materials; prevent learners from building the necessary mental links between relevant materials, and seduce them by "priming inappropriate existing knowledge" (Clark & Mayer, 2003, pp. 111 – 112). Multimedia should not be used for its own sake if there is no pedagogical rationale to do so.

Their personalization principle suggests that the colloquial use of language may humanize the learning. Animated pedagogical agents are helpful because they focus learner attention. There did not seem to be a difference between the effectiveness of real or fictional learning agent characters. One caveat is that these agents need to be there for instructional purposes, not entertainment ones (Clark & Mayer, 2003, p. 144).

ADDITIONAL TECHNOLOGICAL AFFORDANCES IN AUTHORING

Beyond the usual authoring tools for those engaged in e-learning, there are plenty of more advanced technological affordances. Objects from videos may be cut and pasted (Li, Sun, & Shum, 2005, pp. 595 – 600). Haptic or force feedback human interfaces are growing more sophisticated in their interactions with computerized systems (Michelitsch, Williams, Osen, Jimenez, & Rapp, 2004, pp. 1305 – 1308). 3D objects may be morphed (Reyes, Hodges, & Gaither, 2004). Vortex detection and visualization have become more sophisticated (Stegmaier & Ertl, 2004, pp. 195 – 202). Digital books now may come in 3D as digital equivalents of "movable books" (Cubaud, Dupire, & Topol, 2005, pp. 244- 245).

AVOIDING MISCONCEPTIONS

Visualizations communicate through graphical language, which may have subconscious and affective overtones. Viewers work through layers of perceptions and thought to get to the meanings.

Ambiguity may be introduced with poor design, or the inappropriate use of the technologies to communicate certain information. "The use of two (or three) varying dimensions to show one-dimensional data is a weak and inefficient technique, capable of handling only very small data sets, often with error in design and ambiguity in perception. These designs cause so many problems that they should be avoided: The number of information-carrying (variable) dimensions depicted should not exceed the number of dimensions in the data" (Tufte, 2001, p. 71).

A central figure in informational design, Tufte offers six principles, which offer guidance:

- The representation of numbers, as physically measured on the surface of the graphic itself, should be directly proportional to the numerical quantities represented.
- Clear, detailed, and thorough labeling should be used to defeat graphical distortion and ambiguity. Write out explanations of the data on the graphic itself. Label important events in the data.

- Show data variation, not design variation.
- In time-series displays of money, deflated and standardized units of monetary measurement are nearly always better than nominal units.
- The number of information-carrying (variable) dimensions depicted should not exceed the number of dimensions in the data.
- Graphics must not quote data out of context (Tufte, 2001, p. 77).

This field will need much more research to define parameters for quality visualization design. "As Meyer points out, there are no generally accepted guidelines for the optimal display of data (Meyer 2000, p. 1480). Part of the problem lies in the lack of empirical evidence for or against the use of different approaches to visualization. Despite the important role that visualizations play in information interfaces, it has been noted that the evaluation of data visualizations is rarely undertaken (Morse, Lewis & Olsen 2000)" (Lee, Reilly, & Butavicius, 2003, n.p.)

For visualizations to have long-term informational value, they need to be designed with the highest quality informational value possible. The data that a visualization draws from should be objective and factual. Value-judgments, cultural overlays, and subjectivity should not be built into visualizations. Visualizations should be as non-biased, non-politicized, and objective as possible.

Because of the affective and surface features of images and the possibilities of subconscious effects, those who would design visualizations need to be careful how they convey information. The application of logical analysis to an image will be important. Inductive logic refers to the amassing of information, the analysis of that data, and then coming to a conclusion. This suggests that those using a visualization should have access to sufficient information before drawing a conclusion. If a visualization only offers limited relevant data, that should be clear. Deductive logic involves the uses of syllogisms to reorder existing information and relationships. Syllogisms may be ineffectual if the premises used are inaccurate. Toulmin logic suggests that there should be evidentiary groundings or "proofs" before assertions may be made.

Some logical risks include the following:

- Over-generalizing from a small dataset to the larger situation
- Mixed scales in imagery should be avoided, so size factors do not confuse users
- Shifting the meaning of key symbolic terms or metaphors used in the visualization
- Over-simplifying an issue to one aspect or factor
- Basing a visualization on a debatable premise
- Misfocusing a visualization on personality (like using a politician's caricature to symbolize a particular stance)
- Over-simplifying with either-or reasoning by not including sufficient information in the visualization
- Disconnecting the facts of a visualization from the conclusions that are drawn from it (a kind of red herring argument)
- Falsely assuming cause-and-effect relationships simply because of chronology
- Over-valuing historical events in implying the future
- Using an anomalous situation to generalize about other situations
- Using a circular argument to suggest a particular stance like a (factually) unanchored simulated projection to argue for changes in the real world

- Assuming a foregone conclusion based on a particular set of facts, by building a visualization that only depicts a limited, set outcome
- Presenting information as from high authority, without the possibility of dissenting views]
- Building a false analogy with an inappropriate metaphor

Beyond the above efforts to build cleanly, designers may set up visualizations with the proper information and design the visualization in an e-learning context that is gradual, with the foundational learning first. The language used should be simple and clear. In-domain terms will require clear definitions, so there are no semantic confusions. Any areas that may lack clarity should be fully annotated. There should be a clear feedback loop for people to test their ideas from the visualization, so that misinterpretations may be addressed.

The Evaluation of Information and Visualization Imagery

Judging the efficacy of information and visualization imagery necessarily involves the larger context of the information and its use. "Visualization has to be *effective* and *efficient*. In other words, visualization should do what it is supposed to do, and has to do this using a minimal amount of resources. One immediate and obvious implication is that we cannot judge visualization on its own, but have to take into account the context in which it is used" (van Wijk, 2005, p. 79).

"Evaluating the Efficacy of Visual Imagery" offers a basic checklist of some factors to consider when evaluating a visualization for efficacy (Table 1).

The "Objectives and Outcomes" will vary depending on the purpose of the visualization.

CONCLUSION

With the numerous affordances of image capture and authoring tools, information-rich visualizations likely will be used with greater frequency in e-learning. There will likely be deeper levels of realism, both in raw real-world captures and in synthetic digital imagery. The pushes towards synaesthesia may involve more sensory channels for visualizations, with the inclusion of digital smells. The computer-mediated communications affordances may promote increased collaboration around digital image creation.

More visualizations will likely be created for open-source distribution through data warehouses, libraries and repositories, especially as these become more portable and interchangeable. As augmented reality and ambient intelligent spaces become less unwieldy and as more channels are built for mobile delivery, there will be more real-space visualizing and building. An acknowledgment of the importance of the Internet in the porting of geospatial imagery to Internet-friendly delivery methods to enhance accessibility and usability via multimedia warehouses (Barclay, Gray & Slutz, 2000, pp. 307 – 318). There will be more datamining endeavors across heterogeneous platforms "that encompass high end servers, desktop computer, laptops, personal digital assistants, cell phones, and other devices" (MacEachren & Rhyne, Aug. 2004, p. 1).

Visualizations will continue to add value through information extractions. They add value in a range of applications for learning, depiction, analysis, and live situational awareness. More research in the domain-specific builds of visualizations and fresh pedagogical approaches would enhance this field.

Table 1. Evaluating the efficacy of visualization imagery (Hai-Jew, 2009)

Area of Evaluation	Factors for Evaluation
Meaning-Making	User orientation User focus Clear semantics (text and visuals) Effective metaphor Feedback loop quality Transparency of the visualization
Technological Affordances	Interactivity / user control Intuitive interface Accessibility Stand-alone or dependent Design updatability and malleability
Informational Aesthetics	Information quality Information timeliness Information completeness Information relevance, applicability to the real-world (fidelity) Elegant design and sparseness Uniqueness and originality
Objectives and Outcomes	Memory retention Accurate visual depiction Analysis Decision-making Problem-solving Discovery and new learning Research value The predictability of the visualization

REFERENCES

Aerial photograph vs. digital orthophoto. (n.d.). *US Geological Survey*. Retrieved November 8, 2008, from http://en.wikipedia.org/wiki/Image:AerialDigitalPhoto.JPG

Ahmad, F., de la Chica, S., Butcher, K., Tumner, T., & Martin, J. H. (2007). Towards automatic conceptual personalization tools. In *Proceedings of the 7th ACM/IEEE-CS joint conference on Digital libraries* (pp. 452-461). New York: ACM.

Alexander, P. A., & Judy, J. E. (1988). The interaction of domain-specific and strategic knowledge in academic performance. *Review of Educational Research, 58*(4), 375–404.

Angles, R., & Gutierrez, C. (2008). Survey of graph database models. *ACM Computing Surveys, 40*(1), 1:1-1:2.

Bakshi, R., Knoblock, C. A., & Thakkar, S. (2004). Exploiting online sources to accurately geocode addresses. In [New York: ACM.]. *Proceedings of the GIS, 04*, 194–203. doi:10.1145/1032222.1032251

Balakrishnan, A. D., Fussell, S. R., & Kiesler, S. (2008). Do visualizations improve synchronous remote collaboration? In *Proceedings of CHI 2008*, Florence, Italy (pp. 1227-1236). New York: ACM.

Barclay, T., Gray, J., & Slutz, D. (2000). Microsoft TerraServer: A spatial data warehouse. *SIGMOD Record, 29*(2), 307–318. doi:10.1145/335191.335424

Becks, A., & Seeling, C. (2004). SWAPit: A multiple views paradigm for exploring associations of texts and structured data. In *Proceedings of the AVI '04,* Gallipoli, Italy. New York: ACM.

Chen, C.-C., Knoblock, C. A., Shahabi, C., Chiang, Y.-Y., & Thakkar, S. (2004). Automatically and accurately conflating orthoimagery and street maps. In *Proceedings of the GIS '04*, Washington, DC, USA (pp. 47-56).

Chen, H., Liu, Z., Rose, C., Xu, Y., Shum, H.-Y., & Salesin, D. (2004). Example-based composite sketching of human portraits. In *Proceedings of the 3rd international symposium on Non-photorealistic animation and rendering* (pp. 95-102). New York: ACM.

Cheok, A. D., Goh, K. H., Farbiz, F., Liu, W., Li, Y., Fong, S. W., et al. (2004). Human Pacman: A wide area socio-physical interactive entertainment system in mixed reality. In *Proceedings of the CHI 2004* (pp. 779-780). New York: ACM.

Chi, E. H.-H., & Riedl, J. T. (1998). An operator interaction framework for visualization systems. In *Proceedings of the 1998 IEEE Symposium on Information Visualization (InfoVis '98).* Washington, DC: IEEE.

Clark, R. C., & Mayer, R. E. (2003). *E-Learning and the Science of Instruction.* San Francisco: Pfeiffer, John Wiley & Sons.

Crawford, D., Ma, K.-L., Huang, M.-Y., Klasy, S., & Ethier, S. (2004). Visualizing gyrokinetic simulations. In [Washington, DC: IEEE.]. *Proceedings of the IEEE Visualization, 2004*, 59–66.

Crisp, D. J., Perry, P., & Redding, N. J. (2003). Fast segmentation of large images. In *Proceedings of the Twenty-Sixth Australasian Computer Science Conference, Conferences in Research and Practice in Information Technology*, Adelaide, Australia.

Cubaud, P., Dupire, J., & Topol, A. (2005). Digitization and 3D modeling of movable books. In *Proceedings of the JCDL '05* (pp. 244-245). New York: ACM.

Daniel, G., & Chen, M. (2003). Video visualization. In *Proceedings of the 14th IEEE Visualization Conference (VIS '03)* (pp. 409-416). Washington, DC: IEEE.

Davis, S. B., & Moar, M. (2005) The amateur creator. In *Proceedings of the C&C '05,* London, UK, (pp. 158-165). New York: ACM.

Dorsey, J., Rushmeier, H., & Sillion, F. (2008). Advanced material appearance modeling. In *Proceedings of the SIGGRAPH 2008, ACM Special Interest Group on Computer Graphics and Interactive Techniques*, New York, USA. Retrieved November 15, 2008, from http://portal.acm.org/toc.cfm?id=1401132&idx= SERIES382&type=proceeding&coll=ACM&dl=ACM&part=series&WantType=Proceedings&title=SI GGRAPH&CFID=11068648&CFTOKEN=87519326

Douglas, S., Hundhausen, C., & McKeown, D. (1995). Toward empirically-based software visualization languages. In *Proceedings of the 11th International IEEE Symposium on Visual Languages* (pp. 342-349). Washington, DC: IEEE.

Duchastel, P. (2003). Learnability. In *Usability Evaluation of Online Learning Programs.* Hershey, PA: Information Science Publishing.

Ebert, D. S., Shaw, C. D., Zwa, A., & Starr, C. (1996). Two-handed interactive stereoscopic visualization. In *Proceedings of the Seventh IEEE Visualization 1996 (VIS '96).* Washington, DC: IEEE.

Fahnestock, J., & Read, C. H. (2000). Potential utility and needs for imagery fusion technology. In *Proceedings of the ISIF 2000.* Washington, DC: IEEE.

Grønbæk, K., Vestergaard, P. P., & Ørbæk, P. (2002). Towards geo-spatial hypermedia: Concepts and prototype implementation. In *Proceedings of the thirteenth ACM conference on Hypertext and hyper-media* (pp. 117-126). New York: ACM.

Gyllstrom, K., Miller, D., & Stotts, D. (2007). Techniques for improving the visibility and 'sharability' of semi-transparent video in shared workspaces. In *Proceedings of the ACMSE '07*, Winston-Salem, NC (pp. 425-430). New York: ACM.

Hai-Jew, S. (2008). Building mental models with visuals for e-learning. In *Proceedings of the MERLOT: Still Blazing the Trail and Meeting New Challenges in the Digital Age.*

Han, J., Altman, R. B., Kumar, V., Mannila, H., & Pregibon, D. (2002). Emerging scientific applications in datamining. *CACM, 45*(8), 54–58.

Hsieh, H., & Shipman, F. M., III. (2002). Manipulating structured information in a visual workspace. In *Proceedings of the UIST '02*, Paris, France (pp. 217-226).

Huang, J., Liu, X., Bao, H., & Guo, B. (2005). Clustering method for fast deformation with constraints. In *Proceedings of the 2005 ACM symposium on Solid and physical modeling* (pp. 221-226). New York: ACM.

Hyman, J., Graham, E., & Hansen, M. (2007). Imagers as sensors: Correlating plant CO_2 uptake with digital visible-light imagery. In *Proceedings of the 4th International Workshop on Data Management for Sensor Networks (DMSN '07),* Vienna, Austria (pp. 25-30).

Kazemi, L., Shahabi, C., Vincent, L., & Sharifzadeh, M. (2007). Optimal traversal planning in road networks with navigational constraints. In *Proceedings of the 15th International Symposium on Advances in Geographic Information Systems, ACM GIS 2007*, Seattle, Washington (pp. 1-7).

Kemp, C. C., Anderson, C. D., Nguyen, H., Trevor, A. J., & Xu, Z. (2008). A point-and-click interface for the real world: Laser designation of objects for mobile manipulation. In *Proceedings of the HRI '08* (pp. 241-248). New York: ACM.

Kovar, L., & Gleicher, M. (2004). Automated extraction and parameterization of motions in large data sets. *ACM Transactions on Graphics, 23*(3), 559–568. doi:10.1145/1015706.1015760

LaMar, E., & Pascucci, V. (2003). A multi-layered image cache for scientific visualization. In *Proceedings of the IEEE Symposium on Parallel and Large-Data Visualization and Graphics (PVG '03)* (pp. 61-67). Washington, DC: IEEE.

Laramee, R. S., Weiskopf, D., Schneider, J., & Hauser, H. (2004). Investigating swirl and tumble flow with a comparison of visualization techniques. In . *Proceedings of the IEEE Visualization, 2004*, 51–58.

Lau, A., & Moere, A. V. (2007). Towards a model of information aesthetics in information visualization. In *Proceedings of the 11ᵗʰ International Conference Information Visualization (IV '07)*. Washington, DC: IEEE.

Leberl, F., Bischof, H., Grabner, H., & Kluckner, S. (2007). Recognizing cars in aerial imagery to improve orthophotos. In *Proceedings of the 15ᵗʰ International Symposium on Advances in Geographic Information Systems, ACM GIS 2007* (pp. 1-9).

Lee, M. D., Reilly, R. E., & Butavicius, M. A. (2003). An empirical evaluation of Chernoff faces, star glyphs, and spatial visualizations for binary data. In *Proceedings of the Australian Computer Society, Inc. Conferences in Research and Practice in Information Technology*.

Lehikoinen, J., & Röykkee, M. (2003). 1D selection of 2D objects in head-worn displays. *Personal and Ubiquitous Computing, 7*, 44–52. doi:10.1007/s00779-002-0212-9

Li, Y., Sun, J., & Shum, H.-Y. (2005). Video object cut and paste. *ACM Transactions on Graphics, 24*(3), 595–600. doi:10.1145/1073204.1073234

Liu, D., & Chen, T. (2008). Background cutout with automatic object discovery. In *Proceedings of the ICIP 2007*. Washington, DC: IEEE.

Ma, K.-L., Schussman, G., Wilson, B., Ko, K., Qiang, J., & Ryne, R. (2002). Advanced visualization technology for terascale particular accelerator simulations. In *Proceedings of the 2002 ACM/IEEE conference on Supercomputing*.

Marcus, A., Feng, L., & Maletic, J. I. (2003). 3D representations for software visualization. In *Proceedings of the 2003 ACM symposium on Software visualization*. New York: ACM.

Marques, O., Mayron, L. M., Borba, G. B., & Gamba, H. R. (2006). Using visual attention to extract regions of interest in the context of image retrieval. In *Proceedings of the ACM SE '06*, Melbourne, FL. New York: ACM.

Michelitsch, G., Williams, J., Osen, M., Jimenez, B., & Rapp, S. (2004). Haptic Chameleon: A new concept of shape-changing user interface controls with force feedback. In *Proceedings of the CHI 2004* (pp. 1305-1308). New York: ACM.

Moreno, R. (2004). Decreasing cognitive load for novice students: Effects of explanatory versus corrective feedback in discovery-based multimedia. *Instructional Science, 32*, 99–113. doi:10.1023/B:TRUC.0000021811.66966.1d

Nakakoji, K., Takashima, A., & Yamamoto, Y. (2001). Cognitive effects of animated visualization in exploratory visual data analysis. In *Proceedings of the Fifth International Conference on Information Visualisation*. Washington, DC: IEEE.

Nardi, B. A., & Zarmer, C. L. (1991). Beyond models and metaphors: Visual formalisms in user interface design. In *Proceedings of the 24ᵗʰ Annual Hawaii International Conference on System Sciences*. Washington, DC: IEEE.

Newsam, S., & Yang, Y. (2007). Comparing global and interest point descriptors for similarity retrieval in remote sensed imagery. In *Proceedings of the 15th International Symposium on Advances in Geographic Information Systems*, Seattle, Washington (pp. 1-8). New York: ACM.

Nocke, T., Böhm, U., & Flechsig, M. (2003). Information visualization supporting modeling and evaluation tasks for climate models. In *Proceedings of the 2003 Winter Simulation Conference* (pp. 763-771).

North, C. (2006). Toward measuring visualization insight. *IEEE Computer Graphics and Applications*, *26*(3), 6–9. doi:10.1109/MCG.2006.70

Pettersen, O., Bordes, N., Ulm, S., Gwynne, D., Simmich, T., & Pailthorpe, B. (2008). Grid services for e-archaeology. In *Proceedings of the Sixth Australasian Workshop on Grid Computing and e-Research*. Australian Computer Society.

Pothos, V. K., Theoharatos, C., Economou, G., & Ifantis, A. (2007). Texture retrieval based on Non-parametric measure for multivariate distributions. In *Proceedings of the CIVR '07*, Amsterdam, The Netherlands (pp. 502-509). New York: ACM.

Qian, Y., Zhang, K., & Qiu, F. (2005). Spatial contextual noise removal for post classification smoothing of remotely sensed images. In *Proceedings of the 2005 ACM Symposium on Applied Computing* (pp. 524-528).

Qiu, F., Zhao, Y., Fan, Z., Wei, X., Lorenz, H., & Wang, J. (2004). Dispersion simulation and visualization for urban security. In . *Proceedings of the IEEE Visualization, 2004*, 553–560.

Reyes, R., Hodges, W., & Gaither, K. (2004) Visualizing the evolution of horned lizards using 3D morphing techniques. In *Proceedings of the conference on Visualization '04*.

Rhyne, T. M., & MacEachren, A. (2004). Visualizing geospatial data. In *Proceedings of the ACM SIGGRAPH 2004*.

Riggins, F. J., & Slaughter, K. T. (2006). The role of collective mental models in IOS adoption: Opening the black box of rationality in RFID deployment. In *Proceedings of the 39th Annual Hawaii International Conference on System Sciences (HICSS'06) Track 8*.

Sanderson, A. R., Johnson, C. R., & Kirby, R. M. (2004). Display of vector fields using a reaction-diffusion model. In . *Proceedings of the IEEE Visualization, 2004*, 115–122.

Seitz, S. M., & Kutulakos, K. N. (1998). Plenoptic image editing. In *Proceedings of the 6th International Conference on Computer Vision*. Retrieved November 28, 2008, from ftp://ftp.cs.rochester.edu/pub/papers/robotics/97.tr647.Plenoptic_image_editing.ps.gz

Silverman, B. G. (2007). Human terrain data—What should we do with it? In *Proceedings of the 2007 Winter Simulation Conference*. Washington, DC: IEEE.

Stegmaier, S., & Ertl, T. (2004). A graphics hardware-based vortex detection and visualization system. In . *Proceedings of the IEEE Visualization, 2004*, 195–202.

Steiger, N. M., & Steiger, D. M. (2007). Knowledge management in decision making: Instance-based cognitive mapping. In *Proceedings of the 40ᵗʰ Hawaii International Conference on System Sciences* (pp. 1-2).

Suter, M., & Nüesch, D. (1995). Automated generation of visual simulation databases using remote sensing and GIS. In *Proceedings of the 6ᵗʰ IEEE Visualization Conference*. Washington, DC: IEEE.

The elements of nature: Interactive and realistic techniques. (2004). *SIGGRAPH 2004*. New York: ACM.

Thomas, D. M., & Bostrom, R. P. (2007). The role of a shared mental model of collaboration technology in facilitating knowledge work in virtual teams. In *Proceedings of the 40ᵗʰ Hawaii International Conference on System Sciences 2007*. Washington, DC: IEEE.

Tory, M. (2003). Mental registration of 2D and 3D visualizations (an empirical study). In . *Proceedings of the IEEE Visualization, 2003*, 371–378.

Tory, M., & Möller, T. (2004). Human factors in visualization research. *IEEE Transactions on Visualization and Computer Graphics, 10*(1), 72. doi:10.1109/TVCG.2004.1260759

Toward improved geographic information services within a digital government. (1999). Report of the NSF Digital Government Initiative, Geographic Information Systems Workshop. 1.

Tufte, E. R. (1997). *Visual Explanations: Images and Quantities, Evidence and Narrative.* Cheshire, CT: Graphics Press.

Tufte, E. R. (2001). *The Visual Display of Quantitative Information.* 2ⁿᵈ Ed. Cheshire: Graphics Press. 56– 57, 71, 74.

Urness, T., Interrante, V., Marusic, I., Longmire, E., & Ganapathisubramani, B. (2003). Effectively visualizing multi-valued flow data using color and texture. In *Proceedings of the 14ᵗʰ IEEE Visualization Conference (VIS '03)* (pp. 115-121).

Van Wijk, J. J. (2005). The value of visualization. In *Proceedings of the IEEE Visualization 2005*. Washington, DC: IEEE.

Vasile, A., Waugh, F. R., Greisokh, D., & Heinrichs, R. M. (2006). Automatic alignment of color imagery onto 3D laser radar data. In *Proceedings of the 35ᵗʰ Applied Imagery and Pattern Recognition Workshop (AIPR '06)*. Washington, DC: IEEE.

Wang, J., Xu, Y., Shum, H.-Y., & Cohen, M. F. (2004). Video 'tooning. In *Proceedings of the International Conference on Computer Graphics and Interactive Techniques* (pp. 574-583). New York: ACM.

Ware, C. (2004). *Information Visualization: Perception for Design* (2ⁿᵈ ed.). San Francisco: Morgan Kaufmann Publishers.

Wei, Y., Ofek, E., Quan, L., & Shum, H.-Y. (2005). Modeling hair from multiple views. *ACM Transactions on Graphics, 24*(3), 816–820. doi:10.1145/1073204.1073267

Weiskopf, D. (2004). On the role of color in the perception of motion in animated visualizations. In . *Proceedings of the IEEE Visualization, 2004*, 305–312.

Wells, J. D., & Fuerst, W. L. (2000). Domain-oriented interface metaphors: Designing Web interfaces for effective customer interaction. In *Proceedings of the 33rd Hawaii International Conference on System Sciences-Volume 6.* Washington, DC: IEEE.

Williams, E., Maraviglia, C., & Moran, A. M. M. (2002). From x-rays to radar: Using color to understand imagery. In *Proceedings of the 31ˢᵗ Applied Imagery Pattern Recognition Workshop.* Washington, DC: IEEE.

Winterbottom, C., & Blake, E. (2004). Designing a VR interaction authoring tool using constructivist practices. In *Proceedings of the 3rd international conference on Computer graphics, virtual reality, visualisation and interaction in Africa* (pp. 67-71). New York: ACM.

Wittenburg, K., Forlines, C., Lanning, T., Esenther, A., Harada, S., & Miyachi, T. (2003). Rapid serial visual presentation techniques for consumer digital video devices. In *Proceedings of the UIST '03,* Vancouver, BC, Canada (pp. 115-124). New York: ACM.

Wössner, U., Schulze, J. P., Walz, S. P., & Lang, U. (2002). Evaluation of a collaborative volume rendering application in a distributed virtual environment. In *Proceedings of the Eighth Eurographics Workshop on Virtual Environments.*

Wu, C., Liu, C., Shum, H.-Y., Xu, Y.-Q., & Zhang, Z. (2004). Automatic eyeglasses removal from face images. *IEEE Transactions on Pattern Analysis and Machine Intelligence, 26*(3), 322–336. doi:10.1109/TPAMI.2004.1262319

Zhang, J., Zhou, K., Velho, L., Guo, B., & Shum, H.-Y. (2003). Synthesis of progressively-variant textures on arbitrary surfaces. *ACM Transactions on Graphics, 22*(3), 295–302. doi:10.1145/882262.882266

Zhou, G., & Xie, W. (2006). Accuracy improvement of urban true orthoimage generation using 3D R-tree-based urban model. In *Proceedings of the ACM International Conference Proceeding Series,* San Diego, CA. Retrieved November 15, 2008, from http://doi.acm.org/10.1145/1146598.1146755

KEY TERMS AND DEFINITIONS

Absolute Orientation (n): Total correlation between two images, such as an aerial photograph and a map

Afterimage (n): A residual image that persists after the original stimulus has disappeared

Ambient Visualization (n): An informative display that conveys information in the periphery of attention

Analytic Tractability (n): The ease with which something may be analyzed or understood, as through well designed visualizations

Attention (n): The act of focusing the mind on something; observance

Augmented Reality (n): The addition of digital information and functionality in live, real-space, through head-mounted devices, mixed reality enhancements, and wearable computers

Callout (n): The extraction of a portion of an image in order to add more details or elaboration

Data Warehouse (n): Digital data storage that also disseminates the warehouse contents

Datamining (n): Capturing and analyzing information captured from a site's usage

Digital Annotation (n): The inclusion of digital information to an augmented reality space or ambient intelligence-enhanced space

Digital Image Registration (n): The process for the most accurate relative orientation between two or more images, acquired under different circumstances or with different tools

Forefeel (v): To have a presentiment

Fractal (n): A complex geometric structure or pattern that cannot be represented by classical geometry; a computer modeling of irregular patterns and structure (that may be represented as algorithms and formulas)

Geocoding (n): The act of converting an address to geographic coordinates

Geographic Information Systems (GIS) (n): An area of study that combines "computer and information sciences, statistics, geography, ecology, and cognitive science" ("Toward Improved Geographic Information Services within a Digital Government," June 1999, p. 1)

Gyrokinetic (adj): Unstable, turbulent (movement) depicted in a simulation

Information Aesthetics (n): A quantitative and cumulative measure of aesthetics based on the information content of an image's various parts

Linework (n): Lines drawn over an image to annotate or add useful information

Loosely Coupled (adj): Connected in a distant way

Mental Model (n): An individual's personal concept of a thing, phenomena, or system

Metaphor (n): A figure-of-speech comparison between two essentially different things which may share a resemblance

Morphogenesis (n): A digital representation of the development of structural features of a living organism, an organ or tissues, or a part, as in artificial life (A-life)

Multivariate (adj): Involving multiple variables or factors

Negative Knowledge (n): Misleading or wrong information, often accidentally conveyed by poorly designed simulations

Orthophoto or Orthoimage (n): An aerial photograph that has been corrected or "orthorectified" for a more correct geometry and therefore can be used as a map because of the topographical and camera distortion corrections

Orthorectification (n): The geometric correcting of an image for accuracy

Overlay (n): An add-on to a photo or image to add information to that image

Panoptic (adj): Viewing all elements, often from various angles; an all-inclusive or broad view

Photorealism (adj): A style of imagery that emulates the details and effects from photography, a form of high realism

Plenoptic (adj): Viewing from multiple (or all) possible viewpoints

Primitive (n): A primary geometric form used to build 3D objects and shapes

Region of Interest (ROI) (n): An area of an image that may have useful information [as defined by the viewer(s)]

Semantics (n): Sense-making, meaning, informational value

Sense-Making (n): Creating an understanding about a particular phenomena or situation

Simulation (n): An enactment, a recreation; a modeling of a limited aspect of the real world's internal processes

Spatial Hypermedia (n): Digital information in which spatiality or geographical location is an important aspect of its semantic value

Streamline (n): The path of a particle flowing steadily; the path of least resistance for fluid flow (as in a digital visualization)

Tensor Field (n): A geometric or topological space

Tightly Coupled (adj): Connected in a close way

Vector Field (n): A visualization to show the speed and direction of a moving fluid; a region with a vector assigned at each point; an image field defined by lines that may be resized and proportionally scaled; an array of data

Videorealism (n): The quality of authenticity in videography, in terms of lighting, movement, and other aspects

Visualization (n): A graphical representation of information or ideas, either theoretical or factual; data art; an image-based model or simulation

Wearable Computer (n): An item of clothing that has computer parts and functionality integrated; computers worn on the body

Chapter 6
Capturing and Authoring Tools for Graphics in E–Learning

ABSTRACT

A wide range of capturing and authoring tools for the raw image capture, creation and deployment of digital imagery for e-learning exists. Image information may be captured using light and sound. The digital images may be captured from realia, as in digital archival efforts; they may be wholly "born digital" and not have much relation to reality. They may be still images or dynamic ones. Some technologies offer continuous image capture and live analysis or annotation of the information. This chapter covers common capturing and authoring tools. A sidebar by Dr. Jason Caudill, a professor, addresses the use of open –source software for creating digital images.

CHAPTER OBJECTIVES

- Introduce some technologies used for the raw capture of images (including the far limits of imagery capture)
- Provide an overview of image editing tools
- Investigate open-source solutions for the creation and integration of digital imagery into e-learning
- Describe authoring tools for digital image creation
- Emphasize the importance of digital image interchangeability, transferability, and portability
- Describe the art of videography for e-learning

DOI: 10.4018/978-1-60566-972-4.ch006

INTRODUCTION

The tools created for image capture (of real or synthetic visual information) have broadened in terms of their use in higher education. These include a range of high functioning cameras, scanners, and sensors, used in different arrays and combinations. The technologies for the capture of raw images enable an impressive range of capture of microscopic subject matter to large-scale segments of land, sea or sky. "Nature has produced ten different eye layouts — indeed every way of capturing an image has evolved at least once in nature, with the exception of zoom and Fresnel lenses" ("Eye," 2008, n.p.).

Image capture devices (spectroscopes, sonar-based devices, radar, lidar, and others) may capture imagery not only in the visible range of lightwaves but radio, microwave, infrared, ultraviolent, x-ray and gamma rays for the collection of information as imagery; this is called hyperspectral imaging. There are "no precisely defined boundaries between the bands of the electromagnetic spectrum" with these different bands sharing some properties ("Electromagnetic spectrum," Sept. 2008, n.p.). How the universe appears varies with the wavelength of observation (Williams, Maraviglia, & Moran, 2002).

Authoring tools that help create digital imagery from the imagination or a mix of digital objects and images have strengthened faculty members' and content developers' abilities to depict the theoretical, the imaginary, and the real. These tools include digital pens and tablets, photo editing tools, diagramming software, 3D image editors, and others. There are also sophisticated editing and rendering tools once an image has been captured, for the manipulation of the imagery and their delivery in various ways.

TECHNOLOGIES FOR THE RAW CAPTURES OF IMAGES

A broad variety of image capture devices are available for the various uses in higher education. This equipment needs to capture imagery with a high degree of realism and potentially add informational value. The more common ones are addressed first, and then the more specialized ones.

Cameras and Digital Video Cameras

Still digital cameras may capture images in various lighting situations, circumstances (low-light, underwater, in high altitudes), and with various sizes of subjects (from the microscopic to the meso-scale and larger). At the low-end of the commercially available cameras are the light compact ones. The more advanced of these include manual controls (vs. automatic controls, which are more common). These often offer "scene modes" for different image capture circumstances. More advanced models include high quality lenses and control features for a wider range of possible, creative outputs. For example, there may be telephoto zooms, wide angle lenses, and interchangeable lenses, filters, remote controls, external flashes and complex accessories. Single-lens reflex (SLR) cameras capture fast-action with continuous shooting with sub-second lag-times between shots.

A variety of methods are used to more accurately capture visual information of different materials, such as moving from geometric capture models to capturing reflectance fields, which more accurately represent materials with surfaces like fur, jade, ivory, and gems (Hawkins, Cohen, & Debevec, 2001). There is an endeavor to include geographic location tags on digital images for richer automated metadata collection (Toyama, Logan, Roseway & Anandan, 2003).

Some high-end digital cameras are able to capture images in three dimensions. "Stereoscopic imaging" involves the recording of 3D visual information and then creating the illusion of depth in the resulting image. There has been growing sophistication for visual captures through the use of camera arrays for 3D information delivered through a television screen (Matusik & Pfister, 2004). Some high-definition cameras capture 3D images for animation frames, with the characters and props extracted using computer algorithms (Hourcade, Perry, & Moore, 2007). Some other image captures offer a "depth-enhanced panorama" (Bahmutov, Popescu, & Sacks, 2004). (Back-end software enables 2D captures to display as 3D.)

Digital camcorders and digital video cameras capture moving images. Cameras may be collecting digital imagery for a finalized product or only intermediary contents, with high-level processing of the imagery before final rendering and outputs.

Digital cameras for surveillance have become part of the "digital enclosure" in many societies, where the unblinking eyes of the cameras never stop watching and recording (Andrejevic, 2007). Digital camera systems now include ways to collecting rich live information, such as through foveation (focusing on a moving target with high resolution (Bagdanov, del Bimbo, Nunziati, & Pernici, 2006) and ways to extract helpful information, such as comparing facial imagery against a facial database. 3D video recording (Würmlin, Lamboray, Staadt, & Gross, 2002, n.p.) has become more common.

Some "cameras" are embedded software coding for the capturing of *machinima* or "machine cinema." This involves live and non-playable character avatars in 3D immersive spaces. These may include authoring tools with storytelling elements (Reidl, Rowe & Elson, 2008, n.p.).

Cameras are also being used for more immersive captures of the world. Audiophotography captures may be taken from innocuous devices for various personal and professional uses (Martin & Gaver, 2000, pp. 55 – 65). Here, eavesdropper cameras that are triggered by sounds that reach a certain decibel level. There's the capture of "spherical imagery" and "spherical motion imagery" with a 360-degree camera capture in real time ("iMove Spherical Imagery," n.d., pp. 1 – 20).

Not all visual capturing endeavors are about absolute accuracy for informational purposes. For example, one project created the digital equivalent of a creative lomography practice, part of a creative picture-taking movement using old Russian analogue cameras with optical defects that "create unpredictable effects." The culture and rules of engagement of these spontaneous amateur images create an aesthetic that offers "the joy of the unpredictable." These image captures involve such effects as pixel effects, color effects, wave and gray effects, and a "zoom+grey-effect" (Ljungblad, 2007, pp. 357 – 374).

Scanners

Scanners come in a range of sizes, with some types that may capture large engineering or architectural blueprints, drawings, maps, and other types of imagery. Different types of commercially available scanners include flatbed, sheetfed, photo, portable, and other types of scanners. These are based in part of the type of capture needed, based on the shape and pliability of what is being scanned.

Flatbed scanners are the most common desktop type, with a flat glass platen covered by a flip-up cover. These may scan documents, transparencies (or viewfoils), drawings, and photos. These may work with a scanning head as single pass or multi-pass. Some flatbed scanners have the glass platen in a well, to hold three-dimensional objects more comfortably. The bed may move, or the scanning head may move—for the image capture. (Dedicated transparency scanners may be the most effective for regular capture of visual information from transparencies.)

Photo scanners require high-resolution captures. These may involve the capturing of film negatives and slides, with some of these capable of capturing dozens of images simultaneously. These often involve software to de-noise images. Slide scanners often need resolutions in the 5,000 – 6,000 ppi (pixels per inch) range.

Sheetfed scanners may handle numerous pages at once in batch operations but do not capture using high-resolution. Rather, these work well to process many pages that need digitizing and rendering using optical character recognition (OCR) to change the print text into readable words in digital files.

Portable scanners may be handheld and used in the field. Pen scanners can capture text line-by-line. Others may capture whole pages. These are often usable between computers, but are not as accurate in their captures.

Drum scanners (rotary scanners) scans images mounted on a rotating drum; here, the drum spins in front of a stationary reading head. These may capture high-resolution images to the range of 12,000 dpi (dots per inch). These have a large scanning area. These require the original image to be thin and flexible enough to be wrapped around the drum. These scanners capture images with greater dynamic range and visual detail accuracy.

Laser Sensors

Laser scanning range sensors are used for capturing

high-precision, high-density three-dimensional (3D) reconstruction and inspection of the surface of physical objects. The process typically involves planning a set of views, physically altering the relative object-sensor pose, taking scans, registering the acquired geometric data in a common coordinate frame of reference, and finally integrating range images into a nonredundant model (Scott, Roth, & Rivest, 2003, p. 64).

Satellite Imagery

Remote sensing satellite systems capture the absorption and reflection of electromagnetic radiation off of different materials on the earth's surface.

Usually, there are many detectors in a satellite sensor, with each detector designed to record a specific portion of the electromagnetic spectrum, emitted heat, or some other information. These recorded values are translated into discrete values, and scaled to a particular bit range depending upon the characteristics of the sensor system (Heileman & Yang, Oct. 2003, p. 121).

This information results in a multi-spectral image with each pixel representing a particular location of reflected radiation and heat. Pixels "from different image bands are often combined in order to reveal particular features in a scene" (Heileman & Yang, 2003, p. 121).

Invisible Light Captures

Hyperspectral imaging refers to the collection of information from across many parts of the electromagnetic spectrum, including ultraviolet and infrared light. "Certain objects leave unique 'fingerprints' across the electromagnetic spectrum. These 'fingerprints' are known as spectral signatures and enable identification of the materials that make up a scanned object. For example, having the spectral signature for oil helps mineralogists find new oil fields" ("Hyperspectral imaging," 2008). Hyperspectral sensors capture images in sets, which are combined into a 3D hyperspectral cube for analysis. Such data may include tens to hundreds of bands. While hyperspectral data involves contiguous bands, multispectral data involves selected non-contiguous bands collected from multiple sensors. Collection devices may range from satellites to spectrometers, and others. These may be used in situations where direct measurement is invasive or impossible.

Computational Photography

Computational photography involves the use of a digital computer to enhance the traditional capabilities of digital photography.

Computational photography combines plentiful computing, digital sensors, modern optics, many varieties of actuators, probes and smart lights to escape the limitations of traditional film cameras and enables novel imaging applications. Unbounded dynamic range, variable focus, resolution, and depth of field, hints about shape, reflectance, and lighting, and new interactive forms of photos that are partly snapshots and partly videos, performance capture and interchangeably relighting real and virtual characters are just some of the new applications emerging in Computational Photography (Debevec, Raskar, & Tumblin, 2008, p. 1).

The deployment of different sensor networks may be enhanced with more sophisticated back-end strategies: "Recent advances in sensor networks permit the use of a large number of relatively inexpensive distributed computational nodes with camera sensors linked in a network and possibly linked to one or more central servers. We argue that the full potential of such a distributed system can be realized if it is designed as a distributed search engine where images from different sensors can be captured, stored, searched and queried" (Yan, Ganesan, & Manmatha, 2008, p. 155).

Radar and Lidar

Radar (radio detection and ranging) uses electromagnetic waves to "identify the range, altitude, direction, or speed of both moving and fixed objects such as aircraft, ships, motor vehicles, weather formations, and terrain" ("Radar," 2008). Acoustical imaging results in 2D and 3D imagery.

A 2D sonar generates a fan of acoustic energy and using a line array of sensors, generates receiver beams in a similar fan. Mechanical scanning sonars use a number of acoustic transmit and receive cycles in order to fill in the fan. A 3D system fills the entire viewing volume—which may be for example 50 by 50 degrees—with acoustic energy and receives the reflected energy by a large number of hydrophones simultaneously. The data from one time slot is processed electronically and a 2D image is generated (Hansen & Anderson, 1998, n.p.).

Lidar (light detection and ranging) is an optical remote sensing technology that examines scattered light to find information about a distant target such as coastal mapping (Wozencraft, 2002, pp. 1194

– 1198). Lidar uses laser pulses. "The range to an object is determined by measuring the time delay between transmission of a pulse and detection of the reflected signal. LIDAR technology has application in archaeology, geography, geology, geomorphology, seismology, remote sensing and atmospheric physics" ("Lidar," 2008). This technology helps capture information about elusive objects that may have no visible reflections.

Real-Time Image Sonification

This concept may be captured in an art installation, as described:

Techniques for image sonification are coupled with users' physical navigation of the image data and a visual representation of the correspondence between the image and sound. One application of this research, an interactive art installation titled Sonic Panoramas, is discussed. Through the use of vision-based motion tracking, immersive projection, image analysis and real-time spatialized sound, a multimodal representation of landscape image data is deployed (Kabisch, Kuester, & Penny, 2005, p. 156).

Video Media Spaces

Video media spaces connect dispersed users to each other's physical spaces via "always-on" video captures.

Via these video channels, people gain informal awareness of others' presence and their activities. This awareness permits fine-grained coordination of frequent, light-weight casual interactions" (Boyle & Greenberg, 2005, p. 329). The video links may display as occasional "snapshot-only video portholes," intermittently open links, persistent links, or links to shared visual workspaces (Boyle & Greenberg, 2005, p. 329).

IMAGE EDITING

Image editing is used to enhance the initial capture or to focus on particular aspects of the image. "Seldom does a photograph record what we perceive with our eyes. Often, the scene captured in a photo is quite unexpected — and disappointing — compared to what we believe we have seen" (Agarwala, Dontcheva, Agarwala, Drucker, Colburn, Curless, Salesin, & Cohen, 2004, p. 294). In a sense, image editing may allow people to render an image closer to the effect they want to show. Once a digital image has been captured, there is a range of ways to process it for greater information value and use in a learning environment.

Photo-editing software, widely available, allows digital images to be extracted, manipulated, and edited. Scenes may be "jumped" for color processing. The lighting may be changed. Different filter effects may be overlaid on a particular image for artistic effects. Images may be "de-noised" for more useful analysis and learning.

People may age objects by application of various weathering or aging masks (Clément, Benoit, & Paquette, 2007, p. 151; Chen, Xia, Wong, Tong, Bao, Guo, & Shum, 2005). They may change the material textures of various objects in a scene (Khan, Reinhard, Fleming, & Bülthoff, 2006). They may change the colors of an image to highlight particular information (Williams, Maraviglia, & Moran, 2002). Details as fine as paint strokes may be decomposed for analysis (Xu, Xu, Kang, Salesin, Pan, & Shum, 2006). There are fine-attention improvements to the photorealistic rendering of knitwear (Xu, Chen, Lin, Zhong, Wu, Guo, & Shum, 2001), with interpenetrating objects and complex visual relationships depicted. There are technological solutions towards less lossy image compression techniques (Cheng & Vishwanathan, 2007) in rendered output images.

Reality may be abstracted, with a video turned into a cartoon animation—purely through computerized processing. The authors explain:

We describe a system for transforming an input video into a highly abstracted, spatio-temporally coherent cartoon animation with a range of styles. To achieve this, we treat video as a space-time volume of image data (Wang, Xu, Shum & Cohen, 2004, p. 574).

AUTHORING TOOLS FOR DIGITAL IMAGE CREATION

Authoring tools are those that allow for "born-digital" imagery creation. A suite of authoring tools involve screen captures, video frame grabs, screen shots; *machinima* captures; pen-tablet input devices; diagramming and illustration software; modeling systems; gaming engines, and some unexpected devices. One article describes an interface for drawing pixel-based imagery using the keys on a mobile phone handset (Poupyrev & Willis, 2008, p. 2361). Authoring tools may be used in a range of different phases—from prototyping to design to modeling to production.

Screen captures are often used for animated tutorials. Video keyframe grabs capture high-quality still images from a video. Screenshots capture still images from a computer screen. *Machinima* (machine + cinema) may be captured from 3D immersive spaces. Tablet PCs capture doodles and drafting ideas using a pen-to-computer screen interface (Brandl, Haller, Oberngruber & Schafleitner, 2008, p. 31). Pentablet setups offer comfortable haptics, with the electronic pen and tablet interface. There are designs that allow the taking of a scanned image of words and text and being able to differentiate the different types for manipulation and handling (Ao, Li, Wang, & Dai, 2006). Various software programs allow for freehand drawing, 2D and 3D diagram creation (with plenty of pre-set forms and templates); these often include a light table effect with back-ground grids and rulers for measures. Different modeling systems for wireframe, 3D and other types of design enhance human capabilities. Gaming engines offer 4D functionality, including the design of artificial intelligence agents, such as realistic human crowd behaviors (Ulicny, Ciechomski, & Thalmann, 2004).

Various effects may be created such as digital engraving that mimics copperplate engraving (Ostromoukhov, 1999). Digital gravure imitates an intaglio process of photomechanical printing, such as photogravure or rotogravure. High-end digital characters may be created in 3D digital clay with volumetric shape representation and surface detailing (Perry & Frisken, 2001). Textural frottage (rubbing) effects may be used for visual information capture (Lee, Pak, Kim, Kim & Lee, n.d.). There are improvements in the portrayal of progressively-variant textures on arbitrary surfaces (Zhang, Zhou, Velho, Guo, & Shum, 2003).

Pen and tablet setups allow users to have a larger sense of tactile control over the input device to draw or paint digitally into graphics editing software programs. Handwriting, freehand drafting, and other types of artwork inputs may be created using such setups. Some pen and tablet setups now include audio file linked to the imagery and text created by these electronic pens.

INTERCHANGEABILITY, TRANSFERABILITY, AND PORTABILITY

In considering which authoring tools to use, it is important to choose those that do not constrain creativity but still output digital contents that may be widely used across different systems. Authoring tools need to be developed that allow "learning designs that, on one hand, do not prescribe any learning approach and, on the other, guarantee the reusability and exchangeability of those learning designs" (Berlanga & Garcia, 2005, p. 190). Digital information is delivered in so many different ways—through learning /course management systems (L/CMSes), data repositories, mobile devices (Kim, Oh, Jeong & Kim, 2004), computerized accessories, head-mounted displays, and 3D display machines.

CONCLUSION

This chapter has covered a range of imaging modalities and tools. For those who create digital imagery for e-learning, they need to learn how to use the devices accurately. They need to know the limitations of the input and output of the devices, so they may more accurately use the visual information. They should also be versed in the extraction of information from data-mining. They should also be aware of post-processing that may be done for the extraction of more information and the enhancement of the captured data.

A few concepts are important takeaway ones. The triangulation of visual information is important for quality. As an example, real-time sonic capture of sea floor imagery is compared with optical sensing "to confirm interpretations made from sonar data. Optical digital imagery of seafloor sites can now provide very high resolution and also provides additional cues, such as color information for sediments, biota and divers rock types" (Rzhanov, Mayer, & Fornari, 2002, pp. 647 – 652).

Another helpful concept is that of bracketing from photography—where a photographer takes a series of images of the same scene at different exposures to "*bracket* the metered exposure (or manual exposure)" (Askey, 2004, as cited in Roberts, 2004, p. 188). This sampling of adjacent parameters reveals how the different exposures change the image and the visual data. Capturing visuals with different levels of details may be revelatory.

REFERENCES

Agarwala, A., Dontcheva, M., Agrawala, M., Drucker, S., Colburn, A., Curless, B., et al. (2004). Interactive digital photomontage. In *Proceedings of the International Conference on Computer Graphics and Interactive Techniques*. New York: ACM.

Allen, I., & Seaman, J. (2008). *Staying the Course: Online Education in the United States, 2008*. Sloan Consortium. Retrieved January 26, 2009, from http://www.sloan-c.org/publications/survey/pdf/staying_the_course.pdf

Andrejevic, M. (2007). *iSpy:Surveillance and Power in the Interactive Era.* Lawrence, KS: University Press of Kansas.

Ao, X., Li, J., Wang, X., & Dai, G. (2006). Structuralizing digital ink for efficient selection. In *Proceedings of the IUI'06* (pp. 148-154). New York: ACM.

Bagdanov, A. D., del Bimbo, A., Nunziati, W., & Pernici, F. (2006) A reinforcement learning approach to active camera foveation. In *Proceedings of the VSSN '06*, Santa Barbara, California.

Bahmutov, G., Popescue, V., & Sacks, E. (2004). Depth enhanced panoramas. In *Proceedings of the IEEE conference on Visualization '04*. Washington, DC: IEEE.

Berlanga, A. J., & Garcia, F. J. (2005). Authoring tools for adaptive learning designs in computer-based education. In *Proceedings of the 2005 Latin American conference on Human-computer interaction*. New York: ACM.

Boyle, M., & Greenberg, S. (2005). The language of privacy: Learning from video media space analysis and design. *ACM Transactions on Computer-Human Interaction, 12*(2), 329. doi:10.1145/1067860.1067868

Brandl, P., Haller, M., Oberngruber, J., & Schafleitner, C. (2008). Bridging the gap between real printouts and digital whiteboard. In *Proceedings of the AVI '08*. New York: ACM.

Chen, Y., Xia, L., Wong, T.-T., Tong, X., Bao, H., Guo, B., & Shum, G.-Y. (2005). Visual simulation of weathering by y-ton tracing. *ACM Transactions on Graphics, 24*(3), 1127–1133. doi:10.1145/1073204.1073321

Cheng, L., & Vishwanathan, S. V. N. (2007). Learning to compress images and videos. In *Proceedings of The 24th International Conference on Machine Learning*, Corvallis, OR (pp. 161-168).

Clément, O. Benoit, J., & Paquette, E. (2007). Efficient editing of aged object textures. In *Proceedings of the Afrigraph 2007*, Grahamstown, South Africa. New York: ACM.

Dalziel, J. (2003). Open standards versus open source in e-learning. *EDUCAUSE Quarterly, 26*(4), 4–7.

Debevec, P., Raskar, R., & Tumblin, J. (2008). Computational Photography: Advanced Topics. In *International Conference on Computer Graphics and Interactive Techniques*. New York: ACM.

Dick, W., Carey, L., & Carey, J. (2005). *The Systematic Design of Instruction* (6th ed.). Boston: Pearson, Allyn & Bacon.

Dorman, D. (2005). The Coming Revolution in Library Software. In *Proceedings for the ALA Midwinter Conference*.

Electromagnetic spectrum. (2008). *Wikipedia*. Retrieved September 13, 2008, from http://en.wikipedia.org/wiki/Electromagnetic_spectrum

Eye. (2008). *Wikipedia*. Retrieved December 6, 2008, from http://en.wikipedia.org/wiki/Eye

Hansen, R. K., & Anderson, P. A. (1998). The application of real time 3D acoustical imaging. In [Washington, DC: IEEE.]. *Proceedings of the OCEANS, 98*, 738–741.

Hawkins, T., Cohen, J., & Debevec, P. (2001). A photometric approach to digitizing cultural \artifacts. In *Proceedings of the 2001 conference on Virtual reality, archeology, and cultural heritage.*

Heileman, G. L., & Yang, Y. (2003). The effects of invisible watermarking on satellite image classification. In *Proceedings of the DRM '03* (pp. 120-132). New York: ACM.

Helsinki, Finland (pp. 357-374). New York: ACM.

Hourcade, J. P., Perry, K. B., & Moore, J. L. (2007). *Vuelta:* Creating animated characters and props using real-world objects. In *Proceedings of the CHI 2007*, San Jose, CA, USA (pp. 2429-2434).

Hyperspectral imaging. (2008). *Wikipedia.* Retrieved December 13, 2008, at http://en.wikipedia.org/wiki/Hyperspectral_imaging

iMove Spherical Imagery. (n.d.). *Digital Government Society of North America* [Slideshow]. Retrieved January 24, 2009, from http://delivery.acm.org/10.1145/1130000/1123141/p42-ripley.pdf?key1=1123141&key2=2830513221&coll=portal&dl=ACM&CFID=5114638&CFTOKEN=62118861

Kabisch, E., Kuester, F., & Penny, S. (2005). Sonic panoramas: Experiments with interactive landscape image sonification. In *Proceedings of the ICAT 2005, HIT Lab NZ*, Christchurch, New Zealand.

Khan, E. A., Reinhard, E., Fleming, R. W., & Bülthoff, H. H. (2006). Image-based material editing. *ACM Transactions on Graphics, 25*(3), 654–663. doi:10.1145/1141911.1141937

Lakhani, K., & vol Hippel, E. (2002). How open source software works: "Free" user-to-user assistance. *Research Policy, 32*(6), 923–943. doi:10.1016/S0048-7333(02)00095-1

Leamnson, R. (2001). *Does Technology Present a New Way of Learning? Educational Technology & Society, 4*(1). Retrieved January 21, 2009, from http://www.ifets.info/journals/4_1/leamnson.html

Lee, W., Pak, J., Kim, S., Kim, H., & Lee, G. (2007). TransPen & MimeoPad: A playful interface for transferring a graphic image to paper by digital rubbing. In *Proceedings of the International Conference on Computer Graphics and Interactive Techniques*, San Diego, CA. New York: ACM.

Lidar. (2008). *Wikipedia.* Retrieved December 13, 2008, from http://en.wikipedia.org/wiki/Lidar

Ljungblad, S. (2007). Designing for new photographic experiences: How the lomographic practice informed context photography. In *Proceedings of the Designing Pleasurable Products and Interfaces*

Martin, H., & Gaver, B. (2000). Beyond the snapshot: From speculation to prototypes in audiophotography. In *Proceedings of the DIS '00*, Brooklyn, NY (pp. 55-64). New York: ACM.

Matusik, W., & Pfister, H. (2004). 3D TV: A scalable system for real-time acquisition, transmission, and autostereoscopic display of dynamic scenes. *ACM Transactions on Graphics, 23*(3), 814–824. doi:10.1145/1015706.1015805

Novak, J., & Canas, A. (2008). *The Theory Underlying Concept Maps and How to Construct and Use Them.* Institute for Human and Machine Cognition. Retrieved January 23, 2009, from http://cmap.ihmc. us/Publications/ResearchPapers/TheoryCmaps/TheoryUnderlyingConceptMaps.htm

Ostromoukhov, V. (1999). Digital facial engraving. In [New York: ACM.]. *Proceedings of the SIG-GRAPH, 99,* 417–424.

Perry, R. N., & Frisken, S. F. (2001). Kizamu: A system for sculpting digital characters. In *Proceedings of the ACM SIGGRAPH 2001* (pp. 47-56). New York: ACM.

Pharr, M., Lefohn, A., Kolb, C., Lalonde, P., Foley, T., & Berry, G. (2007). *Programmable graphics—The future of interactive rendering* (Neoptica Tech. Rep.).

Poupyrev, I., & Wilis, K. D. D. (2008). TwelvePixels: Drawing & creativity on a mobile phone. In *CHI 2008 Proceedings: Interactivity,* Florence, Italy. New York: ACM.

Radar. (2008). *Wikipedia.* Retrieved December 13, 2008, from http://en.wikipedia.org/wiki/Radar

Reidl, M. O., Rowe, J. P., & Elson, D. K. (2008). Toward intelligent support of authoring machinima media content: Story and visualization. In *Proceedings of the ICST INTETAIN '08,* Cancun, Mexico.

Roberts, J. C. (2004, May). Exploratory visualization using bracketing. In *Proceedings of the AVI '04* (pp. 188-192). New York: ACM.

Rzhanov, Y., Mayer, L., & Fornari, D. (2002). Deep-sea image processing. In *Proceedings of the OCEANS '04. MTTS/IEEE TECHNO-OCEAN '04* (pp. 647-652). Washington, DC: IEEE.

Scott, W. R., Roth, G., & Rivest, J.-F. (2003). View planning for automated three-dimensional object reconstruction and inspection. *ACM Computing Surveys, 35*(1), 64–96. doi:10.1145/641865.641868

Toyama, K., Logan, R., Roseway, A., & Anandan, P. (2003). Geographic location tags on digital images. In [New York: ACM.]. *Proceedings of the MM, 03,* 156–166.

Ulicny, B., & Ciechomski, P. dH., & Thalmann, D. (2004). Crowdbrush: Interactive authoring of real-time crowd scenes. In *Proceedings of the Eurographics: ACM SIGGRAPH Symposium on Computer Animation.*

Wang, J., Xu, Y., Shum, H.-Y., & Cohen, M. F. (2004). Video 'tooning. In *Proceedings of the International Conference on Computer Graphics and Interactive Techniques* (pp. 574-583). New York: ACM.

Williams, E., Maraviglia, C., & Moran, A. M. M. (2002). From x-rays to radar: Using color to understand imagery. In *Proceedings of the 31st Applied Imagery Pattern Recognition Workshop.* Washington, DC: IEEE.

Wozencraft, J. M. (2002). Complete coastal mapping with airborne lidar. In *Proceedsing of the MTS/IEEE OCEANS '02* (pp. 1194-1198). Washington, DC: IEEE.

Würmlin, S., Lamboray, E., Staadt, O. G., & Gross, M. H. (2002). 3D video recorder. In *Proceedings of the 10th Pacific Conference on Computer Graphics and Applications (PG '02).* Washington, DC: IEEE.

Xu, S., Xu, Y., Kang, S. B., Salesin, D. H., Pan, Y., & Shum, H.-Y. (2006). Animating Chinese paintings through stroke-based decomposition. *ACM Transactions on Graphics*, 25(2), 239–267. doi:10.1145/1138450.1138454

Xu, Y.-Q., Chen, Y., Lin, S., Zhong, H., Wu, E., Guo, B., & Shum, H.-Y. (2001). Photorealistic rendering of knitwear using the Lumislice. In *Proceedings of the ACM SIGGRAPH 2001* (pp. 391-398). New York: ACM.

Yan, T., Ganesan, D., & Manmatha, R. (2008). Distributed image search in camera sensor networks. In *Proceedings of the SenSys '08*, Raleigh, NC, USA.

Yanosky, R., Harris, M., & Zastrocky, M. (2003). *Higher education e-Learning meets open source.* Gartner.

Zhang, J., Zhou, K., Velho, L., Guo, B., & Shum, H.-Y. (2003). Synthesis of progressively-variant textures on arbitrary surfaces. *ACM Transactions on Graphics*, 22(3), 295–302. doi:10.1145/882262.882266

KEY TERMS AND DEFINITIONS

Acoustical Imaging (n): The use of sound waves to capture images, as of the bottom of the ocean or internal organs of the human body

Camera Array (n): An arrangement of interrelated cameras used for a particular image capture

Computational Photography (n): The extension of the power of digital imagery capture through digital cameras by the use of computational processes and tools (digital sensors, optics, and lighting, for example)

Data Logger (n): A device that is connected to a computer and that collects information as an integrated, stand-alone unit

Digital Rubbing (n): A digital image capture that simulates the rubbing of a leaded pencil over a ridged or textural surface

Frottage (n): A technique in the visual arts for capturing textural images by rubbing chalk on paper laid over a surface

Granularity (n): The size of a digital learning object

Hyperspectral (adj): A type of imagery that involves information collected from a broad range of the electromagnetic spectrum (including those invisible to the human eye), usually from contiguous bands collected from one sensor

Lidar (n): A device that uses infrared laser light to detect particles in the atmosphere

Multispectral Imagery (n): An image that is composed of a range or spectrum of image information, both radiation from the invisible and the visible parts of the electromagnetic spectrum, often from selected spectral bands that are not contiguous and which were collected from multiple sensors

OCR (n): Optical character recognition

Optics: The distinguishing between two separate adjacent objects or sources of light

Resolution (n): The level of detail depicted via the dots per linear inch or number of pixels; the sharpness of the digital image

Sensor (n): A device that captures information either as a stand-alone device or part of a larger interconnected array

Video Media Spaces (n): Physical spaces where video cameras may be constantly (or sporadically) capturing visual information (in real time and for archival), with video feeds made available to a dispersed group of individuals; this may involve synchronous video awarenesses of each group with each other's situations

SIDEBAR 1

The Art of Videography for E-Learning

Brent A. Anders
Kansas State University, USA

Introduction

Simply having video in an online course doesn't improve its educational quality, but having *good* video within an online course can definitely improve learning and retention. So the question arises, "What is *good* video for E-Learning?" This is where the art, and science, of videography come into play.

First it is important to ascertain if video is really needed and why. What is the true goal of including the video in the first place? Do you have a video or can you create a video that will truly accomplish this goal? Could text, a picture or simple audio accomplish the same thing? In viewing an E-Learning course in a Systems Approach Model framework, these are the questions that would be addressed within the development of an instructional strategy (Dick, Carey & Carey, 2005). The media used would be part of the overall plan for the instruction, not something thrown in or added at the last second.

There are many reasons why videos could and should be used within an E-Learning environment, but identifying a real need for the video and properly implementing the video are two very different things. The proper mechanics of creating a good video are beyond the scope of this entry. Important aspects such as: good lighting and sound, the use of a tripod, the rule of thirds, and proper editing won't be addressed. Instead the focus is on the art of properly using video within E-Learning.

Problems

A common scenario in E-Learning is the use of a video of an "on-campus" class. This is where an instructor simply has his or her regular class (which meets in a real-life classroom, "on-campus") captured via video and then places that video online for his or her E-Learning class to view (see Figure 1). The thought is that this would fully replicate what "on-campus" students are experiencing and would then yield the greatest educational experience. Without going into problems dealing with that, based simply on educational principles, it is important to understand how viewing a one-hour video of one's "on-campus" class online is not the same as actually being there.

- **Viewing Angle, Image Quality:** Viewing the video online limits you to one viewing angle. If you were actually attending you could move to find the angle that best suited you and would give you the best-detailed view.
- **Action:** While in a live classroom, a student views many things, not just the "talking head" of the instructor. At times the student may focus in on the instructor's hands and/or body if it is pertinent to the understanding of the instructor's description or explanation.
- **Interaction:** While watching the video, there is no interaction. The student is receiving the instructor's message and that is it. A student who is actually in the classroom could ask for clarification or pose his or her own thoughts and ideas about what was being addressed. Additionally, a student actually in the classroom could ask questions or make comments to other students.

Figure 1. A video screenshot (Anders, 2009)

- **Physiological and Cognitive Investment:** In a real life class, a student would have traveled and physically moved to actually get to the class. They would have found their seat and set everything up to be ready to receive the class from the instructor. If the instructor where to come out and give a ten minute lecture a student would be upset that they had invested all of this time and effort for only 10 minutes worth of education. A lecture of at least an hour is typically expected. Online however it is a very different story. Having video broken down into much more manageable chunks (with frivolous content edited out) would be of great educational benefit.
- **Learning Environment:** The students present at the live classroom are much more of a captive audience than E-Learning students. This is an important difference in the way the students are learning the content. In order for learning to take place two components are required: concentration and repeated reconstruction (Leamnson, 2001). Repeated reconstruction is not to be confused with simple practice or rote memory. Instead it represents being able to reconstruct the content or idea in multiple ways with multiple connections to prior knowledge, "cognitive structure" (Novak & Canas, 2006).

Solutions

With these important differences identified, there are ways that each can be addressed to enhance the E-Learning video overall.

- The viewing angle and image quality can be improved by using high quality video cameras (High Definition would be the best), and either altering the recording angle or using multiple cameras placed at various angles.
- The action within a video can be accomplished by varying what is shown to student depending on what is going on with the instruction. Instead of having a "talking head" where just the instructor's head is shown, the video would be more dynamic, which would be interesting, which would aid in motivation.

- In asynchronous video (in this case meaning one-way video viewed at a later time), interaction is not really possible. But interaction can still take place within the E-learning class by referencing the video or by mentioning specific interactive content within the video. As an example, imagine an online student comes to the conclusion of a ten-minute video dealing with the Visual Sensory System. A closing segment that includes something like "now that we have learned about the Visual Sensory System go to the message board and write your views with respect to bottom-up versus top-down processing of the brains visual perception. Also read another student's entry and explain why you agree or disagree with their view point." This addition to the actual content of the video's data would work to personalize the video as well as start the needed interaction to fully learn the content or idea.

- The physiological and cognitive investment mentioned earlier can easily be addressed by simply editing the videos. Do the online students need to see five minutes of the instructor passing out papers or discussing special issues dealing specifically with the on-campus class? The answer is no, so the content should be edited and if possible broken up into meaningful chunks to make it easier for online students to download and use.

- Although an instructor does not have control of an E-Learning student's learning environment, the content of the video can definitely affect the students' motivation to learn which then translate to concentration and the students' connection to the educational material presented. Instructors should strive to present the content within the video in more than one way. Examples, analogies and humor can go a long way to personalize the information, allow for more reconstructive connections and make it all less abstract and easier to understand.

Conclusion

The use of videos within E-Learning is a powerful tool that if used correctly can accomplish many things such as: explaining complicated concepts, demonstrating the kinesthetics of a subject, presenting analogies and examples to aid in the teaching of abstract content as well as personalizing and humanizing the course in general. The video, however, must be properly created so as to truly accomplish its goal

Figure 2. Brent A. Anders teaching a course (Anders, 2009)

and enhance the educational experience. Real thought and planning must be done during the design of the course so as to identify if videos should be used, if so, what types of videos should be used, where it should be placed throughout the course and what type of interaction will be utilized. Selected or created video content should always be evaluated and edited to maximize its usefulness and eliminate any unneeded material so as to enhance the students' educational experience.

E-Learning is continuing to become more and more competitive (Allen & Seamen, 2008), students are looking at more than simply attaining their degree. They want to truly master the content and have a good educational experience. Quality video that is educational, motivational, exciting and interesting is what educators need to strive for in order to be the most effective and offer the best educational experience.

SIDEBAR 2

Open Source Solutions for Digital Imagery Creation and Integration into E-Learning

Jason Caudill
Carson-Newman College, USA

Introduction

As electronic communication and electronic learning grows and expands it is becoming increasingly media rich. The Internet and the ever-increasing variety of devices we use to access networks have undergone a literally visible shift from text and simple images to sites with extensive graphics, and video integration is becoming common. Throughout the history of organized education technological shifts in society have translated to technology integration in the classroom, and the advent of digital imagery is proving no exception.

To integrate digital imagery into the eLearning environment, instructors and students must have access to the appropriate software to create digital images. One solution to providing this access is the use of open source software. What open source software is, and how to select and implement it, is the focus of this work. A selection of popular open source software packages for digital imagery is also presented.

Open Source Software

Software is expensive. Students are not wealthy. Institutions do not have unlimited technology budgets. Commercial software can be slow to update and slower to recognize and correct errors or failures. These perfectly valid complaints and many more can be responsible for instructors abandoning the use of technology in their teaching, even in the context of eLearning. While no single solution exists to fix everything that is wrong with the world of software the open source community is making great strides at fixing a sizable portion of it, and it is projected that eLearning environments will lead the way into the integration of Open Source software for academia (Yanosky, Harris, & Zastrocky, 2003).

Open source software is perhaps best known by the computing public as free software. This is accurate as there is no charge to download or use software that is distributed under an open source license, but it is by no means the end of the discussion. The availability of source code to independent developers, the community of developers and their contributions to software's success, multi-platform compatibility, and compatibility with commercial file formats are all important components of the open source world (Dalziel, 2003).

Open source software is distributed at no cost to the user. Most often the software is downloaded but some distributions also offer to send out the software on CD. If a user opts for the CD version it is not free, but the charge is just for the media, shipping, and time to create the CD; the software contained on the CD is still free of any license fee. This definition can usually be shared with another no-charge software license called freeware. The difference that makes open source software open source instead of just freeware is that open source software freely distributes the program's source code and freeware does not.

Source code is the programming behind a piece of software that actually makes everything work. The code is what communicates with the computer's hardware and operating system and is really what the software is; the interface that the user interacts with is simply a product of the source code's interaction with the computer hardware and operating system. Making source code freely available is the source of many of open source software's advantages. Because users, and more importantly independent programmers, can access the source code behind open source programs there are an unlimited number of contributors for any open source project.

The real power behind open source software is the independent programming community that supports it (Dorman, 2005). Without the programmers, the software would not exist nor would it ever be repaired or updated. The open source community is an active one. Users and programmers alike participate in online message boards about the software sharing their experiences, their questions, and their ideas (Lakhani & von Hippel, 2002). For programmers, this is where user-discovered bugs or user-requested improvements make their way into the programming community. At times, there may be programmers putting their time and talent into working on open source programs from locations around the world.

What does this community programming effort mean? It means that popular open source programs are developed faster, their problems are more quickly solved, and plug-ins and extensions are developed more rapidly than is often the case with competing commercial software packages. The specific notation of popular open source software is an important one. Just because software is open source does not mean that it is good software or that there is a large community of developers supporting it. Popular programs, however, do enjoy wide community support and a loyal following of users.

The other side of the user community effort is that of education. Just distributing software accomplishes little if the software's users never learn how to start the program. Programmers form part of this educational community by participating in forums and posting answers or explanations for users who have questions. There are also programmers and some instructional designers who independently develop instructional materials that they distribute online for users to learn how to use the software. These materials may take any form, from basic text instructions to animated screen-capture tutorials, but the end result is to produce an educated user. While these efforts are not entirely unique to open source software they are another key example of the power of the open source community working together to support each other.

This community relationship in open source software does not necessarily end with online exchanges of information and programming. One of the oldest issues in computing that has yet to completely go away is that of cross-platform compatibility. Even today there are programs that will work on Windows, or Mac, or Linux, but not others. Or, in some cases, there are distributions for different operating systems but material created in a compatible package on one operating system will not necessarily translate with its formatting intact to the same software running on a different operating system. There is also the problem of some proprietary file formats preventing users from creating a file on one piece of software and allowing another user with another piece of software to access the file. Both of these issues, cross-platform compatibility and proprietary file formats, inhibit communication and collaboration among computer users.

Fortunately, many of the popular open source programs offer solutions to both of these problematic issues. Many of the open source programs, and all of the programs addressed in this sidebar, have versions for multiple operating systems. In the context of education, and particularly e-learning environments, this cross-platform compatibility means that students can work on the operating system of their choice at home and still have access to the same software packages. This gives e-learning instructors the ability to write directions and tutorials for a single piece of software instead of different packages. This also provides students participating in e-learning exchanges the ability to discuss the software with each other knowing that their classmates, whether on Windows, Mac, or Linux, are looking at essentially the same interface when working on the same assignments. Just like the open source community at large, this opportunity creates a small open source community within the e-learning class environment.

Many open source programs also have a large number of compatible file formats built into their design. One of the goals of using computers is to be able to communicate with others and, obviously, if the files a user creates are unreadable by the person he or she wants to communicate with then the media cannot serve its intended purpose. To address this common problem many open source programs include a long list of format options in which to save files. Notably, these options usually include the most popular commercial applications. This allows users to access files created on commercial applications and also to create their own media with open source programs, save the file in a commercial format, and move to a machine with the commercial software package and continue working. This can be of particular importance to users who work at home on open source software and are also at work or on campus with computers that are running the equivalent commercial software.

While open source software is admittedly not the one and only answer to every technical problem it does answer many of the most serious. One of the most significant opportunities, and difficult obstacles, for e-learning is its ability to reach larger communities of learners. Expanding educational access is a wonderful benefit, but providing technological access to these new learners is a challenge.

Integrating Open Source Solutions

Now that the stage has been set for what open source software is, how can open source solutions be integrated into the e-learning environment? The first step in adding open source programs to the e-learning environment is to examine what kinds of media need to be used and which programs best address those needs. Once the software has been selected the method of distribution needs to be decided on and implemented. Also, training needs to be available and the compatibility of the software with other applications should be examined. These steps are not really a one by one process as much as a set of requirements against which to compare available options.

To begin the selection of open source media software the first question that needs to be asked is exactly what kind of media needs to be a part of the learning environment. Does the class need diagrams, flowcharts, graphs, tables, vector drawings, three-dimensional renderings, edited photos, or something entirely different? The answer to this first question will immediately narrow the selection of an open source program to just a few popular, stable distributions.

After deciding on the type of media that will be included in the class there is the question of how sophisticated the media objects need to be. Digital images can be as simple as an arrow drawn between two blocks of text or as complex as a three-dimensional rendering of a building. In between these two extremes are countless levels of media sophistication. Will a plain, two-dimensional pie chart work for the class or does it demand a three-dimensional comparative bar chart? Will flowcharts with just a few shapes and arrows work or are there discipline-specific icons and symbols that have to be included in complex renderings? The answers, first to the big question and then to the more detailed questions, will further narrow down the choice of software.

Once a decision has been made on what kinds of tasks the software needs to perform there is the question of what, if any, other programs the software needs to be compatible with. The environment in which the class is taking place may have a significant impact on this decision. If the e-learning environment is an asynchronous, entirely online class then file format compatibilities may not be a significant issue. In an entirely online environment, where students and instructors are working on personal machines, the chosen open source solution can simply be used on everyone's machine and operated locally. If the course is connected to a campus or other academic facility, however, there may be other issues. If the computing resources available to students at a physical location are using commercial software packages then the corresponding open source solutions should be compatible with the commercial software file formats. Primarily this is an issue of student access. One of the goals of using open source software is to provide students with access to software on their personal machines, but this convenience is lessened if, by working on their own machines with open source software, they are unable to work with campus computers when they are away from their own computers.

After the software choice has been made there is the question of how to get the software to students. Again, this choice will depend on the environment in which the software is being used. Physical meetings versus entirely online environments, student access to high-speed network connections, and the ability of students to afford additional pieces of technology will all factor into the decision of how to get the open source software to the students.

Perhaps the easiest way for an instructor to distribute software to students is to put the software on CD and hand then hand out discs to students in a classroom. This guarantees that every student will get the same version of the software with the same updates, and that everyone will get the software at the same time. While there is no guarantee of when students will install the software, handing CDs to all of them at least avoids any potential issues of a download site not working or other problems that can occur when working with online resources.

The biggest potential problem for distributing software via CD is the learning environment itself. If the class is entirely online and there are no physical meetings then handing out CDs in class is obviously impossible. Mailing the discs to students would be a possible solution, but that entails both a significant expense to the instructor or the institution for mailing materials and postage and the time delay between final registration of students for the course, the packaging and mailing of the discs, and the arrival of the discs at the student's home or workplace. Even if it is a blended course with a few physical meetings, schedules may not work out to get the CDs to the students when they need the software.

To avoid using physical media there is the option of posting links to download sites for the software and giving students instructions for how to download and install the files. This method may require a bit more sophistication on the part of the student, but should not be so much of an issue that it prevents students from being able to complete their work. Providing links to the download sites for software is a very fast way to give students access to the software and the links can be distributed through any type of electronic communication, whether the course uses an e-mail listserv, a web site, or a learning / course management system (L/CMS).

Another approach to network distribution is for the instructor or institution to host the downloads of the software themselves. Students can be directed to the software either through a course website or LMS that links to files located on the server, or they can be given access to an FTP site for downloading. This solution provides the ease of access for students offered by posted links but also gives the instructor more control over the system being used for delivery.

Regardless of the hosting location, there are certain factors which may complicate the downloading of software by students. One of the most serious in the arena of e-learning environments is the risk that students may not have access to a high-speed connection. If a student is still working with a dial-up ISP, or even with a slower DSL connection, downloading large files can be challenging, if not impossible. An institution may have a requirement for high-speed access to participate in an online course, which would provide some assurance that students would be able to download software, but absent this type of requirement network speeds should be taken into consideration when making a decision on how to distribute software to users.

Popular Open Source Media Software

Having explored many of the technical components of open source software for digital imagery it will be useful to know what the actual open source programs are that support digital imagery. This discussion will by no means be an exhaustive list of all the open source possibilities available, but it will present some of the most popular digital imagery applications from the open source community. Applications will include digital image manipulation, flowcharting, vector graphics, and graphing.

Possibly the most popular, best known, and most widely used open source imaging program is the GNU Image Manipulation Program, commonly called The GIMP. The GIMP is a full-featured image manipulation program that can be used for everything from creating basic digital images to advanced editing of digital photographs. As is the case with many of the popular distributions it is multi-platform compatible, offering versions for Windows, Mac, and Linux.

Due in large part to its popularity, The GIMP has a very large base of support from the open source community. The main GIMP site (www.gimp.org) provides users with a variety of tutorials and there are even more available online from independent tutorial developers. In addition to tutorials there is also a very extensive collection of plug-ins and extensions available for The GIMP. These tutorials and add-ons are complimented by active discussion boards where users share tips and techniques, along with troubleshooting advice. Figure 3 is a picture from the website FreeFoto.com. Figure 4 is the image after some quick editing in GIMP to create what might be used as a button or icon for an eLearning environment.

While The GIMP is an excellent tool for advanced digital image and digital photo editing there are times that a simpler, faster program is needed to work with large numbers of digital photos. In the open source arena one of the excellent digital photo workflow choices is RawTherapee. Digital photo work-flow software is basically an interface that allows the user to organize collections of digital photos, view them, perform simple editing functions such as cropping or adjusting the darkness and contrast, and

Figure 3. Building a picture from FreeFoto.com (Caudill, 2009)

Figure 4. Building button created in The GIMP (Caudill, 2009)

export the photos in either the same or a converted file format. RawTherapee is available for Windows and Linux.

To create original vector graphics there is an open source solution called Inkscape. Inkscape is a full-featured drawing program that includes many advanced features and is capable of advanced image creation. As is the case with many other open source programs Inkscape is available on multiple platforms; Windows, Max, and Linux, and also has extensive training and support resources available online. Figure 5 is a sample of a banner that was created in Inkscape. It is worth noting here that Inkscape is a very capable tool; it can create very simple images like a banner or very complex renderings. The author, however, is limited in the creation of original vector graphics.

As another aspect of digital imagery, flowcharts and other diagrams may be incorporated into an eLearning environment. An open source solution that supports this kind of functionality is Dia. Dia is

Figure 5. A banner created with Inkscape (Caudill, 2009)

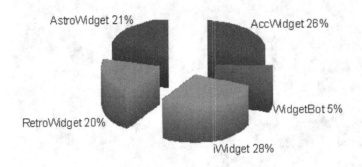

Figure 6. Flowchart created with Dia (Caudill, 2009)

available for Windows and Linux and comes preloaded with diagramming shapes for flowcharts, relationship diagrams, networks, and many other applications. Figure 6 is a simple flowchart that was created with Dia. There are many different shapes, colors, and other formatting tools available, the simple example here is just to illustrate the creation of a basic decision flowchart.

The final aspect of digital imagery that will be explored here is the use of charts. Most frequently seen as output from spreadsheet applications, charts are a good way to convey a large amount of information very quickly. An open source solution for a spreadsheet application that can produce graphs is actually a full open source office suite, OpenOffice. OpenOffice includes not only a spreadsheet application, but also a word processor, presentation software, database, and other office tools. There are editions available that are compatible with Microsoft Office 2007 files and there are versions available for Windows, Mac, and Linux. Figure 7 is a chart that was created with OpenOffice Calc.

This overview of open source media applications for digital imagery is only a preview of everything that is available. It is entirely possible, perhaps even likely, that from the time this sidebar is written to the time it is published a new open source program will be created that serves some aspect of digital imagery. The important thing for practitioners to remember is that they must make an effort to read and stay current with emerging technologies.

Conclusion

In any learning environment it is important to provide students with the information and the tools that they need. In the eLearning environment that need is enhanced by the separation between instructors

Figure 7. OpenOffice chart (Caudill, 2009)

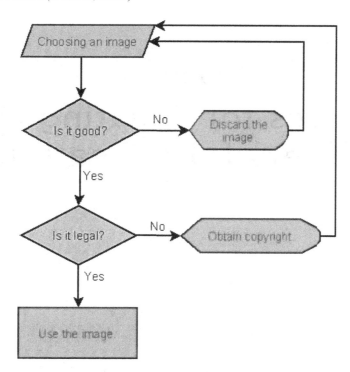

and students; when communication is occurring online the tools and techniques to facilitate that communication must be in place. Ultimately, the goal of integrating open source software solutions into the eLearning environment, whether for digital imagery or some other application, is to support students through technology access.

Beyond the initial provision of access, open source software has the ability to give students long-term access to technology resources. After a student leaves a class, or an institution, they can keep the open source software and use it in the future; the student is not left without access to software after they lose access to commercial licenses in an institutional computer facility. This can be critical for students who go into professions where funding is not available for software but there is still a need for software solutions.

Finally, regardless of what programs a student learns the only guarantee seems to be that either different programs will need to be used at a later time or the program the student already knows will change versions and interfaces. Change, and rapid change, is a fact of life in the world of modern technology. Pedagogically, there is something to be said for exposing students to multiple ways of doing things. By working with different kinds of software students can gain flexibility and an ability to quickly learn how to work with new software. These are skills that will be valuable regardless of what program they may be using.

Open source software is one of the very few instances where you truly do not get what you pay for. You pay nothing, but can get a great deal of functionality, utility, and productivity. Practitioners are encouraged to give open source programs a try. Students need access to the technology and practitioners may find themselves surprised at just how much they move to open source solutions themselves.

Chapter 7
Procedures for Creating Quality Imagery for E–Learning

ABSTRACT

What features describe a quality digital image for e-learning? From concept to actualization, what steps will likely lead to more effective results? This chapter examines the various aspects of successful digital imagery in various e-learning contexts, and it includes strategies for how to identify quality objectives and to execute to achieve these. This includes ideas on how to make the digital imagery for more identifiable, transferable and usable as a visual object in a digital repository.

CHAPTER OBJECTIVES

- Introduce a 12-step procedure for creating quality imagery for e-learning
- Highlight where raw digital imagery may be collected for processing
- Explore ways to make digital imagery for re-usability (through identifiability, transferability, portability, and usability)

INTRODUCTION

Multiple paths may be used to achieve the same end point of an effective digital image for e-learning. The local realities of users, technologies, and teaching and learning aims, all will affect the creation and deployment of such visuals. The purpose of this chapter, then, is to offer a general procedure for creating quality digital images for e-learning. This will focus on process and the decisions and planning that will likely inform this process.

DOI: 10.4018/978-1-60566-972-4.ch007

The main sequential sections are as follows: Needs Assessment and Environmental Scan, Project Management, Setting Standards for Quality, Development and Production Work, Assessment and Revision, and then Launch and Future Planning. This chapter is organized according to these general engineered workflow sequences.

Any variety of customizations may be made to this process, and steps that have been defined by an organization already may simplify and shorten this planning, development and assessment cycle.

There's plenty of flexibility here. These steps are not linear ones but rather recursive, with movement between the steps. As procedures are put into place, various steps may be more efficiently achieved or bypassed in future development cycles. This aims to be an encompassing view of this procedure from start to image delivery. The spirit of these procedures is to support freedom of action within quality structures.

A 12-STEP PROCEDURE FOR CREATING QUALITY IMAGERY FOR E-LEARNING

Needs Assessment and Environmental Scan

Step 1: Defining the Project Scope; Evaluating Extant Resources, and Conducting a Gaps Analysis
Step 2: Assessing the Learning Objectives and Learning Situation; Understanding Learners and their Learning Needs
Step 3: Evaluating the Techno

Project Management

Step 4: Building a Team, a Budget and a Schedule

Setting Standards for Quality

Step 5: Setting Ethical, Pedagogical, Cultural, Domain, Aesthetic, and Technological Stylebook Standards

Development and Production Work

Step 6: The Collection of Rich, Raw Materials
Step 7: Intellectual Property Negotiations, Arrangements and Documentation
Step 8: Creating the Learning Images
Step 9: Accessibility Mitigations

Assessment and Revision

Step 10: Alpha and Beta Testing; Revision, Editing and Metadata Labeling

Launch and Future Planning

Step 11: Deployment for Learning and Archival
Step 12: Planning for Updates

NEEDS ASSESSMENT AND ENVIRONMENTAL SCAN

Step 1: Defining the Project Scope; Evaluating Extant Resources, and Conducting a Gaps Analysis

Defining the needs of the e-learning graphics capture and creation is the first step in understanding the scope of work. For some learning circumstances, only a dozen images may be needed for a particular slideshow. For another circumstance such as ones using data-hungry models (like simulations), thousands of images may be necessary. Some projects may require multi-year capturing of images or even open-ended work into the foreseeable future.

In some situations, the raw capture may also be possible for a limited period of time. The capturing of sonar images mapping the bottom of the ocean depends on the funding for the ship and the expensive equipment used in this endeavor, for example. Satellite imagery captures and telescope-captured images may involve additional costs and complexity. The context then is critical as part of the planning.

Figure 1. A 12-step procedure for creating quality imagery for e-learning

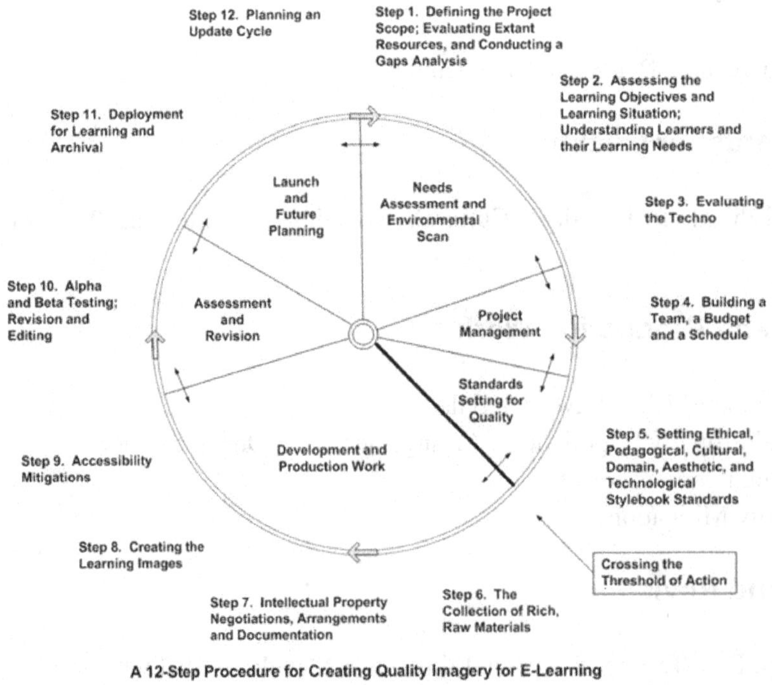

A 12-Step Procedure for Creating Quality Imagery for E-Learning

Plenty of digital imagery and information may already exist for the particular build, with some of the resources available as royalty-free or copyright-released types. Doing some research to find what is available and to analyze whether it's suitable would make this task easier.

A gaps analysis involves a look at the current state of the project and what needs to be done to achieve the full objectives of the project. Defining the gaps between the "final state" and the "present state" will enable the team to move forward strategically to achieve their goals and to close the gap. Strategic debriefings may help the team move forward with continual improvements (Hackman, 2002, p. 186).

The following then offers some ideas of what may be considered to determine the critical information for Step 1: Defining the Project Scope; Evaluating Extant Resources, and Conducting a Gaps Analysis.

Project Scope

- **How many images will be needed?** What are the bare necessary images needed for the earliest deadlines? The ideal level of images?
- **What types of images will be needed?** What image contents will there be? What image file types are desirable, and why? Will there be versioning of images for various uses?
- **What sorts of processing will go into the raw capture of these images?**
- **What processing will go to the revision and creation of the finalized images?**
- **Who will need access to these images?** How will these images be made available to all possible users? Are there unique protections in terms of access?
- **Are some of the images sensitive, with restricted access?** How can safe channels be made for the creation, handling and distributed of sensitive images?

Extant Resources

- **What extant resources are there?** What images exist that are royalty-free or have legal releases and may be used for the image development? What contents are available through existing open-source repositories and digital libraries? What equipment and technologies are available for the creation of these images? What digital repositories will be used? What learning / course management systems (L/CMSes)?

A Gaps Analysis

- **What image contents already exist for educational use?** What progress has already been made towards creating the necessary images, and what more needs to be done?
- **When are the images due?** What flexibility is there in terms of deadlines?

The next step involves a deeper understanding of the particular learners using the materials. The broader the range of possible learners, the more generic the designs may have to be. In particular, this examines learner needs in regards to the e-learning context, and in relation to the digital imagery, in particular.

Step 2: Assessing the Learning Objectives and Learning Situation; Understanding Learners and their Learning Needs

The design of digital imagery for e-learning will vary depending on the learning objectives and context. Learning objectives seem most efficient when listed out as verb phrases with learning outcomes that may be measureable. Learning contexts are the places where situated cognition occurs, places where people will practice their skills.

Images for a scientific lab may require attention to conventions of the field, including proper lighting, appropriate measures, and true color balancing. Images used for a field trip may have to evoke a place and activities. Images to enhance the telepresence of a guest speaker may need to provide a professional image and communicate professional values. Images for a fantastical fictional world may have to evoke a particular tone (threatening, dreamy, or metallic, for example). A digital studio may include images in various stages of development and sophistication. An orientation site may involve plenty of automated learning with self-explanatory and stand-alone visuals.

Considering the unique learners for a particular curriculum may also change the visuals for the widest applicability and use. Factors may involve learners' demographics; attitudes; prior knowledge regarding the domain, related skill levels; general learning styles; cultural backgrounds; main language(s); visual and multimedia literacy; access to technologies, and other factors that may be considered relevant. These factors may determine how much development work and scaffolding needs to be done to make the images effective for learning; this may determine if "antecedents" and "debriefings" may enhance the learning both pre- and post- presentation of the imagery. Designers of learning images may take these factors and put together the various solutions that may support learners in making mental connections.

Other stakeholders may also be considered. Are there those in private industry that may be affected by the curriculum and learning? Administrators? Professionals in the field? The general public? Global learners in other national or cultural contexts? Applying stakeholder evaluation as part of the design process may enhance the development of educational imagery.

Using pedagogical theories and research will enhance the coherent and aligned build of the e-learning visuals with the rest of the pedagogical build. What learning theories are at play—behaviorism? Constructivism? Affective theories? Cognitive theories? What actual roles do the images play in evoking particular thought and learning processes? How do the images enhance recall and the storage of information into long-term memory?

There is a line of research that explores human vision and perception, which may enrich the building of visuals.

The human vision system evolved to extract information about surface properties of objects, often at the expense of losing information about the quality and quantity of light entering the eye. This phenomenon, the fact that we experience colored surfaces and not colored light, is called color constancy. When we are talking about the apparent overall reflectance of a surface, it is called lightness constancy. Three terms are commonly used to describe the general concept of quantity of light: luminance, brightness, and lightness (Ware, 2004, p. 80).

The following are questions that may be used for consideration in assessing the learning objectives, the learning situation, and the particular learner needs.

Assessing the Learning Objectives and Learning Situation

- **What are the learning objectives that these images will be supporting?** How will the images support those objectives?

- **What is the learning domain?** What unique aspects of this learning domain or field will affect image capture, image processing, and image storage and use? (The study of live and active volcanoes, ocean terrain, microbial biological agents, and outer space, for example, will involve different image challenges.)

- **What unique user considerations are there for accessing and viewing the images?** Are there certain unique compression methods necessary to process the images?

- **What is the e-learning context in which the image(s) will be used?** Will the images be used in a lecture? An assignment? A slideshow? A digital gallery? A video? A downloadable sample? A mobile repository?

- **What will the main intention of each image be?** For comparison and contrast? For identification? For the development of individual or group "telepresence"? For marketing? For advertising? For primary research and testing? For branding? For portraying a range of creative solutions? For showing different image capture techniques?

Understanding Learners and their Learning Needs

- **What are the main demographics of the learners in this situation?** Which of the demographics may be relevant to the learning situation? What cultural background issues are there? What various language fluencies are there? What about graphical fluency and graphical literacy among the learners? What about adult learning preferences and needs?

- **What are their attitudes about the subject matter?** Are there pre-existing misconceptions?

- **What are their backgrounds with the learning materials? Related skill sets?** What scaffolding may be needed to make the images more accessible for learning value? What planning is needed for the amateurs and non-experts in the group? What planning is needed for the experts in the group?

- **What are their general learning styles?** Do they tend to be visual learners? Textual learners? What are their preferences in terms of engaging materials?

- **What accessibility challenges may they have in accessing and using the images?** Will files need to be versioned differently? Will there need to be extra tools to make the learning more accessible? What quality annotations, labels, metadata and captions are made to enhance the accessibility of the images?

- **What languages do the learners speak and read?** How fluent are they? How well do the materials translate from English to the foreign language (if relevant)?

- **What insightful value may these learners bring to the images?** How may the ideas and insights of the learners be captured in relation to the digital images? How may their insights be used to enhance learning?

- **What technologies will the main "installed base" of learners be using to access the digital imagery?** Do they all have equal access to the information? Will the learners themselves be capturing images as part of their own studies? If so, how may this be effectively facilitated?

Step 3: Evaluating the Techno

The digital image creation pipeline involves the use of various types of technologies. There are technologies for raw image captures (scanners, webcams, cameras, sensors, and other devices). There are many authoring and editing tools that may adjust color, crop images, add effects, and label or annotate the imagery. There's technology for digital image storage. And there's technology for deploying the imagery (see Figure 2).

The affordances of new technologies for high quality image creation has expanded human capabilities to create images in a variety of forms, including icons (Brami, 1997), diagrams, photos, 3D immersive images, macro-and micro-scale images, and remote sensor captures.

Setting up shop effectively means setting up appropriate work spaces (sometimes mobile), with the proper hardware, and software for the entire sequence of the digital imagery pipeline—from capture and creation to the deployment.

Techno for Raw Image Capture

Here, technologists and instructional designers need to find the right tool for the task. Defining the tool essentially requires a consideration of the functions and features required.

- What level of imagistic details is required? Will close-ups need to be done? Pans? Live image captures with modifiability of images?
- What image capture conditions exist in the environment? Will waterproof, heat-proof, or rugged equipment be necessary?
- Will special studios be needed for scanned image captures of 3D objects? Live objects?
- What tools exist to enhance the image capture and to mitigate for hand shakiness, variable lighting, and other real-world features?
- What add-on equipment will be needed to strengthen the particular devices? Will there need to be microphones?
- Will there need to be unique customizations made to the equipment for the image capture?
- Will the camera need to be used in combination with other equipment like microscopes, telescopes, computers, or other visual information capture devices?
- What sorts of from-digital / born-digital images will be helpful for the learning? Are screenshots or screen captures desirable? Video grabs? *Machinima* from 3D immersive spaces?
- What sorts of digital file outputs are desired?

Figure 2. General Techno in the Digital Imagery Pipeline

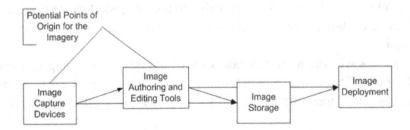

Techno for Authoring and Editing

Authoring tools allow for the creation of digital diagrams and objects directly through drawing or image development. Such tools may include visualization ones, in both 2D and 3D. Also, once raw images have been captured, invariably, they will all need processing: color adjustments, cropping, and compression for desired file type, size and applied-use output.

Some points that may be considered in selecting authoring and editing tools may include the following:

- What sorts of diagrams and drawings and figures will need to be created using authoring tools?
- What particular tools will be needed for 2D images?
- What particular tools will be needed for 3D images?
- Will 4D (the inclusion of movement and time) images be necessary? What tools will be needed for 4D?
- For image editing, what functionalities will be desired? What special effects or filters will be needed?
- Will 2D images need to be translated into 3D for more panoramic experiences? What other high-end functions may be needed?
- How may the visuals be made "interoperable" and useful in various circumstances?

Techno for Storage

Once the digital images have been created and labeled with metadata, they may be stored for multiple instructional users in digital libraries or repositories. The images may be deployed for learning in an automated way through recommender systems (which rank the relevance of items for particular uses) or automated learning designs (which deliver unique learning based on learner profiles, learner behaviors, or other information).

- What sort of digital storage would be optimal for the images and digital learning objects?
- Will the repository be fully accessible or partially "dim" or "dark"—protected against wide distribution?
- What sorts of metadata can the system collect?
- How strong are the authentications into the particular repository system?
- Can federated referatories point to particular digital objects that may be useful for other faculty?
- How easy is it to batch-upload images into the system? How easy is it to "port" off objects to other databases, digital libraries, repositories and storage devices?

Techno for Deployment

Digital images and learning objects also need to be deployed to the learners. The deployment may be through public websites; pass-word protected learning / course management systems, and tangibles like CDs, DVDs, or portable memory devices. RSS-syndicated contents may be sent to mobile devices.

- What are the optimal ways to make the images available in e-learning contexts?
- How may images be deployed with digital rights management protections?

PROJECT MANAGEMENT

Step 4: Building a Team, a Budget and a Schedule

In most situations where images are built for e-learning, this occurs in a workplace, which defines the "authorizing environment." This environment defines the politics and social expectations about the work. It limits the work scope based on the available technologies, the budgets and schedules. To manage such complexity requires project management.

Building a Team

Various skill sets are needed to support the "graphics processing pipeline," so those skills are addressed here. Different individuals bring different skill sets, so several of these roles may be included in one person; likewise, several of these roles may require several people to actuate depending on abilities, and project needs.

An overall manager of the project is important to identify, to make sure that the work stays on track and meets standards. "Hot" teams may have distributed leadership on a particular project. There are different team configurations, but the critical piece is to have project oversight and individual accountability.

The raw image capture—by digital cameras mounted on microscopes, scanners, digital cameras—may often be done by those in the domain field (the professors, graduate students) or professional videographers and photographers hired out of other units (or internal departments or offices in a college).

The processing of the imagery using photo editing tools also requires a combination of domain knowledge and high-tech skills. The proper handling of images and the correct use of annotation are critical.

The instructional design surrounding the imagery requires subject matter expertise in order to appropriately represent the image contents and learning. Depending on the complexity of the building of digital learning objects with the imagery, code developers may have to be brought in. High level instructional designers may also use authoring tools to script the learning.

Intellectual property management should be handled as part of the image capture and editing work. As learning objects are built with the images, and as images are integrated from various sources, the rights management of these sources needs to be pursued and documented. The metadata should involve clear provenance or lineage of the information and also documentation of the ownership of the imagery and learning objects.

The storage and deployment of the digital imagery and digital learning objects may be done through data repository and learning / course management systems (L/CMSes). Often, those who are building the learning objects are the ones who shepherd the work into storage and into live use. Having clear labeling of the objects and their various stages of completion would be critical.

Budgeting

Determining a budget is an important part of the work especially since the "memorandums of agreement" define not only the work expected but the cost of the work. A memorandum of agreement (MOA) should define the scope of the work; the technological outputs; the raw image or video captures that will be done; the standards for the work; the deadlines, and the expected costs. [Sometimes, memorandums of understanding (MOUs) are used, which are essentially the same types of agreements.]

The MOA should also project future needs—especially if the project will be handed over to the faculty or department. How will the imagery be kept fresh and relevant? How can the learning objects be revised and updated? What accessibility mitigations will be made to the work? If new work is added during the course of the project, how will that be negotiated and billed?

Plenty of mutual understanding and good will should underlie MOAs. These should be treated like contracts. Some offices in higher education will use outright negotiated contracts. Others use word-based agreements and simple budgets. Much of this depends on the familiarity that principals have with each other.

A project manager collects this information after thoroughly ascertaining the requested work from the potential faculty and administrative clients. It usually helps to have a meeting of the entire technological team to consider the work given the nuances various types of image capture, processing, instructional design builds, storage and deployment.

From there, the hours for the work are estimated. Some extra layer of time is usually added to cover potential challenges (re-shoots, camera malfunctions, system crashes, mis-editing, and iterating). Some overhead needs to be added for maintaining equipment and the management. A draft budget is proposed, negotiated over, and finally approved.

In this process, it's critical to note that the larger number of stakeholders there are, the slower it may be to fully actualize a project. Projects that involve alpha and beta testing of the online curriculum will require revisions, and that should be proposed in the budget.

Setting a Schedule

The schedule set for the work determines what may be feasible, its quality, and cost. The faster something needs to be done, the more expensive that may be. Oftentimes, the dictates of a grant or a course launch will determine scheduling.

There are some strategies to speed up the work. One is to have a technological design team that is familiar with each other and that works well together. It helps to plan properly and intelligently, to prevent the team from wasting time or failing at any step of the process. This may mean making sure all equipment is maintained, stored properly, checked regularly, and stocked well with backup tapes and batteries. There may be well scripted behaviors and double-checks in image captures. Storing raw images for potential later re-editing and re-rendering may be important (to avoid lossiness in the compressed image outputs). Properly labeling of images and having clear naming protocols will be critical. Maintaining clear communications and documentation of work will be important for the record-keeping and the usability of the contents. Proper labeling is not a trivial endeavor and likely will require team norming and practices, as well as standards, to execute well.

One way to speed up image processing work is to use batch processing to render images appropriately, but the setup for this is critical so as not to process incorrectly.

Deadlines should be reasonable, but technological teams also need to be able to go into the occasional emergency capture and development mode in some situations.

SETTING STANDARDS FOR QUALITY

Step 5: Setting Ethical, Pedagogical, Cultural, Domain, Aesthetic, and Technological Stylebook Standards

To have a team working efficiently from the same playbook, it's critical to set expectations before the work starts. The ethical standards should be defined for expectations about how images will be captured and how handled. The pedagogical standards will address ways of capturing and editing and integrating the images for high learning value. Cultural standards define what images may be captured and portrayed, without offense. Domain-specific standards require an awareness of how imagery is used in a domain field and in-field conventions. Aesthetic standards deal with issues of brand and artistry. Stylebook standards define the fundamentals of image size (dpi, cropping), technological outputs, and other factors.

Planning correctly may save plenty of trouble later on. Cobbling on massive changes later on in the development cycle may be costly in time and frustrations. Indeed, there should be flexibility in adjusting the standards as the project progresses.

Ethical Standards

Ethical standards refer to the values applied to the decision-making in terms of how truth is represented, legal permissions are attained, information is vetted, and the effects of the digital imagery are planned. Ethics also affects how contributors to a project are treated and rewarded for their endeavors.

Truth Representation

- How may truth be depicted in imagery?
- How will images be captured in lawful ways? What are the laws that might apply?
- How may images be edited without corrupting the original information and meanings?
- In setting up dramatizations or fictionalized scenes, what ethical guidelines should be followed for representing truth?

Legal Permissions

- Do those taking photos have permission to capture the images from the people in the photo?
- Do those capturing images have permission to be on private property?
- Do those capturing images represent correctly what the images will be used for?
- How are privacy rights respected?
- How may intellectual property rights be upheld?
- How may the images be made accessible per federal law?
- What sort of "informed consent" should be created for people involved in imagery?

Maintaining Informational Value

- How are the images provenanced? What were the situational details of their capture?
- How will users know the history of the images as informational or educational artifacts?
- How are chains of custody followed to avoid corruption of the images?

Responsible Effects

- How may the images be created so as to first "do no harm"? How can image creators not release sensitive information or information that may have negative consequences?
- How may emotional or cognitive manipulation of people be avoided?
- How may mistaken ideas stemming from digital images be avoided?
- How are people depicted to maintain their dignity? How are representations of people made to avoid stereotypes?

Crediting

- How may those who captured or created the images be properly credited?

Pedagogical Standards

Pedagogical standards consider the educational strategies applied to a particular curriculum or digital imagery build.

- What educational standards must be upheld with the images?
- What information do the images have to contain?
- What sorts of annotations will enhance the learning?
- What sorts of accompanying learning objects need to be built around the images for effective learning?
- How may images have explanatory value?
- Will the images be stand-alone or part of a larger learning context? In either situation, how are the images strengthened to contribute to the overall learning goals?
- What dimensions (of the 7 defined by Dowhal) should be used to convey particular information and to build knowledge? (Dowhal, 1996)
- Do the images need to be photo-realistic or non-photo-realistic? What are the benefits of each in the learning situation? Which form offers more credibility for the particular context?
- How may negative learning or misconceptions be avoided?

Cultural Standards

Cultural standards address how cultural sensitivities may be addressed in the context of the particular learning domain.

- What images would be considered taboo and offensive? What may not be depicted?
- What are the cultural standards for image acceptability?
- How may popular tastes and values not be offended?
- When should cultural standards be flouted for learning value?

Domain Field Standards

Different learning domains have different professional values in the field. These values may define how valid research is done. These may address paradigmatic understandings. These may laud particular practitioners as exemplars.

- What conventions in the domain field will apply to the image capture?
- Which works are considered high quality standards that may inform future image capture? What aspects of these works show the high quality?

Aesthetic Standards

Artistic or aesthetic values often affect an image capture and processing. Articulating and defining these standards early on will enhance the understandings and work done by the team.

- What aspects of the images will appeal to the human senses of beauty and balance?
- How may the imagery be logically consistent and aligned?
- How may the aesthetic values of the images be enhanced (without compromising the other standards)?
- Will the images be photorealistic or synthetic? Or a mix of realistic and "CG" (computer graphics / computer generated)?
- What are the definitions of beauty in the particular imagistic context?
- How may images be made elegant?
- How are images original and fresh?
- How are images memorable? Attention-getting?
- What tone is being conveyed in the images?
- What back story is being conveyed in immersive alternate reality spaces? How are such stories contexted and internally congruent?
- How may the viewpoint be logical and appropriate? If mixed viewpoints are used, are each justified and value-added?
- How will the various theories of color, shape, design and immersiveness, apply to the designs?
- What sort of branding will be applied to the digital imagery and learning?

Technological Stylebook Standards

Defining technology standards early on is critical given the many ways that images may be created and output. For members of a team to effectively edit the raw digital files and to use the final processed images, they must have interchangeable and portable files with the proper file types.

- What are the technological standards for the image captures?
- What are the technological standards for moving images?
- What are the technological standards for the processed and compressed images?
- What performance benchmarks will be used for 3D? (Scott, Roth, & Rivest, 2003)
- What standards are there for synthetic models and depictions?
- What sorts of annotations and metadata are needed at each step of the processes?
- What naming protocols will be used for the image captures?
- What information will be collected about the sourcing of the images? And why?

Framework for Evaluation

Once standards have been decided by the administration and those on the team, there then needs to be checklists, rubrics, or other devices used to evaluate whether the standards are being met.

Sample Work for Norming

It may also help to create initial sample images for critique, so the team becomes familiar with the instruments for evaluation and for the expected standards. It helps them acclimate to the upper and lower ranges of what is acceptable quality. This process may spawn useful discussions among the team members and may result in richer learning from outside the team. Adjustments may be made to the policies and procedures based on the learning from these experiences.

DEVELOPMENT AND PRODUCTION WORK

Step 6: The Collection of Rich, Raw Materials

Development refers to the pedagogical design and planning of the digital image capture and processing. The production refers to the execution of that work.

The collection of raw images may come from a variety of sources. Extant repositories may offer treasure troves of contents, many that are available through royalty-free copyright releases and open-source availability. Many such images tend to be useful for decorative and branding purposes, but for analytical depth, these may be harder. The challenge with freeware is that the provenance of the images may not be clearly defined or able to be established. The quality controls for these images were set by others, and once a raw image has been captured and compressed, there's much less imagistic manipulation that may be done. To support the digital imagery processing, it's a good idea to maintain continuing awareness of possibly relevant graphics as they come online and are in the public domain or free-use or involve reasonable costs. As with most information, updating is a critical aspect of maintaining quality.

Third-party content providers may also make customized images available. Commercial businesses often offer stock photos and digital video as well.

The self-capture of raw images often means a much clearer provenance (origins of the imagery), direct control of quality, and clearer intellectual property rights establishment. (Not all image captures are copyright-free, depending on what the image depicts. If a person takes a photo of someone else's copyrighted image, the photographer does not have free use to use that derived image.) The point-of-capture is a critical moment in a live situation. New technologies have been evolved to capture spatial, temporal and social contexts at this moment—for automated semantic or metadata annotation of the images (Davis, King, Good, & Sarvas, 2004).

Images in controlled situations like laboratories, studios, and classrooms may be much easier to control than those taken in the outdoors, in unplanned image captures, or where weather, temperatures, lighting, and other factors may cause challenges for capture. Web cams and sensors may capture images in the field. Some capture images continually while others have to be triggered with sufficient informational input to register on the sensor (such as a light amplitude threshold).

High speed image captures, telescope captures, nano-level imagery, and night imagery may also offer challenges to generate high-value images.

In-house capture of images will require the talent to capture images to quality—which means their ability to capture images in the proper contexts, with the proper lighting (for proper color representation), focus, size information, and creation of images to the standards of the domain field. There needs to be effective annotation and documentation of that information. They need to have clear sourcing of each of the images. They must have an awareness of how the capture device (the camera, the scanner, the sensor) may skew the informational capture and to be able to adjust for it in later visual editing. The naming protocols of the images need to be accurate, succinct and informational.

Individuals who work on capture need to practice sensible habits by having the right equipment, spare batteries and image storage devices, and other relevant materials. They need to be able to regularly evaluate their materials in case an image recapture is needed. They need to provide information-rich captures efficiently. The images themselves need to be high-fidelity and useable downstream after processing.

Captures of images may meld multiple sources of information. For example, images may be generated from existing historical digital information as in geospatial repositories.

In the cases where the subject matter expert is the only one who has access to the imagery capture, it may help to have additional trainings on the equipment. Having downloadable sheets of the steps needed in the image capture would be helpful. Also, having live access to a tech consultant by phone, text messaging, or email may enhance the ease of the digital captures.

The technologies for digital image captures are growing in sophistication, with increasing details. There are successful endeavors to capture and view gigapixel images (Kopf, Uyttendaele, Deussen & Cohen, 2007).

Multimedia transcoding involves the use of capturing information from different file formats. Stills may be extracted from digital videos and rendered with high salience, high resolution, and data integrity; these may be captured in an automated, live and high definition image for street surveillance (Teodosio & Bender, 2005). Systems are improving, too, to remove ghosting, noise, and other visual echoes that may detract from the focus of the visuals.

Step 7: Intellectual Property Negotiations, Arrangements and Documentation

Building a project "clean" from the beginning means following all extant laws regarding raw image capture, image processing, image conceptualization and creation, metadata capture, storage and deployment, and use in learning. One critical aspect deals with the ownership and use of images, which falls under the general area of intellectual property (see Figure 3).

A special note should be made about the situations when digital imagery and e-learning contents go "commercial". Once such objects are no longer under the auspices of non-profit, accredited higher educational university use, they will no longer fall under fair use protections under the US Copyright Act, which may mean liabilities for using copyrighted images.

If trademarks or registration marks are used in an image, that should be clearly observed in related annotation, so as to acknowledge that. An image of information that is undergoing a patent process should also be labeled as such, and depictions of patented processes should also be labeled clearly (see Figure 4).

Step 8: Creating the Learning Images

"Beginners don't understand 'less is more.'" – Nicholas Negroponte in *Being Digital* (1995)

Learning imagery differs from generic ones because of the learning value. Images highlight contents for a learning purpose—to explain, to exemplify, to contrast, to encourage analysis, and ultimately, to support decision-making. "The idea is to make designs that enhance the richness, complexity, resolution, dimensionality, and clarity of the content" (Tufte, 1997, pp. 9 – 10). These are images with utility. Images also support memory retention. They may concretize elusive concepts. They may offer evidentiary proof of particular phenomena. They may feed mental models of complex relationships and interactions.

Optimally, learning images would be co-developed with the e-learning course materials. Images may be created prior to the curricular build, or as an afterthought if unanticipated course build funds are available. It's important to note that digital images contribute to overall learning and works in a

Figure 3. Intellectual Property Checklist

Intellectual Property Checklist

Raw Image Capture

❑ Do those capturing or generating the images have rights releases to copy something which may involve intellectual property value?

Image Processing

❑ Have all raw digital materials been clearly provenanced and ownership established (and copyright releases attained) before use?

Image Conceptualization and Creation

❑ If a certain branding or style is being emulated, do the creators have the permissions of whomever may own copyright?

Metadata Capture

❑ Do the metadata captures properly represent true copyright and ownership of the image?
❑ If images have been combined, is the copyright clear about which part originated where?

Storage and Deployment

❑ Is there accurate registration of the copyright for the image?
❑ If the images are deployed for use by others, are there clear guidelines and restrictions for the image use?
❑ Is there clear crediting if the digital imagery is shared?

Uses in Learning

❑ Is there a clear intellectual property policy that encourages users of the images in the course or training to respect the IP rights of others?
❑ Are the images properly and clearly labeled in terms of ownership?
❑ Are there provisions made for fair use?

cumulative way. Having an over-arching pedagogical plan for image use and creation will be a critical aspect of learning. The integration of images into a learning flow also may enhance their effectiveness. The learning context is a critical aspect. Even a brief "economic modeling" approach of depicting what would be needed in a sketch, prototype or storyboard may be helpful. These brief approaches generally do not require deep detail or fidelity.

Editing and Annotation

The simplest level of imagery processing involves image editing and annotation. Image editing aims to de-noise or remove irrelevant visual data. These eliminate elements that may upstage the learner focus or the learning value of the contents. Unintended visual effects—like rosette or moiré patterns, interference patterns from cross-hatching, screen wire effects—need to be removed, particularly if the images will be used in print form and may carry these unintended patterning. Text may be anti-aliased, or smoothed of the stair-step jaggedness of curved lines. Images may have information airbrushed, or relevant elements may be pulled out or highlighted.

Figure 4. Evolving raw contents into digital imagery for e-learning (an overview of some IP considerations)

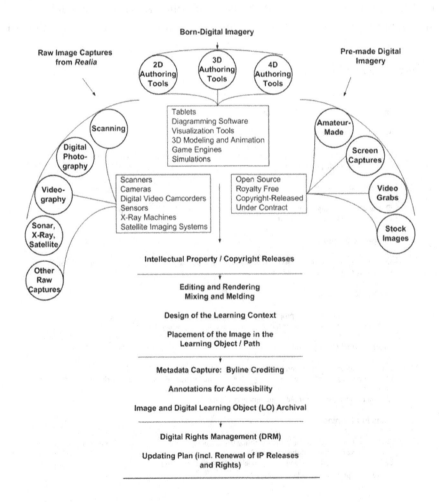

Labeling and captioning control for viewer misunderstandings. Written well, these explanations infuse photos with cognitive value beyond the sensory and affective. Substantive information should be as high profile as the images themselves, with back-end annotations stored invisibly. This informational hierarchy adds value to users' understanding of the imagery. For many learning situations, having a repository of such images is sufficient for samples for learning. For others, these may be integrated into discussions on discussion boards. These may be used to evoke scenarios in case studies. Or many of these may be used for a photo-realistic simulation or branched logic decision-making by learners in an automated learning situation.

Adjusting for Accuracy

Scale is an important aspect of many images, particularly in the hard sciences. Self-representing scales define sizes based on the contexts and relationships to other objects in a scene. Photo captures may be integrated with diagrams or map overlays, for composite images. They may be combined with other types of visuals for value-added combinations and glyphs. Users of images need a clear sense of orientation (Which way is true north? Which way is up and down? How do the elements in the image relate to each other? What is the depth field of the view? The breadth? The volumetric data? What is the larger context?) and spatial relationships.

Imagery annotation will play a critical role in the processing of digital imagery for e-learning. Images often need elaboration—through informative legends, informational overlays, proper notations, metadata captures, and captioning. In 3D and 4D digital imagery, there may be textual narratives to add accessibility and value to the scenes and immersive experiences.

Artificial Overlays

Illustrations may be informative and involve clear design artificiality—with superimposed images, overlays, filters, color effects, and textual data. Illustrations may be abstract and theoretical. One main design principle is to create clarity with the glyph; another is to avoid excessive information or a data-dump.

Information Salience

Because of people's limited abilities to intake and process information, there has to be a high selectivity of relevant information to focus the learning through design cues. Informational salience plays a major role in people focusing on what is relevant and not forming incorrect conclusions. The presented imagery needs to active the correct prior knowledge for proper future learning (Albers, 2007, pp. 80 – 86). If people's prior knowledge about a topic is incorrect, it would be better for them to have had no prior knowledge than incorrect initial priming (Lipson, 1982; Recht and Leslie, 1988, as cited in Albers, 2007, p. 83).

Interactivity

Imagery may be created into image maps that may involve low-level interactivity. Here, certain parts of the image link to further information or visual effects. 3D imagery may be handled by learners for multi-layered views or different angles. One example would include digital crystals that may be viewed from various perspectives. Glyphs may offer interactive access to the effects that come from adjusting various inputs like locale, time, and other factors.

Remixes

Visualization conventions will affect how the images may be remixed for learning values. "Our examples have inventoried all sorts of design strategies that collate like with like: pairing, orientation, simultaneity, overlap, superimposition, flowing together on a common track, codes, pointer lines, sequence, adjacency, analogy, similar content. Parallelism provides a coherent architecture for organizing and learning from images—as well as from words and numbers, the allies of images. And by establishing a structure of rhythms and relationships, parallelism becomes the poetry of visual information" (Tufte, 1997, p. 103).

Relating Visuals to Each Other

An important aspect of learning may relate to the relationships between digital images. Series of panels—in diptychs, triptychs and even more complex combinations—may show sequencing, implied contrasts and relationships. There may be echoes between the images. Visual concepts may be intensified or amplified. Visual motifs may be repeated through parts of the learning experience. Images may create a sense of "situated cognition" to place learners mentally into a particular learning context.

Processing Agent Personalities and Behaviors

Pedagogical agents, whether photo-realistic or not, may communicate personality and promote help-seeking in the e-learning. Avatars may be designed to create a sense of automated interactivity and camaraderie in e-learning; their design may not only involve surface features but deep personality pieces and even the choreography of movements and animations. Series of 2D images may be evolved into a 3D experience.

Virtual crowds may be created using "body envelopes" that are then imbued with unique heads, hands and feet to simulate individuality. Crowd behaviors may be coded in immersive spaces for particular macro effects as well as close-up interactions with human avatars.

Created Backgrounds and Immersive Spaces

Digital video may be enriched with editing, sound, and inserted sequences and still slides. Video shot on green screens may be placed on top of imaginary or photo-realistic backgrounds. Digital simulated background effects may also be used, to highlight the focus on the principal figure(s).

Digital universes (often coded with physical impossibilities) may be created in immersive 3D spaces, with embedded digital visuals. Here, objects may act without gravitational pull, for example.

Real-world imagery may be used as patterns for hypotheticals. Points of interest may be pulled out and integrated onto blank backgrounds. These may be used as information-gathering for more complex projects for students. Digital imagery may have value in various stages of rough development, depending on their learning application.

The aesthetic aspects of an immersive build should not encourage learners to lose their critical distance. Ludologist Gonzalo Frasca (2004) argues that dominant versions of immersion are Aristotelian and that video games are dominated by this perspective. In his view: "*One of the biggest problems of Aristotelian poetics, as explained by such theorists as Bertolt Brecht, is that spectators get immersed in the stories and lose their critical distance from what is happening on the stage or screen...this effect is seen as narcotic only by authors whose intentions go further than simple entertainment and want to trigger critical thinking in their audience—for educational, social and / or political reasons*" (Frasca 2004: 87, as cited in Dovey & Kennedy, 2006, pp. 9 - 10).

Building Rich Learning through Augmentation

Image captures in their various forms may be insufficient to portray the full complexity of the learning situation in reality. To mitigate for the gaps in information, it may help to build materials around the actual capture (see Figure 5). R.J. Spiro, B.P. Collins and A. Ramchandran advise: "If the goal is presenting complexity as it naturally occurs in order that learners may acquire knowledge of that complexity, then video is obviously a big step forward. Can video present full complexity? Obviously not. Can a fuller presentation of complexity be approximated? Yes. Is one camera angle too limiting? Add another. Still too limiting? Add more. Provide auxiliary material not captured on video. Add commentaries from different perspectives" (2007, pp. 94 – 95).

Figure 5. A screen capture of the back end of a visually rich automated learning module (Screen Shot of Lyra™, courtesy of Dr. Howard W. Beck, 2007)

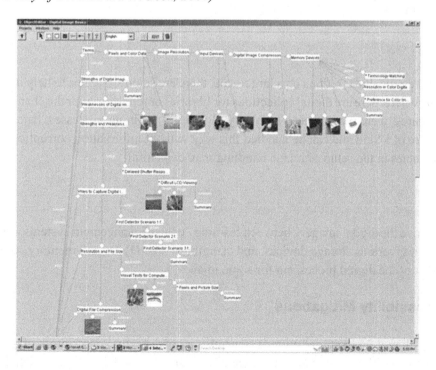

Avoiding Information Lossiness

Throughout the processing, while there may be some lossiness of visual information from the file compression, the process should help focus the learning value of each image. There should also be retention of the sourcing and intellectual property (IP) information.

Hidden Annotations and Encapsulation of some Visual Information

And hidden annotations may also be helpful for information-rich use by researchers, faculty, staff and students. Purposeful "encapsulation" (the hiding of irrelevant or distracting or extraneous elements) of some visual information from users may also be helpful to enhance focus.

Standards and Stylebook Guidelines

The team building the digital images may refer to the stylebook and standards to know when a particular image is complete. Others may use a sample or template as a guide. Analyzing images to read for the sub-text and point-of-view for objectivity and neutrality may be important.

The Protection of Raw Imagery

The raw images should always be protected because it is information-rich. If new edits and outputs are needed somewhere down the line, having these will protect the original capture work. Also, digital images may corrupt, so having a back-up copy of the raw and the processed images will be helpful to protect the investment.

Scaling Up

If the image processing must be done on a large scale, there are some strategies to help individuals scale up. In situations where there are digital collections for libraries or repositories or the changeover of *realia* into digital captures, there may need to be plenty of images. Defining processes, batch processing of images (if they're of a kind and can be handled this way without information corruption and loss), and planning efficiencies in the setup of image handling may be helpful.

Portability

The ability to move the digital imagery between learning / course management systems, digital libraries, digital repositories, various storage devices, and "tangibles" like DVDs and memory sticks, will be an important aspect of the digital processing for some images.

Step 9: Accessibility Mitigations

Accessibility in digital imagery and visuals generally involve textual descriptors of still visuals (alt text), the labeling of table cells for informational clarity, and sequential and detail-rich descriptions of live motion and interactivity in immersive visuals. A critical aspect is understanding what is relevant for learners.

Color contrasts of created illustrations should be sufficient for those with color blindness issues. Particular colors which do not register with those who have color acuity challenges should be avoided.

ASSESSMENT AND REVISION

Step 10: Alpha and Beta Testing / Revision, Editing and Metadata Labeling

Alpha testing typically refers to in-house testing before a curriculum goes live. This involves an analysis of all the links and technologies linked to the e-learning. Beta testing brings in users for further testing once there's a clean bill for the alpha testing stage. The following are some questions to consider when building an alpha test and a beta test for the images and e-learning. The standards decided on by the team should be used for the alpha and beta testing.

Sample Alpha Questions:

- Do all the links work?
- Does the interactivity work?
- Are the images able to be manipulated by viewers?
- Do the images work in the various browsers?
- Are the images rendering properly?
- Are the images clearly labeled?
- Is the metadata easy to find for each image?
- Does each image contribute to the quality of the learning?
- Are the images accessible?
- Are the images legally created?
- Do the images contravene ethical standards?

Sample Beta Questions:

- How do learners engage with the images?
- What is the quality of the e-learning?
- Are there strategies to improve the capture, processing and deployment of the images?

Metadata Labeling

After the alpha and beta testing comes the revision and editing of the images. Once the images have been finalized, the final metadata captures need to be done. There are no widely accepted standards for the preservation, provision or communication of the provenance of information. The speed of digital imagery creation may " quickly exceed their ability to track how it was created" (Lanter, 1990, as cited in Bose & Frew, 2005, p. 5). This means that more attention must be paid to the development of the resources with proper metadata labeling.

It would help to decide what metadata systems to use, such as Dublin Core or IEEE LOM. Many projects will base a metadata scheme on one of the main ones but will add fields for labeling that may be special to the particular learning situation or domain field. Others use a combination of metadata systems to meet the various needs of a variety of different users.

Metadata supports data quality; it also supports the shareability and re-usability of digital imagery via repositories and learning / course management systems (L/CMSes). "While metadata may be a technical necessity, recent studies of data quality, decision theory and knowledge management suggest it has significant business implications as well," suggest Shankaranarayanan and Even, Feb. 2006, p. 90). These authors highlight the importance of organizations not creating metadata islands that are fragmented and disconnected (p. 91). Centralized oversight over metadata policies is critical for an organization, they suggest (p. 92).

LAUNCH AND FUTURE PLANNING

Step 11: Deployment for Learning and Archival

The next step in the image creation cycle is to launch the materials for learning. There are a number of vehicles that may be used for this—such as learning / course management systems, course cartridges, tangibles, wireframes for planning, and repositories. Some images may be archived, whether for internal access and use or even public deployment. Gallery sites may be publicly available. Ontologies built around databases may capture data values (entities) and data structures (relationships) (Bertin, 1977, as cited in Ware, 2004, p. 23). These often have nodes and connectors, with nodes representing entities and the connectors representing relationships. Some 3D images may be bound to a particular proprietary immersive space, but these are starting to be able to be ported out to 3D repositories.

The digital imagery should have clear copyright ownership. If a team worked on an image, it may be too much to track the versioning of the evolving imagery and to assign ephemeral partial copyright credits for certain phases and contributions, but that may be helpful if there are ever future disagreements over the lineage or ownership of a digital image.

Beyond the structure of image archival is the issue of digital rights management (DRM), or the protection of the intellectual property of the images. Technology systems may offer various ways to protect images by not making them downloadable, embedding watermarks (and sending spiders out to capture any versions of digital imagery hosted on others' servers above the authentication layers), capturing IP addresses for those downloading images, and others. There may be file protections based on user identifications. And some files may be programmed to be unreadable after a certain day. However, for the various technologies used to protect images, there are others that may be used to gain unauthorized access. Persistent identifiers may be assigned to particular resources for easier location and reference.

Protecting digital imagery may involve creating multiple versions in different file formats and also in protecting the raw original images, with annotations about the work.

Works that are shared via open source should be output in ways that are accessible and portable on and off of different systems. The copyright releases should be clearly spelled out, and the proper digital rights management should be applied in the service of enforcing those rights. And there should be clear records kept of where works are deployed to and where content is housed. These should be checked regularly for live linking and accuracy. And if changes are made to the locations of various resources, it'll be important to back-track to all the links that connect to that digital object to correct the paths. Many builders of digital contents are hesitant to build for interoperability and reusability because of the extra costs in production (Berlanga & Garcia, Oct. 2005, pp. 190 – 201). Reusability requires that the objects be easily identifiable, so potential users may assess their value relative to their own learning needs. Identifiability may also refer to the clear labeling of the different versions of a digital learning object as it evolves over time. Transferability refers to the ease with which the digital contents may be moved between repositories and learning/course management systems (L/CMSes), sites, and computer-mediated communications systems. Portable objects are easy-to-move. The "usability" of digital learning objects refers to their ease-of-use in different circumstances by different users. A sub-set of usability involves accessibility or the widest possible use of a digital learning object for people who are differently abled in terms of visual, mental, and auditory functioning as well as physical range-of-motion mobility.

Step 12: Planning an Update Cycle

All information dates out. Over time, it becomes less relevant, less engaging. It may also be less applicable to the domain field. Depending on the turnover cycle of such images, it may help to determine an update cycle for the imagery.

Planning Digital Imagery Updates

- Have there been central changes to the domain field?
- Are new models and paradigms available?
- Have the authoring tools for digital objects been updated? Have file types been updated? Are there new technologies for design that would add value to the learning?
- Have new relevant knowledge and contents come online?
- Are there new types of raw imagery that would be relevant?

Having an audit trail of the sequential steps taken in creating digital imagery will be helpful for data quality and for future building onto the image. Deviations from this general approach should be recorded, for a sense of awareness, easier transfer of work to other team members, and smoother workflow. Different teams or organizations may find that adjustments need to be made to this workflow, with an emphasis on some phases more than others. There may be some step dependencies that do not apply to the particular work, and those may be omitted.

CONCLUSION

Teams that would build quality and applicable e-learning images clearly need to do plenty of front-end collaborative standards discussions, decision-making, and planning; they need to be flexible enough to make changes as they proceed in their work. This chapter provides an overview of the general work required from concept to raw image capture to content creation to deployment.

REFERENCES

Albers, M. J. (2007). Information salience and interpreting information. In *Proceedings of the SIGDOC '07*, ElPaso, TX, USA (pp. 80-85). New York: ACM.

Berlanga, A. J., & Garcia, F. J. (2005). Authoring tools for adaptive learning designs in computer-based education. In *Proceedings of the CLIHC '05*, Cuernavaca, Mexico (pp. 190-201). New York: ACM.

Bose, R., & Frew, J. (2005). Lineage retrieval for scientific data processing: A survey. *ACM Computing Surveys, 37*(1), 5. doi:10.1145/1057977.1057978

Brami, R. (1997). Icons: A unique form of painting. *Interaction, 4*(5), 15–28. doi:10.1145/264044.264046

Clark, R. C., & Mayer, R. E. (2003). *E-Learning and the Science of Instruction.* San Francisco: Pfeiffer, John Wiley & Sons.

Davis, M., King, S., Good, N., & Sarvas, R. (2004). From context to content: Leveraging context to infer media metadata. In *Proceedings of the MM '04*, New York (pp. 188-195).

Dovey, J., & Kennedy, H. W. (2006). *Game Cultures: Computer Games as New Media.* New York: Open University Press.

Dowhal, D. (1996). A seven-dimensional approach to graphics. In Proceedings of the SIGDOC '96 (pp. 149-160). New York: ACM.

Hackman, J. R. (2002). *Leading Teams: Setting the Stage for Great Performances.* Boston: Harvard Business School Press.

Kenworthy, J. (2006). Simulations—Bridging from thwarted innovation to disruptive technology. *Developments in Business Simulation and Experiential Learning, 33*, 149–158.

Kim, J.-W., Oh, J.-O., Jeong, C.-H., & Kim, J.-H. (2004). 3D graphics accelerator platform for mobile devices. In [Washington, DC: IEEE.]. *Proceedings of the ICFPT, 2004*, 387–390.

Kopf, J., Uyttendaele, M., Deussen, O., & Cohen, M. F. (2007). Capturing and viewing gigapixel images. *ACM Transactions on Graphics, 26*(3).

Scott, W. R., Roth, G., & Rivest, J.-F. (2003). View planning for automated three-dimensional object reconstruction and inspection. *ACM Computing Surveys, 35*(1), 64–96. doi:10.1145/641865.641868

Shankaranarayanan, G., & Even, A. (2006). The metadata enigma. *Communications of the ACM, 49*(2), 88–94. doi:10.1145/1113034.1113035

Spiro, R. J., Collins, B. P., & Ramchandran, A. (2007). Reflections on a post-Gutenberg epistemology for video use in ill-structured domains: Fostering complex learning and cognitive flexibility. In R. Goldman, R. Pea, B. Barron, & S. J. Derry (Eds.), *Video Research in the Learning Sciences* (pp. 94-95). Mahwah, NJ: Lawrence Erlbaum Associates, Publishers.

Teodosio, L., & Bender, W. (2005). Salient stills. *ACM Transactions on Multimedia Computing . Communications and Applications, 1*(1), 16–36.

Tufte, E. R. (1997). *Visual Explanations: Images and Quantities, Evidence and Narrative.* Cheshire, CT: Graphics Press.

Ware, C. (2004). Foundation for a science of data visualization. In *Information Visualization:Perception for Design* (2ⁿᵈ ed.). San Francisco: Morgan Kaufmann Publishers.

Weiskopf, D. (2004). On the role of color in the perception of motion in animated visualizations. In *Proceedings of the IEEE Visualization.* Washington, DC: IEEE.

KEY TERMS AND DEFINITIONS

Abstract (adj): Non-figurative, theoretical, elusive; difficult to understand

After-Image (n): A visual sensation retained by the retina of the eye after the original image has disappeared

Airbrush (v): To alter an original image using digital editing devices

Amplitude Threshold (n): The point at which there is sufficient informational input to register on a sensor

Animation (n): An image that involves movement or the simulation of life and activity

Anti-Aliasing (n): The act of smoothing the stair-step jaggedness of curved or diagonal lines for a smoother appearance

Augmentation (n): An add-on or addition to improve the learning experience or clarity of a digital visual

Body Envelopes (n): Virtual human figures without heads, hands or feet

Economical Modeling (n): A design approach that depicts only what will be needed in a sketch or prototype, without unnecessary detail

Encapsulation (n): The hiding of information into a particular instructional design build, to avoid confusion or distraction of learners

Figurative (adj): Based on a likeness or shape

Glyph (n): A visual that displays one or more data variables

Instructional Design (n): The purposive creation of digital learning materials, assignments, syllabi, e-learning paths and learning programs based on a number of pedagogical factors (and often instructional design models)

Lossiness (n): The degradation of an image or the loss of visual data through editing and outputting in different forms

Memorandum of Agreement (MOA): A formal, contractual writing that defines the work that will be accomplished within a certain defined budget and timeframe

Memorandum of Understanding (MOU): A formal, contractual writing that defines the work that will be accomplished within a certain defined budget and timeframe

Moiré (adj): An interference pattern of dots

Node (n): A hub, a center point, an intersection of connected contents

Norming (n): Establishing a quality standard through collaborative evaluative efforts

Photo-Realistic (adj): An image that is based off of a photograph, something derived from a photograph and such realism

Rosette (adj): An unobtrusive circle of dots formed in color separations by the arrangement of the color plates at different angles; an undesirable visual effect

Synthetic (adj): Artificial, created digitally without necessarily drawing from real-world imagery

Transcoding (n): Translating digital information (such as imagistic data) into different computer languages

Volumetric (adj): Related to measurement by volume (a mass or quantity)

Wireframe (n): A design tool used to visualize Web site development, with functions, navigational structures and contentsy

Chapter 8
Building Interactive and Immersive Imagery

ABSTRACT

The influence of immersive gaming and simulations on e-learning cannot be understated. While there has been some successful harnessing of interactivity and immersive spaces for e-learning, more awareness of related fundamentals may enhance e-learning. This chapter discusses the role of graphics in interactivity (live and automated) and immersion and strategies for creating effective interfaces, virtual spaces, contexts, agents, and 3D digital learning objects.

CHAPTER OBJECTIVES

- Define people-to-people and automated interactivity in the e-learning context
- Explore examples of interactivity in the e-learning context
- Define the "Z-axis" or immersiveness in the e-learning context
- Explore examples of immersiveness in the e-learning context (including ubiquitous immersion)
- Investigate a continuum of types of immersion in e-learning
- Discuss ways to set up, facilitate and debrief immersive e-learning
- Offer ways to evaluate immersive e-learning
- Explore the uses of live and automated imagery in interactive and immersive spaces
- Consider various image strategies in interactivity and immersiveness

INTRODUCTION

Some of the most complex digital imagery stems from interactive and immersive imagery. Digital imagery offers functionalities well beyond print in terms of interactivity and immersive experiential learning.

DOI: 10.4018/978-1-60566-972-4.ch008

Experiential learning exists in a cycle, with the individual first experiencing the event or set of events. That event is reinforced through the description and sharing of the event and observations from it. The events are interpreted, and relationships between the elements in that experience are formed. The learner then develops generalizations of the event and relates that experience to both the past and the future. Next, the individual prepares for the next experiences and determines how he or she may approach the future events differently (Jacques, 1985, as cited in Gredler, 1992).

Interactivity refers to the learners engaging with artificial intelligence robots; live communications and interactions with real people; branching simulations with particular actions and decisions expected of learners. Immersion involves full-sensory engagement (sight and sound inputs) in digital environments. Here, learners may be "disembodied" but enabled through avatars in multi-faceted, creative multiverses. To echo Isaac Newton's "Clockwork Universe" idea, some game designers create immersive digital universes with certain physics engine codes and then let it run with minimal inference—so participants in the immersive spaces engage each other without a larger game creator presence.

Immersiveness indicates the experiential engagement with three-dimensional environments that encompass and surround a user, with multiple sensory details. To enhance situated cognition, such spaces are used for social learning, systems learning, and open-ended self-discovery learning. Simulations may be actualized in immersive spaces:

Simulations find application in training, decision-making and research in science, education and a vast number of applied areas, such as national defense, ecology, manufacturing and economic forecasting. Sometimes simulations are cost effective substitutes for hands on experience, but increasingly they are used to facilitate decision-making and applied or theoretical research (Doubleday & Kurtz, Oct. 2004, p. 145).

Non-immersiveness may be used to describe some types of virtual reality that are partially virtual (Slater, Howell, Steed, Pertaub, Gaurau, & Springel, 2000).

INTERACTIVITY IN E-LEARNING

Interactivity may be human-facilitated and social (between people), or it may be automated and delivered by a computing machine. It may be live and synchronous, or it may be asynchronous. Interactivity may form just a portion of a curriculum, or interactivity may involve the whole learning. Interactivity offers opportunities to customize learning to individual users. It also offers strategies to make the learning engaging.

The goals from an interactive learning environment may involve the following, according to Barker (1994),

knowledge acquisition, skill development, skill rehearsal, problem solving and self-realization. Some things he suggests designers should consider to achieve these outcomes include: the learning theory mix; instructional position mix; machine character mix; environmental factors; mode of use; locus of control; extent of instructor intervention; aesthetic features; content; and role of technology (as cited in Withers, Aug. 8, 2005, p. 23).

Some Types of People-to-People Interactivity

The enhancement of Net-enabled real-time and asynchronous communications has improved people's abilities to communicate through distance and time. Studies have explored the effects of virtuality on people's communications and their qualities of interactions, and these have found that some live personas have little overlap with the real-life identities, and people tend to be more aggressive online than in real life. Anonymity provides more of a sense of individual agency for people to self-reveal only as much as they want (Raybourn, 2003).

For complex and innovative learning, human-based interactivity may be expressed in case analysis:

Case-based teaching has a constructivist and experiential approach to learning. The main advantages according to literature are that students: 1) Acquire knowledge when they analyze the case. 2) Actively discuss it with peers. 3) Increase understanding of ill-structured and complex situations. 4) Bring practice into the classroom relating the case to own work-experience (Colbert, Desberg & Trumble 1996, Mauffette-Leenders, Erskine & Leenders 1997, as cited in Orngreen, Feb. 2004, p. 168).

There may be role-playing, decision-making scenarios, desktop team-coordination exercises, live simulations. Live human mentoring may add value to e-learning by providing tailored motivation (Ahdell & Andresen, Mar. 9, 2001). Peer-to-peer learning for collaborative interactivity may result in powerful problem-solving and innovations, with a rich social dimension (Houle 1996, as cited in Thomas, 2001). The participants in a participatory simulation often bring the rich learning and open-ended outcomes to some simulation experiences. Through reflection and dialogue with other learners, the actual learning will occur (Levin, 2003).

Human-based interactivity may be used in distributed problem-based learning, where an instructional problem draws on the experiences of individuals to richer learning. "The analysis and study of this problem comprises several phases that are spread over periods of group work and individual study" (Barrows & Tamblyn, 1980; Evensen & Hmelto, 2000; Schmidt, 1983, as cited in Ip & Naidu, 2001, p. 6).

Simulations have been described as a kind of "interactive pretending" (Prensky, 2004) that allow for practice learning in a discovery-oriented environment (Galarneau, 2004, p. 5). Taylor and Walford (1978, p. 7) describe simulations by three features: a taking on of roles by participants; experiential consequences from their actions, and a monitoring of these results and an ensuing reflection on their decisions and consequences (Schönwald, Euler, Angehrn, & Seufert, 2006, p. 14).

Practices for "cyclical content" may be revamped for visual variations for learning that is mapped to a specific "real" activity and often consists of plenty of practice. "The brave, new world of e-learning will be predicated on our ability to build engaging, realistic scenarios that enable discovery learning," observes one author (Wilkinson, 2004, p. 214). Self-discovery learning theoretically involves plenty of investment in the build on the front end but less effort in maintaining the learning over time. Different types of learning may be connected to simulations: directed learning, self-directed learning, and collaborative learning (Babich, Senk, & Mavrommatis, 2005, p. 2).

Traditionally, simulation games have been thought of as contrived situations without direct real-life consequences (Thiagarajan & Stolovitch, 1978). The "game conceit" was that the rules of play suspended the real world for a time, and the play happened in a "magic circle" (Huizinga, as cited in Bartle, 2006, p. 34). Further, games are supposed to be inconsequential and irrelevant to the larger world

(Castronova, 2005). The feelings of play in a digital game or simulation create feelings of "tension, joy, and the consciousness that it is 'different' from ordinary life'" (Huizinga, 1955, p. 28, as cited in Dovey & Kennedy, 2006, p. 24). The play itself may be relatively risk-free. However, the learning from these spaces is supposed to carry on in near- and far-transfer learning in the real world, with potentially serious implications. The use of such games now in higher education and training for learning belies these traditionalist ideas.

Human-centered learning environments draw on constructivist and social constructivist learning theories. "Common characteristics of technology-enhanced constructivist learning environments include cognitive and collaborative tools, various types of scaffolding (conceptual, procedural, metacognitive coaching), and access to resources, models, and exemplars (Hannifin et al, 1999; Jonassen, 1999). A critical asset of constructivist learning environments is that students are provided with opportunities for interacting within and upon the environment Johnson & Johnson, 1996). The theoretical assumption is that learners construct understandings by interacting with information, tools, and materials, as well as by collaborating with other learners" (Dickey, 2005, p.441). "Simulation games provide an effective tool for affective growth—the areas of feelings, emotions, attitudes, beliefs, and values. Simulation games help participants gain empathy for real-life decision makers and provide gut-level referents to abstract words" (Thiagarajan & Stolovitch, 1978, p. 60).

People may engage in problem-solving via goal-based scenarios (GBS). These scenarios are "essentially simulations in which there is a problem to resolve, or a mission to complete, require learners to assume the main role in the resolution of the problem or the pursuit of their mission" (Schank, 1997; Schank, 1990, as cited in Ip & Naidu, 2001, p. 2).

Knowledge-building communities may spring up around multi-object oriented domains. "These communities provide opportunities for peer role models, open classrooms and role reversal, and the presence of an appreciative audience amongst the community. Riner's (1996) research of educational MOOs further supports many of Bruckman's findings. According to Riner (1996), educational MOOs promote an interactive style of learning, opportunities for collaboration, and meaningful engagement across time and space, both within and across classrooms" (Dickey, 2005, p. 440).

Some Types of Automated Interactivity

Automated interactivity may range from formula-based and simplistic to complex computational modeling, which point to complex conceptual frameworks and knowledge schemas.

Rhodes and Azbell (1985) created three levels of interactivity: reactive (with low learner control of the content structure), co-active (with some learner control over "sequence, pace and style"), and proactive (with learner control over structure and content. Another model focuses on the levels of interaction based on "the instructional quality of the interaction" in terms of effects on cognitive processing (Sims, 1995, after Schwier & Misanchuk's model, as cited in Ahdell & Andresen, Mar. 9, 2001, pp. 60 - 61). This model considers user abilities to manipulate objects and the trajectory of the learning. Here, learners receive performance support via messages and tutorial systems. There's also a strong feedback loop that is responsive to user input. Users receive "reflective interactivity" or feedback from former users or experts. "Hyperlinked interactivity" allows learners to access the Internet. "Non-immersive contextual interactivity" combines interactive elements into a "complete virtual training environment," and "immersive virtual interactive" puts learners fully into virtual spaces (Ahdell & Andresen, 2001, pp. 60 - 61).

One aspect of user feedback that may be helpful may involve reflection of their own performance by giving them control over saving and restoring their particular state of the simulation. They should be able to annotate their own play to focus attention (Thomas, 2001, pp. 7 - 8).

The more complex the simulation, the more important it is to offer high-value feedback to learners. "But with sophisticated large-scale simulations where the stakes are high, participant interaction and collaboration are focal points. The participants must have a time and a place to interact, exchange ideas and synthesize their experiences. 'You can't simply put a full-scale experiential learning experience up on a learning management system platform by itself and expect it to be effective,' says Billhardt" (Boehle, 2005, n.p.). Feedback will be critical to head off misconceptions from the learning (Alexander and Judy, 1988). Optimally, personalized feedback may be the richest type but also the most challenge to design (Summers, 2004).

Thomas suggests that meaningful interactivity must go beyond navigating contents; he suggests that simulations and models encapsulate the best examples of complex and meaningful interactivity currently: "Such applications model a real or theoretical system, allowing users to manipulate input variables to change the system behaviour and view the results. With such applications, learners can construct and test hypotheses and receive feedback as a result of their actions. There are great benefits to the learner if a static image such as a diagram in a textbook is replaced with a simulation" (Thomas, 2001, p. 3). Shared simulations between learners and facilitators and tutors may enhance "group experiential learning," the exploration of multiple perspectives, and collaboration around alternate views (Thomas, 2001, p. 4). Simulations are seen as promoting transferability of learning into analogous situations as it is a model of reality (Greenblatt, as cited in Thiagarajan & Stolovitch, 1978).

The degree and quality of interactivity are critical for meaningful interaction (Bork, 1992, as cited in Ahdell & Andresen, 2001). The interactions need to engage the total learning process to enhance learner motivation. Time needs to be set aside for learning reflection.

Virtual reality has been found to provide support for constructivist learning by engaging learning contents and experiences through a first-person point-of-view.

Research in educational VR reveals that 3D interactive environments provide support for constructivist-based learning activities by allowing learners to interact directly with information from a first-person perspective (Bricken & Byrnes, 1993; Dede, 1995; Winn, 1997). Winn (1993) argues that information taught in schools is often presented as "third-person symbolic experiences," whereas innately, much of how we learn is through first-person nonsymbolic experiences. According to Winn (1993), VR can help bridge the gap between experiential learning and information representation (Dickey, 2005, p. 440).

Augmented reality involves learning in real-spaces in real-time with an overlay of digital information and sensory inputs; augmented reality may mean the inclusion or the omission of sensory data (via sight, smell, taste, touch or hearing). Co-located groups in a shared physical space may collaborate and interact. This allows for more view-dependent, location-sensitive learning. Some augmented reality spaces allow less deterministic ways to interact—with more ludic and user-determined goals that focus on "curiosity, openness and ambiguity" (Feltham, Vetere, & Wensveen, 2007, p. 61), and still others combine various haptic objects and tangible high-tech digital interfaces to promote "inquiry, spontaneity, and causality as children explore the relationships of physical components with their subsequent digital visualizations" (Frederking, Cruz, Baskinger, & Overbeeke, 2008, p.158).

Figure 1. An interactivity continuum in immersive spaces (Hai-Jew, 2009)

Other augmented reality (AR) digital installations combine tangible interfaces with a simulation agent that reflects the users' actions back to them. Research has gone into making wall-size displays more reachable:

Researchers have proposed a variety of interaction techniques to address this issue, such as extending the user's reach (e.g., push-and-throw) and bringing potential targets to the user (drag-and-pop) (Collomb, Hascoët, Baudisch, & Lee, 2005, p. 25).

In one, users move sand (as a haptic surface) around and have the changes in the sand surface reflected digitally on a nearby wall (Seevinck, Candy & Edmonds, 2006, pp. 143 – 150). This experience is designed to be compositional and explorative. Another installation uses the digital space to publicize digital services and materials within the physical space of the library in informative art exhibitions (Grønbæk, Rohde, & Bech-Petersen, 2006, p. 21).

Figure 1, "An Interactivity Continuum in Immersive Spaces" shows the possible ranges of interactivity.

In the continuum above, at the left could be something simple like Java applet games (Blejec, 2003, p. 3). These are focused narrowly and experienced in discrete time segments. "Java applets also are developed using very simplified models in order to illustrate trends, but not up-to-date research results of the type provided by very sophisticated simulators needing several hours or several days of calculations" (Bonnaud, Danto, Bertrand, Lewis, Fouillat & Schrimpf, 2004, p. 372). These are sometimes referred to as mobile code simulations (applets).

The structure of an electronic simulation is a simple one. Underlying the visualization is a model, with code controlling the system behavior. The visualization layer is the learner's view of the system. The underlying model provides input variables to the visualization, and the learner's actions provide "output variables" back to the model, with the actions changing what the learner experiences (Thomas, 2001, p. 10). The interactivity then may fall along a range of manipulating different aspects of the model or interacting with different parts.

At the far right would be immersive continuous learning environments, virtual learning environments, massively multiplayer online role-playing games (MMORPGs pronounced as "mor-pegs") and pervasive simulations.

These may include infrastructure games (infra-games) with immersive environments in which applied multi-stakeholder "pluri-centric" decision-making may occur (Bekebrede, Mayer, van Houten, Chin & Berbraeck, 2005, p. 4). One researcher explains the rationales for these types of simulations: "Infrastructures are essential for our social and economic life. Yet the world of infrastructures is becoming more complex due to changes in technology, policy, and demand and therefore difficult to understand

and manage. Business managers in infrastructure-based industries are facing strategic and operational problems with long-term decision horizon. Public policy makers and politicians are confronted with unexpected effects of their policies of liberalization of the markets and privatization of the utility companies and students and young professionals have problems with getting the big picture and acquiring the necessary professional skills. Therefore managers, policy makers and young professionals need support to understand the complexity of infrastructures and to get the big picture" (Burgos, Tattersall, & Koper, 2005, n.p.)

Some games may be connected with live databases of information for authentic information flow and more effective decision-making (Bekebrede, et al., 2005, pp. 1 – 7). Very sophisticated simulations may involve projections into the future. The look and feel of simulations has been embellished by more polygons and mesh (Dovey & Kennedy, 2006, pp. 53 – 54). Complex imagery may be created with more ease.

Sophisticated Interactivity Tools

The capturing devices for visualizations have become more high-functioning. "Digital computers are powerful tools for studying natural phenomena at large-scales. Nevertheless, custom-made methods have to be developed to digitalize, simulate and finally visualize these phenomena. First, the numerous data of the real-world have to be digitalized to be stored into a computer. Then, as dynamics of large-scale natural phenomena are usually not obvious to understand, computation-based simulation models have to be developed. Finally, Virtual Reality (VR) techniques are better than 3D visualization on conventional computer graphic displays to observe and manipulate real and large-scale data, to compare them with simulation ones. Consequently, in a first interdisciplinary effort, we present some new solutions to design a VR platform for the analysis and simulation of large-scale phenomena. Original digitalization and visualization techniques (in an immersive environment) constitute the main contribution of this paper" (Muzy, Fauvet, Bourdot, Bosseur & Gouinaud, 2005, p. 155).

Some automated interactions involve the use of video realistic speech animation (Ezzat, Geiger, & Poggio, 2002, pp. 388 – 398), which originates with video captures but adds synthetic audio and simulated speech. The initial video capture is enhanced by a multidimensional morphable model "to synthesize new, previously unseen mouth configurations from a small set of mouth image prototypes" and a "trajectory synthesis technique based on regularization, which is automatically trained form the recorded video corpus, and which is capable of synthesizing trajectories in MMM space corresponding to any desired utterance" (Ezzat, Geiger, & Poggio, 2002, p. 388). This system gives the impression of talking to a live human on video. Natural language tools are coded into intelligent tutoring systems.

Emotional agents may be responsive to the users' expressions through "soft controlling" (Gao & Zhang, 2001, p. 1351). Affective computing enables training in social and relational skills. "Much work has been now carried out in the affective computing domain to perform the detection an inference of emotional state detection from physiological correlates, facial expressions, vocal-non-verbal features, verbal speech content, questionnaires or self-report measures and the detection of behavioural events (e.g. mouse-clicking)" (Anolli, Mantovani, Mortillaro, Vescovo, Agliati, Confalonieri, Realdon, Zurloni, & Sacchi, n.d., n.p.).

Image creation authoring tools are widely popular, with different game engines. There are specific tools for unique circumstances, such as rapid 3D insect construction based on insect taxonomy (Buron & Matthews, 2003, n.p.).

Educational Games

Educational games, also known as intelligent learning games (ILGs), are those with a serious purpose—to promote learning. Gameplay—defined by Prensky as "all the activities and strategies game designers employ to get and keep the player engaged and motivated to complete each level and an entire game"—involves "all the doing, thinking and decision making that makes a game either fun or not" (Prensky, 2002, pp. 8 – 9). The game design principle goes: "Make games easy to start, but hard to master" (Raab, 2003, p. 4).

Educational games are built around particular learning objectives. Games involve a range of factors: an environment, non-playable characters, playable characters (with different points-of-view), skill sets, tools, and a rewards structure. Some games are close-ended, with a defined range of action possibilities. The more complex games are open-ended (or with so many possible endings that there's a de facto open-endedness). Empirical studies suggest that learners may not be used to complex and open learning environments and so need instructional supports on how to proceed (Schönwald, Euler, Angehrn, & Seufert, 2006, p. 17). Simulation games in general should involve learning supports for effectiveness: "Given the scarcity of time for formal staff development outside the workplace, the design of the simulation should incorporate substantial 'cognitive scaffolding' so users can learn at their own pace inside and outside of formal training (Bransford, 1993, as cited in Hallinger, 2005, p. 3.2). A learning scaffold serves as a "transitional support strategy or mechanism" (Naidu, 2001, p. 13).

Most games have mixed scales, which refers to the lack of relation between the sizes of real-world objects.

The people in strategy games (such as Rise of Nations™) are smaller than cars, but only half as small. Cities are bigger than cars, but perhaps only five times as big. (This is not just a computer game thing. We also see this in almost all illustrations of the solar system, where a planet's size is scaled to other planets' sizes, their distance to the sun is scaled to the other planets' distances to the sun, but the size and distance to the sun are not scaled to each other) (Aldrich, Learning by Doing, 2005, p. 86).

There's also a mix of scales regarding time, with some events taking a short time and others with extended play time. For example, the many choices of a player may be run through a game or simulation in seconds but represent interchanges that took days or weeks of simulated time. Costs for objects may not have any tie to a real-world economy. Games do not need a sense of "fidelity" or mimetic realism in the way a simulation may require.

Interactive virtual reality "fidelity" may exist in a number of sensory ways. "Much recent and historical research in the field of virtual reality (VR) has focused on the question of how much and what type of fidelity (visual, auditory, haptic, proprioceptive, etc.) we need to maintain between a virtual and real experience in order to enable participants to achieve similar results from their VR experience as they would in reality" (Interrante, Anderson, Ries, O'Rourke, & Gray, 2007, p. 144).

Excessive fidelity may cause learners to get bogged down in the details. Musselwhite suggests that abstract learning concepts should be expressed in abstraction for the simulation, so learners may focus on the bigger issues of the simulation. "If you want to teach highly conceptual content, Musselwhite recommends using a simulation that is a metaphor for what you do, but not identical to it" (Boehle, 2005, n.p.). Educational games may also be modified ("modded") from commercial off-the-shelf games with changed playability and context. This may be augmented with pre-game learning and post-game debriefings.

Virtual Labs

Electronic (or virtual) labs may simulate the work of wetlabs. Remote labs allow distance access to actual live labs to actualize particular functionalities. These offer opportunities to conduct experiments and tests of principles of suppositions. Self-discovery learning in rich lab designs may possibly offer innovative ideas for further research, particularly if this experience is coupled with relevant published information.

The context of laboratories in higher educational learning in particular fields (science and engineering) is critical, to enable learners to test theoretical knowledge in practical situations.

These interactions can involve local, remote or virtual laboratories. In a local laboratory, students operate real devices and manipulate and measure real objects while being directly co-located with the devices and objects in the same room. In a remote laboratory students and devices are at different locations and students work through a computer that is connected online to a real experiment device. Virtual laboratories contain software simulations of experiments and pre-recorded measurements, pictures and videos, possibly as learning objects associated with metadata (Pastor et al. 2003) (Tuttas & Wagner 2001), *but do not manipulate real objects* (Nejdl & Wolpers, 2004).

Critical success factors for virtual laboratories may include the following:

1. Laboratories should be fundamentally investigative, encouraging active learning by actually doing it.
2. Formats used should include active collaboration among students, and between students and lecturers.
3. Laboratories and problem assignments should be based on complex, real-world problems.
4. Exercises and laboratories should inculcate higher order thinking skills, and intellectual maturity (Coman, 2002, n.p.).

The idea is to create these to emulate the real-world labs as closely as possible, with a mix of experiment and theory. In the theoretical hard sciences, simulations may be the only way to illustrate theories. In the applied sciences, there are more down-to-earth goals:

Here it is important to include both the presentation of the characteristic features of the basic phenomenon and the experience of the 'real' experiment (e.g. how to set up a realistic experiment correctly and how to choose and handle the equipment to measure the desired effects) (Jeschke, Richter, Scheel, Seiler & Thomsen, 2001, pp. 1 – 5).

Virtual lab learning is enhanced with extant computer mediated communications tools (Leleve, Prevot, BenMohamed, & Benadi, n.d., n.p.).

If designed and executed well, interactivity may offer a level of situated cognition and learning engagement, and immersiveness may involve even more. The persistence of immersive spaces as continuing networked "games" or 3D social networking sites offers continuity to learners. Many such spaces are designed to enhance longevity (the number of hours that an individual will interact with a game). The ability to move 3D objects off into 3D repositories and to transfer the objects into other immersive spaces will enhance the usefulness of these spaces as continuous learning environments (CLEs). The portability encourages user investment into digitally building these spaces.

THE "Z-AXIS": IMMERSIVENESS IN E-LEARNING

Immersiveness occurs in pervasive spaces, which last more than the length of a simulation or an interactive session. It involves the spatiality of the so-called Z-Axis, which extends into 3D space. It involves virtual spatial perception with a full-wrap experience. 3D games are immersive because of the full-sensory wraps and the "longevity" in play that they encourage. The immersiveness may lead to more learner engagement, but too much information may lead to "channel saturation". Immersion refers to how engaged learners are. Hemphill asks: "How immersed is the user, has she or he lost the sense of self and entered into a state of flow?" and "Does the system make the user feel like he or she is collaborating with a responsive entity?" to understand the depth of the immersion (Hemphill, 2001, p. 35), along with other questions.

Immersive environments must involve convincing terrains, which include an "aerial perspective (atmospheric effects lending a sense of scale), and procedural textures for coloring and modeling appurtenant features such as clouds and water" (Musgrave, 1996, p. 92). Wayfinding strategies for navigating the spaces also are an important part of this virtual experience (Abásolo & Della, 2007), with a focus on lowering the cognitive load of participants. One strategy for making a 3D space more accessible for novice users is to use "humanoid animated" characters to conduct guided tours (Chittaro, Ranon, & Ieronutti, 2003, p. 27). Such immersive spaces often need a high level of "constructability" or the capability of users to easily co-construct within the virtual environment.

Basic components of immersiveness do not only involve the nature of the space and pervasiveness, but these often include complex backstories and histoires to make the learning more engaging and fun.

A-Life

Artificial life (A-life) environments that imitate biological systems are also immersive and are known as massively single player games (where the player engages the immersive designed space without the presence of other human players). "A-life is part of the science of complex systems. A-life scientists use simulations to study evolution and self-organization in large, complex system (Langton, 1989). For example, rather than studying ecosystems through the use of a system of equations, A-life scientists use agent-based models to simulate the organisms and environment "in-silica" (Summers, 2004, p. 235). Biologically inspired artificial intelligence may be brought in for flocking, herding, crowd actions and other such behaviors (Charles, Fyfe, Livingstone, & McGlinchey, 2008). Generic "body envelopes" are created to represent characters, and then unique physical aspects and unique faces may then be created for each one. Code developers discovered emergent patterns out of simple agent behaviors.

Such immersive spaces use physics engines to define the movements and behaviors in-world. Non-playable characters are guided by walking engines, to help them navigate the virtual spaces. Various in-world creatures are guided by back-end codes that generate their behaviors as well as their interactions with other digital life forms online.

Cyber Worlds

Other terms for these alternate digital realities may be the following: microworld, virtual world, MMOR-PG, cyberspace, metaverse, proskenion, hyperstage, synthetic world, authentic learning environments, synthetic environments, and immersive environments (Castronova, 2005, p. 11). These different terms do have different nuances though. These environments do tend to be persistent and to maintain avatar characteristics and "reputations" over time (Castronova, 2005, p. 105). These spaces encourage explorative learning (Papert, 1980, as cited in Withers, 2005).

Plenty of research into human behaviors and motivations has gone into the millions of lines of code that undergird game worlds. These codes involve image rendering, digital physics, artificial intelligence –driven behaviors of agents, music, and other functions. Participants in these immersive spaces may use open-ended modeling tools to create and change the in-world contents (Merrick & Maher, 2007).

Educational Immersive Sims

Simulations are considered so important for next-generation learning that computerized simulations will likely be integrated as a critical component in off-the-shelf and customized e-learning courseware (Boehle, 2005, .n.p.). Automated immersive simulations are models built around

a device, equipment, principle, process, situation etc. (Alessi & Trollip, 1991, Driscoll & Carliner, 2005). *To describe the state of the simulated situation and the results of changes, simulations use underlying qualitative or quantitative models. Models use variables and rules to grasp relationships between the variables. Especially in educational settings, simulations have mechanisms to change the settings of variables. When outputs of a simulation change over time due to successive alternations in the variables, the learner can observe these* (Quinn, 2005). *Thus, the learner can undergo an interactive, engaging learning experience* (as cited in Kreiger, 2006, p. 2).

Simulations may teach about something (physical simulations and process simulations) and those that teach how to do something (procedural and situational simulations) (Alessi & Trollip, 1991). Aldrich (2005) identifies four different genres of computer-based simulations, namely, branching stories, interactive spreadsheets, virtual labs / virtual products, and game-based models" (as cited in Kreiger, 2006, p. 2).

While the learning efficacy of simulations will be discussed later in this chapter, most automated and immersive sims strive for verisimilitude and fidelity—to accurately and authentically represent the world. The more applicable the learning to a real situation, the more robust a simulation is. They also are designed for intuitive usability: "Usability can be defined in terms of live salient properties of an interactive system: task efficiency, reuse, user-computer communication, robustness and flexibility" (Hussey, MacColl & Carrington, 2001, p. 40).

The design of simulations does not mean that there is inherent teaching in the experience.

While people can learn by participating in any simulation (e.g., observing types of cause / effect relationships), simulations do not inherently teach. Instructional designers need to use a systematic approach to designing simulations by inserting instructional supports such as virtual coaches, scaffolding, and job aids while using debriefing techniques. By structuring simulated events that force specific learner actions, we can create simulation-based environments that actually do teach...The ideal is for training environments to look exactly like the job environment thus, improving transfer of skills to job performance (Mihal, Kirkley, Christenberry & Vidali, 2003, pp. 11 - 12).

Simulations facilitate the attaining of tacit knowledge building and the development of expertise "as opposed to explicit or declarative learning" (Kirriemuir & McFarlane, 2004, as cited in Withers, 2005, p. 20).

Another way to describe this is "decoding" learning during electronic gameplay.

Playing requires this decoding of its structure or system (of levels, or architectural organization, of scoring systems, timing of events, of non-player characters' actions and interactions, etc.). This process must take place with each new genre of game, as each has its own mode of interaction, its own conventions and controls—and each game within the genre invents its own variations, different combinations of buttons to press or peripherals to add. Mastering the controls of each game is essential, and a fundamental pleasure in its own right. Video games are, as Provenzo has argued, 'literally teaching machines that instruct the player....in the rules...as it is being played' (1991:34) (Dovey & Kennedy, 2006, p. 7).

Experiential learning serves as a way for people to experience the substructure of a system and to understand its unspoken rules.

This interaction between the learner and learning material allows students to develop a feel for the relationship between the underlying factors governing a system, promotes an appreciation of appropriate ranges for system parameters, and gives a qualitative feel for the system before the introduction of theory (Thomas & Neilson, 1995). Simulations can be used as cognitive tools, allowing students to manipulate the parameters to test hypotheses, trying out 'what if' scenarios without a real consequence or risk, and in a time frame which is convenient and manageable to them, they enable the learner to ground their cognitive understanding of their action in a situation (Laurillard, 1993, as cited in Thomas & Milligan, 2004, n.p.).

Continuous learning environments (CLEs) offer opportunities for rich analysis of the interactive learning (p.14) and opportunities to fine-tune the training. Continuous learning environments provide multiple methods to support learner "negotiation of understanding." Learners engage in a process of inquiry based on authentic problems or cases: "As they examine these cases or problems, they use real world resources, tools, and people. Three of these learning methodologies; problem-based learning, case-based reasoning, and anchored instruction, provide good examples of methodologies that can be used effectively within continuous learning environments" (Mihal, Kirkley, Christenberry & Vidali, 2003, p. 8).

To immerse may not necessarily mean to interact, in some cases. Simulations do not have to be necessarily interactive, according to Aldrich. A simulation may be a "created atmosphere" similar to the real-world one (Aldrich, Learning by Doing,, 2005, p. 83) in which learning and decision-making may occur.

The work of created immersive environments should be done for particular types of learning only, partially because of the extensive development work required for mixed realities: "In their study, Windschitl and Winn found that the 'extra cost of immersion only pays off when the content to learn is complex, three-dimensional and dynamic' and when the student does not need to communicate with the outside world (Liu, Cheok, Mei-Ling, & Theng, 2007, pp. 65 – 66). Some educational simulations include ways to record the learning in a learning log (whether automated or learner-created) to capture their thinking as they progress and which may be used in a learning debriefing afterwards.

Ubiquitous Immersion in the Real and the Virtual

With the advent of wireless fidelity (wifi), e-learning has entered the realms of augmented reality (the addition of digital information into real spaces), augmented virtuality (the integration of real-time live information feeds into virtual environments; the use of haptics or physical interaction objects to communicate with the virtual ones), and mobile learning via mobile devices and learning platforms. Ubiquitous immersion engages three of the four points on the virtuality continuum. The much-cited "Virtuality Continuum" moves from the real environment to augmented reality (the real world enhanced by digital visuals and sounds), to augmented virtuality (the adding of live real-world data feeds into an online virtual space and / or use of haptic input devices), and then a fully virtual environment (fully online) (Milgram & Kishino, 1994, as cited in Christian, 2006, p. 2). Haptic interactions may between textured models with coordinated digital visualizations (Otaduy, Jain, Sud, & Lin, 2004, pp. 297 – 304).

Augmented reality involves digital information flowing to and supporting reality perceptions. These may be digital voice files corresponding to the location of the individual in a particular area. This may include the use of information delivered via head-mounted displays (HMDs) in a real-time, context-sensitive way. Various systems now may display using "mutual occlusion"—which means that the augmented reality display may have real objects occluding virtual ones, and virtual ones occluding real objects (Cakmakci, Ha, & Rolland, 2004, n.p.).

This may involve surface computing with computers embedded into furniture, clothing, and common everyday devices. Augmented reality not only involves the senses of sight and sound but also touch (via haptics or skin-level sensory data). Augmented reality installations involve the following:

1. Small-scale, single-user through head-mounted displays and desktop stereoscopic displays; 2. Medium-scale displays for small groups of collaborative users (CAVEs, reality centers, power walls), and 3. Large-scale displays designed for group immersions as through IMAX, simulator rides and domes (Lantz, 2007, n.p.).

Much research work has gone into creating displays that work with the human viewing systems that enable human stereoscopic vision: accommodation and convergence. "The ambiguous depth cues can cause users to experience symptoms of asthenopia, such as nausea, dizziness and eye fatigue," according to Grossman and Balakrishnan (2006, p. 193).

Examples of augmented reality installations run the gamut. One intelligent environment uses purposive ambiguity to tell the tragic story of Narcissus with an installation that used "projections, water reflections, sound, and distorted visual imagery to present a scripted experience of fixed duration" to participants (Otitoju & Harrison, 2008, p. 193). Similar works cited by these authors involve the following: "A number of projects have explored interactive technologies in art gallery settings. Notable examples are: Grinter et al., that considers how to augment curatorial didactics using portable handheld devices; Bannon et al., that explores how interactive technologies might deepen informational content in historical museums; Harrison et al that explored how reading varies based on time and place, and Hindmarsh et al., who conducted an ethnography of the social construction of interactive museum-going" (p. 194).

Those in the field predict more combined or mixed spaces that include the digital and the physical for an embodied immersive experience.

As the boundaries and reference points between physical and digitally grounded imagery become less defined, the possible duality and interplay for a combined image space moves towards a seamless self-referencing and continuous activity (Gwilt, 2004, p. 120).

There is a clear need for flexible configurability in mixed-media environments that combine digital and non-digital artifacts (Binder, De Michelis, Gerevautz, Jacucci, Matkovic, Psik, & Wagner, 2004).

Researchers are exploring ways to display 3D objects in 3D virtual spaces through a variety of techniques: "While a great deal of computer generated imagery is modeled and rendered in 3D, the vast majority of this 3D imagery is shown on 2D displays. Various forms of 3D displays have been contemplated and constructed for at least one hundred years (Lippman 1908), but only recent evolutions in digital capture, computation, and display have made functional and practical 3D displays possible (Jones, McDowall, Yamaada, Bolas & Debevec, 2007, n.p.). Other researchers are exploring the Wii controllers as a way to offer 3D gesture-based input into a 3D virtual world (Sreedharan, Zurita & Plimmer, 2007). Work is being done towards understanding spatial hypermedia and spatial information management.

Augmented virtuality may involve desktop team coordination exercises, such as those related to weather emergencies. Digital information captures could involve video captures, including those that may capture spherical motion (360-degrees of activity), with foveation technologies that may focus on individual faces with more detail. Such informational capture may be helpful in areas of exploration, training, architecture, security, "situational awareness," navigation, and reconnaissance ("imove spherical imagery," n.d.). These may also include the use of haptic devices to simulate surgery or handle virtual molecules (Qi, Martens, van Liere, & Kok, 2005).

Mobile e-learning involves the delivery of contents and information to devices such as cell phones and personal digital assistants (PDAs). Context-aware devices (with global positioning systems, for example) may offer digital contents that will appear when the individual carrying the device is in a particular location.

Several research results present important technical and technological aspects of computer-based simulations. One study compared the adequacy of Palm hand-helds and wearable computers for participatory simulations. It was revealed that both platforms were equally capable of engaging students in a problem-solving task with a simulation (Klopfer, Yoon & Rivas, 2004, as cited in Kreiger, 2006, p. 4).

There are many challenges of delivering and rendering 3D graphics for mobile terminals (Tack, Morán, Lafruit, & Lauwereins, 2004, pp. 109 -117).

The limitations of mobile devices present technological and delivery challenges for designers, particularly in delivering heavy geographic information systems (GIS) information.

Platforms and devices for mobile 3D GIS technology manipulating geographic data and information provide some limitation to design and implement: limited CPU and memory, absence or limited performance of graphic accelerators, small size of display panel, and so on (Lee, 2007, n.p.).

Figure 2, "A Continuum of Types of Immersion in E-Learning," compares the different depths of immersion with the types of learning that are most often connected to them. Then, there are examples of the pedagogical and technological structures used to enhance the learning.

SETTING UP, FACILITATING AND DEBRIEFING IMMERSIVE E-LEARNING

Simulations may be used to enhance workplace decision-making, develop empathy with others' job positions, and change mindsets and behavioral patterns (Boehle, 2005); enhance tactical skills (Radcliff, 2005); share stories to enhance collective memory and reasoning (Schank, 1990, as cited in Ip & Naidu, 2001); promote proper laboratory-based learning (Nejdl & Wolpers, 2004); "demo" new software technologies; teach "procedures, principles, and problem-solving" (Kapp, 2007, pp. 84 – 85); promote learner cooperation (Maldonado, Lee, Brave, Nass, Nakajima, Yamada, Iwamura, & Morishima, n.d.); spotlight critical incidences in a workplace (Ip & Naidu, 2001); encourage individual initiative and learning (Schank, 2002, as cited in Lee, 2005), and other endeavors.

Even back in 1978, Thiagarajan and Stolovitch suggested that the elements of a simulation game must involve four main steps: the preliminaries, the playing of the game, the termination of the game, and then debriefing with an elaboration of the underlying model (p. 28). Some suggest that the real learning begins only after the end of the game. Radcliff (2005) proposes a "content flow" learning model which involves a briefing, the model, the experience, the debriefing and a follow-up with a continuous learning mechanism to protect the learning and mastery (p.5).

Figure 2. A Continuum of types of immersion in e-learning (Hai-Jew, 2009)

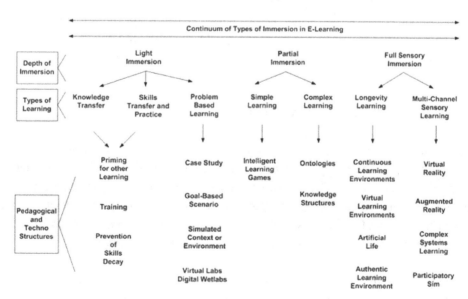

Setting up an immersive experience may involve preparatory learning, so the learners have the skills to engage and benefit from the simulation. Then, there's the introduction of the immersion, the roles, the strategies, and other relevant details.

There may be benefits to facilitation during the simulation or immersive experience itself. "Educators may wish to focus the learner's use of the simulation by setting the scene, providing objectives, directions, context, tasks and problems. The need for additional support, in the form of guidance, feedback and scaffolding has been recognized for some time (Thomas & Neilson (1995), Pilkinton & Grierson 1996, as cited in Thomas & Milligan, 2004, n.p.).

Post-immersion, learners may benefit from various types of de-briefing. These include the following:

- **Plenary Debriefing:** The facilitator triggers reflection and discussion by asking selective reflection-triggering questions according to the relevant learning goals.
- **Individual Reflection:** Introducing the debriefing with an individual reflection phase can help to explore the experiences of reserved individuals. The participants receive a questionnaire to fill out in order to reflect their individual experiences on relevant aspects of the gaming session.
- **Team Debriefing:** The participants form pairs and interview each other on their experiences and insights.
- **Small Group Debriefing:** As each team has made its specific experiences a team debriefing can be fostered by providing the teams with a list of questions that they should discuss within the teams (Kriz & Nöbauer, 2002, as cited in Schönwald, Euler, Angehrn, & Seufert, 2006, p. 23).

Group debriefing may involve one of two approaches:

One is the development of generalizations from the interpretation of learner perceptions (the Lewinian model). The other is that of beginning to address the cognitive conflict that has arisen from challenges to the learners' intuitive beliefs or methods of thinking (the Piagetian model) (Gredler, 1992, p. 7)

The Piagetian model suggests that when learners encounter new information, they either assimilate it into their existing worldview, or they must make greater systemic mental changes to accommodate the new information that may not fit with the former worldview (Van Eck, 2007).

EVALUATING IMMERSIVE E-LEARNING

Various thinkers suggest that there should be a formalized process for the evaluation of the efficacy of sims (Boehle, 2005, n.p.). The designs of sims should be based on clear pedagogical theories and on measurable learning goals. "The design of any delivery environment must be pedagogically rooted, reflecting the transposition of an abstract pedagogical model to a tangible system design" (Coman, 2002, n.p.). Galarneau summarizes C. Aldrich's structural conceptualizations of the ideal learning experience, as consisting of "pedagogical elements, simulation elements and game elements":

In his view, pedagogical elements wrap the other elements in a directed learning context, providing a theoretical basis, assessment, and opportunities for reflection. Simulation elements refer to the compo-

nents that make the simulation executable, be it a simple branching simulation or more complex game-like simulation. Game elements, on the other hand, refer to the aspects that are simply there to make a game fun: competition, reward, discovery, etc. (Galarneau, 2005, n.p.).

Relevant Pedagogical Theories

Any number of pedagogical theories may be brought to bear on the creation of immersive learning. Lave and Wenger's situated cognition, Paivio's dual coding theory, and mental models are cited, too.

For software and hard skills training, simulations can offer unlimited opportunities to practice, which supports learning via the behaviorist approach of drill and repetition. Simulations also offer the learner the opportunity to test new knowledge, strategies, skills and techniques in a virtual, risk-free environment. Many educators believe that experiencing failure such as this is a critical component in the learning process (Schank, as cited in Galarneau, 2005; Withers, 2005, p. 14). Designing for different learning styles has been advocated. One model groups learners as pragmatists, reflectors, theorists, and activists (Honey & Mumford, 1992, as cited in Thomas, 2001, p. 3). Some suggested ways to improve simulations: "providing multiple examples, highlighting critical features, providing ongoing and relevant feedback, and offering adjustable levels of challenge" (Strangman, Hall, & Meyer, 2003, as cited in Kim, Graesser, Jackson, Olney & Chipman, 2005). Others suggest increasing the realism of the scenario and the value of the experience in terms of triggering insights at the individual and team levels (Schönwald, Euler, Angehrn, & Seufert, 2006, p. 7).

Static media theory suggests that the limited cognitive channels of learners should not be spent on extraneous information.

Basically, this theoretical framework states that a learner's attention span is limited; however, during the learning process, their attention can be directed either to intrinsic, germane, or extraneous processing. Intrinsic processing describes a learner's focus on the Learning Object and its key features. Germane processing describes a deeper processing of the Learning Objects by its organization to cognitive representations and its integration with existing representations. Extraneous processing describes cognitive demands during learning, which do not foster the actual objectives of the Learning Object. Consequently, static media (for example text or images) demand less extraneous processing due to the fact that learners are only provided with relevant information (for example: key images of a physical process), whilst animations require the perception and the integration of a complete timeline of images. Moreover – in contrast to animations – static media allow learners to manage intrinsic processing by controlling the pace and order of the presentation (Holzinger, Kickmeier-Rust, & Albert, 2006, n.p.).

Some Immersive Simulation Building Models

Aldrich's "The Iterative Order of Design" shows the importance of developing learning objectives first, then building the simulation, getting feedback, then creating the game, the story specifics, the introduction, and then the background. Contrarily, learners experience the story differently, with the background experienced first, then the introduction, then the story, then the sim, and then the feedback (Aldrich, Learning by Doing, 2005, p. 220).

Simulation models must pass muster both with internal and external validity (Kenworthy, 2006, p. 153). This theorist's "Building a Standard Evaluation Framework (for Simulations)" shows a range of factors on a sliding scale that may be evaluated. These examine issues of competition, user group size, visual fidelity, realism, usage environment, purpose, epistemology, pedagogical philosophy, underlying psychology, goal orientation, experiential value, teacher role, program flexibility, value of errors, motivation, accommodation of individual differences, learner control, user activity, cooperative learning, and cultural sensitivity (p. 155).

Schönwald, Euler, Angehrn, and Seufert (2006) suggest that a build may begin with a definition of the desired learning outcomes in three main categories: Subject Matter Competencies, Social Competencies, and Self Competencies. Within these, there would be the different outcomes based on Knowledge, Attitudes and Skills.

The more learners know about a particular domain field, the better their ability to strategize ways of functioning within that field. Offering instructional tools to enhance learner metacognition may be helpful. "Research in cognitive psychology during the past two decades has produced two undisputed findings about academic performance. First, those who know more about a particular domain generally understand and remember better than do those with only limited background knowledge e.g., Chi, 1985; Glaser, 1984). Second, those who monitor and regulate their cognitive processing appropriately during task performance do better than those who do not engage in such strategic processing"(Alexander & Judy, 1988, p. 375).

The Efficacy of Immersive Sims

A meta-analysis of various research on simulation efficacy has found mixed results. "Many studies have investigated the use of simulations as an instructional technology within computer-based learning environments (Bourque & Carson 1987; Choi & Gennaro 1987; Gorsky &Finegold 1992; Hupper, Lomast, & Lazarowitz 2002; Michael 2001; Roberts & Blkeslee 1996). For example, Dekker and Donatti (1981) conducted the meta-analysis of 93 studies and found mixed results on the effects of simulations (Dekker 1981). The question arises as to why their evidence is inconclusive. Potential flaws in the studies might include poorly designed simulations, speed of display, difficulty of subject matter, and flexibility of user control" (Kim, Graesser, Jackson, Olney & Chipman, 2005).

Others concur that the methodology for evaluating simulations has been somewhat lacking. "In spite of the extensive literature, many of the claims and counterclaims for the teaching power of business games and simulations rest on anecdotal evidence or inadequate or poorly implemented research. These research defects, according to Keys and Wolfe (1990), have clouded the business gaming literature and hampered the creation of a cumulative stream of research. Gredler (1996) notes, as did Pierfy (1977) that a major design weakness of most studies evaluating simulation based training is that they are compared to regular classroom instruction even when the instructional goals for each differ (Kenworthy, 2006, p. 150).

One model used extensively in business environments employing immersive simulations is Kirkpatrick's (1998) four-tiered Evaluation Process

- **Level 1 (Reaction):** Did the learner enjoy himself? (Ask)
- **Level 2 (Learning):** Does the learner know what he learned? (Test)
- **Level 3 (Behavior):** Did the user change his behaviour? (Observe)

- **Level 4 (Results):** What are the results of the learning? (Measure) (Ahdell & Andresen, 2001, p. 28)

AUTOMATED AND LIVE IMAGERY IN INTERACTIVITY AND IMMERSIVE E-LEARNING

Visuals play a critical part in both interactivity and in immersiveness; these are a main channel for branding, communications, interactivity and engagement. Now that a basic context has been created regarding interactivity and immersiveness, the role of digital imagery will be explored. Graphics is a universal language that may help cross cultural and language boundaries (Blejec, 2003). Immersiveness involves storytelling as a cultural universal that may be shared through sociomedia (Mazalek & Davenport, 2003).

Multimedia and imagery have been found to motivate learning and retention.

But it is well documented that multi-sensory approaches, utilizing graphics, sound and interactive elements, not only appeal to different learning styles, but also positively affect motivation and retention among the general population. This approach is supported by research and wholeheartedly encouraged by experts: 'Multimedia presentations encourage learners to engage in active learning by mentally representing the material in words and pictures and by mentally making conn4ectiions between the pictorial and verbal representations' (Clark & Mayer 2002). Learning theories abound that also support these ideas. 'Imagery has been shown to facilitate recall in many studies,' and Dual Coding Theory suggests 'recall / recognition is enhanced by presenting information in both visual and verbal form' (Kearsley 2002, as cited in Galarneau, 2004, p. 3).

Research on the fidelity of the imagery offered deeper insights. While some suggest that high realism results in high learner engagement (Radcliff, 2005, p. 7), the research has been mixed. Physical fidelity matters in the development of skills which do not require much cognitive effort, according to Allen, Hays and Buffardi, 1986; however, functional fidelity—which shows cause-and-effect relationships—are important for tasks that require deeper cognitive processing and thought (Thomas & Milligan, 2004, n.p.). Too much fidelity may be distracting for learners (Alessi, 1988, as cited in Thomas & Milligan, 2004).

Lower fidelity visuals of computer agentry did not affect their evaluation by learners or the learning achieved (Reeves & Nass, 1996, as cited in Hollandsworth, 2005, p. 6). There's no strong evidence that animated graphics are more effective than still ones in a learning situation (Mayer et al., 2005, as cited in Holzinger, et al., 2006, n.p.)." However, it is interesting that most of the research carried out was on standard animations (e.g., "on how lightning works" or the typical "how a toilet tank works") and most of the experiments took place in a laboratory setting (Mayer, 2005) (Holzinger, et al., 2006, n.p.). Some research not finding favoring towards either static media or animations include the following: (Betrancourt &Tversky, 2000; Hegarty, et al., 2003; Lowe, 1999; Tversky, et al., 2002, as cited in Holzinger, et al., 2006, n.p.).

Interface and Interactivity

Imagery helps learners orientate themselves to the digital context. Digital imagery lets learners know how to interact with the space. The behaviors of the digital objects show what may be manipulated for effects. Indicators show the status of the person interacting, with feedback and some scoring. Visual indicators (often augmented with sound such as music or effects) may help human-driven avatars interact with the larger environment and with other live avatars, with rich degrees of freedom. Greater degrees of motion, anatomically-based avatars, and design for ballistic motion and kinetics all enhance virtual avatar realism.

In immersive spaces, feedback on the learner's performance comes through the digital environment and through characters. This is designed for learning value: "This feedback can be both formative, as the learner progresses through the interaction, and often summative at the completion of the curriculum" (Maldonado, Lee, Brave, Nass, Nakajima, Yamada, Iwamura & Morishima, n.d., p. 409).

Setting the Scene

Imagery also helps set the scene. The setting may involve a sense of place, with history, an atmosphere, a back story, and even an institutional memory. The digital images are 2D or immersive 3D or 4D (3D with the addition of time). The gestalt laws of pattern perception emphasize the importance of context in making meaning and sense (Westheimer, Koffka, & Kohler, 1912, 1935, as cited in Ware, 2004, pp. 189 – 197). Imagery has to be designed to human visual perceptions for effectiveness. "There is more visual interference within channels. The basic rule is that, in terms of low-level properties, like interferes with like. If we have a set of small symbols on a textured background, a texture with a grain size similar to that of the symbols will make them hard to see (Ware, 2004, p. 185).

There may be annotations of a scene to further enhance meaning-making.

Annotations in virtual spaces may include features such as comments on objects in the environment, guided tours through the virtual space, and a history mechanism so that the evolution of objects or portions of the space can be replayed and examined. In general terms, an annotation is simply a relationship between one object and another and we examine several methods of displaying these relationships. To extend annotations across communities, the system architecture supports naming and packaging object and meta-information and integration of content into a shared digital repository. By distributing to users the power to create, edit, store, and retrieve objects and annotations, we promote development and re-use of meaningful content. Such systems can have great utility for the development of virtual environments for learning and research (Kadobayashi, Lombardi, McCahill, Stearns, Tanaka, & Kay, 2005, p. 255).

A non-photorealistic scene may offer designers more versatility in rendering such as through artistic expression, selection of details, and the adding in of other semantic information (Klein, Li, Kazhdan, Corrêa, Finkelstein & Funkhouser, 2001, p. 527). There are a number of semantic channels for interactivity and immersiveness. Digital pyrotechnics may create a scene of fire with embers and dust with computational fluid dynamics (CFD).

A scene may be set in a live way with remote sensing, camera captures, and live data streams (such as through satellite or GIS technologies). There are 3D multidirectional captures in a studio (Matsuyama & Takai, 2002, n.p.). Computers are being designed that allow for analytics of these raw captures for value-added analysis. There are ways to integrate terrain data from various databases that includes the following: "terrain, ocean, atmosphere, 3D icons/models, features, topology, sound, textures, symbols, and special effects" (Schiavone, Sureshchandran, & Hardis, 1997, p. 335). These all may enhance the setting of a scene for e-learning.

Learning Artifacts

Digital imagery offer learning artifacts that convey meaning and experiences. Diagrams, for example, may enhance case studies. Videotaped case studies may enhance experiential learning. Sound effects may enhance the lived reality of the depicted situation.

Various rules of digital imagery apply in the conveyance of meaning through 2D. The proximity of objects may indicate relatedness and may group them perceptually. Similarly shaped pattern elements may be placed closed together. Objects that are connected may be linked via lines in node-link diagrams (Palmer & Rock, 1994, as cited in Ware, 2004, p. 191). Visually, people tend to "construct visual entities out of visual elements that are smooth and continuous, rather than ones that contain abrupt changes in direction" (Ware, 2004, p. 191). When people view an object, their mind tends to fill in missing information to create a sense of symmetry—for a visual whole constructed of two sides of an object. A closed contour tends to be viewed as an object, with the concept of inside and outside (Palmer, 1992, as cited in Ware, 2004, p. 195). The sizes of objects may affect how an object is perceived. Smaller components of a pattern are seen as objects (p. 196). People's eyes tend to focus on what is in the foreground, with whatever is seen beyond as the background.

Avatars and Characters

Modern-generation avatars may be formed into any sort of entity in 2D or 3D, as anthropomorphic (human-based) or non-human characters, and with evolving appearances and effects. People use avatars to provide an embodiment of their digital selves in online, immersive spaces; avatars convey their personal telepresences. Visuals may enhance the role profiles of specific characters used in role-play simulations. The gaze and non-verbals of avatars help human interactors focus on the avatars and engage in more directed ways (Garau, Slater, Vinayagamoorthy, Brogni, Steed & Sasse, 2003).

In Figure 3, a live avatar engages with her digital surroundings at the National Oceanic and Atmospheric Administration (NOAA) space.

Non-playable characters (NPCs) have become more sophisticated, too, with wider ranges of locomotion and full-jointed movement. They may display realistic body language and expressive behaviors (Gillies & Ballin, 2004), such as posture and gesture, facial expressions, and gaze. Their choreography of movements may be smoother, with greater visual detail, and frame-to-frame coherence. Such digital characters now may have more capabilities. Many are designed with back-end intelligence and emotions; some are imbued with histories and tendencies. Such intelligent characters act based on cognitive modeling about what it knows, for deeper character builds (Funge, Tu, & Terzopoulos, 1999). Intelligent agents may tap into rich data repositories for responding in natural language.

Automated avatars respond to human learners with more naturalness:

The avatar's conversational behaviors and gestures are autonomously derived from the directions given by the human learner and the learner's answers to the teacher's questions. Research suggests this com-

Figure 3. Hattie Williams' avatar in the NOAA Space in Second Life (Williams, 2009)

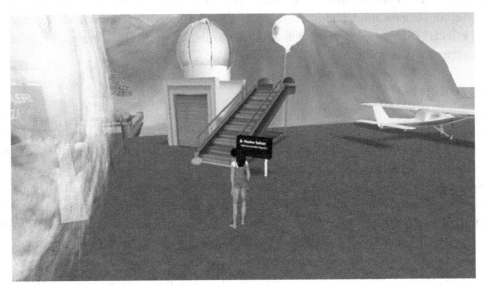

bination of high-level directions and autonomous behavior is perceived as more natural than avatars whose behaviors are minutely controlled by the users, leading to increases in perceived expressiveness of the conversation, and greater sense of user control (Maldonado, Lee, Brave, Nass, Nakajima, Yamada, Iwamura & Morishima, n.d., p. 409).

Some act as tutor agents. Others are digital co-learners.

The colearner, or classmate, as its name indicates, is learning alongside the human student and has no additional knowledge on the subject nor explanations to provide. It is not privy to additional information than the student views on the screen, and is called to answer questions as often as the student, on average. The colearner exchanges friendly banter with the student's avatar before the teacher poses a question, or after the answer is revealed. We have introduced this presence in the learning environment to determine the effects that learning alongside a social animate character has upon the student's performance and attitudes, rather than using the colearner to elicit nuanced explanations form the student, or model understanding, as is the case with some intelligent tutoring systems (Maldonado, Lee, Brave, Nass, Nakajima, Yamada, Iwamura & Morishima, n.d., p. 410) .

There are intelligent avatars that use sign languages with human users and display the signing from multiple angles for greater clarity (Farhadi, Forsyth & White, 2007). There are digital tools to capture the facial and body motion of those in Korean deaf society as a visual-spatial language (Oh, Park & Bien, 2007).

This intelligent avatar communications system uses "a non-verbal sign-language based on body gesture, facial expression, and model information to overcome the linguistic barrier between different languages." The system's sign language involved the following characteristics:

(1) What differs from verbal or written languages is the fact that there is no auxiliary words in sign-languages. (2) The syntax structures of sign languages are simple because they use only basic patterns in their verb conjugations. (3) The sign-language of one country is easily translated into that of another country in a different way from natural languages. Therefore, a sign-language communication system between different languages to get over the linguistic barrier including cultural barrier had been considered (Kim, Li & Aoki, 2004, p. 747).

Digital characters play a critical role in cinematography. McLaughlin (2006) describes how creatures are created conceptually; defined as 3D maquettes; captured on digital stills; embedded in sequential storyboards; captured on story reels for dramatic timing; used in animatics for lighting cues, detailed settings, and effects animations, and further enhanced. He explains that they are designed only to the level of detailed needed for the filming, whether it's up close in "hero" form, mid-ground, or back-ground. Technologies now enable facial action co-digitization, by following an actor's talking and emoting (Havaldar, 2006, pp. 1 – 20). This technology has application in films, animations, and gaming. Some "synthetic thespians" take the place of live actors as digital stunt doubles.

IMAGE STRATEGIES IN INTERACTIVITY AND IMMERSIVENESS

The high variability in interactive and immersive e-learning makes it near-impossible to define anything but general principles for approaching the digital imagery design for these contexts.

Some Principles

1. **Pedagogical Underpinning:** Immersive learning outcomes should be clearly programmed, without unintended messages or effects. Digital images should be used in a similar focused way.
2. **Selective Fidelity:** The images should be as accurate and specific as necessary to the desired learning (and the level of abstraction of the learning).
3. **Aesthetics Alignment:** The digital imagery should be aligned with the aesthetics of the learning—such as branding, character development, and the values of the particular domain field.
4. **Ethics:** Digital imagery should not convey stereotypes or inaccurate ideas. They should not be derivative of others' designs or concepts.
5. **Accessibilty:** Digital imagery should be designed in a way to be accessible to those with color vision challenges. Images should include alt text. Motion should include some sort of text-based narration for accessibility.
6. **Portability:** The digital imagery—whether interactive or immersive or both—should be able to be deployed from various repositories, learning / course management systems, and other venues. This also assumes a kind of interoperability: "Variations in media formats, systems standards, platforms, networks, programming languages and delivery formats are just a few of the issues that arise. In an effort to manage these, there is a current trend towards creating simulations that are modular or object-oriented and support interoperability between Learning Management Systems (LMS), platforms and delivery formats" (Withers, 2005, p. 21).

Many factors—not least the popularity of simulations and immersive and interactive gaming—support the research developments in this field.

CONCLUSION

The field of interactivity and immersiveness in e-learning holds immense promise for the ability to offer full-surrounds for simple-to-complex learning. Digital imagery lies at the heart of these learning designs and structures because of their communications abilities. Much more work will need to be done in this area. This chapter offers an initial perusal of the pedagogical issues that may enhance the building of interactive and immersive digital imagery.

REFERENCES

Abásolo, M.J., & Della, J.M. (2007). Magallanes: 3D navigation for everybody. In Proceedings of the GRAPHITE 2007, Perth, Western Australia (pp. 135-142). New York: ACM.

Ahdell, R., & Andresen, G. (2001). Games and simulations in workplace eLearning: How to align eLearning content with learner needs. Unpublished master's thesis, Norwegian University of Science and Technology.

Aldrich, C. (2005). Learning by doing: A comprehensive guide to simulations, computer games, and pedagogy in e-learning and other educational experiences. San Francisco: Pfeiffer.

Alessi, S., & Trollip, S. R. (1991). Computer-Based Instruction: Methods and Development (2nd ed.). Upper Saddle River, NJ: Prentice Hall.

Alexander, P. A., & Judy, J. E. (1988). The interaction of domain-specific and strategic knowledge in academic performance. *Review of Educational Research, 58*(4), 375–404.

Anolli, L., Mantovani, F., Mortillaro, M., Vescovo, A., Agliati, A., Confalonieri, L., et al. (n.d.). A multimodal database as a background for emotional synthesis, recognition and training in e-learning systems. In Affective computing and intelligent interaction (LNCS 3784, pp. 566-573). Berlin, Germany: Springer.

Babich, A., Senk, D., & Mavrommatis, K. (2005). Combination of lab experiments and online simulations in master course. Tainan, Taiwan: Exploring Innovation in Education and Research.

Bartle, R. A. (2006). Virtual Worldliness. In J. M. Balkin & B. S. Noveck (Eds.), The State of Play: Law, Games and VirtualWorlds. New York: New York University.

Binder, T., De Michelis, G., & Gervautz, M., Jacucci, Gl., Matkovic, K., Psik, T., & Wagner, I. (2004). Supporting configurability in a mixed-media environment for design students. *Personal and Ubiquitous Computing, 8*, 310. doi:10.1007/s00779-004-0294-7

Blejec, A. (2003). Teaching statistics by using simulations on the Internet. In Proceedings of Statistics and the Internet, Berlin, Germany.

Bekebrede, G., Mayer, I., van Houten, S. P., Chin, R., & Verbraeck, A. (2005). How serious are serious games? Some lessons from infra (infrastructure)-games. In Proceedings of the DiGRA 2005 Conference: Changing Views—Worlds in Play (pp. 1-7).

Boehle, S. (2005). Simulations: The next generation of e-learning. *Training (New York, N.Y.), 42*(1), 22–31.

Bonnaud, O., Danto, Y., Bertrand, Y., Lewis, D., Fouillat, P., & Schrimpf, R. D. (2004). The importance of mental calculations in multimedia and e-learning approaches that emphasize simulation and modeling in electrical engineering studies. In Proceedings of the Fifth International Conference on Information Technology Based Higher Education and Training (pp. 371-376). Washington, DC: IEEE.

Burgos, D., Tattersall, C., & Koper, R. (2005). Repurposing existing generic games and simulations for e-learning. *Computers in Human Behavior, 23*(6), 2656–2667. doi:10.1016/j.chb.2006.08.002

Buron, G., & Matthews, G. (2003). Rapid 3D insect model reconstruction from minimal 2D image set. In Proceedings of the 14th IEEE Visualization Conference (VIS '03).

Cakmakci, O., Ha, Y., & Rolland, J. P. (2004). A compact optical see-through head-worn display with occlusion support. In Proceedings of the Third IEEE and ACM International Symposium on Mixed and Augmented Reality (ISMAR 2004). Washington, DC: IEEE.

Castronova, E. (2005). The Right to Play.In J. M. Balkin & B. S. Noveck (Eds.), The State of Play: Law, Games, and Virtual Worlds (pp. 66-85). New York: New York University Press.

Castronova, E. (2005). Synthetic Worlds. Chicago: The University of Chicago Press.

Charles, D., Fyfe, C., Livingstone, D., & McGlinchey, S. (Eds.). (2008). Biologically Inspired Artificial Intelligence for Computer Games. Hershey, PA: IGI Global.

Christian, J. (2006). Augmented reality in corporate pervasive e-education: Novel ways to support aviation maintenance training. In Proceedings of the Innovation North Research Conference 2006, Leeds Metropolitan University, UK (pp. 1-10).

Chittaro, L., Ranon, R., & Ieronutti, L. (2003). Guiding visitors of Web3D worlds through automatically generated tours. In Proceedings of the eighth international conference on 3D Web technology (pp. 27-38). New York: ACM.

Collomb, M., Hascoët, M., Baudisch, P., & Lee, B. (2005). Improving drag-and-drop on wall-size displays. In Proceedings of Graphics Interface 2005. Victoria, British Columbia, Canada: The Canadian Human-Computer Communications Society.

Coman, P. G. (2002). Critical success factors for eLearning delivery. In Proceedings of the International Conference on Computers in Education (ICCE '02).

Dickey, M. D. (2005). Three-dimensional virtual worlds and distance learning: Two case studies of Active Worlds as a medium for distance education. *British Journal of Educational Technology, 36*(3), 439–451. doi:10.1111/j.1467-8535.2005.00477.x

Doubleday, N., & Kurtz, S. (2004). Shared extensible learning spaces. In Proceedings of the SIGITE '04, Salt Lake City, Utah.

Dovey, J., & Kennedy, H. W. (2006). Game Cultures: Computer Games as New Media. New York: Open University Press.

Ezzat, T., Geiger, G., & Poggio, T. (2002). Trainable videorealistic speech animation. In Proceedings of the 29th annual conference on Computer graphics and interactive techniques (pp. 388-398). New York: ACM.

Farhadi, A., Forsyth, D., & White, R. (2007). Transfer learning in sign language. In Proceedings of the IEEE Conference on Computer Vision and Pattern Recognition (pp. 1-8). Washington, DC: IEEE.

Feltham, F., Vetere, F., & Wensveen, S. (2007). Designing tangible artefacts for playful interactions and dialogues. In Proceedings of the 2007 conference on Designing pleasurable products and interfaces. New York: ACM.

Frederking, J., Cruz, M., Baskinger, M., & Overbeeke, K. (2008). Beyond the screen: Designing immersive collaborative experiences for children through digital and physical interaction. In Proceedings of the DIS 2008. New York: ACM.

Funge, J., Tu, X., & Terzopoulos, D. (1999). Cognitive modeling: Knowledge, reasoning and planning for intelligent characters. In Proceedings of the SIGGRAPH 99 (pp. 29-38). New York: ACM.

Galarneau, L. (2004). The eLearning edge: Leveraging interactive technologies n the design of engaging, effective learning experiences. In Proceedings of e-Fest 2004, Wellington, New Zealand (pp. 1-10).

Galarneau, L. (2005). Authentic learning experiences through play: Games, simulations and the construction of knowledge. In Proceedings of DiGRA 2005 Conference: Changing Views – Worlds at Play.

Gao, Y., & Zhang, H. (2001). Avatar control by facial expressions. In Proceedings of the 2001 IEEE International Fuzzy Systems Conference (pp. 1351-1354).

Garau, M., Slater, M., Vinayagamoorthy, V., Brogni, A., Steed, A., & Sasse, M. A. (2003). The impact of avatar realism and eye gaze control on perceived quality of communication in a shared immersive virtual environment. *CHI, 5*(1), 529–536.

Gibson, D., Aldrich, C., & Prensky, M. (Eds.). (2007). Games and simulations in online learning: Research and development frameworks. Hershey, PA: Information Science Publishing.

Giddings, S. (2005). SimAcademy. Games and Simulations, Interact. The Learning Technology Support Service, University of Bristol.

Gillies, M., & Ballin, D. (2004). Affective interactions between expressive characters. In Proceedings of the 2004 IEEE International Conference on Systems, Man and Cybernetics. Washington, DC: IEEE.

Gredler, M. (1992). The role of post-simulation activities. In Designing and Evaluating Games and Simulations: A Process Approach (pp. 1-15).

Grønbæk, K., Rohde, A., & Bech-Petersen, S. (2006). InfoGallery: Informative art services for physical library spaces. In Proceedings of the JCDL '06 (pp. 21-30). New York: ACM.

Grossman, T., & Balakrishnan, R. (2006). An evaluation of depth perception on volumetric displays. In Proceedings of the AVI '06, Venezia, Italy. New York: ACM.

Gwilt, I. (2004). Interface as image: Image making and mixed reality. In Proceedings of the International Conference On Computer Graphics and Interactive Techniques, Los Angeles, CA (pp. 120-123).

Hallinger, P. (2005). Making change happen: A problem-based computer simulation. In Proceedings of the Second International Conference on eLearning for Knowledge-Based Society (pp. 3.1-3.7).

Havaldar, P. (2006). Course Notes: Performance driven facial animation. Sony Pictures Imageworks.

Hemphill, H. (2001). Instructional syntax analysis: Beyond CBT. *TechTrend*, *45*(1), 35. doi:10.1007/BF02763376

Hollandsworth, R.J. (2005). The theoretical and developmental applications of online simulations.

In Proceedings of the International Simulation and Gaming Association 2005 Conference (pp. 1-10).

Holzinger, A., & Ebner, M. (2003). Interaction and usability of simulations & animations: A case study of the Flash technology. In Proceedings of the Human-Computer Interaction INTERACT 2003 (pp. 777-780).

Holzinger, A., Kickmeier-Rust, M. D., & Albert, D. (2006). Visualizations, animations and simulations for computer engineering education: Is high tech content always necessary? In Proceedings of the 10th IACEE World Conference on Continuing Engineering Education (WCCEE).

Hua, T.G. (n.d.). Exploring simulation in teaching and learning – Part 1: Game, simulation and simulation game.

Hussey, A., MacColl, I., & Carrington, D. (2001). Assessing usability from formal user-interface designs. In Proceedings of the 2001 Australian Software Engineering Conference. Washington, DC: IEEE.

iMove Spherical Imagery. (n.d.). Digital Government Society of North America [Slideshow]. Retrieved January 24, 2009, from http://delivery.acm.org/10.1145/1130000/1123141/p42-ripley.pdf?key1=1123141&key2=2830513221&coll=portal&dl=ACM&CFID=5114638&CFTOKEN=62118861

Interrante, V., Anderson, L., Ries, B., O'Rourke, E., & Gray, L. (2007). Experimental investigations into the feasibility of using augmented walking to facilitate the intuitive exploration of large scale immersive virtual environments. In Proceedings of the APGV 2007, Tübingen, Germany. New York: ACM.

Ip, A., & Naidu, S. (2001). Experienced (sic)-based pedagogical designs for elearning. *Educational Technology*, *41*(5), 53–58.

Jeschke, S., Richter, T., Scheel, H., Seiler, R., & Thomsen, C. (2001). The experiment in eLearning: Magnetism in virtual and remote experiments. Retrieved from http://prints.mulf.tuberlin.de/28/01/Experiment_in_eLearning-Magnetisminvirtual_and_Remote_Experiments.pdf

Jones, A., McDowall, I., Yamada, H., Bolas, M., & Debevec, P. (2007). An interactive 360o lightfield display. In Proceedings of the SIGGRAPH 2007. New York: ACM.

Kadobayashi, R., Lombardi, J., McCahill, M. P., Stearns, H., Tanaka, K., & Kay, A. (2005). Annotation authoring in collaborative 3D virtual environments. In Proceedings of the ICAT 2005 (pp. 255-256).

Kapp, K. M. (2007). Gadgets, Games and Gizmos for Learning. San Francisco: John Wiley and Sons.

Kapp, K.M. (2005). Learning by doing: A comprehensive guide to simulations, computer games and pedagogy in e-learning and other educational experiences by Clark Aldrich. ELearn Magazine, 2005(9), 4.

Kenworthy, J. (2006). Simulations—Bridging from thwarted innovation to disruptive technology. *Developments in Business Simulation and Experiential Learning, 33*, 149–158.

Kim, H.-J. J., Graesser, A., Jackson, T., Olney, A., & Chipman, P. (2005). The effectiveness of computer simulations in a computer-based learning environment. In G. Richards (Ed.), Proceedings of World Conference on E-Learning in Corporate, Government, Healthcare, and Higher Education 2005 (pp. 1362-1367). Chesapeake, VA: AACE.

Kim, S.-W., Li, Z.-X., & Aoki, Y. (2004). On intelligent avatar communication using Korean, Chinese and Japanese sign-languages: An overview. In Proceedings of the 2004 8th International Conference on Control, Automation, Robotics and Vision.

Kirriemuir, J. (2005). Commercial games in the classroom. Games and Simulations. Interact, (31), 20-21.

Klein, A. W., Li, W., Kazhdan, M. M., Corrêa, W. T., Finkelstein, A., & Funkhouser, T. A. (2000). Non-photorealistic virtual environments. In Proceedings of the SIGGRAPH 2000 (pp. 527-534). New York: ACM.

Kreiger, H. (2006). Simulation-based learning content: How might simulation-based learning contribute to performance-based, meaningful employee learning? In Proceedings of the INN Faculty Research Conference 2006 (pp. 1-9).

Lantz, E. (2007). A survey of large-scale immersive displays. In Proceedings of the EDT 2007. New York: ACM.

Lee, K.-T. (2005). E-learning: The quest for effectiveness. *Malaysia Online Journal of Instructional Technology, 2*(2), 61–72.

Leleve, A., Prevot, P., Benmohamed, H., & Benadi, M. (n.d.). Generic e-lab platforms and eLearning standards. In Proceedings of International Conference on Computer Aided Learning in Engineering Education (CALIE 2004), Grenoble, France.

Levin, D. (2003). Preparing future education leaders through simulation-enhanced learning[Draft].

Liu, W., Cheok, A. D., Mei-L, C. L., & Theng, Y.-L. (2007). Mixed reality classroom – Learning from entertainment. In Proceedings of the DIMEA '07 (pp. 65-66). New York: ACM.

Liu, Y., Wenyin, L., & Jiang, C. (2004). A structural approach to recognizing incomplete graphic objects. In Proceedings of the 17th International Conference on Pattern Recognition (ICPR '04). Washington, DC: IEEE.

Luley, P. M., Paletta, L., & Almer, A. (2005). Visual object detection form mobile phone imagery for context awareness. In Proceedings of the Mobile HCI (pp. 385-386). New York: ACM.

Maldonado, H., & Lee, J.-E. R., Brave, S., Nass, C., Nakajima, H., Yamada, R., Iwamura, K., & Morishima, Y. (2005). We learn better together: Enhance eLearning with emotional characters. In Proceedings of the Computer Supported Collaborative Learning 2005: The Next Ten Years! (pp. 408-417).

Mazalek, A., & Davenport, G. (2003). A tangible platform for documenting experiences and sharing multimedia stories. In Proceedings of the 2003 ACM SIGMM workshop on Experiential telepresence (pp. 105-109). New York: ACM.

McLaughlin, T. (2006). Taxonomy of digital creatures: Defining character development techniques based upon scope of use. In Proceedings of the International Conference on Computer Graphics and Interactive Techniques, ACM SIGGRAPH 2006. Retrieved January 24, 2009, from http://doi.acm.org/10.1145/1185657.1185808

Merrick, K., & Maher, M. L. (2007). Motivated reinforcement learning for adaptive characters in open-ended simulation games. In Proceedings of the ACE '07, Salzburg, Austria (pp. 127-134). New York: ACM.

Mihal, S., Kirkley, S., Christenberry, T. C., & Vidali, A. (2003). Continuous learning environments: Incorporating performance metrics into next generation simulation-based eLearning environments for military and law enforcement. Institute for Operational Readiness and Continuous Education in Security.

Musgrave, F. K. (1996). Fractal landscapes in context. *Interaction*, *3*(6), 92–95. doi:10.1145/242485.254739

Muzy, A., Fauvet, N., Bourdot, P., Bosseur, F., & Goulnaud, C. (2005). A VR platform for field-scale phenomena: An application to fire spread experiments. In Proceedings of the 3rd international conference on Computer graphics and interactive techniques in Australasia and South East Asia (pp. 155-158). New York: ACM.

Naidu, S. (2001). Designing instruction for eLearning environments. The University of Melbourne.

Nejdl, W., & Wolpers, M. (2004). European eLearning: Important research issues and application scenarios. In L. Cantoni & C. McLoughlin (Eds.), Proceedings of World Conference on Educational Multimedia, Hypermedia and Telecommunications 2004 (pp. 2054-2068). Chesapeake, VA: AACE.

Oh, Y.-J., Park, K.-H., & Bien, Z. (2007). Body motion editor for sign language avatar. In Proceedings of the International Conference on Control, Automation and Systems 2007 (pp. 1752-1757).

Orngreen, R. (n.d.) CaseMaker: An environment for case-based e-learning. Academic Conferences Limited. Electronic Journal on e-Learning, 2(1), 167-180.

Otaduy, M. A., Jain, N., Sud, A., & Lin, M. C. (2004). Haptic display of interaction between textured models. In Proceedings of the IEEE Visualization 2004 (pp. 297-304).

Pinho, R. R., & Tavares, J. M. R. S. (2004). Morphing of image represented objects using a physical methodology. In Proceedings of the 2004 ACM Symposium on Applied Computing, SAC '04 (pp. 10-15).

Prensky, M. (2002). The motivation of gameplay or, the REAL 21st century learning revolution. *Horizon, 10*(1), 1–14.

Qi, W., Martens, J.-B., van Liere, R., & Kok, A. (2005). Reach the virtual environment—3D tangible interaction with scientific data. In Proceedings of OZCHI 2005, Canberra, Australia (pp. 1-10). New York: ACM.

Raab, M. (2003). Games and eLearning: Attempt to identify reasons why games are popular and how they can be applied to make eLearning more popular. Unpublished master's thesis, Trinity College, Dublin, Ireland.

Radcliff, J. B. (2005). Executive Viewpoint: Why soft-skills simulation makes a hard case for sales training. CompeteNet Publications.

Ramsden, A. (2005). Low cost, low tech web-based simulations. Games and Simulations. Interact, (31), 15.

Raybourn, E. M. (2003). Design cycle usability evaluations of an intercultural virtual simulation game for collaborative learning. In C. Ghaoui (Ed.), Usability Evaluation of Online Learning Programs. Hershey, PA: Information Science Publishing.

Schiavone, G. A., Sureshchandran, S., & Hardis, K. C. (1997). Terrain database interoperability issues in training with distributed interactive simulation. *ACM Transactions on Modeling and Computer Simulation, 7*(3), 332–367. doi:10.1145/259207.259221

Scholz-Reiter, I. B., Echelmeyer, W., Morales, E., & Gavirey, S. (2003). Enhanced approach for new cooperative e-learning environments. In Proceedings of the International Conference on Network Universities and e-Learning. Retrieved February 21, 2009, from http://www.hsh.no/menu

Scholz-Reiter, I. B., Hamann, T., Echelmeyer, W., Gavirey, S., & Doberenz, R. (n.d.). Developing a virtual tutorial system for online simulation games. In Proceedings of the 30th SEFI Annual Conference.

Schönwald, I., Euler, D., Angehrn, A., & Seufert, S. (2006). EduChallenge Learning Scenarios: Designing and evaluating learning scenarios with a team-based simulation on change management in higher education (SCIL Report 8).

Seevinck, J., Candy, L., & Edmonds, E. A. (2006). Exploration and reflection in interactive art: Glass pond. In Proceedings of the OZCHI 2006 (pp. 143-150).

Slater, M., Howell, J., Steed, A., Pertaub, D.-P., Gaurau, M., & Springel, S. (2000). Acting in virtual reality. In Proceedings of the CVE 2000, San Francisco, CA, USA. New York: ACM.

Sreedharan, S., Zurita, E. S., & Plimmer, B. (2007). 3D input for 3D worlds. In Proceedings of the OzCHI 2007, Adelaide, Australia (pp. 227-230). New York: ACM.

Summers, G. J. (2004). Today's business simulation industry. In Simulation & Gaming (pp. 208-241). SAGE Publications.

Tack, N. Morán, F., Lafruit, G., & Lauwereins, R. (2004). 3D graphics rendering time modeling and control for mobile terminals. In Proceedings of the ninth international conference on 3D Web technology (pp. 109-117). New York: ACM.

Thiagarajan, S., & Stolovitch, H. D. (1978). Instructional Simulation Games. Englewood Cliffs, NJ: Educational Technology Publications.

Thomas, R. (2001). Interactivity & simulations in e-learning. MultiVerse Publications.

Thomas, R. C., & Milligan, C. D. (2004). Putting teachers in the loop: Tools for creating and customizing simulations. *Journal of Interactive Media in Education*, 15.

Turner, J. (2006). Destination space: Experiential spatiality and stories. In Proceedings of the 2006 international conference on Game research and development (pp. 87-94). New York: ACM.

Van Eck, R. (2007). Building artificially intelligent learning games. In D. Gibson, C. Aldrich, & M. Prensky (Eds.), Games and Simulations in Online learning: Research and Development Frameworks. Hershey, PA: Information Science Publishing.

Ware, C. (2004). Foundation for a science of data visualization. In Information Visualization: Perception for Design (2nd ed.). San Francisco: Morgan Kaufmann Publishers.

Weber, M., Pfeiffer, T., & Jung, B. (2005). Pr@senZ-P@CE: Mobile interaction with virtual reality. In Proceedings of the Mobile HCI '05 (pp. 351-352). New York: ACM.

Wilkinson, D. L. (2004). The intersection of learning architecture and instructional design in e-learning. In Proceedings of the 2002 ECI Conference on e-Technologies in Engineering Education: Learning Outcomes Providing Future Possibilities.

Withers, D. (2005). Authoring tools for educational simulations. Retrieved February 20, 2009, from http://www.sfu.ca/~dwithers/articles/publications/WithersEdSimReport.pdf.

Zualkernan, I. A. (2004). Using simulations to automatically generate authentic constructivist learning environments. In Proceedings of the IEEE International Conference on Advanced Learning Technologies (ICALT '04).

KEY TERMS AND DEFINITIONS

Agent (n): A simulation object or entity that determines its own behavior based on artificial intelligence

Ambient Light (n): Total light in the visual field, natural light without artificial light

Ambient Shading (n): Illumination produced by other objects redistributing the light from the main light source, in an environment

Articulated (adj): Jointed, with often full motion

Artifact (n): A human-made object

Artificial Life (n): The digital simulation of biological life, with biological principles

Aspect Ratio (n): The relation of a viewing screen's height to its width

Automated Cinematography (n): The capturing of a digital movie in a machine-driven way

automated design (n): The planning of machine-driven interactivity

Autonomous (Behavior) (adj): Independent actions determined by each 'bot

Avatar (n): A symbolic or graphical representation of a person, an embodiment

Boid (n): A model for the animation of the behavior of flocks proposed by Craig Reynolds, this boid model proposes cohesion or flock centering; alignment or "velocity matching" in movement, and separation or "collision avoidance"

Configurability (adj): The ability of a system to be flexibly changed to accommodate other situations, able to be modified or arranged / re-arranged

Constructability (n): The ease with which users of an immersive space may build to the environment

Context-Aware (adj): A device that has a GPS-reading of its location

Cybernetics (n): The theoretical study of communications and control processes in systems

Emergent Behavior (n): Unplanned or unexpected actions

Emotive (adj): With emotion.

Filtering (n): The selecting of relevant digital contents based on particular search criteria

Flexibility (n): The range in enabling user customizations of the system

Immersive (adj): 3D, full-sensory, encompassing

Interactivity (n): Involving the intercommunications and interrelating between individuals

Interactive Speed (n): The rate at which a user engages with the machine

Light Effects (n): The simulation of indoor, outdoor, strobe, and other light effects

Maquette (n): A 3D sculpture used as a model for a digital creature

Microworld (n): Self-discovery-based exploratory learning environments

Mobile 3D (n): The delivery of 3D images and objects to mobile devices

Model Driven Architecture (MDA) (n): The technical structure of a simulation that runs based on an underlying model

Presence (Personal, Social and Environmental) (n): The sensation of being in a particular digital space as an individual entity, in a social grouping with other autonomous individuals, and in a particular digital manifestation of a physical context

Neutral Photography (n): The images captured by camera for matching size, proportion, texture and color information

Proprioceptor (n): A sensory receptor that detects motion and body position; sensors in muscles, tendons, joints and the inner ear that help a person be aware of his or her body position

Task Efficiency (n): Minimizing user efforts to execute varied tasks

Reference Photography (n): The images captured by camera for reference, particularly when the digital creature has a live counterpart

Reuse (n): The ability to save and retrieve previous work.

Robustness (n): The facilitation of recovery from errors, system resiliency

Story Reel (n): A filmed version of a storyboard to evaluate dramatic timing

Tangible Interface (n): A physical object that can interact with a virtual environment in a computerized system

Telepresence (n): A sense of a virtual identity, situatedness in a virtual situation ("social presence" usually refers to the presence of a group)

Usability Audit (n): A test (often involving users) to verify the usability of a system

Virtual Lab (n): A digital simulation of a laboratory, often used in the empirical sciences. These may include simulations of chemical processes, extractions, the effects of various forces on various materials, and other types of experiments

Chapter 9
Collaborative Image Creation

ABSTRACT

With multi-institution multi-state collaborative funding grants and consortium-based e-learning endeavors, the occurrence of collaborative image creation has become much more common-place. Even within an institution, cross-departmental or cross-college endeavors exist. This chapter addresses collaboration around digital imagery creation for e-learning, both via face-to-face (F2F) and virtual teaming. This captures some workflow practices and highlights ideas for encouraging quality builds and innovation.

CHAPTER OBJECTIVES

- Explore the steps to collaborative digital image creation
- Define face-to-face (F2F) co-located collaborative teams for creating digital imagery
- Define distributed virtual teaming for digital imagery creation
- Describe a virtual design studio and some of the technologies needed
- Emphasize the importance of verbose communications for digital imagery collaboration, design, and development
- Review cultural sensitivity in teaming
- Explore efficient workflow practices for encouraging collaborative quality image builds and innovation

INTRODUCTION

Few digital imagery creation shops are go-it-alone individualistic ventures. Rather, this work usually involves a team of individuals with differing skill sets who collaborate around the work. This is usually

DOI: 10.4018/978-1-60566-972-4.ch009

necessary because mixed skill sets are required for the creation of digital imagery for learning. Digital imagery creation requires complex skills with a variety of digital hardware and software. The concepts required for the accurate representation of visuals in a field require subject matter expertise from a variety of domains. The images that are created need to be legal and accessible; they need to be ethical. They must be technologically sound and portable. They need clear metadata labels. Visuals need to be versioned for a variety of potential needs—from print to versioning for slideshows to integration with 3D immersive spaces.

Also, a wider range of users of digital imagery may provide more eyes on the work to co-evolve the quality and creativity. And lastly, the talent for executing on some of the needs for digital imagery creation may not exist in one location. This requires drawing in talent from other locations. Those who use collaborative work structures may need to make the business case for the value of collaboration (Bodenstaff, Wombacher, Reichert & Wieringa, 2007).

COLLABORATIVE IMAGE CREATION

Some collaborations are formal with clearly defined teams and goals; others involve informal peer-to-peer networks connected by computer mediated communications. Some are co-located teams within the same organization; others are virtual teams that may or may not be from the same organization. Collaborative work via outsourcing is another factor that has fed collaboration.

Some teams are regular work ones, with plenty of research addressing different ways that these function. Then, there are the anomalous "hot groups" that coalesce spontaneously around cutting-edge work, deliver creative results, and tend to be short-lived (Lipman-Blumen & Leavitt, 1999, pp. 11 – 13). Underlying collaborative image creation is the idea of equifinality, a principle that suggests that "an open system such as a person, team, or organization can behave and still achieve the same outcome…" (Hackman, 2002, p. 216). Yet, even given the different paths, some general phases of digital imagery capture and development may be understood to be the work of such teams.

Collaborative digital image creation for e-learning involves five general steps:

1. design,
2. planning (for execution),
3. capture and collection,
4. processing and development, and
5. deployment and archival.

These steps actualize both the digital imagery and the digital learning object (DLO) pipelines, which progress in a parallel way, as indicated in Figure 1: Collaborative E-Learning Image Creation. The design phase involves conceptualizing the digital imagery and the pedagogical design. The planning phase involves both the planning for the digital imagery capture as well as the practical instruction planning. The capture and collection phase involves the capture of the raw imagery as well as pedagogical information and artifacts that may be used with the imagery. The next step—processing and development—involves image and digital learning object (DLO) processing. Lastly, the deployment and archival phase involves user testing, live use, and the archival of the images and DLOs in a repository for e-learning purposes.

Figure 1. Collaborative e-learning image creation

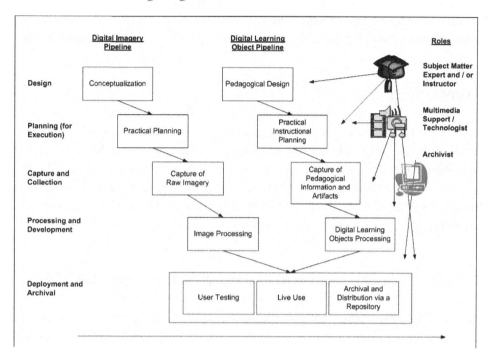

The members of a team may serve discrete and separate roles, or they may take on multiple and overlapping roles. Based on the above diagram, there may be some initial observations about setting up a team.

Setting up a Team

The harmonizing effect of being digital is already apparent as previously partitioned disciplines and enterprises find themselves collaborating, not competing. A previously missing common language emerges, allowing people to understand across boundaries. -- Nicholas Negroponte in Being Digital (1995)

A variety of functions and skill sets are necessary. The expertise of the subject matter expert (SME) or instructor is critical for proper representation of imagery for a particular field. Instructional design help may be necessary in many cases, except where the SME or instructor has e-learning expertise. Technological expertise will be needed for the multimedia developers, archivists, camera-people, graphics designers, and editors. A staff writer may be needed to help create some of the digital learning objects. There may need to be scripters or coders for the multimedia pieces. A team leader (and project manager) may be needed to keep the project focused and with proper technical direction. A project documenter may also be retained to handle the grant documentation along with the in-house documentation. In a higher education environment, There are different ways to conceptualize roles beyond task function. Another approach is to look at the social dynamics for communications: "task leader, social-emotional leader, active listener, tension releaser, information provider, central negative, questioner, silent observer, and recorder" (Wang, Huang, & Wang, 2006, n.p.).

Clearly, unique project needs may dictate the need for other skill sets and team members. Setting up a successful team will require having sufficient staff with the proper skill sets to execute on the work. Changing work situations will require adaptability and the possible need to acquire new skills on-the-fly.

Setting Expectations

A team needs to have a clear sense of its objectives early on. It needs to know what its deliverables are and the deadlines for those deliverables. They have to know what quality standards will be upheld. They need a clear sense of their own roles and those of others, and which ones will be shared responsibilities (and with whom). They need a sense of the larger workflow. They need to know what technologies will be used. They need a sense of what is expected of each of them in terms of design and creativity as well as decision-making. They need a sense of how authority is apportioned and shared.

FACE-TO-FACE (F2F) COLLABORATION AROUND DIGITAL IMAGERY

A co-located team shares the synergies of live interactivity. There may be easier coordination with fewer logistical considerations. Information may be more easily shared both through formal and informal interactions.

Teamwork Phasing

Traditionally, it was thought that group development might move through universal sequences of stages, such as preparing to perform and then performing (Hare, 1977; McGrath, 1984, as cited in Hackman, 1990). The stages of teaming have been explored, with no findings of a universal sequence of activities, except for the idea of "punctuated equilibrium" (Eldredge & Gould, 1972), which suggests sudden patterns that appear, persist for a time, and then change in "compact, revolutionary bursts" (as cited in Hackman, 1990, p. 100). Groups were found to have immediate working framework assumptions, which included "behavior patterns (as the group did things) and premises (ways the group construed things) about its task, its environment, and its internal interaction" (p. 100).

Then, at the midpoint, groups first "completed (or dropped) major aspects of their starting frameworks (Gersick, n.d.)…Second, groups showed fresh awareness of their deadlines at transitional meetings… Third, transitional meetings broke routines of meeting times, places, styles, and sometimes attendance… Fourth, teams' supervisors played important roles in their transitions…Fifth, transitions yielded specific new agreements on the ultimate directions teams' work should take, and teams made a burst of progress on their projects" (Hackman, 1999, pp. 106 – 107).

The Collaboration Life Cycle

The Collaboration Life Cycle involves four phases: initiation, formation, operation and decomposition. These are interlinked and contain several tasks and subtasks each (Tellioğlu, 2008). This cycle starts with a determined need for collaboration and the building of a workgroup in the initiation phase. In the formation phase, the team defines a common goal, defines roles, and sets up a coordinated work environment (CWE). In the operation phase, the team works within the CWE, preserve the results of their work and "manage change processes." In the last stage, decomposition, the workgroup publishes results and decomposes both the CWE and the workgroup (Tellioğlu, 2008).

Selecting Team Members

The business literature includes plenty of admonitions to hire wisely—based on "character, work ethic, basic intelligence, dedication to fulfilling commitments, and values" as more critical than specific knowledge or skills, which are teachable (Collins, 2001, p. 51). Clearly, having both quality human traits and a well developed skill set would be optimal. The ability to communicate well with different individuals from different backgrounds and with different personalities will also be important.

Some common mistakes in coalescing a team would be including too many people instead of building lean. The research suggests that the optimal work group size is 4.6 members, with an optimal at not more than 6 members: "Indeed, a team may function better when it has slightly *fewer* members than the task actually requires" (Hackman, 2002, pp. 118 - 119).

Team structure does affect performance and outcomes. There are lower group attention spans when teams are larger (Karayaz & Keating, 2007, p. 2596). Smaller teams may be more effective to deal with complexity, and some dyads (the smallest size teams) were found to outperform four-person teams Karayaz & Keating, 2007). Some teams' compositions may be too homogeneous, without sufficient diversity (Hackman, 2002).

Some have suggested a flat (non-hierarchal) structure for virtual teaming, but the research has pointed to more effectiveness with "an *informal hierarchical structure* (that) was associated with more smooth coordination in distributed teams" (Hinds & McGrath, 2006, p. 343). Transparency in team structure should be *de rigueur* for team members.

Goal Setting

No matter what the backgrounds of the various team members, there must be some convergence around shared expectations and goals. There need to be clear understandings of roles, so individuals do not repeat each other's works or infringe on others' territory. There often needs to be greater understandings of the shared technologies to be used and practice uses of the various tools. Shared groupware, socio-technical systems, and repositories also have to be introduced.

Teams need to co-create (or inherit) a stylebook that defines the expectations for the work project quality. The team members have to understand and accept the shared standards for finalizing the work.

There have to be clear workflows and work documentation. There have to be understandings of when meetings will be held and who will communicate with whom and when. Major decision junctures have to be decided and addressed. Security protocols have to be addressed for the proper handling of the digital objects and information that the team will use.

The team leader needs to work to garner resources to enable the team's works and to maintain the most contemporaneous technological outputs. He or she needs to have a sufficient understanding of e-learning pedagogy, digital imagery, related technologies, and the higher education context in which the digital imagery and learning objects will be used.

Manager-led teams will have the leader set the overall direction, design the team and its organizational content, monitor and manage the work process and progress. The team task is then executed by the team members. Self-managing teams will have management set the overall direction and design the team, but the team members themselves will monitor and manage their work process and progress and execute the team work. Self-designing teams will do all tasks except set the general direction. Self-governing teams take over all roles from management ones to line staff ones, according to Hackman's "The Authority Matrix: Four Levels of Team Self-Management (2002, p. 52).

Hackman suggests that leaders must create an environment where teams will thrive, after getting them started on a strong trajectory (2002). A compelling direction challenges team members and motivates them. It sets a clear common purpose, and it is consequential, engaging "the talents of members and encourages the team to identify and use well the full complement of members' knowledge and skills" (Hackman, 2002, p. 72).

This researcher offers five conditions of a successful team: "having a real team, a compelling direction, an enabling team structure, a supportive organizational context, and expert team coaching" (Hackman, 2002, p. ix). The research offers general terms for leadership because of the wide diversity of work-based teams. "Specifically, I suggest that effective team leaders have the following four qualities: (1) they *know* some things, (2) they know how to *do* some things, (3) they have *emotional maturity* sufficient for the demands of the leadership role, and (4) they have a good measure of personal *courage*" (Hackman, 2002, p. 222). A team is successful when the product is acceptable to clients; the team's capabilities have grown, and the group experience has been "meaningful and satisfying for members" (Hackman, 2002, p. 30). Teams with a stable membership will perform better than those that are in constant flux. These members build a familiarity and so can work more efficiently.

Techno for F2F (and Hybrid and Virtual Teaming)

Even teams that are working out of the same location will need shared virtual work spaces for the sharing of work and collaborations (both synchronous and asynchronous. They will need digital ways to archive their work—from the raw in-progress work to the finalized ones; they will need a way to archive their metadata and in-house work documentation. They'll need computer mediated communications technologies to communicate in real-time and also asynchronously. And most co-located teams will still work with others from a distance. Technologies may enhance F2F interactivity. They add value to hybrid communications. In addition, they are critical for mediating virtual teaming.

The following technologies may be used for collaboration in rich ways with co-located teams, hybrid teams, and totally virtual ones. Table 1, "Connectivity Technologies and their Uses in Collaborations" lists common collaborative technologies.

Teams have to select which technologies are useful for their tasks and which are accessible to all the team members.

Sustaining Hot Groups

Hot groups are groups that are highly innovative that may appear as disrupting factors in an organization but which may contribute massively to the organization and field. To create an ecosystem to support the spawning and support of such groups, these authors advise less organization, fewer bureaucratic controls, fewer deadlines and no individual performance evaluations. These groups should have expanded managerial powers (Lipman-Blumen & Leavitt, 1999, p. 228).

DECENTRALIZED COLLABORATION AND VIRTUAL TEAMING

In this networked economy, talent may be brought together from different time zones and geographies. These groups go by different names: global virtual team, remote teams, and virtual teams. These are

Table 1. Connectivity technologies and their uses in F2F, hybrid and virtual collaborations

Connectivity Technologies	Information Rich Uses
Asynchronous	
Email	• Sharing files • Sharing timely information • Maintaining back-channel communications • Offering electronic trails for communications • Coordinating meetings
Fax	• Visuals sent in print form
Listservs	• Connecting groups around shared interests • Maintaining electronic trails
Discussion Forums	• Sharing ideas • Collaborating on issues that are generally not time-sensitive • Documenting electronic communications
Blogs	• Capturing team member ideas • Recording various types of relevant multimedia files • Publishing out privately, semi-privately, and publicly
Wikis	• Co-evolving ideas together through mutual writing and revision • Disseminating information and files • Maintaining a controllable record of information
Collaborative virtual spaces	• Maintaining a coherent space for shared digital files • Asynchronous sharing of multimedia visuals, designs and policies • Coordinating meetings • Offering private development spaces for team members • Providing semi-public spaces for team members
Synchronous	
Telephone	• Real-time voice interactivity • Real-time video interactivity with video phones
Chat and Instant Messaging	• Communicating via real-time textual interactivity • Interactions via real-time voice and conversation • Preserving digital records
Whiteboard	• Sharing live drawing • Sharing annotations of digital files and visuals
Video Conferencing / Teleconferencing	• Live audio, visual interaction • Using body language in communications
Webinars	• Real-time live audio and video interactivity • Shared annotation of digital files
Collaborative virtual spaces	• Real-time chat, IM, video-conferencing, and whiteboard • Holding live small-group meetings • Broadcasting and micro-casting guest presentations
Immersive 3D spaces	• Communicating via avatars • Sharing 3D digital imagery

dispersed teams that are working on separate sub-tasks, with collaborations both within-team and between team.

The definitions read as fairly similar.

Virtual teams are small work/project teams that are geographically dispersed and collaborate via computer-mediated technology, predominantly over the Internet, with a potential face-to-face initiation in order to work for a specific purpose and / or specific piece of work (Karayaz, 2004, as cited in Karayaz & Keating, 2007, p. 2593).

Another group writes:

*A virtual team is an evolutionary form of a network organizatio*n (Miles & Snow, 1986) *enabled by advances in information and communication technology* (Davidow & Malone, 1992; Jarvenpaa & Ives, 1994). *The concept of virtual implies permeable interfaces and boundaries, project teams that rapidly form, reorganize, and dissolve when the needs of a dynamic marketplace change, and individuals with differing competencies who are located across time, space, and cultures* (Kristof et al, 1995; Mowshowitz, 1997)...*virtual teams promise the flexibility, responsiveness, lower costs, and improved resource utilization necessary to meet ever-changing task requirements in highly turbulent and dynamic global business environments* (Mowshowitz, 1997; Snow et al, 1996, as cited in Jarvenpaa & Leidner, n.d., n.p.).

Connected by powerful collaboration technologies, these teams are "thinking together apart" (Larsson, Nov. 2003, p. 153). "Effective virtual teaming requires high trust, high communications, well-defined goals, a culture of informational sharing (without the corrosive effects of informational withholding), and conscious Machiavellian personal bonding and creation of 'social presence'" (Nemiro, 2004, as cited in Hai-Jew, 2006, p. 20).

Surfacing the assumptions of virtual organizations and teams may help a team more freely discuss concerns and solve shared issues. "Much like typical organizations that exist in buildings, virtual organizations have beliefs and values manifested in norms that form behavioral expectations and that give members guidelines for "the way to do things around here" (Elliott & Scacchi, 2003, p. 21).

Some Challenges of Virtual Teams

Remote teams are not without challenges. There have been differences found in the relative awareness between co-located team members vs. remote ones, with the research suggesting a need for further cues to augment the work (Epps, J. & Close, B.S., Apr. – May 2007, p. 2363). More supervision is needed to help "break the ice" between team members, with one intervention based on team building games founded on social psychological theory (Ellis, Luther, Bessiere, & Kellogg, 2008, p. 295).

Managers fear the loss of control in going to telework. "Managers are also concerned that telework may require them to change their management style since they cannot rely on visual contact for monitoring and control. Researchers suggest that a more results-oriented management style is needed (Duxbury, Higgins, and Irving 1987; Metzger and Von Glinow 1988; Olson 1988) and that a shift in management from being a passer of information to a leader or coach is necessary (Duxbury, Higgins, and Irving 1987; Lallande 1984; Savage 1988). Trust is suggested as being a key ingredient to effectively manage teleworkers (Duxbury, Higgins, and Irving 1987; Savage 1988). Managing perceptions of corporate culture in a remote worker is also seen as a possible obstacle, requiring additional investment from managers" (Hendricks and McMains 1989; Olson 1988, as cited in Staples, Borstad, Dusdar, Pliskin, Romm & Tan, 1998, p. 429). Extra efforts must be made to bridge the psychological distance of telework employees (Rathod & Miranda, 1999, pp. 268 – 275).

Silences may be misunderstood. Time zone differences have added a layer of challenge to the work, with some members not very reachable. Multicultural differences may cause challenges to the team members and team leader(s). There may be higher levels of deception and higher reticence to cooperate initially with perceptions of distance, but this may be changed with more interaction (Bradner & Mark, 2002).

Time separations between team members have an impact on coordination costs.

The most salient findings are that: (1) time separation has a strong impact on coordination costs, particularly delay and effort, but this increased effort helps teams achieve coordination success; (2) as more time zones are involved in a project collaboration, the challenges and effort required to achieve success escalate rapidly, thus the importance of understanding how different team configurations across time zones affect team coordination patterns and how teams need to coordinate (Espinosa & Pickering, 2006, p. 9).

One strategy (albeit expensive) is to use a "temporal bridge" for "critical synchronous information seeking" with social information sources across time zones (Milewski, Tremaine, Egan, Zhang, Köbler, & O'Sullivan, 2007, p. 1) for one corporation. The costs of organizing synchronous meetings via virtual meeting spaces may be more challenging. There also may need to be more oversight in terms of enforcing deadlines and pacing the work, which will require on-ground awareness at each of the team members' locations.

Within virtual teams, there is much ambiguity and artificiality, a concept that they call 'team opacity'. Because the team members are in an environment of an increased level of abstraction due to their technology-mediated communication, and because of the influence of the external environment on their work, they run the risk of having lower cohesion and trust than in teams who communicate face to face (F2F). It is discussed that focused on pre- and post process interventions to keep a virtual team functioning at a high level when creating a virtual team (Wang, Huang, & Wang, 2006, n.p.).

The risks of "poor coordination among team members (i.e., lack of simultaneity of effort) or decreased social motivation" are higher for virtual teams (Wang, Huang, & Wang, 2006, n.p.). Team members may misread others' meanings or intentions. The transparency necessary for smooth coordination may be somewhat harder to achieve.

Others have pointed to the risks of losing novel ideas in virtual intercommunications and brainstorms. There may be a lack of critical evaluation of perspectives in distributed collaboration (Farooq, Carroll & Ganoe, 2007, p. 31).

Going virtual has strengths and weaknesses, depending on the team composition and tasks. Virtual teams, as compared to face-to-face ones, have "fewer tendencies to develop constructive or aggressive styles and more tendencies to develop passive interaction styles…Constructive teams tend to do well regardless of the communication mode, and passive teams tend to do poorly regardless of the communication mode. Aggressive teams tend to do poorly, and more so in virtual settings" (Wang, Huang, & Wang, 2006, n.p.).

A Virtual Design Studio

The metaphor of a virtual design studio is helpful in this situation because this is "creative, collaborative, and most-of-all *highly material*—that is the space is dominated by material objects, surfaces for sharing ideas and inspiration, making ideas and activities visible and tangible by means of physical materials such as post-it notes, sketches, magazine scraps, models, and physical prototypes." There are private creative spaces and shared ones. There are serendipitous objects in the space that may evoke cross-contextual ideas for breakthrough designs (Blevis, Wolf, Lim, Sato, & Stolterman, 2007, pp. 2821 – 2822). A virtual design studio should offer works-in-progress in clear view to all participants to invite feedback "*early and often*" (p. 2822). The creative aspects of digital visual creation for e-learning apparently has some overlaps with co-authorship networks (Huang, Zhuang, Li, & Giles, 2008), which draw widely on creativity and mutual productivity. Using virtual means to rapidly prototype and share ideas may make for smoother digital-based innovations.

Virtual Teaming Techno

A range of technologies may be used to enable virtual teaming. Dubé and Paré point to video conferencing, intranets, shared collaborative sites, virtual private networks, telephones, fax machines, emails, and desktop Web conferencing (2001), in a cobbling of technologies. In general, it's easier to use a unified main system for most of the work and interactions, with some additional side technologies.

The functionalities needed are the following:

- Asynchronous collaboration and communication—to allow for non-time-dependent work
- Synchronous collaboration and communication—to allow for real-time, closely-coupled communications and collaboration
- Authenticated commentary and sign-offs—to validate the work
- Authoring tools—to co-create digital imagery and digital learning object (DLO) contents
- Private spaces—for the development of contents
- Semi-public spaces—for the publishing out of evolving work for feedback and critique; for "attunement to others' contributions" (Bryan-Kinns, Healey, & Leach, 2007, p. 224)
- Repository and data storage—with the ability of differentiating raw, evolving and finalized digital imagery

For others, they name some other collaboration functionalities.

In terms of supported functionality we take a bottom up approach and try to address the basic collaboration needs first: distributed storage, distributed search to discover information, self-organized setup of the infrastructure, management of simple (un-)structured data with known semantics, efficient and flexible communication taking into account user mobility, and efficient dissemination of notifications according to current user needs (Hauswirth, Podnar & Decker, 2005, n.p.).

Others suggest that such a collaboration system requires on-demand access to the techno for whenever needs arise; adaptivity in that the right collaboration elements are available for the work context, and integration in that the technology brings together elements from "multiple sources, multiple modalities, and multiple vendor technologies. In addition, it integrates structured collaborative activities with ad hoc peer collaboration tools, and with the business processes at large" (Lei, Chakraborty, Chang, Dikun, Heath, Li, Nayak, & Patnaik, 2004, n.p.).

The ability to communicate information across rich interfaces is critical, particularly given the perception by virtual team members that the help that they're getting from their peers is often that it is poor or non-existent. "These possibilities have somewhat different implications for collaboration tools, since the first would require tools that help with effectively carrying out the work, while the latter places more importance on communication tools that help convey more context, and perhaps more emotional content. In any case, this is a particularly urgent problem since it is directly related to delay, and the responses suggest that people in general will see no need to take any action" (Herbsleb, Mockus, Finholt & Grinter, 2000, p. 327).

Security is an important concern. Any member of a distributed team may compromise the work by sharing information that they shouldn't, for unplanned "downstream" uses. Systems may be hacked. "In many collaborative situations not controlled with specialized tools, all users will likely have equal rights to the work in the mutually shared directories. This strategy makes it relatively simple for users to read and modify work done by the group" (Price, 2007, p. 107).

To prevent project compromise and data loss, team members need to build their work to the system (even if it's in their private folders), and the team leader (and a backup) must have high level access to access even the private folders in case of a team "churn" or team member turnover. There must be endeavors to preserve and protect the work. Some cross-training on the team may make the work easier to protect and less prone to a one-point-of-failure phenomena.

Various systems and combinations of systems in the market today offer the above functionality. These go by various general names: tele-immersive environments, virtual work environments, collaboration suites, collaborative virtual environments, tabletop groupware systems (with worktable interfaces), group support systems, and others.

Richer Mediated Interactivity Range

The technologies have actually evolved beyond these to offer a richer range of interactivity. There's much more seamless moving from desktop workstations to small handhelds for collaboration (Marsic, Krebs, Dorohonceanu, & Tremaine, 2002.) Mobile or ubiquitous collaborations are possible, with lightweight distributed peer-to-peer (P2P) collaboration infrastructures for mobile collaboration. There's research work on the most effective ways to collaborate on physical tasks using head-mounted and scene-oriented video systems (Fussell, Setlock & Kraut, 2003), for more kinetic and physically embodied learning. Others are working to mix augmented reality with virtual reality for more mixed collaborations; in this approach, the augmented reality provides the exocentric, third-person viewpoint, and the virtual reality offers the egocentric, subjective viewpoint (Grasset, Lamb & Billinghurst, 2005).

The collaborative spaces may combine a range of input devices to the shared computing space. One system:

explores the multimodal fusion of pen, speech and 3D gestures, coupled to the dynamic construction of a semantic representation of the interaction, anchored on the sketched diagram, to provide feedback that overcomes some of the intrinsic ambiguities of pointing gestures (Barthelmess, Kaisser, Huang, & Demirdjian, 2005, p. 10).

There are endeavors to capture more direct body language and gesturing in distance communications for richer "disambiguated" communications. Remote gesturing technologies include: use of laser pointer and digital sketching, projecting the hands of the helper into the worker's workspace, viewing the hands of the helper into a separated monitor overlayed (sic) onto the view of the worker's workspace..." (Wickey & Alem, 2007, p. 87). Collaborative virtual environments may closely couple synchronous interactions of team members for manipulating shared artifacts for close real-time learning (Otto, Roberts, & Wolff, 2008), such as the demonstrating of how to assemble a complex detailed object.

There are networked haptic collaboration environments: "Networked haptic virtual environments (NHVEs) are those in which multiple users collaborate and experience force feedback at the same time" (Sankaranarayanan & Hannaford, 2007, n.p.). Social software such as wikis and blogs has been used for "distributed agile development environments" (Abbattista, F., Calefato, F., Gendarmi, D., & Lanubile, F., 2008, pp. 46 – 51). User interfaces are more visually appealing, with a transparent video interface with a personal computer (Stotts, Smith, & Gyllstrom, 2004).

The integration of physical objects in a virtual collaboration are more common now, where "objects that are physical in one space are electronic in the other space, and vice versa. Our distributed system is designed for two groups, with multiple users at each end. Our tangible approach is the first system to enable simultaneous, multi-input across locations" (Klemmer & Everitt, 2002, p. 878).

IMPORTANT TYPES OF "VERBOSE" INTERCOMMUNICATIONS

Given "the loss of the rich, subtle interactions" (Herbsled, Mockus, Finholt & Grinter, 2000, p. 319) in virtual communications, it should be no surprise that a mitigating factor is to increase the richness of intercommunications consciously. High and low-performing virtual design teams were similar in "the number of messages exchanged, the amount of communication devoted to aspects of design, and the amount and proportion of communication spent on team coordination, supportive commentary, and 'other' topics." Where they differed was in verbosity, with the high performing teams using more words. While they spent less time in brainstorming activities, the high performing groups "engaged in more critical commentary and active debate, compared to low performing teams. High performing teams conducted more in-depth discussions in the form of argumentation, as ideas were developed through an interactive debate of the pros and cons of issues" (Ocker & Fjermestad, 2008, p. 51). Other researchers suggest that having more social-based interactions among virtual team members enhance the work experience and the work, but only if they're work-focused: "In addition, conversations in virtual teams have been shown to be more task-focused, to the exclusion of social interaction, although this effect lessens over time" (Ellis, Luther, Bessiere, & Kellogg, 2005, p. 295).

MEDIATING CULTURAL UNDERSTANDINGS

Many virtual teams are global ones, and even those that are not, teams often include diverse members—with cultural differences stemming from more than nationality, language, race and ethnicity, but those "springing up from age, gender,, income, national(ity), sexual orientation, or physical or mental disabilities" (Duryea, 1992, as cited in Golemon, 2003, p. 231). A global virtual team spans national and people group boundaries. Such teams are "culturally diverse, geographically dispersed, and electronically communicating work group" (Massey, Hung, Montoya-Weiss & Ramesh, 2001, p. 207).

Culture informs the total communications framework between people, and it is "comprised of words, actions, nonverbal behaviors, the handling of time, space, and materials, world view, beliefs, and attitudes passed over time from generation to generation. Culture often serves as a perceptual filter with which we determine that which is important to us, and that which is not. In many ways, it is necessary to unlearn the lessons of culture in order to effectively communicate with others whom we perceive to be different from ourselves" (Raybourn, Apr. 2000, p. 28). Another challenge involves the lack of some communications cues: "One of the major disadvantages of a GVT is the lack of physical interaction, nonverbal cues, and synergies that often accompany face-to-face communications" (Dubé & Paré, 2001, p. 73).

What may compound cross-cultural communications challenges in virtual team situations is the lack of shared understandings of terminology, differing technological proficiency levels, and different work situations and technological infrastructures.

Hofstede's Cultural Dimensions model focuses on power distance (vs. egalitarianism), individualism (vs. collectivism), masculinity (vs. femininity), uncertainty avoidance (vs. risk-taking), and long-term orientation (vs. short-term considerations) as key differentiating factors between groups with different cultures. These concepts affect human interrelationships, communications habits, behaviors, the handling of conflict, risk-taking, and world-views, among other aspects.

Hall differentiates between perceptions of time as either monochromatic ("emphasize schedules, segmenting activity, and promptness") or polychromatic ("do several things at once. They value involving themselves with others and completing tasks over keeping schedules") (Golemon, 2003, p. 231), with the differences more about a comparison between traditionally Western and Eastern values.

The West-East divide is addressed also by another theorist, who looks at thought patterns. "In Nisbett's theory, there are reliable differences in the modes of thinking between people from the East and the West. In greater detail, the Western way of thinking is characterized by Nisbett as analytical, meaning that the people tend to "think in a line." However, the Eastern way of thinking seems to be more holistic in that they tend to "think in a circle" (Shi & Clemmensen, 2008, p. 2813). Cultural differences inform communications habits and interpretations (Massey, Hung, Montoya-Weiss & Ramesh, 2001, p. 207).

Cultural contexts (defined as "traditions, practices, metaphors, values, and stories and legends") may inform the interpretation of "movement grammars" and "shape grammars" in visual communications (Asokan & Cagan, 2005, p. 4). Movement may involve various aspects—which the authors label "emotion, action, rhythm, gender, speed, timing, firmness and lighting" (Asokan & Cagan, 2005, p. 9).

Cultural diversity is seen as a positive, in some ways, such as offering more innovative problem-solving. Those working on global teams may consider some of the following factors.

- Inter-cultural considerations, e.g., the language and cultural backgrounds of users and project staff;

- Methodology, e.g., selecting techniques that will provide the same quality of results across countries;
- Logistics, e.g., recruiting users globally, setting up and resourcing international sessions;
- Project management, e.g., planning, coordinating multiple user groups and remote usability teams, and delegating responsibilities among the teams" (Gorlenko & Krause, 2006, p. 160).

The research literature on cultural adjustments is positive in terms of the ability of people to make the necessary adjustments in understandings. Team members can "adapt their behavior in both spoken and written communication as well as allowing for religious beliefs and time zone differences" (Anawati & Craig, 2006, p. 44). They can learn how to understand each other's silences (Anawati & Craig, 2006). They know to use visual supplements to aid in the communications, and they engage in both formal and informal communications.

Team managers themselves know how to "enforce a higher level of collaboration and integration across the team" (Williams & Stout, 2008, p. 356) through more regular meetings with their large (30 member) global team. They use planning to set expectations, and they strategically co-locate part of their team. They bring on members with high expertise and strong technical skills. And for synchronous meetings, usually held in virtual conference rooms, they control the size to not more than 7 – 10 at a time for the greatest productivity (p. 361).

ENCOURAGING QUALITY IN COLLABORATIVE IMAGE DESIGN

Virtual collaboration must involve awareness of ways to create "*mutually engaging* interaction between people – interaction in which creative sparks fly and we lose ourselves in the joint action" (Bryan-Kinns, Healey & Leach, 2007, p. 223). J. Nemiro suggests that such innovations on virtual teams are based on "design, climate, resources, norms and protocols, and continual assessment and learning" (Nemiro, 2004, p. xxvii) and four stages of creation: "idea generation, development, finalization and closure, and evaluation" (Nemiro, 2004, as cited in Hai-Jew, 2006, p. 20). There are a range of computer tools to encourage brainstorming—by tapping into intuition and linear problem-solving and visualizations. Various ingredients may help spark creativity. Some team members identified six necessary factors as "autonomy and freedom, challenge, clear direction, diversity / flexibility / tension, support for creativity, trust, and participative safety" (Wang, Huang, & Wang, 2006, n.p.).

DEFINING WORKFLOW PRACTICES

Y. Benkler uses the term "centralization" to describe how to create coherence from the work of individual agents for an effective result (Benkler, 2006, p. 62). That seems fitting in a virtual teaming context. The centralization not only includes proper team management and a clearly defined stylebook for quality but also possibly sample work, for the team members' learning and norming. The concept of "encapsulation" includes the hiding of complexity from users of a technology so as to ease its use. This concept applies also to collaboration around digital image creation.

The following (Table 2) is an outline from Chapter 7 about the steps to creating quality images in e-learning. Some of this clearly belongs in the management purview, while the "Development and

Production Work" clearly falls to the development team. That's not to say that there's not value from soliciting line-level insights about these other issues, but selectively assigning the work would be a good strategy.

Documentation and IP Rights Management

Team-created collaborative digital image creation will require much closer attention to documentation (Figure 2). This will involve the sourcing of the raw images, the proper metadata, and the work documentation about what was done with each image and how it fits in with the larger project. The person in charge of each change should be clearly recorded for easier tracking. The work annotations should use a proper semantic base, so that images that have already been used are not used again.

Finalizing Work and Dissemination Check-offs

Deadlines are often set by grants or the timing of national conferences or other on-ground realities for the team leaders. Delays in any phase of the digital image capture, creation, testing (user-based, and alpha- and beta-testing) and deployment may slow down the finalizing of portions of the project. It's clearly important not to freeze a version until it meets the standards set by the instructor and the development team.

CONCLUSION

Bringing together a collaborative team around a shared project is actually a lot more common than many may imagine. Planning ahead, setting standards, selecting team members with care, identifying the right technologies for the project, and providing astute and culturally sensitive leadership may enhance the

Table 2.

Needs Assessment and Environmental Scan
Step 1: Defining the Project Scope; Evaluating Extant Resources, and Conducting a Gaps Analysis
Step 2: Assessing the Learning Objectives and Learning Situation; Understanding Learners and their
Learning Needs
Step 3: Evaluating the Techno
Project Management
Step 4: Building a Team, a Budget and a Schedule
Setting Standards for Quality
Step 5: Setting Ethical, Pedagogical, Cultural, Domain, Aesthetic, and Technological Stylebook Standards
Development and Production Work
Step 6: The Collection of Rich, Raw Materials
Step 7: Intellectual Property Negotiations, Arrangements and Documentation
Step 8: Creating the Learning Images
Step 9: Accessibility Mitigations
Assessment and Revision
Step 10: Alpha and Beta Testing; Revision, Editing and Metadata Labeling
Launch and Future Planning
Step 11: Deployment for Learning and Archival
Step 12: Planning for Updates

Figure 2. A more documentation-heavy workflow in collaborative image design

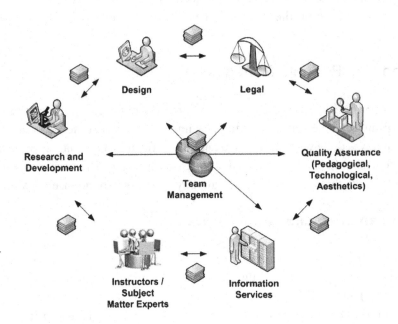

work of virtual distributed teams creating digital imagery for e-learning. The flexibilities of digital image editing and creation allow rich flexibility in evolving digital imagery. The immersive spaces that have been created for collaboration offer plenty of functionalities for team members and leaders.

REFERENCES

Abbatista, F., Calefato, F., Gendarmi, D., & Lanubile, F. (2008). Incorporating social software into distributed agile development environments. In *Proceedings of the 23rd IEEE/ACM International Conference on Automated Software Engineering* (pp. 46-51). Washington, DC: IEEE.

Agarwala, A., Dontcheva, M., Agarwala, M., Drucker, S., Colburn, A., Curless, B., et al. (2004). Interactive digital photomontage. In *Proceedings of the International Conference on Computer Graphics and Interactive Techniques* (pp. 294-302). New York: ACM.

Anawati, D., & Craig, A. (2006). Behavioral adaptation with cross-cultural virtual teams. *IEEE Transactions on Professional Communication, 49*(1), 44–56. doi:10.1109/TPC.2006.870459

Asokan, A., & Cagan, J. (2005). Defining cultural identities using grammars: An exploration of cultural languages to create meaningful experiences. In *Proceedings of the 2005 conference on Designing for User eXperience* (pp. 2-11). New York: AIGA.

Barthelmes, P., Kaiser, E., Huang, X., & Demirdjian, D. (2005) Distributed pointing for multimodal collaboration over sketched diagrams. In *Proceedings of the ICMI '05*, Trento, Italy (pp. 10-17). New York: ACM.

Benkler, Y. (2006). *The Wealth of Networks.* New Haven, CT: Yale University Press.

Blevis, E., Wolf, T. V., Lim, Y.-K., Sato, K., & Stolterman, E. (2007, April-May). Workshop extended abstract: Supporting design studio culture in HCI. In *Proceedings of the CHI 2007*, San Jose, California, USA (pp. 2821-2822).

Bodenstaff, L., Wombacher, A., Reichert, M., & Wieringa, R. (2007). Monitoring collaboration from a value perspective. In *Proceedings of the 2007 Inaugural IEEE International Conference on Digital Ecosystems and Technologies (IEEE DEST 2007)* (pp. 134-140).

Bradner, E., & Mark, G. (2002). Why distance matters: Effects on cooperation, persuasion and deception. In *Proceedings of the CSCW '02*, New Orleans, LA (pp. 226-235). New York: ACM.

Bryan-Kinns, N., Healey, P. G. T., & Leach, J. (2007). Exploring mutual engagement in creative collaborations. In *Proceedings of the C&C '07*, Washington, DC (pp. 223-232). New York: ACM.

Clark, R. C., & Mayer, R. E. (2003). *E-Learning and the Science of Instruction.* San Francisco: Pfeiffer, John Wiley & Sons.

Collins, J. (2001). *Good to great: Why some companies make the leap...and others don't.* New York: Harper Collins Books.

Dubé, L., & Paré, G. (2001). Global virtual teams. *Communications of the ACM, 44*(12), 71–73. doi:10.1145/501317.501349

Elliott, M. S., & Scacchi, W. (2003). Free software developers as an occupational community: Resolving conflicts and fostering collaboration. In *Proceedings of the GROUP '03*, Sanibel Island, FL (pp. 21-30). New York: ACM.

Ellis, J. B., Luther, K., Bessiere, K., & Kellogg, W. A. (2008). Games for virtual team building. In *Proceedings of the DIS 2008*, Cape Town, South Africa (pp. 295-304). New York: ACM.

Epps, J., & Close, B. S. (2007). A study of co-worker awareness in remote collaboration over a shared application. In *Proceedings of the CHI 2007*, San Jose, CA. New York: ACM.

Espinosa, J. A., & Pickering, C. (2006). The effect of time separation on coordination processes and outcomes: A case study. In *Proceedings of the 39th Hawaii International Conference on System Sciences* (pp. 1-10). Washington, DC: IEEE.

Farooq, U., Carroll, J. M., & Ganoe, C. H. (2007). Supporting creativity with awareness in distributed collaboration. In *Proceedings of the GROUP '07*, Sanibel Island, FL, USA (pp. 31-40). New York: ACM.

Fussell, S. R., Setlock, L. D., & Kraut, R. E. (2003). Effects of head-mounted and scene-oriented video systems on remote collaboration on physical tasks. *CHI, 5*(1), 513–520.

Goleman, P. (2003). Communicating in the intercultural classroom. *IEEE Transactions on Professional Communication, 46*(3).

Gorlenko, L., & Krause, S. (2006). Managing international usability projects: Cooperative strategy. In *Proceedings of the CHI 2006*, Montréal, Québec, Canada (pp. 159-164). New York: ACM.

Grasset, R., Lamb, P., & Billinghurst, M. (2005). Evaluation of mixed-space collaboration. In *Proceedings of the International Symposium on Mixed and Augmented Reality (ISMAR '05)*. New York: ACM.

Hackman, J. R. (1990). *Groups that work (and those that don't): Creating conditions for effective team work.* San Francisco: Jossey-Bass.

Hackman, J. R. (2002). *Leading teams: Setting the stage for great performances.* Boston: Harvard Business School Press.

Hai-Jew, S. (2006, Spring). Deploying virtual teaming for high creativity [Review]. *Journal of Interactive Instruction Development, 18*(4), 20–21.

Hauswirth, M., Podnar, I., & Decker, S. (2005). On P2P collaboration infrastructures. In *Proceedings of the 14th IEEE International Workshops on Enabling Technologies: Infrastructure for Collaborative Enterprise (WETICE '05).*

Herbsleb, J. D., Mockus, A., Finholt, T. A., & Grinter, R. E. (2000). Distance, dependencies, and delay in a global collaboration. In *Proceedings of the CSCW*, Philadelphia, PA (pp. 319-328). New York: ACM.

Hinds, P., & McGrath, C. (2006) Structures that work: Social structure, work structure and coordination ease in geographically distributed teams. In *Proceedings of the CSCW '06*, Banff, Alberta, Canada (pp. 343-352). New York: ACM.

Huang, J., Zhuang, Z., Li, J., & Giles, C. L. (2008). Collaboration over time: Characterizing and modeling network evolution. In *Proceedings of the WSDM '08*, Palo Alto, CA (pp. 107-116). New York: ACM.

Jarvenpaa, S.L., & Leidner, D.E. (n.d.). *Communication and trust in global virtual teams.* Retrieved

Karayaz, G., & Keating, C. B. (2007, August). Virtual team effectiveness using dyadic teams. In *Proceedings of the 2007 PICMET*, Portland, OR (pp. 2593-2603).

Klemmer, S., & Everitt, K. (2002). Bridging physical and electronic media for distributed design collaboration. In *Proceedings of the CHI 2002*, Minneapolis, MN (pp. 878-879). New York: ACM.

Larsson, A. (2003). Making sense of collaboration: The challenge of thinking together in global design teams. In *Proceedings of the GROUP '03*, Sanibel Island, FL (pp. 153-160). New York: ACM.

Lei, H., Chakraborty, D., Chang, H., Dikun, M. J., Heath, T., Li, J. S., et al. (2004). Contextual collaboration: Platform and applications. In *Proceedings of the 2004 IEEE International Conference on Services Computing (SCC '04).*

Lipman-Blumen, J., & Leavitt, H. J. (1999). *Hot groups: Seeding them, feeding them, and using them to ignite your organization.* Oxford, UK: Oxford University Press.

Marsic, I., Krebs, A. M., Dorohonceanu, B. l., & Tremaine, M. (2002). Designing and examining PC to Palm collaboration. In *Proceedings of the 35th Hawaii International Conference on System Sciences.*

McLaughlin, T. (2006). Taxonomy of digital creatures: Defining character development techniques based upon scope of use. In International Conference on Computer Graphics and Interactive Techniques. New York: ACM.

Milewski, A. E., Tremaine, M., Egan, R., Zhang, S., Köbler, F., & O'Sullivan, P. (2007). Information 'bridging' in a global organization. In *Proceedings of the 2007 conference of the center for advanced studies on Collaborative research* (pp. 1-10). New York: ACM.

Nemiro, J. (2004). Key components for creativity in virtual teams. In *Creativity in Virtual Teams: Key Components for Success.* San Francisco: John Wiley and Sons.

November 30, 2008, from http://hyperion.math.upatras.gr/commorg/jarvenpaa/

Ocker, R. J., & Fjermestad, J. (2008). Communication differences in virtual design teams: Findings from a multi-method analysis of high and low performing experimental teams. *The Data Base for Advances in Information Systems, 39*(1), 51–67.

Otto, O., Roberts, D., & Wolff, R. (2006). A review of effective closely-coupled collaboration using immersive CVEs. In Proceedings of the VRCIA 2006. Hong Kong (pp. 145-154). New York: ACM.

Price, S. M. (2007). Supporting resource-constrained collaboration environments. *Computer, 40*(6), 106–108. doi:10.1109/MC.2007.220

Rathod, M. M., & Miranda, S. M. (1999). Telework and psychological distance: The mediating effects of culture and technology in four countries. In *Proceedings of the SIGCPR '99*, New Orleans, LA, USA (pp. 268-275).

Raybourn, E. M. (2000). Designing an emergent culture of negotiation in collaborative virtual communities: The case of the DomeCityMOO. *SIGGROUP Bulletin, 21*(1), 28–29.

Sankaranarayanan, G., & Hannaford, B. (2007). Comparison of performance of virtual coupling schemes for haptic collaboration using real and emulated Internet connections. In *Proceedings of the 1st international conference on robot communication and coordination.* New York: ACM.

Shi, Q., & Clemmensen, T. (2008). Communication patterns and usability problem finding in cross-cultural thinking aloud usability testing. In *Proceedings of the CHI 2008*, Florence, Italy (pp. 2811-2816). New York: ACM.

Staples, S., Borstad, A., Pliskin, N., Romm, C. T., Tan, M., & Dusdar, S. (1998). Telework practice across national cultures. In Proceedings of the International Conference on Information Systems, Helsinki, Finland (pp. 429-430).

Stotts, D., Smith, J. M., & Gyllstrom, K. (2004). FaceSpace: Endo- and exo-spatial hypermedia in the transparent video facetop. In Proceedings of the HT '04, Santa Cruz, CA, USA (pp. 48-57). New York: ACM. –Tellioğlu, H. (2008). Collaboration life cycle. In *Proceedings of the International Symposium on Collaborative Technologies and Systems* (pp. 357-366). Washington, DC: IEEE.

Wang, Q. P., Huang, H., & Wang, X. (2006). Intelligent virtual team in collaborative design. In *Proceedings of the 7th International Conference. on Computer-Aided Industrial design and Conceptual Design 2006, CAIDCD '06.*

Wickey, A., & Alem, L. (2007). Analysis of hand gestures in remote collaboration: Some design recommendations. In *Proceedings of the OzCHI 2007*, Adelaide, Australia (pp. 87-93). New York: ACM.

Williams, W., & Stout, M. (2008). Colossal, scattered, and chaotic (Planning with a large distributed team). In *Proceedings of the Agile 2008 Conference* (pp. 356-361). Washington, DC: IEEE.

KEY TERMS AND DEFINITIONS

Co-location (n): The state of being in the same location or place

Collaboration (n): People working together on a shared project; human cooperation

Cross Functional Team (n): A group of work collaborators who represent different areas of expertise or domain knowledge

Design (n): A plan, a blueprint, a purposive schema, a diagram

Distributed (adj): Spread out over distances, not co-located

Graphics Stylebook (n): A digital publication that defines the parameters of a project's design such as the technological, aesthetic and pedagogical guidelines

Knowledge Management (n): The storage and dissemination of information and knowledge via socio-technical systems

Process Loss (n): The loss of efficiencies often stemming from poor coordination or poor work processes

Prototype (n): An initial design, an original model

Raw Files (n): Unprocessed or unrefined images, sketches, diagrams and other elements used in the creation of digital imagery

Remote Gesturing Technology (n): Communications technology that capture human gestures and body language

Team Opacity (n): The ambiguity and artificiality in a team; the lack of transparency in a team in terms of information, work processes, or members

Virtual Teaming (n): The grouping of individuals around a shared project using computer mediated communications (CMC)

Virtual Workspace (n): A virtual space where virtual team members may interact, store and share documents, create digital artifacts, and collaborate

Chapter 10
Effectively Integrating Graphics into E-Learning

ABSTRACT

Pedagogical theories and practices inform the effective integration of digital graphics in e-learning. This chapter examines how digital images may enhance e-learning at critical junctures, based on the learning context, learning objectives and learner needs. This also offers some insights on the procurement and / or creation of existing digital imagery to fit the learning context. This offers strategies for updating e-learning graphics for continuing applicability to a learning situation. Diana Marrs addresses how to maximize digital content quality in live interactive television and video conference courses, in a sidebar.

CHAPTER OBJECTIVES

- Suggest some ways to integrate digital imagery with the electronic learning
- Differentiate between loose and tight coupling of images in an e-learning situation
- Explore the learning roles of visuals in e-learning
- Show how digital imagery may enhance learning at critical junctures
- Offer a method to effectively integrate digital visuals into an e-learning context and learning path
- Introduce some applied theories and practices to the integration of digital imagery in e-learning
- Show the importance of consistent aesthetics in the use of digital imagery
- Demonstrate the importance of efficacy testing of digital imagery with live users
- Discuss ways to maximize digital content quality on live ITV and video conference courses

DOI: 10.4018/978-1-60566-972-4.ch010

- Recommend how to update imagery effectively
- Explore how digital imagery needs to be archived effectively for later reference

INTRODUCTION

Digital imagery may be inherited from a number of sources. They may be open-source, royalty-free works or those in the public domain, hosted off of websites or repositories. These may be images released for various uses through Creative Commons™ or other types of releases. They may be imagery that have been integrated into reusable learning objects (RLOs) that have been created using various instructional models. They may be images that may be created live from websites that offer access to satellite imagery or visual captures.

Effectively integrating digital graphics and imageries into a learning trajectory depends on the learning context, the learning objectives, the learners (and their needs) and the domain knowledge. Whether the imagery is used in a training experience, a simulation, a short course or a long course, it is important to consider how digital imagery adds value pedagogically. Digital imagery costs money, time and effort to create, find, purchase, and integrate. Having a strategic approach in deciding how to use digital imagery will be critical for effective e-learning.

Imagery may be freestanding or integrated with other contents for learning. Loose integration or loose coupling means that the visuals are not innately connected with other images. These may be "loose" digital slides, slideshows, diagrams, a screenshot, or a video still. These may be experienced in a range of different orders and with or without any organizational structure.

Tight integration or tight coupling means that the visuals link inextricably with other contents, as in an immersive space or simulation, a video, or a visualization. Ontologies and taxonomies of images involve defined inter-relationships between them.

Figure 1, "Imagery Types and Integration Methods," illustrates this concept.

Discrete visuals are more flexible in versioning for different uses. The atomistic sizes of these images make them more interchangeable and able-to-be-integrated into multimedia builds. The smaller the granularity, the fewer dependencies (on context, on technologies) there are, the better. Discrete visuals may be used at a point-of-need or juncture in the learning. Tightly coupled visuals may have less applicability for a variety of learning applications but are more pre-packaged for particular learning purposes. These images would be contents related to reusable learning objects, for example, or imagery integrated with compressed video sequences. Some visual resources may be used only for reference, for additional learning or enrichment.

Figure 2, titled "The Integration of Digital Imagery in E-Learning: Loose to Tight Coupling Continuum," gives a range of digital imageries as they fit on this continuum. It is important to view the imagery as its own form before analyzing how it connects to the larger gestalt for contextual learning.

As noted in the diagram above, digital visuals may be use anywhere along the Virtuality Continuum by Milgram and Kishino—from the real environment to augmented reality to augmented virtuality to fully virtual environments (Milgram & Kishino, 1994, as cited in Christian, 2006).

Digital imagery used in an e-learning training or course may be in various states of completeness. They may be non-existent but only textually defined (or defined as a set of directions), partially created, or complete (either static or evolving). Some imagery for assignments may not even be pre-defined; they may be a requirement for a learner assignment that hasn't yet been designed or engineered. In other

Figure 1. Imagery types and integration methods

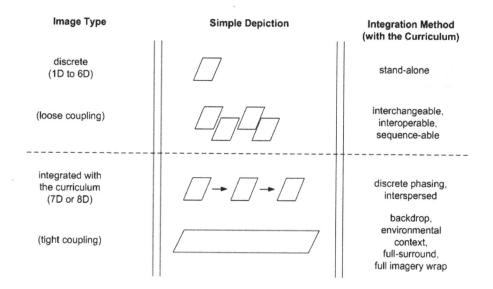

words, that image may be open-ended, without the subject matter expert or faculty member "seeing" what the imagistic outcome may be (Zarzycki, 2004).

Again, it is helpful to conceptualize of digital imagery in a rich range. Some may be manipulable, and others may be in fixed form. Some are static, and some are dynamic. Some are photo-realistic; some are synthetic, and some are a mix of both. The imageries may be professionally created, or they may be works of amateurs and learners. The data value of the imagery may range from "info-light" to "info-heavy."

Another way to conceptualize the contributions of digital imagery is to use Bloom's taxonomy in terms of the level of learning that may be addressed with the imageries. This model builds foundationally: knowledge, comprehension, application, analysis, synthesis, and evaluation. Learners may use imagery to capture knowledge; learn about real-world realities; question ideas; predict potentialities in the future; organize information; exemplify concepts; elaborate on ideas; summarize key points about particular phenomena or entities; interpret events or sequences, or experience different realities. Beyond Bloom's taxonomy, they may even innovate or create new understandings in a field.

Some early thoughts in integrating digital imagery may involve the following questions.

- How should the image be used?
- What should individuals do with the image?
- What information or meaning(s) do individuals need to see in the image?
- How may the image be used for learning purposes?

What are learners expected to do with the images in terms of thought? Should they have a sensory response? Will they engage in deductive reasoning? Will they draw inferences from the imagery? Will they interact *with* the imagery (as through a graphical user interface) or will they interact *through* the imagery (as through an avatar)?

Figure 2. The integration of digital imagery in e-learning: loose-to-tight coupling continuum

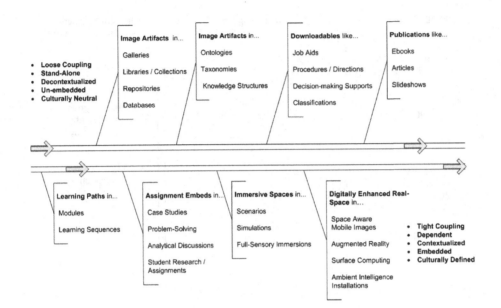

INTEGRATING DIGITAL IMAGERY

What is meant by integrating digital imagery into e-learning? This integration may be conceptualized first in various layers: the e-learning trajectory at the highest level, then the particular application of the image in an assignment, assessment, or other specific learning context.

Levels of Integration

The highest level of e-learning may be visualized as a trajectory or e-learning path, within the context of the curriculum or course or the overall learning process. This may be sequential; this may be branched based on learner performance and needs; this may be a la carte, based on learner choice. Here, imagery may be used throughout an e-learning trajectory; it may be inserted at discrete points.

A more learner-direct level is the lesson level, where imagery fits in with an assignment, assessment, project, survey, or e-learning environment. The imagery may support various learning purposes.

Imageries used in learning often appear in assignments, lectures, experiential learning, and preparatory (antecedent) learning. Those used in assessments are integrated with questions, case studies, design questions, and problem-solving. Those used in research projects involve the setting of contexts and understandings. Digital images used in surveys help make surveys more accessible (Christian, Dillman & Smyth, 2007, as cited in Lewis, Dishon, Johnson, & Firtion, 2008). Visuals used in intercommunications enhance the creation of individual or group telepresence and promote the creation of shared peopled virtual spaces. Visuals may enhance the building of environments and brand them for sensory and cognitive immersiveness (as in metaphors for virtual spaces). They may be used for a navigational structure. Visuals may also be used for practice—for rote memorization—as in the use of flashcards, repeatable experiences and games, and other aspects.

Figure 3. Central-to-peripheral roles of digital imagery in e-learning

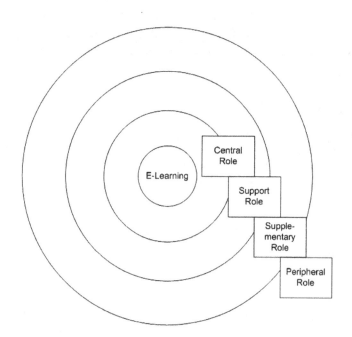

The Learning Roles of Visuals in E-Learning

One early conceptualization of the integration of digital imagery may be the role of the visuals to the e-learning (see Figure 3). One simple view is to see what the visuals contribute to the learning.

In a learning trajectory, a visual may fit into the lesson in ways that are central to the direct learning. Here, the imagery is a main cause for the learning. In simulations, immersive learning, visual-based learning (maps, visual designs, and diagrams), geographical information systems, the images are a core part to the learning. A graphical user interface is at core visual and is important for some e-learning experiences. Complex visualizations require the imagery as a core part of the communications. Learning here cannot happen without this necessary imagery. Without the central imagery, the learning objectives would not be attainable.

Images the next "orbit" out are those that play a support role in learning. Here, the images contribute to the learning; they're value-added, such as through the use of images to illustrate a point, provide visual examples, define categories by visual factors, compare and contrast various points, or enrich a case study. Here, images may be evidentiary. They may show cause and effect. The imagery is not *the* learning, but it contributes core understandings. The imagery works in unison with text and other curricular materials. Supportive imagery contributes to the achieving of the learning objectives.

In the next orbit out, the digital imagery is more peripheral to the central learning: here, images may be supplementary—as in antecedent learning, scaffolding (for pre-learning and post-learning), and pedagogical agentry (in support roles). They may be part of the opt-in learning. They may be part of extra credit. Supplementary imagery supports the "lesser" learning objectives, or they help prepare learners to address the more challenging ones. Such imageries may offer redundancy in the learning.

The outermost orbit is the peripheral one. Here, imagery has a small effect on the direct learning. These may be decorative images (for flourish); they may be part of general telepresence or look-and-feel to enhance the learning context. The images may serve to "brand" a learning experience or virtual space by giving it a core identity. Here, the digital imagery may not relate directly to the stated learning objectives but rather add aesthetic value.

Effective Digital Imagery for E-Learning

For efficacy, imagery needs to fit its particular circumstance. Also, these objects must work on the content, values, and technological standards levels. Tables 1, 2 and 3 highlight some of these factors.

The creation of such effective visuals then will require focused planning and design work in these above areas.

SOME APPLIED THEORIES AND PRACTICES

The relative efficacy of images in a particular learning context, sequence or applied situation really depends on the learning domain, the instructor's pedagogical approach, and the needs of the learners. Still, some of the research-based principles for multimedia design may apply. Mayer proposes the following elements for principled design:

Table 1. Effective digital imagery for e-learning: Contents

Area of Digital Imagery Integration Efficacy	Features
Domain Field / Informational Value	• Meets the standards of the field • Provides quality and relevant visual information • Offers credible information • Represents truth • Presents timely information • Demonstrates originality of vision or aesthetics • Meets legal evidentiary standards for collection and capture • Properly represents physical realities (if relevant)
Pedagogy	• Offers support for the learning situation / context • Shows sensitivity to the various types of learners and stakeholders to the learning situation • Aligns with the applied pedagogical theories
Culture	• Works across cultures • May be culturally neutral or at least culturally non-offensive • May strive to offer universally valuable information • May offer cultural insights
Message Clarity	• Provides clear message(s) • Eliminates noise in the message • Is not misleading; does not support misconceptions • Has accurate informational provenance • Has standard metadata information • Is clearly labeled and captioned
Coherence	• Offers frame-by-frame coherence in motion / in sequence • Presents a unified experience and deeper understanding

Table 2. Effective digital imagery for e-learning: Values

Area of Digital Imagery Integration Efficacy	Features
Ethics	• Presents accurate information • Does not mislead viewers • Does not offer stereotypical images of people • Does not cause harm • Does not offend societal values and mores

Table 3. Effective digital imagery for e-learning: Technology standards (Hai-Jew, 2009)

Area of Digital Imagery Integration Efficacy	Features
Technology	• Offers seamless portability to digital repositories, L/CMSes, databases, and websites • Follows international standards for interchangeability • Fits the technological situation whether in a real environment, augmented reality, augmented virtuality, or a wholly virtual environment • Is compressed into durable visual formats • Is editable • Is updatable • May be enhanced for accuracy (as in orthophotographs)
Accessibility	• Follows federal, state and local laws and accessibility guidelines; adheres by international standards • Is machine readable • Is fully annotated • Involves alt-text and captioning descriptions with "equal" learning value

- *Multimedia principle:* present an explanation using words and pictures rather than solely in words…
- *Spatial contiguity principle*: present corresponding text and pictures near each other on the page or screen rather than far from each other…
- *Temporal contiguity principle:* present corresponding speech and pictures at the same time rather than at different times…
- *Modality principle:* accompany an animation with concurrent narration rather than on-screen text…
- *Coherence principle:* minimize extraneous words, pictures, and sounds when giving a multimedia explanation (Mayer, 2000, pp. 372 – 373).

Image Requirements for the E-Learning

Planning for digital imagery requirements for a course from the beginning will be helpful. Images have a high potential of enhancing learning, not only for visual learners but for the majority of learners. Images are conveyed through a critical sensory channel, and they may integrate a rich depth of information.

Defining the learning needs and uses of the imagery in the learning will help set parameters for the digital image design environment. It may help to ensure that there is a consistent pool of available images for the length of the studies or for the length of the course. This availability would optimally be for the reasonable length of the course. For many courses, that may require the purchase or release of rights "into perpetuity" for future reference and use, without the continual need to return to the issue of renewing rights and paying regular subscription fees.

Analysis of the Image Requirements for the E-Learning

- What images are needed?
- Where may legally-obtained images be acquired from?
- How may the images be vetted for quality choices?
- How may these images be named for consistent reference?
- How may the images be well organized and synthesized for learning purposes?
- How may the images be presented for learning?
- How may these images be evaluated for learning efficacy?

Proper Atomistic Size

For most digital imagery, there are ways to disaggregate pieces for learning value. Screen shots, screen captures, video keyframes, video stills, and still image pull-outs may all be taken from digital images. To elaborate, there are ways to decouple images from digital resources. Within the limits of intellectual property releases, those who use or create digital imagery in e-learning may rework image sources for optimal learning.

USING IMAGERY TO FIT THE LEARNING CONTEXT

Learning domains may generally be understood to include particular types of digital imagery. For example, history may involve scans of documents, photos of historical figures, timelines, diagrams (like family trees), and maps. Computer science graphics may include network diagrams and models. The life sciences may involve photomicrographs, photographs, illustrations, and diagrams. Art courses may feature sketches, paintings, drawings, computerized images, logos, and other designs. English courses may use images for writing prompts and diagrams of writing and analytical reading processes. Landscape architecture may involve geospatial data, maps, and aerial images. Oceanography and geology may involve live sensor data.

Visualizations are used to enhance human understandings and analysis, and ultimately to promote new learning and insights. Imagery may be offered at the point-of-need. They may be a constant reference resource. They may be part and parcel of the learning, as in immersive simulations.

Digital imagery is always used in a context of constraints—of equipment, of expertise, of time, and of money. Within these limits, there may be various channels to acquire these images. They may be created; they may be attained through open source or copyright releases, or they may be captured from a third-party content provider. For many instructors, they choose to use pre-determined images for particular learning purposes. Some will also use finite and open-ended sources, such as public image sites. Most e-learning courses and trainings may pull from multiple sources, depending on needs.

Online Environmental Design

For learners, imagery may be used for the online environmental design. Their virtual learning spaces may be portrayed as offices or cafes or factory floors. A particular field may be envisioned with pieces that are both informative and decorative, such as a shared student club site with related symbols and image artifacts.

Conveying Assignments

A number of design fields will use imagery to convey assignments. Learners may receive topographical information, climate and water flow information, a budget, and a definition of client needs to design land use plans. Or they may receive images of a building's exterior, its blueprints, and a task to redesign the building's interior spaces. Many such tasks may be based on real-world spaces. Prior to a field trip, learners may get visuals of the site they are to visit.

Sometimes, incomplete imagery may be provided, with learners asked to complete the imagery based on a set of principles and rules. Learners may be expected to create their own imagery based on various prompts and assignments.

Work Samples

Learners may view various images that are captures of live former student work samples or professional work. This creates a sense of professional context for the learning work.

Illustrating Selves

Learners may be asked to illustrate themselves in avatar form, with their instructor and teaching assistants embodied virtually. The telepresence piece is critical in shared virtual spaces to represent selves and to promote interactivity.

Memorization and Practice

Imagery may be used in e-learning "games" such as mix-and-match. Unusual images may be used to enhance memorability or evoke affects that may enhance memory. Sometimes, for example, images are linked to particular foreign language learning. In agronomy, images may be used to help identify particular plants. Various visuals may be used as mnemonic devices.

Augmented Reality

Augmented reality involves the use of digital imagery (and audio) in a live real-world situation. The imagery may be delivered via head mounted displays or digital projectors or touch screens. Augmented reality is used in museum tours, military training, art installations, and training that involves muscle memory.

Mobile Environments

The use of imagery in mobile environments must consider the limits of small screens and how little visual information may comparatively be deployed through them. Podcasts of multimedia are an example of digital visuals that may be delivered through these devices. Laptops are so light now that they are considered a valid tool for mobile learning.

A key design issue involves learning in a live, synchronous way based on a wireless geographical location. Learning in a mobile environment may involve context-awareness or location-awareness of the devices, so that particular multimedia contents are pushed out when an individual is at a particular location.

Live mediated communications are also a common feature in mobile environments, so images need to be interchangeable among learning participants in their live learning.

Such environments usually involve training in architecture, military trainings, and e-tourism.

Augmented Virtuality

Augmented virtuality spaces are online spaces that involve the streaming of value-added real-world data through cameras or sensors or other devices. The real-world cameras add overlays of information or individual streams of content that enhance the virtuality (often simulations or data visualizations). In-world immersive spaces may be added to with real-world information channels. Another definition involves the inclusion of haptic devices like data gloves that may reach interactively into immersive virtual spaces (Qi, Martens, van Liere, & Kok, 2005).

For example, a simulated digital casino table training may be enhanced by a live video cam of a live casino floor. Or a live 360-degree webcam capture of a street scene may enhance virtual connection in a traffic flow training.

CONSISTENT AESTHETICS

No matter how the images are used, it is good practice to have consistent aesthetics in terms of image quality. These will vary between fields, and these should be defined early on in a course design or redesign. These involve issues of image sizing, color depth, sourcing, metadata, image processing, and other factors.

Beyond image data quality, aesthetics also apply to a sense of style. A consistent look and feel is important for experiential learning. The design aspects here involve deciding on particular color sets and consistent aesthetic messages.

A Future Stylebook

Evolving a stylebook for the integration of imagery into the future will require changing specific requirements to more generalized ones or higher-level principles.

THE IMPORTANCE OF EFFICACY TESTING (WITH LIVE USERS / LEARNERS)

Digital imagery contains a number of meanings, some inherent to it, and some imposed upon it by outside viewers. Imagery that will reach a global learning audience in particular will need extensive user testing to understand the ranges of understandings. Images should also be tested for accessibility by those with visual acuity challenges. Seeing is "selective" and dependent upon the viewer's prior experiences and learning, so the testers should involve novices as well as experts in the field.

Imagery should be evaluated within its learning context, too, based on learning objectives. Images need to align with the learning and the other learning objects around it. Each digital artifact in a learning sequence must have learning value on its own and as part of a larger learning trajectory. If the learning is individualistic, it needs to be effective for each learner. If the learning is collaborative and group-based, the imagery needs to be valuable in that context.

Images need to hold their meaning well not only for the present but into the future. There must be coherence in what is depicted.

For imagery that is part of an interface to guide user behaviors (as in virtual self discovery learning spaces), learners need to proceed through such spaces with a minimum of confusion. If help-seeking behavior is desirable, those that would benefit from such assistance should be encouraged to seek such help based on the visual formatting and design.

Avoiding Negative Learning

Part of the planning should involve consideration of how to avoid unintended messages or effects. Image clarity refers not only to the fidelity of the image but also to the clarity of the messages it conveys, both intentionally and unintentionally. Images have to attract the proper attentional level for proper analysis. A work that is not set up properly for analytical depth may also result in improper insights.

One factor that complicates the clarity of an image involves the use of multimedia, in which imagery may be embedded or integrated. The rationale is to improve learning accuracy, speed of acquisition, and long-term retention and applicability. "Students retain 20% of what they see, 30% of what they hear, 50% of what they see and hear, and 80% of what they see, hear, and interact with" (Shelly, Waggoner, Cashman & Waggoner, 1998, as cited in Eskicioglu & Kopec, 2003, p. 205).

There are a number of ways to test for negative learning. One is to deploy the images with a user group, consisting of novices along with experts, and to ask for interpretations and understandings. The wider the cultural range of the group, optimally, the more useful their responses regarding the global deployment of the imagery. Another is to query subject matter experts to analyze the various meanings of the imagery.

Another angle is to test for the cognitive linkages that are made from the imagery and the larger gestalt perceived from the digital image artifacts. What sorts of knowledge discovery may be made? What contexts and frameworks do learners use to approach semantic meaning with the imagery?

Eliciting an idea of where the images may have come from, how they were captured, and what image processing they went through may be helpful in terms of visual literacy.

Another way to head off negative learning in the use of digital imagery is to possibly allow users to handle the imagery by zooming in and out and analyzing various aspects. They may be able to share the imagery with others in order to discuss the various meanings. Some digital imagery systems may allow them to revise, restructure, organize, and "handle" the imagery in ways that may add value.

Table 4. A Checklist for Updating Digital Imagery

A Checklist for Updating Digital Imagery
The Learning
Content Updates
□ Has the information in an informational graphic been updated?
□ Is there more accurate visual information out and available?
□ Have there been changes in the academic field or learning domain that needs to be reflected in the curriculum?
Pedagogical Approaches
□ Are there new paradigms in a particular field that should be reflected in an updated curriculum?
Aesthetics
Branding Approach
□ Is there a new look-and-feel in the learning / course management system?
□ Is there a new visual theme for the learning course or module?
Aesthetic Approaches
□ Are there new aesthetics that should be conveyed?
Technological Advancements
Technology Updates
□ Has the technology structure underlying the images changed?
□ Are there more efficient technologies to deliver the imagery?
□ Are there more visually rich ways of communicating information?
Problematic Former Imagery
Information Accuracy
□ Is the old visual information inaccurate?
□ Are the images misleading?
Accessibility
□ Is the old information inaccessible to users?
Unclear Imagery Provenance and Ownership
□ Are the former images in use of unclear origin and intellectual property ownership?
□ Are the digital images liabilities to use?

Accurate captioning of the provenance of the digital imagery and the intended effects will be critical metadata for enhancing the value of digital imagery in e-learning.

Instructional methods may add value to digital imagery, too. A pedagogical approach could help learners contextualize photo-realistic images into a larger context and with greater depth of understanding.

UPDATING DIGITAL IMAGERY

Digital imagery for most learning situations will require some updating and revision for learning relevance. Updates should be pursued in most of the following circumstances (Table 4).

ACCESS FOR LATER REFERENCE

Digital imagery may need to be archived for later reference and use. Some institutions of higher education store imagery in learning / course management systems (L/CMSes), or digital repositories. The images need to be saved in a form that is the most flexible for all possible uses—including the high-end printing needs vs. the more low-end WWW needs. The original raw images that are captured should likely be kept in digital form, too, because those are the least lossy images. Every edit and compression thereafter usually involves some loss of visual information. There are finite amounts of information carried within an image.

Accurate metadata needs to be kept for each of the images in terms of provenance, ownership, copyright release, date, geographical location (of the image capture), sizing of the image, and other details. The naming protocols of the images will be important.

The instructors who maintain their own raw and processed digital imagery files need to maintain clear labeling of the image artifacts, their storage folders, and related assignment builds from those images.

The repositories themselves need to track the resources with clarity and maintain the integrity of the visual information. The images themselves need to be portable between learning and storage systems. If images are used by a range of individuals, there will need to be a more professional and systemic way of organizing digital imagery and storage methods for easier collaborations and individual work.

CONCLUSION

The integration of digital imagery into various types of e-learning really enhances a range of learning through an important sensory channel. The effective integration of such imagery depends on pedagogical rationales, the learning context, the learning domain, and the learners themselves. Considering where imagery may be used most effectively and understanding some ways in which they may be effectively used is critical. Designing imagery to fit the technology through which they are delivered is also important. Planning for long-term use of digital imagery as an integrated part of e-learning also benefits the course build.

REFERENCES

Ahmad, F., de la Chica, S., Butcher, K., Tumner, T., & Martin, J. H. (2007). Towards automatic conceptual personalization tools. In *Proceedings of the 7th ACM/IEEE-CS joint conference on Digital libraries* (pp. 452-461). New York: ACM.

Alexander, P. A., & Judy, J. E. (1988). The interaction of domain-specific and strategic knowledge in academic performance. *Review of Educational Research, 58*(4), 375–404.

Christian, J. (2006). Augmented reality in corporate pervasive e-education: Novel ways to support aviation maintenance training. In *Proceedings of the Innovation North Research Conference 2006*, Leeds Metropolitan University (pp. 1-10).

Ebert, D. S., Shaw, C. D., Zwa, A., & Starr, C. (1996). Two-handed interactive stereoscopic visualization. In *Proceedings of the Seventh IEEE Visualization 1996 (VIS '96)*. Washington, DC: IEEE.

Eskicioglu, A. M., & Kopec, D. (2003). The ideal multimedia-enabled classroom: Perspectives from psychology, education, and information science. *Journal of Educational Multimedia and Hypermedia, 12*(2), 205.

Lewis, T. L., Dishon, N., Johnson, K. T., & Firtion, M. (2008). Creating surveys for the visualizers generation: The use of affective imagery to capture perceptions of the computing discipline. In *Proceedings of the Consortium for Computing Sciences in Colleges*.

Mayer, R. E. (2000). The challenge of multimedia literacy. In A. W. Pailliotet & P. B. Mosenthal (Eds.), *Reconceptualizing Literacy in the Media Age* (pp. 372-373). Stamford, CT: JAI Press, Inc.

Moreno, R. (2004). Decreasing cognitive load for novice students: Effects of explanatory versus corrective feedback in discovery-based multimedia. *Instructional Science, 32*, 99–113. doi:10.1023/B:TRUC.0000021811.66966.1d

Nardi, B. A., & Zarmer, C. L. (1991). Beyond models and metaphors: Visual formalisms in user interface design. In *Proceedings of the twenty-fourth Hawaii international conference on system sciences* (p. 478-493). Washington, DC: IEEE.

Paulos, E., & Jenkins, T. (2005). Urban probes: Encountering our emerging urban atmospheres. In *Proceedings of the CHI 2006: PAPERS: Design Thoughts & Methods* (pp. 341-350). New York: ACM.

Qi, W., Martens, J.-B., van Liere, R., & Kok, A. (2005). Reach the virtual environment—3D tangible interaction with scientific data. In *Proceedings of the OZCHI 2005*, Canberra, Australia (pp. 1-10). New York: ACM.

Riggins, F. J., & Slaughter, K. T. (2006). The role of collective mental models in IOS adoption: Opening the black box of rationality in RFID deployment. In *Proceedings of the 39th Annual Hawaii International Conference on System Sciences (HICSS'06) Track 8.* Washington, DC: IEEE.

Steiger, N. M., & Steiger, D. M. (2007). Knowledge management in decision making: Instance-based cognitive mapping. In *Proceedings of the 40th Hawaii International Conference on System Sciences.*

Thomas, D. M., & Bostrom, R. P. (2007). The role of a shared mental model of collaboration technology in facilitating knowledge work in virtual teams. In *Proceedings of the 40th Hawaii International Conference on System Sciences 2007* (pp. 1-8). Washington, DC: IEEE.

Tory, M. (2003, October). Mental registration of 2D and 3D visualizations (an empirical study). In . *Proceedings of the IEEE Visualization, 2003*, 371–378.

Tory, M., & Möller, T. (2004). Human factors in visualization research. *IEEE Transactions on Visualization and Computer Graphics, 10*(1), 72. doi:10.1109/TVCG.2004.1260759

Tuttle, H. G. (1996). Learning: The star of video conferencing. *Multimedia Schools, 3*(4), 36.

Wang, J., Xu, Y., Shum, H.-Y., & Cohen, M. F. (2004). Video 'tooning. In *Proceedings of the International Conference on Computer Graphics and Interactive Techniques* (pp. 574-583). New York: ACM.

Ware, C. (2004). *Information Visualization* (2nd ed.). San Francisco: Elsevier, Morgan Kaufmann.

Wells, J. D., & Fuerst, W. L. (2000). Domain-oriented interface metaphors: Designing Web interfaces for effective customer interaction. In *Proceedings of the 33rd Hawaii International Conference on System Sciences-Volume 6.* Washington, DC: IEEE

Zarzycki, A. (2004) Abstracting design, designing abstractions: Use of computer graphics in early stages of architectural design. In *Proceedings of the International Conference on Computer Graphics and Interactive Techniques.* New York: ACM. Amirian, S. (2008). Pedagogy & video conferencing: A review of recent literature. In *Proceedings of the First NJEDge.NET Conference*, Plainsboro, NJ.

KEY TERMS AND DEFINITIONS

Conceptual Model (n): An expert's mental model of a particular domain field or aspect of the domain field

E-Learning (n): Electronic learning, learning online

Immersive (adj): Full-sensory, encompassing, 3-dimensional

Interactive Television (ITV) (n): Live, synchronous interactivity via Internet connectivity or satellite

Loose Coupling (n): Connected loosely with other elements, decontextualized

Mental Model (n): A learner's conceptualization of how something works or exists

Module (n): A stand-alone unit of study as a separate component (often interchangeable with others to create a larger sequence or course of study)

Negative Learning (n): Unintended messages and learning that may result from the incorrect interpretation of a digital image or immersive virtual experience

Photomosaic (n): A composite image created by a combination of photos or images, often aerial ones

Reusable Learning Object (RLO) (n): A digital learning object that is built around a learning objective (or multiple ones) and that are portable and may be used in various learning situations

Stand-Alone (adj): Independent, self-contained, operating independently, not connected with other learning objects with learning dependencies

Student Retention (n): The act of keeping students enrolled and continuing with their studies

Synaesthesia (n): The sensing of one type of sensation created by a different sensory stimulation, such as the evoking of color by a sound

SIDEBAR

Maximizing Digital Content Quality in Live ITV and Video Conference Courses

Diana Marrs
University of Kansas, USA

Plenty of literature exists to support the use of graphic material to enhance the learning experience. In the case of live interactive television (iTV) or video conference courses, the use of graphic content becomes even more essential. Consider a typical news program on TV. The view switches between different speakers, often with images shown behind them, or the view of the speakers is replaced with a short video clip or graphics. Notice how quickly the view changes. As instructors teaching in a live TV environment, we must follow some of the same rules. But what are those rules and how can we improve the quality of the live iTV learning experience?

Presentation Techniques

Picture the multi-tasking, multi-modal learner of today and imagine how hard it would be to sit for an hour watching a talking head (the instructor) with no other stimulus. Using TV news as a model, we can begin to create a format for teaching live via a distance. For example, a good rule of thumb is that each power point slide be displayed for only 15 seconds (Tuttle, 1996, p. 36) – either switch back to instructor camera view for further discussion, or move to a new graphic, slide, or short video clip. Another overall rule when teaching synchronously at a distance is to break the lecture into 15 minute segments (Amirian, 2002). No matter how entertaining your graphic content is, viewing a TV or screen for 10-15 minutes is about the maximum time the far side viewers can focus their attention before they start to wander. The result is disruptive behavior on the far side – students using IM, leaving the room, talking to each other. The absence of physical presence significantly reduces the urgency to pay attention. Changing the view gives them new focus and if you combine that with breaks in the presentation for discussion it is easier to retain their involvement in the learning process. During discussion breaks also consider changing the camera view to show the students at each site to enhance the feeling of a face-to-face discussion and facilitate interaction while providing another visual display.

Technical Issues

Now beyond these timing rules and breaks for interaction, there are technical issues that must be taken into account. Because satellite and microwave connections are typically TV quality when transmitted, high graphic quality is not an issue and will not be discussed here. Video conferencing is entirely different however. The connection speed, the type of cabling, the font size, and the quality of the original content critically impact the quality of your power point, video, website, or any other graphic image that is seen by the far side.

236

Bandwidth

Let's start with connection speed. If you have equipment that allows for a direct computer connection (such as Polycom's "People + Content") then you need to have at least a 384K connection speed, and frankly I would recommend 768K. When using this feature, you are sending two signals at the same time - the instructor and the computer - and this really requires higher bandwidth. Furthermore, the best recommendation to insure quality is for your network personnel to program configure the port and the router to "tag" this signal as video conferencing. What this means is that your video signal gets priority over all the other traffic on your internet (other computers connecting to websites, downloading, etc. on your network). This is called QOS, or Quality Of Service, and will significantly improve your ability to send content during your class. To be most effective, this QOS must be provided "end-to-end". Your network router may identify the video conference as highly important and give it priority, but if the receiving school has not also coded for tagging for QOS, then once your signal reaches their network, it begins competing with all the other traffic in that school system and you lose any advantage in quality. When video conferencing without QOS and on limited bandwidth, the result is choppy video, a "freezing" screen for brief moments as the signal fights through, and audio that breaks up like a bad cell phone connection.

Cabling and Equipment

Cabling is another area where improvements can be made, and like bandwidth and QOS, the quality of the cabling must be consistent from end-to-end. For example, in the "People + Content" configuration previously mentioned, the computer is connected to the video conference equipment using a VGA cable – the same kind of cable used to connect your computer to your monitor. On the far end, the video conference equipment should be connected to a projector also using a VGA connection. The result is a high quality clear image of whatever your are doing on your computer – Powerpoint, web browsing, etc.

On the other hand, most low to mid-range video conference equipment uses S-video to display either on a TV monitor or through a projector onto a screen. This works well for the camera that displays the instructor but a computer sends a much higher resolution than S-video can display. The result is a blurred image because the high quality computer signal is compressed. Another complication is that this level of equipment does not allow a direct computer connection and to make the connection externally, another device called a scan converter is commonly used. Many K-12 schools have special interactive distance learning (IDL) classrooms built at great expense. These rooms allow instruction to multiple sites at the same time, have touch panels, and a display monitor for each site, yet they are built using the low end scan converter, reducing a computer presentation to a blur because a scan converter compresses the signal even more. Figure 4 illustrates the problem. This SPSS program was sent from and IDL room (using a scan converter) to a far site that used S-Video to connect to a projector. The result is unreadable for the students at the far site.

This is a view of SPSS as seen by the far side. It is sent through a scan converter in an IDL room and displayed on an 8'x10' projection screen using S-video. As you can see, it is completely unreadable.

Finally at the top end, there is High Definition (HD) video conferencing equipment but to work effectively, an HD unit must be purchased with HDMI cabling and either LCD display or an HD projector. Buying the HD equipment without the HD display results in the same blurred image you get with S-Video. This is beyond reach for most schools and not really necessary if some basic techniques are followed.

Figure 4. A View of SPSS (Marrs, 2009)

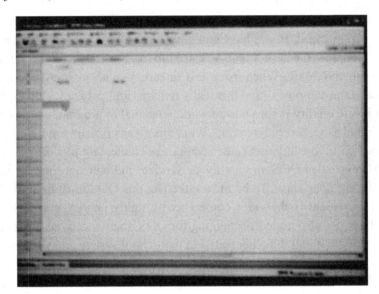

Solutions and Techniques

As discussed, where possible, purchase equipment that can connect directly to the computer and then use VGA cabling to the display. Ask your network administrator or internet provider if QOS can be set keeping in mind that both sites need to have this for it to work. These are ideals and many schools may not have these options yet there are still steps the instructor can take to increase quality graphics even with low-end equipment and connections.

With your PowerPoint™, use sans serif font, 24 pt font (minimum), bold type and strongly contrasting color. Many of the built-in themes look great on the computer but become difficult to read if the display is not clear so choose simple, less busy backgrounds. If you follow this formula, your presentation will still be readable even when using a scan converter or with S-video connection. Figure 5 is an example of a PowerPoint™ slide that follows this rules. If you are using photos, consider adding in a red arrow or circle onto the image to highlight the area of interest. This is especially useful in classes using aerial photos and geography. Once you start your PowerPoint™ slideshow, right click and select a pointer option like felt tip pen or highlighter and use it to emphasis points on the slides as you lecture. If you visit websites, your browser has an option under view to increase text size or to zoom in, thereby increasing the font (some websites do not allow this to work so be sure to check). When writing, avoid using the white board which will either throw a glare or be too dark depending on the lighting. Switch to a document camera and dark marker.

Finally and most importantly, take the time to test your digital content in the actual room and with the equipment you will be using. You will need to connect to the far side and have someone there to provide feedback. If you find that the quality is just too low, then you still have two alternatives - provide the content through your CMS and require students to bring it or have the digital content displayed at each local site with the help of a facilitator, a GTA, or student at that location while you remain on camera on

Figure 5. Digital Media in Video Conferencing (Marrs, 2009) This is a PowerPoint™ slide created using most of the rules to maximize readability – 24-28pt font, bold, not too much text, with a solid background.

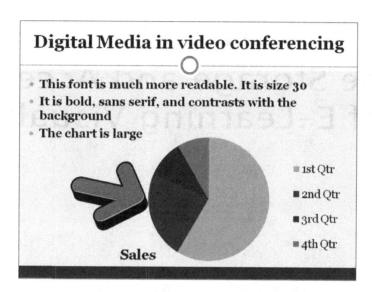

a second display. This is the best option if your school does not have the bandwidth or the equipment available for high quality content display. For a visual demonstration of some of these concepts, visit: http://facweb.bhc.edu/TLC/learn/hottopics/distlearn/visuals.mov .

Chapter 11
The Storage and Access of E-Learning Visuals

ABSTRACT

Rich image repositories and digital libraries exist for the collection, labeling, archival and delivery of digital graphics. Understanding the ingestion of such images into digital repositories will be helpful not only for those searching for resources but also for those creating digital imagery for such storage and distribution. This chapter addresses some of the latest research going on currently for the labeling of digital graphics, their storage, their protection, and their distribution to users.

CHAPTER OBJECTIVES

- Introduce image repositories and digital libraries as storehouses for digital imagery
- Introduce use cases for image repositories and digital libraries
- Explore the digital preservation, born-digital, and other origination paths for digital imagery, and their ingestion into digital repositories
- Show what elements are necessary for the metadata labeling of digital imagery for e-learning
- Promote more efficient access to and searching of digital image repositories
- Explore the efficient download and delivery of imagery from secure repositories
- Discuss security issues related to image repositories and digital libraries
- Probe the socio-technical and collaborative aspects of image repositories and digital libraries

INTRODUCTION

Digital imagery used in e-learning are archived and distributed via websites and learning / course management systems (L/CMSes), but they are also stored and delivered via digital repositories for reusability

DOI: 10.4018/978-1-60566-972-4.ch011

in other learning contexts. The storage of digital visuals, their protection, and their distribution, all have implications on how digital images are captured, rendered, and labeled. Digital repositories and libraries have been around for several decades but have recently come into more popular use (Rowe, Razdan, & Simon, 2003).

The memory capacities of digital repositories will affect how large the digital images may be. [Some geographic information systems contents contain so much information that each artifact may well be in the terabytes (Reuning & Jones, 2005)]. Yet, it may be in the best interests of those curating such collections to store objects in the least-lossy formats, so the raw contents may be versioned for the most possible practical uses.

For digital imagery to retain their value over time (and have value in the current near-term), the annotations must be high-value (Tangelder & Veltkamp, 2004, n.p.). In addition, most two-dimensional (2D) methods of identification and retrieval for shape-matching do not generalize to the three-dimensional (3D) model matching. This will explore some of the issues raised in relation to the archival of digital imagery for uses in e-learning, in the present and for the future.

Various learning / course management systems (L/CMSes) link into digital libraries and repositories. Others access course cartridges with visual contents. Interoperability gaps are being addressed.

Lastly, this chapter will explore the uses of online repository and library spaces for the co-development of images and the collaboration around work. Informatics communities have sprung up around topics of shared interests in digital repositories. With the integration of computer-mediated communications tools into digital storage spaces, plenty of powerful collaborations may be actualized.

IMAGE REPOSITORIES AND DIGITAL LIBRARIES

A digital image repository is a storehouse for various types of contents, without curatorial oversight. A digital image library consists of collections of materials based around topic areas and usually curated by an expert in the respective field. All variety of digital imagery may be archived: maps, photos, geospatial resources, 3D objects, aerial images, satellite images, and remotely sensed image captures. The imagery may be photo-realistic or wholly synthetic.

Repositories and digital libraries may be high-prestige and formal, controlled by designated subject matter experts in a field. They may be wholly public and open to any user. In between are those repositories that may capture less formal imagistic information but which still has value through projects or dissertations (Tschimer & Zipf, 2005) or community contributions (Kennedy & Naaman, 2008).

Because of the influences of interdisciplinary academic traditions—library and information science, information retrieval, and human-computer interaction communities, different definitions of terms have emerged regarding digital libraries (Goncalves, Fox, Watson & Kipp, 2004). "Information retrieval, human-computer interaction, computer supported collaborative work, machine learning, user modeling, hypermedia and information science" all inform the design of these digital repositories (Callan, Smeaton, Beaulieu, Borlund, Brusilovsky, Chalmers, Lynch, Riedl, Smyth, Straccia, & Toms, 2003, p. 2). Subject matter experts (SMEs) and data archivists vet contents and add form to the visual information.

Such collections may be publicly accessible or privately held (as by companies, organizations, or families. Some contents may be for-profit; free and open-source (with copyright releases for academic use), or free and public-domain. Some are closed-access systems that are available from certain locations, and others are Web-accessible. Some are stand-alone digital collections, and others are open to federated searches.

Repositories that include imagery support fields like medicine (Nikolaidou, Anagnostopoulos, & Hatzopoulos, 2003; McIntyre, Dennis, Uijtdehaage, & Candler, 2004), archaeology (Gorton, Shen, Vemuri, Fan, & Fox, June 2006), engineering (Wong, Crowder, Wills & Shadbolt, Oct. 2006); global climate change (McCaffrey & Weston, 2005); ethnomusicology (Dunn & Cowan, 2005), and others.

Digital Preservation and Long-Term Storage

To emphasize the challenges of maintaining digital repositories, it has been said: "Scale, longevity, economy—pick any two" (Janêe, Mathena & Frew, 2008, p. 136). Some researchers define long-term preservation as "exceeding the lifetimes of the people, applications, and platforms that originally created the information," which this group defined as 100 years.

In our experience in building and running digital library and storage systems, a ten-year-old system is nearing the end of its lifetime in terms of supportability...Storage systems change much more frequently, with turnovers in technology occurring every 3-5 years. Even entire institutions come and go. Few institutions can guarantee their continued existence, let alone support for preserving a specific piece of information, for 100 years; and that still leaves the issue of changes in curatorship within institutions (Janêe, Mathena & Frew, 2008, p. 134).

Current ways to protect "legacy" digital data has been compared to a "relay" or a "migration", the handing over impermanent digital information from an obsolescent technology to a newer one, from repository to repository—while trying to maintain data integrity and the original context of the digital information. D.E. Geer writes:

If this prediction of a data-rich, data-mobile future is true, then you do not have to be a professional paranoid to imagine that data eclipses CPUs (central processing units) as the primary focus of attacks carried out over ever-faster networks" (2006, p. 45).

Image Co-Storage with Multimedia

Digital imagery is often stored with other types of multimedia information, and they may include "raw data; analyzed data; imagery; analysis environments; simulations; notes, letters, and reports, and published articles" (McGrath, Futrelle, Plante, & Guillaume, 1999, p. 188).

USE CASES FOR IMAGE REPOSITORIES AND DIGITAL LIBRARIES

There are many stakeholders to such repositories; they include e-learning instructors, course creators, researchers, professionals in the field, learners, non-experts and the general public. These stakeholders are those who may use the materials now and also into the future.

The use cases in the research literature involve work flows in broadcast media (Markkula & Sormunen, 2006; Westman & Oittinen, 2006), telemedicine, art, landscape architecture, and a range of other fields.

Often, imagery needs to be called up for further research or for remixing into other multimedia content. Research in repositories may involve analysis and decision-making. Digital imagery use is central in e-learning. Learners and academics access imagery for research and learning.

ORIGINATION PATHS FOR DIGITAL IMAGERY CONTENTS

A number of origination paths exist for digital imagery contents. Content originators may be subject matter experts and professions in a particular domain field. They may be students or apprentices to a field, who create the digital imagery as part of their work. And yet others may be members of the general public with an interest in the field. Remote sensors may even capture digital imagery.

Given the role of user-generated contents and the low cost of digital video and imagery capture devices, many personal digital images are coming online with some potential use, whether these are from camera-embedded mobile devices ("mobile multimedia") or digital cameras or image sensors. Amateur-shot video may have repurposing value and so would benefit from automated "content-based indexing, retrieval, summarization, and access" (Madhwacharyula, Davis, Mulhem, Clips-Imag, & Kankanhalli, 2007, pp. 358 – 388). Many more individuals have started creating digital imagery contents (Adams, Venkatesh, & Jain, 2005, pp. 211 – 247). Private family history collections with social relevance may be integrated with digital repositories (Callan, et al., 2003).

Digital Preservation

Some contents involve digital preservation of physical objects, such as "models of statues to virtual archeological landscapes" (Brown, Seales, Webb & Jaynes, 2001, pp. 57 – 59). Materials from archaeological digs, artworks, vases, buildings, and other objects have been digitally preserved for posterity. "Techniques such as photography, video, X-ray, 3-D scans, infrared, UV, and laser scans have been used successfully for different art recording purposes" (Chen, Wactlar, Wang & Kiernan, 2005, p. 4).

Born-Digital

Many digital images are born digital or fully created in digital form. This content may have value not only for the creator(s) but other users, with value-added captures (with automatic metadata).

The recent popularity of mobile camera phones allows for new opportunities to gather important metadata at the point of capture … (in a) spatial, temporal, and social context … (l)everaging contextual metadata at the point of capture can address the problems of the semantic and sensory gaps. In particular, combining and sharing spatial, temporal, and social contextual metadata from a given user and across users allows us to make inferences about media content (Davis, King, Good, & Sarvas, 2004, p. 194).

The imagery in repositories comes from a range of channels. Figure 1, "Digital Visual Content Streams in Repositories," shows how the imagery may come from professionals, apprentices, and non-professionals; they may also come from remote or automated cameras or sensors. The metadata should describe the context of the image captures and how much processing went into the development of those images. The digital contents may be photorealistic, video-realistic, synthetic, or some mix of those forms.

THE INGESTION OF IMAGERY

Some repositories allow user uploading of contents. Some referatories point to digital visuals hosted off of other servers by capturing URLs. Still others are curated, with quality standards applied to the submitted contents. Some automatically take in materials such as one that automatically captures and deploys video lectures for deployment on a digital repository (Abowd, Harvel & Brotherton, 2001, pp. 467 – 474). Automated digital libraries with "repurposable" output is a complicated endeavor (Simske & Lin, 2004, para. 1). Generally, the more complex the informational contents, the greater the need for specialized human vetting for proper interpretation, annotation and structuring (Janée, Mathena & Frew, 2008, pp. 134- 135).

The ingestion process ensures that the visual information is somewhat standardized in terms of sizes (granularity) and types. There may be a "cleansing" of the captured data including color adjustments. Rights management may include a vetting of copyright and ownership. The images may be analyzed, and automated metadata information may be extracted for easier future identification and search through "OCR (optical character recognition), speech recognition, cut detection, MPEG-7 visual descriptors"

Figure 1. Digital visual content streams into repositories (Hai-Jew, 2009)

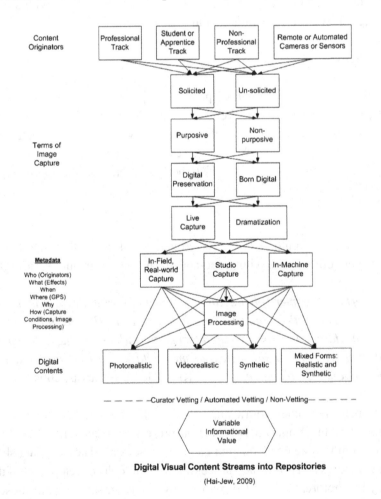

Digital Visual Content Streams into Repositories

(Hai-Jew, 2009)

(Bolettieri, Falchi, Gennaro, & Rabitti, 2007, pp. 21 – 28). Object categorization can already be easily identified through machine intelligence and a "universal visual dictionary" (Winn, Criminisi, & Minka, 2005, pp. 1 – 8). Persistent identifiers may be applied to the imagery. Metadata may be verified, revised or added. Then the imagery may be distributed to the users who have been authenticated and have access.

For greater efficiencies, there are methods to ingest digital artifacts into multiple repositories simultaneously (Rani, Goodkin, Cobb, Habing, Urban, Eke, & Pearce-Moses, 2006, p. 360). It is critical that each image has its own persistent handles or identifiers for easier manageability (Agosti & Ferro, 2007).

METADATA LABELING FOR E-LEARNING

Metadata—data about data or "unstructured data"—is a critical piece of documenting the provenance of digital imagery. Practitioners in the field suggest that there should be formal foundations adopted by those creating digital libraries (Goncalves, Fox, Watson & Kipp, 2004). There are some standardized metadata systems with pre-set fields for the labeling of data that may be built into repositories. Some systems use a combination of metadata labeling systems or "multi-scheme metadata" (Palmer, Zavalina, & Mustafoff, 2007, p. 386), and others even use wholly customized ones that are more fitting for a particular field. Adding metadata enriches the digital imagery; it is sometimes added during ingestion for some repositories (Bainbridge, Thompson & Witten, 2003). Metadata may be added retroactively, but the accuracy of the information will have to be firmly established. These visual semantic systems must both cater to human perceptions and machine processing (Dori, 2004).

Metadata may be captured by people. Human manual annotation presents limits in terms of human judgment, subjectivity and likelihood of human error (Volkmer, Thom, & Tahaghoghi, 2007). There are often semantic disputes (because of heterogeneity or variance) in knowledge domains. The three most common problems with descriptions were "consistent application of the chosen metadata scheme within a project, identification and application of controlled vocabularies, and integration of sets of data, schemes, and vocabularies either within an institution or among collaborators" (Palmer, Zavalina, & Mustafoff, 2007, p. 393). This problem of accurate metadata labeling is magnified in socio-technical systems which are open and which incorporate the works of volunteer contributors.

Human speed is another factor, with some researchers striving to harness rapid image analysis based on human brain signals "by tapping into split second perceptual judgments using electroencephalograph sensors" (Mathan, Erdogmus, Huang, Pavel, Ververs, Carciofini, Dorneich, & Whitlow, 2008, p. 3309). Some repositories begin with the human rating of contents and the application of semantic labels, and then the application of machine-based statistical learning methods to evaluate the other contents (Volkmer, Thom, & Tahaghoghi, 2007, p. 151). This is a form of "image understanding," which "seeks to derive qualitative conclusions from quantitative data" (Canosa, 2006, p. 544).

Graphic design terms have been tested with image tagging for efficacy to allow searches using loosely defined visual properties using descriptors such as the following:

Balance vs Instability, Symmetry vs Asymmetry, Regularity vs Irregularity, Simplicity vs Complexity, Unity vs Fragmentation, Economy vs Intricacy, Understatement vs Exaggeration, Predictability vs Spontaneity, Activeness vs Stasis, Subtlety vs Boldness, Neutrality vs Accent, Transparency vs Opacity, Consistency vs Variation, Accuracy vs Distortion, Flatness vs Depth, Singularity vs Juxtaposition, Sequentiality vs Randomness, Sharpness vs Diffusion, and Repetition vs Episodicity (Laing, 2008, pp. 4 – 5).

While a majority of metadata is textual, some repositories feature a speech or audio interface for annotation. Others have proposed the annotating of multimedia documents with multimedial objects: "Annotations can refer to whole documents or single portions thereof, as usual, but also to multi-objects, i.e. groups of objects contained in a single document" (Bottoni, Civica, Levialdi, Orso, Panizzi, & Trinchese, 2004, p. 55).

Automated captures of metadata may also be used, such as through the deployment of 'bots over the Web in search of imagery. Or capturing devices like context-aware cameras and mobile phones may automatically capture metadata at the point of capture and share the images and metadata via a remote server (Sarvas, Herrarte, Wilhelm & Davis, 2004). Automated tagging has inaccuracies as well. Large image databases are seldom fully tagged, and the tags are often unreliable or inconsistent, with surrounding text treated as tags. There are efforts to generate automated tagging of untagged objects and to clean up the tagging accuracy of objects in a repository (Datta, Ge, Li, & Wang, 2006). Indeed, there's a preference for more efficient, accurate and high-reliability automated means of labeling contents.

Humans and machines work together for metadata labeling, oftentimes. For example, intelligent computers may capture low-level image details such as texture, color, or geometry, or visual-level descriptors like brushwork, color temperature, color palate, and color contrast. People then vet images based on high-level organizational domain-specific concepts, disambiguate the image, and add metadata at that level (Leslie, Chua & Jain, 2007; Bertini, Del Bimbo, Torniai, Grana, & Cucciara, 2007). Hauptmann, Lin, Yan, Yang and Chen found that searches that combine "the combined extremes of human and machine power" trumps findings by either track alone. In their system, the system re-ranks searches "using a number of knowledge sources, such as image similarity, text similarity, and temporal proximity" (2006, p. 385).

Various software are tested for their classification performance, inter-rater reliability (as compared to human labeling), and are mixed with human oversight for greater accuracy. Some systems use cross-referencing of various data sources to interpret the quality of the information found in a federated repository search based on user criteria (Thakkar, Knoblock, & Ambite, 2007). Federated searching may help avoid the problem of missing documents (Zhuang, Wagle & Giles, 2005) and digital artifacts.

Another challenge is to label digital image artifacts so that there's value when a repository is tapped by a federated search. The interoperability of a digital repository should be high, even if there are multi-scheme metadata systems at play. There has to be high metadata integration for objects located in federated searches (Wyss & Robertson, 2005). Without shared understandings, even metadata granularity (relative size) may be up for debate (Foulonneau, Cole, Habing, & Shreeves, 2005). Locally developed metadata schemes may be less desirable in terms of wider accessibility and reuse (Palmer, Zavalina, & Mustafoff, 2007). One example of this challenge stems from the local to federal government endeavors to access governmental spatial data sources, with the resultant barrier of semantic heterogeneity in the labeling of the resources (Gupta, Memon, Tran, Bharadwaja, & Zaslavsky, 2002). Some researchers have proposed designing annotation before it's needed, as a kind of anticipatory approach to ingestion of audiovisual media (Nack & Putz, 2001). Annotations are not merely textual but may include imagery, audio, and video annotations (Agosti & Ferro, 2007).

Metadata and annotations may be viewed as "content enrichment" or as "stand-alone" documents (Agosti & Ferro, 2007, p. 3:9). These annotations may have semantic value independent of the digital imagery. The same visuals may also have a range of annotations created for different layers of access: "a private layer of annotations accessible only by authors of the annotations, a collective layer of annotations, shared by a team of people, and finally a public layer of annotations, accessible to all the users of the digital library. In this way, user communities can benefit from different views of the information resources managed by the DL (digital library) (Marshall 1997; Marshall and Brush 2002, 2004, as cited in Agosti & Ferro, 2007, p. 3:10).

EFFICIENT ACCESS AND SEARCHING

Multimedia information retrieval (MIR) has and continues to be the main focus of attention in relation to image and multimedia repositories. While a lot of back-end technological work is going on to enhance the searching and use of image repositories, much focus is on helping seekers define their search criterion with more efficiency (Albertoni, Bertone, & De Martino, 2005). Seekers of visuals have varying domain knowledge and sophistication levels with query formulations, attributes, and repository structures. Visual-based reasoning may be elusive.

A core usability feature of image repositories involves their searchability, regardless of the digital formats the objects are in (Malazia, 2004, para. 1). Without an adherence to the published interoperability standards for various types of digital objects, a veritable "digital tower of Babel" (Smith, 2005, p. 27) may result (Bainbridge, Ke, & Witten, 2006, pp. 105 – 106). On the back-end of repositories, effective searchability involves the accurate labeling of resources at ingestion, efficient findability by a range of users employing different search approaches, even when there are semantic gaps between the query and the desired image object(s), image evaluation, storage and management. One research approach studies different users of digital libraries to close the "intention gap" (Vuorikari, 2007, p. 207; Blandford, Keith, Connell & Edwards, 2004, p. 27). The success of search is often judged at the individual situational level (Westman & Oittinen, 2006, p. 102).

A semantic gap exists between human and machine understandings of the respective images. "The drawback of the current content-based image retrieval systems is that low-features used by them always could not be interpreted to high-level concepts that are commonly comprehended by humans. This matter is always called 'Semantic Gap'. Some semantic-sensitive image retrieval techniques use relevance feedback to narrow the gap; some use pattern recognition techniques to identify or classify between semantic concepts such as human face, nude pictures; indoor and outdoor, etc.; some use machine learning techniques to learn grouped concept to facilitate image retrieval" (Jiang, Huang, & Gao, 2004, n.p.).

Given the scarce attentional resources of users and their expectations, there's a need for image document triage—or the quick determination of the relevance of the objects in a collection (Badi, Bae, Moore, Meintanis, Zacchi, Hsieh, Shipman & Marshall, 2006, p. 218). This efficiency also requires strategic user interface design for the most effective ways to access the database of resources. To this end, researchers study how people share information to build systems that are more usable and interactive (Crabtree, Rodden & Mariani, 2004).

Image Search Strategies

Textual annotations, while very commonly used for image searches, may have limitations. *"The way of applying keyword annotation to the image resource has low capability to analyze semantic relations among keywords, such as synonym, homonym and antonym. Taking the topic of images as example, it is nearly impossible to include all the synonyms of the topic keyword in the annotation of every image. This will lead to the consequence that if the user input a keyword which has the exact same meaning to the topic keyword of some certain images in the index database but in different terms, those images are not able to be retrieved"* (Fan & Li, 2006, n.p.). People who search the Web tend to use brief queries, approximately 2.3 words in length (Silverstein, et al., 1998, as cited in Xue, Zhou & Zhang, 2008, p. 21:1). Many argue, though, that image semantics should be used for pictorial language and visuals.

The type of digital visuals will affect some of the strategies used in the back-end design for searching. For example, there is a repository of GPS (global positioning satellite) trails overlaid over aerial maps (Morris, Morris & Barnard, 2004, pp. 63 – 71) for an informational visualization. Video abstraction involves the culling of keyframes and video skims to represent the digital video for browsing, searches, navigation, and video metadata (Truong & Venkatesh, 2007, pp. 1 – 37). Audio and video "surrogates" are extracted to help people make sense of a video based on a storyboard, audio, or multimodal information—as shorthand for the longer work. Combined surrogates are more effective than single-channel ones for effective capturing of the "gist" of the video (Song & Marchionini, 2007, pp. 867 – 876). Most 2D methods of identification and retrieval for shape-matching do not generalize to 3D model matching. This situation shows the importance of high-value annotation (Tangelder & Veltkamp, 2004, n.p.). Geometric queries are often used for 3D polygonal models for shape-based retrieval (Funkhouser & Kazhdan, n.d., n.p.).

Searching for 2D and 3D imagery may be achieved through query-by-one-example (QBE) or even by multiple examples arranged in groups. Some repositories are then able to capture the average features from a small number of query images for a bounded set definition. Computers are able to put meaning to that group for a search (Hiransakolwong, Hua, Koompairojn, Vu, & Lang, 2005, pp. 1195 – 1199). While two-dimensional searches generally focus on features like color, texture and shape, 3D data involves higher dimensionality (Funkhouser, Min, Kazhdan, Chen, Halderman, Dobkin, & Jacobs, 2003), such as in image orientation and the positioning of the x, y and z axes. 3D searches are usually achieved with a combination of keyword searches and human sketches (which vary widely in quality) based on shapes or existing 3D models for querying. What then happens on the back end of the repository is crawling, indexing, querying, and matching (Funkhouser, et al., 2003).

Spatio-temporal resources include video, which includes physical movements and time, as well as synthetic *machinima* and animations. The heterogeneous nature of multimedia affects the combination of approaches to query repositories. "To query visual repositories, the visual features of the imagery, such as colors, textures, shapes, motions, and spatiotemporal compositions, are used in combination with text and other related information. Low-level visual features may be extracted with or without human intervention" (Chang, Smith, Beigi, & Benitez, 1997, p. 64).

Sometimes transcript narratives are used to enhance the search for visuals; this allows even cross-lingual retrieval of images (Christel & Conescu, 2005). In video searches, visual information may be extracted for efficient searching. A shot—a single continuous camera operation without a cut or effect—may be captured; a keyframe—a single bitmap image extracted from a shot—may be used for identifying a video for searching as well. Types of information extraction may include "shot detection, story segmentation, semantic feature extraction, and information retrieval" (Christel & Conescu, 2005, p. 70). Some video searches involve textual analysis of closed captioning text. Others use automatic speech recognition captures from videos. Some still image searches involve thumbnail drag-and-drops, with partial image or texture matching.

Researchers have been working to enhance search capabilities, including "the utility of speech recognition, image processing, and natural language processing techniques for improving search and discovery in the video medium" (Christel, 1999, p. 303). Another value-added search feature involves the "chaining" of related digital contents (O'Sullivan, McLoughlin, Bertolotto, & Wilson, 2003, p. 86). Some systems offer simultaneous searching and reference linking across bibliographic resources on the Web (Mischo, Habing & Cole, 2002).

Another search approach involves the relational aspects of objects with each other in a video database management system. One system focuses on the subframe "hot objects" of user interest and uses the spatial relations between two entities in a visual clip to pull out the clip (Jiang & Elmagarmid, 1998, pp. 226 – 238). The relations that are meaningful for searching in this model are the following: "disjoint, touch (or meet), inside, contains, overlap, covers, cover-by and equal" (p. 228).

Geospatial information and georeferenced resources include geographical artifacts, the location, shapes, and relationships among geographic features; these include maps and remotely sensed data (O'Sullivan, McLoughlin, Bertolotto, & Wilson, 2003). To locate this type of information, users may have to specify the location of the information on the Earth's surface (The Alexandria Digital Library Team, June 2004). This same concept applies, too, for the oceanic and coastal environments (Marincioni & Lightsom, 2002). Some researchers propose a task-based annotation of geo-spatial resources in geospatial image databases, based on "intelligence operations, recreational and professional mapping, urban and industrial planning, and tourism systems" (O'Sullivan, McLoughlin, Bertolotto, & Wilson, 2003, pp. 78 – 87).

Avoiding image duplication in a repository is critical for lowering indexing overhead, and promoting greater storage and search efficiencies (deCarvalho, Goncalves, Laender, & da Silva, 2006). Computers may identify similarities between shapes and images to weed out multiple copies (Ko, Maekawa, Patrikalakis, Masuda, & Wolter, 2003). Images may also receive unique and persistent identifiers to "fingerprint" them (Manku, Jain & Sarma, 2007) for originality and a stable point-of-reference. These unique global identifiers may be especially useful when digital artifacts are exchanged, used in different situations, serialized or reassembled (Bekaert, Liu, Van de Sompel, Lagoze, Payette, & Warner, 2006). In terms of applied image search engines deployed in the public realm, these technologies are still fairly rare (Kherfi, Ziou, & Bernardi, 2004, 35 – 67).

Referatories and Metadatabases

Referatories point to objects stored on the Web through links and persistent identifiers. Metadatabases enhance federated searches over a number of repositories; they may add value by recording "the *image templates* as the summaries of the visual contents of the images for remote image databases. Each template is associated with the *statistical metadata* to characterize its similarity distribut6ions with the images in various remote databases" (Wang, Ma, Wu, & Zhang, 2002).

Serendipity in Browsing and Searching

Laing (2008) suggests that building some serendipity in search functions may enhance the work of those using an image database to find helpful resources to solve a visual problem:

Often, visual information from images that appear entirely unrelated by subject offer the potential to encode information, feelings and moods that may then be incorporated into the design. Examples of the types of information that might be gathered from such visual sampling include textures, production methods and their resultant output, styles, fashions and trends, layouts and compositions, typographic samples, complimentary imagery or contrasting imagery (p. 3).

Capturing such information that may appear secondary may add value to a digital image repository. The design of a search may encourage discovery and browsing, with an encouragement of "chance encounters" leading to meaningful experiences (Leong, Howard, & Vetere, 2008, p. 719).

Figure 2, "Successful Search Results: Targeting an Image Database," shows the mix of intended and unintended consequences of an image search, with the value-added of some serendipitous finds.

Visualizing Informational Structures for Searching

Another strategy to enhance searching involves structuring the visual information in a database based on domain-specific schemas, the relationships between the image objects (Nelson, Marchionini, Geisler, & Yang, 2001). Ontological structures "often conceived as a set of classes (concepts), relations, functions, axioms, and instances" organize the digital contents (Jiang, Huang, & Gao, 2004, n.p.). This organizational structure offers high-level concepts in ontologies that people can relate to vs. the specific low-level features (color, texture, shape, and other features) (Zhu, Rao & Zhang, Apr. 2002, p. 226).

Figure 2. Successful Search Results - Targeting an Image Database

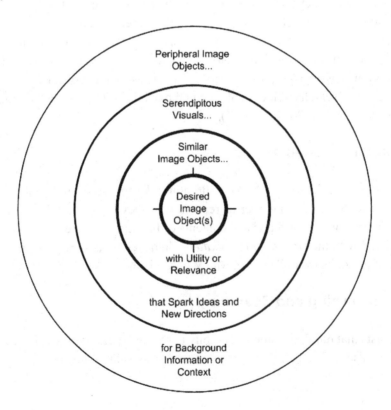

The organization of information protects the prior research work and makes it more efficient to build on existing knowledge structures (Datta, Li, & Wang, 2005).

A simpler version would be topic mapping achieved textually or spatially (Yang, Han, Oh, & Kwak, 2007) or a concept map of the contents in an integrated digital library (Kumar, 2007). Thesauruses may enable users to search with more topic clarity in terms of synonyms (Soergel, 2005). Future browsers of a digital library may benefit from the prior users' browsing behaviors, as captured through machine learning (Krowne & Halbert, 2005), a so-called Web 4.0 twist that personalizes the WWW to the user. Machine learning is employed to enhance the results of searching in terms of finding clustered or like images (Chen, Wang, & Krovetz, 2003). With images in tangible digital archives, search becomes even more complex—because these repositories must house both digital and physical artifacts. Some endeavors have existed to map print and digital artifacts for more interactive documents (Weibel, Norrie, & Signer, 2007).

Those using digital imagery for e-learning are working in complicated information spaces. Most systems rely on user sophistication in their ability to refine queries and to reject inaccurate "false positives" or hits from the candidate result sets. More focused visual findings enhance the recall of those seeking the visual information (Christel, Moraveji, & Huang, 2004, pp. 590–591). A federated "catalog" of searches may enhance a sense of informational structure for searches in educational digital libraries (Pandya, Domenico, & Marlino, 2003).

EFFICIENT DOWNLOAD AND DELIVERY OF IMAGERY

Unique technological challenges have arisen with the delivery of digital imagery to both fixed and mobile clients given the need for connection adaptivity, the low processing power of mobile devices, the small screens, the transient location of the mobile unit, and the security challenges of wireless systems (Alvarez-Cavazos, Garcia-Sanchez, Garza-Salazar, Lavariega, Gomez & Sordia, 2005). Repositories now must deliver not only to fixed computer users but to those who are using mobile devices (Callan, et al., 2003) in ambient, wifi-enabled spaces (Aridor, Carmel, Maarek, Soffer, & Lempel, 2002). Mobile picture sharing has been enabled for the delivery of browsable images (Sarvas, Viikari, Pesonen, & Nevanlinna, 2004). Portability is a critical aspect of objects used in mobile learning, which requires "expediency, immediacy, interactivity, authenticity, accessibility, efficiency and convenience" (Yang & Chen, 2006, n.p.).

SECURITY ISSUES

The secure management of image repositories and digital libraries is crucial to their effective functioning. Digital imagery contains informational value for R&D (research and development), analysis, decision-making, higher learning, and research.

Legal issues and rights management require secure handling of digital contents; these challenges are known as the "ownership problem" of digital imagery and contents (Sencar & Memon, 2005, pp. 93 – 101). Only those with authorized access and proper credentials should be able to access repositories, and those who may make changes to the repository contents should undergo a higher level of vetting yet. This applies to access to e-learning as well. Authentication of users through knowledge-based authentication (like a password), token-based authentication (like a keycard), or biometrics (like fingerprinting or retinal scanning) into an online learning program (Garfinkel & Spafford, 1996, as cited in Adams & Blandford, 2003).

Users accessing a digital repository may have expectations of privacy protections, particularly if the repositories are socio-technical systems that include collaborative virtual environments, or ones that archive user annotations. The provenance or provable histories of digital image information will be important for data integrity. Iverson proposes "a data security model that provides full support for a range of private to semi-public to fully public data and metadata for users and user communities; and simple, flexible and integrated control of privacy, security, and integrity of all such data and metadata" (Iverson, 2004, p. 380).

A culture of security should surround digital image repositories and libraries. Challenges to security come from many sides. The federated or distributed nature of some digital repositories makes security harder to manage. The evolving field of black hacking and malicious attacks increase informational vulnerabilities. "Increased dependence on agent-based architectures for digital libraries and peer-to- peer communications makes them more vulnerable to security threats. Thus, evolving a comprehensively secure distributed digital library system is challenging. In addition to the security guarantees, performance guarantees such as convenience in usage, minimal response time, and high throughput are also required of these systems" (Vemulapalli, Halappanavar, & Mukkamala, 2002). Networked information structures require extra design for security. Common search challenges on the WWW in terms of slow retrieval speeds, communication delays and the level of broken links and noise in the retrieved results cause searcher frustrations (Kobayashi & Takeda, 2000).

An Image Lifespan

Some repositories handle imagery that is complete and stable and likely will not change. Many more deal with imagery that is only relatively complete and may be in evolution. Some digital visuals may need further processing on desktop computers for informational value (Vazhkudai, Ma, Freeh, Strickland, Tammineedi, Simon, & Scott, 2006). Others may be parts of collaborations of virtual teams. Visuals that evolve over various use lifespans may have changing intellectual property rights claims and changing technological formats.

Image lifespans also change based on the "slow fires" that erode images and make them unreadable on current-day devices. The term "slow fires" was applied to the "embrittlement" of paper based on acid decay. For preservation purposes, digital imagery also must be protected against corruption and technological extinction.

Intellectual Property Rights Management

The complexities of multimedia intellectual property rights management may be prohibitive. Then, too, the larger Web 2.0 culture of mash-ups has led to contravention of the rights of many copyright holders. Open –access, Creative Commons and other rights releases have changed the intellectual property landscape and require greater repository flexibility in the recording and release of such contents. Instituting clear use policies will be important.

Image Provenance and Quality

The context of an image capture and its edits will be important information to maintain for informational security (the protection of data, including issues of "privacy, ethics and loss prevention") and data assurance (offering reliable information systems that may "weather untoward events no matter what the cause—whether natural disaster or caused by a malicious individual" (Lewandowski, 2005, p. 184). A repository must guard against information degradation that may occur through system compromises—unauthorized accesses, intrusions, or harmful codes. This is especially important for proprietary and "dim" or "black" data repositories.

User Privacy

Personally identifiable information of individual users should be protected (Callan, et al., 2003, p. 10). User information also should not be exploited for commercial purposes. "Privacy (or the lack thereof) is of a special concern in subscriptions to large data repositories with heterogeneous information, where the service provider can easily profile its users and sell that information to third parties" (Blanton, 2008, p. 217).

Downstream Uses

The downstream uses of information may be the hardest to control. This refers to what happens to information once it leaves a repository and possibly is used in a more open, less secure learning / course management system or is downloaded by users onto their own mobile devices, laptops, or desktop computers. Some systems deploy 3D images in pieces so as to protect them from being downloadable but still letting them be manipulable (for viewing different angles) on the original repository. Some suggest the use of multiple watermarks to head off "ambiguity attacks," due to the high false-positives in watermarking schemes (Sencar, Li & Memon, 2007, pp. 205 – 213), but the use of watermarks may corrupt sensitive images like those on satellite image captures (Heileman & Yang, 2003). Some suggest the use of reversible watermarking so as to allow the recovery of the original host content after verification of the authenticity of the work (Thodi & Rodriguez, 2004). Figure 3 captures the importance of security for an image repository, as a summary to the above discussion.

SOCIO-TECHNICAL AND COLLABORATIVE ASPECTS OF IMAGE REPOSITORIES AND DIGITAL LIBRARIES

Repositories and digital libraries have become socio-technical systems, with the inclusion of computer mediated communications, to make these collaborative environments for researchers and students (Agosti, Ferro, & Orio, 2005). A "collaboratory" offers researchers a space to collaborate around information, multi-modal types of intercommunications, shared software, data storage and "the ability to control remote instruments" (Baecker, Fono, & Wolf, 2007, p. 462). This is about active and evolving knowledge, not inert information. "The class *community* describes business models of digital libraries that expand their services by providing collaborative services for customers" (Markscheffel, Fischer, & Stelzer, 2006, p. 463). These services include both synchronous and asynchronous communications

Figure 3. Some security concerns for an image repository

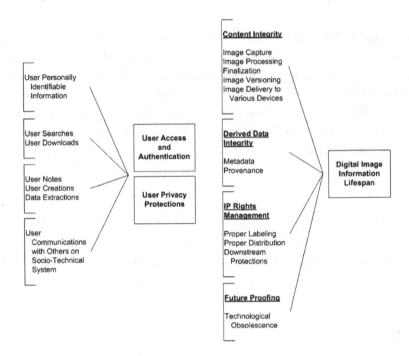

tools. A collaborative digital library is necessarily user centered (Reference models for digital libraries: actors and roles, 2003).

The inclusion of blogs, wikis, and private user spaces on digital repositories has strengthened the call for using these sites as learning communities. Some even build in tools for work-flows—to enhance individual note-taking (Sumner & Marlino, 2004), the annotation of digital artifacts (Frommolz & Fuhr, June 2006), group brainstorming, co-research strategies, citations off-loading, and informational and multimedia literacy. Interactive, immersive, and discovery-based microworlds are being explored to add value to digital library contents but have been time-consuming and difficult to produce (Laleuf & Spalter, 2001).

The long-term health of collaborative repositories will require the building of human relationships and cooperation (Bush & Tiwana, 2005). This will mean converting casual users into return participants for long-term use. "Without converting casual or onetime users into recurring, involved participants, or even members of a community, educational digital libraries will simply be yet another example of, "If you build it, will they come" (Muramatsu, Giersch, McMartin, Weimar, & Klotz, 2004, p. 396). Peer-to-peer self-supervising will need to be enhanced (Cooper & Garcia-Molina, 2005). These sites will need to be persistent to encourage "longevity" in user participation.

The images of a repository may be used for a range of assignments and learner collaborations. Learners may conduct research in image repositories and create presentations from their work; they may engage in "jigsaw" learning and sharing, with different teams covering different parts of the curriculum. Students may hold digital gallery shows of their images, or display eportfolios of their work. Students may conduct information-rich research based on imagery. They may use digital visuals to analyze a situation, solve problems, or create a project in project-based learning. Users may create content resources for the repository to refresh its holdings.

Informatics communities bring people together who have shared interests. Some technologies are brought online for their affordances—to activate groups of experts to extend their work in particular fields, for information gathering. One strives to "rapidly build communities of people (academic taxonomists, amateur natural historians, environmental educators, concerned citizens and students) and institutions (universities, environmental NGOs, governmental agencies and schools) to produce important scientific data about biodiversity" (Stevenson & Morris, 2002, pp. 1 – 4).

CONCLUSION

The storage and distribution of e-learning visuals add powerful functionality to these resources in terms of reusability, research, cross-referencing, and study. Developers have been focused on supporting the manageability, scalability and searchability of digital information in repositories.

With the growing sophistication in federated repositories and cross-repository search techniques, Web-accessible searches will be able to turn up a richer range of resources from various centers of expertise. There will be more powerful ways to capture user-generated contents. More from-life contents may be captured and made available for public use with the Web 2.0 focus on sharing and the open repositories. The growing awareness of the importance of metadata will optimally enhance human metadata labeling of digital imagery, and the technological functionalities of automatic metadata capture from various cameras and sensor devices will output more information-rich visuals. Interoperability ecosystems will need to be supported to promote technical interoperability, legal and public policies, and semantic interoperability (Baird, 2007, p. 65).

Ways to version visual contents mobile and other devices have been in development and will likely affect the quality of ubiquitous and mobile learning. There may be more flexible ways to analyze and visualize image collections and organize the contents into ontologies or taxonomies.

The socio-technical aspects of such virtual spaces may enable cross-domain sharing and collaborations around informatics and shared interests. In specific fields, there will likely be increased abilities to handle larger file sizes that are "high-resolution, high-dimension, and high-throughput" ones (Datta, Joshi, Li, & Wang, 2008, p. 5:49). Ideally, this would be accompanied by more complex ways to compare, integrate, annotate and engage with the digital imagery. An interesting line of inquiry involves researching ways to help individuals share digital personal life artifacts with the requisite levels of safety and ethics via mobile devices (Olsson, Soronen, & Väänänen-Vainio-Mattila, 2008). Various tools to protect the intellectual property, originality, and downstream uses of imagery may encourage controlled sharing through aggregated collections.

Being aware of the roles of digital repositories for images and multimedia should strengthen the uses of these collections; enhance the writing of metadata; promote more sophisticated image capture and deployment for multi-uses, and further promote the uses of digital imagery in e-learning.

REFERENCES

Abowd, G. D., Harvel, L. D., & Brotherton, J. A. (2001). Building a digital library of captured educational experiences. In *Proceedings of the International Conference on Digital Libraries* (pp. 467-474). Washington, DC: IEEE.

Adams, A., & Blandford, A. (2003). Security and online learning: To protect or prohibit. In C. Ghaoui (Ed.), *Usability Evaluation of Online Learning Programs*. Hershey, PA: Information Science Publishing.

Adams, B., Venkatesh, S., & Jain, R. (2005). ICME: Integrated media creation environment. *ACM Transactions on Multimedia Computing . Communications and Applications*, *1*(3), 211–247.

Agosti, M., & Ferro, N. (2007). A formal model of annotations of digital content. *ACM Transactions on Information Systems*, *26*(1). doi:10.1145/1292591.1292594

Agosti, M., Ferro, N., & Orio, N. (2005). Annotating illuminated manuscripts: An effective tool for research and education. In *Proceedings of the JCDL '05* (pp. 121-130). New York: ACM.

Albertoni, R., Bertone, A., & De Martino, M. (2005). Visualization and semantic analysis of geographic metadata. In *Proceedings of the GIR '05,* Bremen, Germany (pp. 9-16). New York: ACM.

Alvarez-Cavazos, F., Garcia-Sanchez, R., Garza-Salazar, D., Lavariega, J. C., Gomez, L. G., & Sordia, M. (2005). Universal access architecture for digital libraries. In *Proceedings of the ITESM* (pp. 1-17). New York: ACM.

Aridor, Y., Carmel, D., Maarek, Y. S., Soffer, A., & Lempel, R. (2002). Knowledge Encapsulation for focused search from pervasive devices. *ACM Transactions on Information Systems*, *20*(1), 25–46. doi:10.1145/503104.503106

Badi, R., Bae, S., Moore, J. M., Meintanis, K., Zacchi, A., Hsieh, H., et al. (2006). Recognizing user interest and document value from reading and organizing activities in document triage. In *Proceedings of the IUI '06*. New York: ACM.

Baecker, R. M., Fono, D., & Wolf, P. (2007). Toward a video collaboratory. In R. Goldman, R. Pea, B. Barron, & S. J. Denny (Eds.), *Video Research in the Learning Sciences* (pp. 461-478). Mahwah, NJ: Lawrence Erlbaum Associates, Publishers.

Bainbridge, D., Ke, K.-Y., & Witten, I. H. (2006). Document level interoperability for collection creators. In *Proceedings of the JCDL '06* (pp. 105-106). New York: ACM.

Bainbridge, D., Thompson, J., & Witten, I. H. (2003). Assembling and enriching digital library collections. In *Proceedings of the 3rd ACM/IEEE-CS joint conference on Digital libraries* (pp. 323-334). New York: ACM.

Baird, S. A. (2007) Government role in developing an interoperability ecosystem. In *Proceedings of the ICGOV 2007*, Macao (pp. 65-68). New York: ACM.

Bekaert, J., Liu, X., Van de Sompel, H., Lagoze, C., Payette, S., & Warner, S. (2006). *Proceedings of the JCDL '06*. New York: ACM.

Bertini, M., Del Bimbo, A., Torniai, C., Grana, C., & Cucchiara, R. (2007). Dynamic pictorial ontologies for video digital libraries annotation. In *Proceedings of the Workshop on multimedia information retrieval on The many faces of multimedia semantics* (pp. 47-55). New York: ACM.

Blandford, A., Keith, S., Connell, I., & Edwards, H. (2004). Analytical usability evaluation for digital libraries: A case study. In *Proceedings of the 2004 Joint ACM / IEEE Conference on Digital Libraries (JCDL '04)* (pp. 27-36).

Blanton, M. (2008). Online subscriptions with anonymous access. In [New York: ACM.]. *Proceedings of the ASIACCS, 08*, 217–227. doi:10.1145/1368310.1368342

Bolettieri, P., Falchi, F., Gennaro, C., & Rabitti, F. (2007). Automatic metadata extraction and indexing for reusing e-learning multimedia objects. In *Proceedings of the MS '07*, Augsburg, Bavaria, Germany (pp. 21-28). New York: ACM.

Bottoni, P., Civica, R., Levialdi, S., Orso, L., Panizzi, E., & Trinchese, R. (2004). MADCOW: A multimedia digital annotation system. In *Proceedings of the AVI '04* (pp. 55-62). New York: ACM.

Brown, M. S., Seales, W. B., Webb, S. B., & Jaynes, C. O. (2001). Building large-format displays for digital libraries. *Communications of the ACM, 44*(5), 57–59. doi:10.1145/374308.374341

Bush, A. A., & Tiwana, A. (2005). Designing sticky knowledge networks. *Communications of the ACM, 48*(5), 67–71. doi:10.1145/1060710.1060711

Callan, J., Smeaton, A., Beaulieu, M., Borlund, P., Brusilovsky, P., Chalmers, M., et al. (2003). *Personalization and recommender systems in digital libraries joint NSF-EU DELOS working group report*. Retrieved from http://dli2.nsf.gov/internationalprojects/working_group_reports/personalisation.html

Canosa, R. L. (2006). Image understanding as a second course in AI: Preparing students for research. In *Proceedings of the SIGCSE '06*, Houston, TX. New York: ACM.

Chang, S.-F., Smith, J. R., Beigi, M., & Benitez, A. (1997). Visual information retrieval from large distributed online repositories. *Communications of the ACM, 40*(12), 63–71. doi:10.1145/265563.265573

Chen, C.-C., Wactlar, H. D., Wang, J. Z., & Kiernan, K. (2005). Digital imagery for significant cultural and historical materials: An emerging research field bridging people, culture, and technologies. *International Journal on Digital Libraries, 5*, 275–286. doi:10.1007/s00799-004-0097-5

Chen, Y., Wang, J. Z., & Krovetz, R. (2003). Content-based image retrieval by clustering. In *Proceedings of the MIR '03*, Berkeley, CA (pp. 193-200).

Christel, M. G. (1999). Visual digests for news video libraries. In *Proceedings of the ACM Multimedia '99*, Orlando, FL.

Christel, M. G., & Conescu, R. M. (2005). Addressing the challenge of visual information access from digital image and video libraries. In *Proceedings of the JCDL '05*, Denver, CO (pp. 69-79). New York: ACM.

Christel, M. G., Moraveji, N., & Huang, C. (2004). Evaluating content-based filters for image and video retrieval. In [New York: ACM.]. *Proceedings of the SIGIR, 04*, 590–591. doi:10.1145/1008992.1009135

Cooper, B. F., & Garcia-Molina, H. (2005). Ad hoc, self-supervising peer-to-peer search networks. *ACM Transactions on Information Systems, 23*(2), 169–200. doi:10.1145/1059981.1059983

Crabtree, A., Rodden, T., & Mariani, J. (2004). Collaborating around collections: Informing the continued development of photoware. In *Proceedings of the 2004 ACM conference on Computer supported cooperative work* (pp. 396-405). New York: ACM.

Datta, R., Ge, W., Li, J., & Wang, J. Z. (2006). Toward bridging the annotation-retrieval gap in image search by a generative modeling approach. In *Proceedings of the MM '06*. New York: ACM.

Datta, R., Joshi, D., Li, J., & Wang, J.Z. (2008). Image retrieval: Ideas, influences, and trends of the new age. *ACM Computing Surveys, 40*(2), 5:1-5:60.

Datta, R., Li, J., & Wang, J. Z. (2005). Content-based image retrieval—Approaches and trends of the New Age. In *Proceedings of the MIR '05*, Singapore (pp. 253-262). New York: ACM.

Davis, M., King, S., Good, N., & Sarvas, R. (2004). From context to content: Leveraging context to infer media metadata. In [New York: ACM.]. *Proceedings of the MM, 04*, 188–195.

De Carvalho, M. G., Goncalves, M. A., Laender, A. H. F., & da Silva, A. S. (2006). Learning to deduplicate. In *Proceedings of the JCDL '06* (pp. 41-50). New York: ACM.

Dori, D. (2004). ViSWeb—the Visual Semantic Web: unifying human and machine knowledge Representations with object-process methodology. *The VLDB Journal, 13*, 120–147. doi:10.1007/s00778-004-0120-x

Dunn, J.W., & Cowan, W.G. (2005). EVIADA: Ethnomusicological video for instruction and analysis digital archive. *TCDL Bulletin, 2*(1).

Fan, L., & Li, B. (2006). A hybrid model of image retrieval based on ontology technology and probabilistic ranking. In *Proceedings of the 2006 IEEE / WIC / ACM International Conference on Web Intelligence*. Washington, DC: IEEE.

Foulonneau, M., Cole, T. W., Habing, T. G., & Shreeves, S. L. (2005). Using collection descriptions to enhance an aggregation of harvested item-level metadata. In *Proceedings of the JCDL '05*, Denver, CO (pp. 32-41). New York: ACM.

Frommolz, I., & Fuhr, N. (2006). Probabilistic, object-oriented logics for annotation-based retrieval in digital libraries. In *Proceedings of the JCDL '06* (pp. 55-64). New York: ACM.

Funkhouser, T., & Kazhdan, M. (n.d.). *Shape-based retrieval and analysis of 3D models* [Online syllabus].

Funkhouser, T., Min, P., Kazhdan, M., Chen, J., Halderman, A., Dobkin, D., & Jacobs, D. (2003). A search engine for 3D models. *ACM Transactions on Graphics, 22*(1), 83–105. doi:10.1145/588272.588279

Geer, D. E. (2006, November). Playing for keeps: Will security threats bring an end to general-purpose computing? *ACM Queue; Tomorrow's Computing Today, 4*(9), 45. doi:10.1145/1180176.1180193

Goncalves, M. A., Fox, E. A., Watson, L. T., & Kipp, N. A. (2004). Streams, structures, spaces, scenarios, societies (5S): A formal model for digital libraries. *ACM Transactions on Information Systems, 22*(2), 270–312. doi:10.1145/984321.984325

Gorton, D., Shen, R., Vemuri, N. S., Fan, W., & Fox, E. A. (2006). ETANA-GIS: GIS for archaeological digital libraries. In *Proceedings of the JCDL '06*. New York: ACM.

Gupta, A., Memon, A., Tran, J., Bharadwaja, R. P., & Zaslavsky, I. (2002). Information mediation across heterogeneous government spatial data sources. In *Proceedings of the 2002 annual national conference on Digital government research*. Retrieved October 7, 2008, from http://portal.acm.org/citation. cfm?id=1123098.1123143

Hatala, M., Kalantari, L., Wakkary, R., & Newby, K. (2004). Ontology and rule based retrieval of sound objects in augmented audio reality system for museum visitors. In *Proceedings of the 2004 ACM Symposium on Applied Computing* (pp. 1045-1050). New York: ACM.

Hauptmann, A. G., Lin, W.-H., Yan, R., Yang, J., & Chen, M.-Y. (2006). Extreme video retrieval: Joint maximization of human and computer performance. In *Proceedings of the MM '06*, Santa Barbara, CA. New York: ACM.

Heileman, G. L., & Yang, Y. (2003). The effects of invisible watermarking on satellite image classification. In Proceedings of the DRM '03 (pp. 120-132). New York: ACM.

Hiransakolwong, N., Hua, K. A., Koompairojn, S., Vu, K., & Lang, S.-D. (2005). An adaptive distance computation technique for image retrieval system. In *Proceedings of the 2005 ACM Symposium on Applied Computing, SAC '05* (pp. 1195-1199). New York: ACM.

Iverson, L. (2004). Collaboration in digital libraries: A conceptual framework. In *Proceedings of the JCDL '04*. New York: ACM.

Janêe, G., Mathena, J., & Frew, J. (2008). A data model and architecture for long-term preservation. In *Proceedings of the JCDL '08* (pp. 134-143). New York: ACM.

Jiang, S., Huang, T., & Gao, W. (2004). An ontology-based approach to retrieve digitized art images. In *Proceedings of the IEEE / WIC / ACM International Conference on Web Intelligence*.

Kennedy, L., & Naaman, M. (2008). Generating diverse and representative image search results for landmarks. In Proceedings of the WWW 2008, Beijing, China (pp. 297-30). New York: ACM.

Kherfi, M. L., Ziou, D., & Bernardi, A. (2004). Image retrieval from the World Wide Web: Issues, techniques, and systems. *ACM Computing Surveys, 36*(1), 35–67. doi:10.1145/1013208.1013210

Ko, K. H., Maekawa, T., Patrikalakis, N. M., Masuda, H., & Wolter, F.-E. (2003). Shape intrinsic fingerprints for free-form object matching. In [New York: ACM.]. *Proceedings of the SM, 03*, 196–207.

Kobayashi, M., & Takeda, K. (2000). Information retrieval on the Web. *ACM Computing Surveys, 32*(2), 144. doi:10.1145/358923.358934

Krowne, A., & Halbert, M. (2005). An initial evaluation of automated organization for digital library browsing. In *Proceedings of the JCDL '05* (pp. 246-255). New York: ACM.

Kumar, A. (2007). Visual understanding environment. In *Proceedings of the JCDL '07*. New York: ACM.

Laing, S. J. (2008). Applying graphic design terms to image tagging. In *Proceedings of the CIVR '08*, Niagara Falls, Ontario (pp. 3-7). New York: ACM.

Laleuf, J. R., & Spalter, A. M. (2001). A component repository for learning objects: A progress report. In *Proceedings of the JCDL '01* (pp. 33-40). New York: ACM.

Leong, T. W., Howard, S., & Vetere, F. (2008). Choice: Abdicating or exercising. In *Proceedings of the CHI 2008 – Sound of Music* (pp. 715-724). New York: ACM.

Leslie, L., Chua, T.-S., & Jain, R. (2007). Annotation of paintings with high-level Semantic concepts using transductive inference and ontology-based concept disambiguation. In *Proceedings of the 15th international conference on Multimedia* (pp. 443-452). New York: ACM.

Lewandowski, J. O. (2005). Creating a culture of technical caution: Addressing the issues of security, privacy protection and the ethical use of technology. In *Proceedings of the SIGUCCS '05*, Monterey, CA.

Madhwacharyula, C. L., Davis, M., Mulhem, P., & Kankanhalli, M. S. (2007). Metadata handling: A video perspective. *ACM Transactions on Multimedia Computing . Communications and Applications*, 2(4), 358–388.

Malizia, A. (2004). A cognition-based approach for querying personal digital libraries. In *Proceedings of the 2004 IEEE Symposium on Visual Languages and Human Centric Computing (VLHCC '04)*.

Manku, G. S., Jain, A., & Sarma, A. D. (2007). Detecting near-duplicates for Web crawling. In *Proceedings of the WWW 2007/Track: Data Mining, Similarity Search. The International World Wide Web Conference Committee (IW3C2)* (pp. 141-149). New York: ACM.

Marincioni, F., & Lightsom, F. (2002). Marine Realms Information Bank: A distributed geolibrary for the ocean. In *Proceedings of the JCDL '02*. New York: ACM.

Markkula, M., & Sormunen, E. (2006). Video needs at the different stages of television program making process. In *Proceedings of the Information Interaction in Context*, Copenhagen, Denmark (pp. 111-118).

Markscheffel, B., Fischer, D., & Stelzer, D. (2006). A business model-based classification approach for digital libraries. In *Proceedings of the First IEEE International Conference on Digital Information Management (ICDIM)* (pp. 457-464). Washington, DC: IEEE.

Mathan, S., Erdogmus, D., Huang, Y., Pavel, M., Ververs, P., Carciofini, J., et al. (2008). Rapid image analysis using neural signals. In *CHI 2008 Proceedings*, Florence, Italy. New York: ACM.

McCaffrey, M., & Weston, T. (2005). The climate change collection: A case study on digital library collection review and the integration of research, education and evaluation. In *International Conference on Digital Libraries, Proceedings of the 5th ACM / IEE-CS Joint Conference on Digital Libraries*, Denver, CO.

McGrath, R. E., Futrelle, J., Plante, R., & Guillaume, D. (1999). Digital library technology for locating and accessing scientific data. In *Proceedings of the fourth ACM conference on Digital libraries* (pp. 188-194). New York: ACM.

McIntyre, S. A., Dennis, S. E., Uijtdehaage, S. H. J., & Candler, C. S. (2004). A digital library for health sciences educators: The Health Education Assets Library (HEAL). In *Proceedings of the JCDL '04* (pp. 387).

Mischo, W. H., Habing, T. G., & Cole, T. W. (2003). Integration of simultaneous searching and reference linking across bibliographic resources on the Web. In *Proceedings of the 2nd ACM/IEEE-CS joint conference on Digital libraries* (pp. 119-125). Washington, DC: IEEE.

Morris, S., Morris, A., & Barnard, K. (2004, June). Digital trail libraries. In *Proceedings of the JCDL '04*, Tuscon, AZ (pp. 63-71). New York: ACM.

Muramatsu, B., Giersch, S., McMartin, F., Weimar, S., & Klotz, G. (2004). 'If you build it, will they come?' Lessons learned from the workshop on participant interaction in digital libraries. In *Proceedings of the 2004 Joint ACM / IEEE Conference on Digital Libraries (JCDL '04)* (pp. 396). Washington, DC: IEEE.

Nack, F., & Putz, W. (2005). Designing annotation before it's needed. In *Proceedings of the MM '01*, Ottawa, Canada (pp. 251-260). New York: ACM.

Nelson, M. L., Marchionini, G., Geisler, G., & Yang, M. (2001). A bucket architecture for the Open Video Project. In *Proceedings of the JCDL '01* (pp. 310-311). New York: ACM.

Nikolaidou, M., Anagnostopoulos, D., & Hatzopoulos, M. (2003). Using a medical digital library for education purposes. In *Proceedings of the 16th IEEE Symposium on Computer-Based Medical Systems (CBMS '03)*.

O'Sullivan, D., McLoughlin, E., Bertolotto, M., & Wilson, D. C. (2003). Capturing task knowledge for geo-spatial imagery. In [New York: ACM.]. *Proceedings of the K-CAP, 03*, 78–87.

Olsson, T., Soronen, H., & Väänänen-Vainio-Mattila, K. (2008). User needs and design guidelines for mobile services for sharing digital life memories. In *Proceedings of the Mobile HCI 2008*, Amsterdam, The Netherlands (pp. 273-282).

Palmer, C., Zavalina, O., & Mustafoff, M. (2007). Trends in metadata practices: A longitudinal study of collection federation. In *Proceedings of the JCDL '07* (pp. 386-395). New York: ACM.

Pandya, R., Domenico, B., & Marlino, M. (2003). Finding and using data in educational digital libraries. In *Proceedings of the Third ACM/IEEE-CS Joint Conference on Digital Libraries (JCDL'03)* (pp. 399). Washington, DC: IEEE.

Rani, S., Goodkin, J., Cobb, J., Habing, T., & Urban, R. Eke, Jn., & Pearce-Moses, R. (2006). Technical architecture overview: Tools for acquisition, packaging and ingest of Web objects into multiple repositories. In *Proceedings of the JCDL '06* (pp. 360). New York: ACM.

Reference models for digital libraries: Actors and roles. (2003). DELOS / NSF Working Group.

Reuning, J., & Jones, P. (2005). Osprey: Peer-to-peer enabled content distribution. In *Proceedings of the JCDL '05* (pp. 396). New York: ACM.

Rowe, J., Razdan, A., & Simon, A. (2003). Acquisition, representation, query and analysis of spatial data: A demonstration 3D digital library. In *Proceedings of the 3rd ACM/IEEE-CS joint conference on Digital libraries* (pp. 147-158). Washington, DC: IEEE.

Sarvas, R., Herrarte, E., Wilhelm, A., & Davis, M. (2004). Metadata creation system for mobile images. In [New York: ACM.]. *Proceedings of the MobiSys, 04*, 36–48. doi:10.1145/990064.990072

Sarvas, R., Viikari, M., Pesonen, J., & Nevanlinna, H. (2004). Mobshare: Controlled and immediate sharing of mobile images. In [New York: ACM.]. *Proceedings of the MM, 04*, 724–731.

Sencar, H. T., & Memon, N. (2005). Watermarking and ownership problem: A revisit. In *Proceedings of the DRM '05*. Alexandra, VA (pp. 93-105). New York: ACM.

Simske, S., & Lin, X. (2004). Creating digital libraries: Content generation and re-mastering. In *Proceedings of the First International Workshop on Document Image Analysis for Libraries (DIAL '04)*. Washington, DC: IEEE.

Smith, M. (2005). Eternal bits: How can we preserve digital files and save our collective memory? *IEEE Spectrum*.

Soergel, D. (2005). Thesauri and ontologies in digital libraries. In *Proceedings of the JCDL '05* (pp. 421). New York: ACM.

Song, Y., & Marchionini, G. (2007). Effects of audio and video surrogates for making sense of digital video. In *CHI 2007 Proceedings*, San Jose, CA (pp. 867-876). New York: ACM.

Stevenson, R. D., & Morris, R. A. (2002). Community science for biodiversity monitoring. In *Proceedings of the 2002 annual national conference on Digital government research* (pp. 1-4). New York: ACM.

Sumner, T., & Marlino, M. (2004). Digital libraries and educational practice: A case for new models. In *Proceedings of the JCDL '04* (pp. 170-178). New York: ACM.

Tangelder, J. W. H., & Veltkamp, R. C. (2004). A survey of content based 3D shape retrieval methods. In *Proceedings of the Shape Modeling International 2004. (SMI'04)*.

Thakkar, S., Knoblock, C. A., & Ambite, J. L. (2007). Quality-driven geospatial data integration. In *Proceedings of the 15th International Symposium on Advances in Geographic Information Systems (ACM GIS 2007)* (pp. 1-8). New York: ACM.

The Alexandria Digital Library Team. (2004). The Alexandria Digital Library and the Alexandria Digital Earth Prototype. In *Proceedings of the JCDL '04*. New York: ACM.

Thodi, D. M., & Rodriguez, J. J. (2004). Prediction-error based reversible watermarking. In *Proceedings of the 2004 International Conference on Image Processing* (pp. 1549-1552). Washington, DC: IEEE.

Truong, B. T., & Venkatesh, S. (2007). Video abstraction: A systematic review and classification. *ACM Transactions on Multimedia Computing . Communications and Applications, 3*(1), 1–37.

Tschimer, S., & Zipf, A. (2005). Finding geodata that otherwise would have been forgotten GeoXchange— A SDI-based portal for sharing free geodata. In *Proceedings of the GIR '05,* Bremen, Germany (pp. 39-43). New York: ACM.

Vazhkudai, S. S., Ma, X., Freeh, V. W., Strickland, J. W., Tammineedi, N., Simon, T., & Scott, S. L. (2006). Constructing collaborative desktop storage caches for large scientific datasets. *ACM Transactions on Storage, 2*(3), 221–254. doi:10.1145/1168910.1168911

Vemulapalli, S., Halappanavar, M., & Mukkamala, R. (2002). Security in distributed digital libraries: Issues and challenges. In Proceedings of the International Conference on Parallel Processing Workshops (ICPPW'02). Washington, DC: IEEE.

Volkmer, T., Thom, J. A., & Tahaghoghi, S. M. M. (2007). Exploring human judgement (sic) of digital imagery. *Conferences in Research and Practice in Information Technology, 62,* 151.

Vuorikari, R. (2007). Can social information retrieval enhance the discovery and reuse of digital educational content? In [New York: ACM.]. *Proceedings of the RecSys, 07,* 207–210. doi:10.1145/1297231.1297276

Wang, W., Ma, D., Wu, Y., Zhang, A., & Mark, D. M. (2002). Webview: A distributed geographical image retrieval system. In *Proceedings of the 2002 annual national conference on Digital government research.* New York: ACM.

Weibel, N., Norrie, M. C., & Signer, B. (2007, August). A model for mapping between printed and digital document instances. In *Proceedings of the DocEng '07,* Winnipeg, Manitoba, Canada (pp. 19-28). New York: ACM.

Westman, S., & Oittinen, P. (2006). Image retrieval by end-users and intermediaries in a journalistic work context. In *Proceedings of the Information Interaction in Context,* Copenhagen, Denmark (pp. 102-110). New York: ACM.

Winn, J., Criminisi, A., & Minka, T. (2005). Object categorization by learned universal visual dictionary. In *Proceedings of the Tenth IEEE International Conference on Computer Vision (ICCV '05)* (pp. 1-8). Washington, DC: IEEE.

Wong, S. C., Crowder, R. M., Wills, G. B., & Shadbolt, N. R. (2006, October). Knowledge engineering—From front-line support to preliminary design. In . *Proceedings of the DocEng, 06,* 44–52.

Wyss, C. M., & Robertson, E. L. (2005). Relational languages for metadata integration. *ACM Transactions on Database Systems, 30*(2), 624–660. doi:10.1145/1071610.1071618

Xue, X.-B., Zhou, Z.-H., & Zhang, Z.-F. (2008). Improving Web search using image snippets. *ACM Transactions on Internet Technology, 8*(4), 21. doi:10.1145/1391949.1391955

Yang, J., Han, J., Oh, I., & Kwak, M. (2007). Using Wikipedia technology for topic maps design. In . *Proceedings of the ACMSE, 2007,* 106–110.

Yang, J. C., & Chen, C. H. (2006). Design of inquiry learning activity using wireless and mobile technologies. In *Proceedings of the Sixth International Conference on Advance Learning Technologies (ICALT '06).* Washington, DC: IEEE.

Zhu, L., Rao, A., & Zhang, A. (2002). Theory of keyblock-based image retrieval. *ACM Transactions on Information Systems, 20*(2), 224–257. doi:10.1145/506309.506313

Zhuang, Z., Wagle, R., & Giles, C. L. (2005). What's there and what's not? Focused crawling for missing documents in digital libraries. In *Proceedings of the JCDL '05* (pp. 301-310). New York: ACM.

KEY TERMS AND DEFINITIONS

Aggregation (n): An assemblage of related digital objects

Candidate Result Set (n): The set of visual objects found as part of a user search

Collaborative Digital Library (n): A user-centered resource that provides services and access to digital multimedia resources

Collection (n): A grouping of objects of a type, usually for a particular purpose, with semantic meaning

Data Stream: A sequence of data units captured often with timing information, from remote sensors, satellites, cameras, and other digital capture technologies

Digital Library (Electronic Library, Virtual Library, and E-Library) (n): A collection of digital objects that are organized and labeled in a coherent and usable way

Field (n): An area of study, a knowledge domain

Georeferencing (n): A way of pointing to information based on the location of the data on the earth's surface, captured through aerial photography, satellite, and other forms of digital image and information capture

Intelligent Agent (n): An often-autonomous computerized entity that has been coded to act upon an environment

Ingestion (n): The acceptance of digital materials into a digital library or repository

Keyframe (n): A single bitmap image extracted from a shot, a sequence of still images extracted from moving video

Keyword Indexing (n): The storage and organization of keywords describing repository or digital library objects

Metadata (n): Information about information, derived information

MIR (n): Multimedia information retrieval from a digital repository

Natural Language Processing (adj): An artificial intelligence function that convert digital information into normal human language and also that convert human languages into machine-understandable contents

Near-Duplicate Keyframes (n): Keyframes of video that are close to exact duplicates of each other but which differ in the environmental capturing conditions, acquisition times, acquisition locations, editing operations and / or rendering conditions

Nested Aggregation (n): An assemblage of digital objects within other digital objects, in a hierarchical structure

Ontology (n): A rigorous structure of defined objects / entities and their relationships that describe a domain field or an aspect of a knowledge domain, a hierarchy of information

Referatory (n): A digital repository that points to various resources on the WWW using links, metadata and value-added information

Relevance Feedback (n): A database query modification technique that uses query refinement and iterative feedback to focus on users' needs

Repository (n): A storehouse for digital objects, with tools for submittal, archival, labeling, search, and extraction / download

Search (n): The identification and location of particular digital information

Semantic Gap (n): The disparity between the image desired and those with high feature similarities described in the query, the differences in meaning between the image desired and those of found images in a search query

Semantics (n): Meanings, definitions

Shot (n): A single continuous camera operation without a cut or transition effect

Socio-Technical (adj): Relating to the systems that involve both human presence and use and computer technologies

Speech Recognition (adj): A software feature that turns voice articulation into machine-recognizable textual speech

University-Based Institutional Digital Repository (n): A system for the management and dissemination of digital materials created by the institution's members, including theses, dissertations, journals, instructional materials, and other contents (often to help the campus retain copyright to some of the intellectual property output of their faculty and staff)

User Interface (n): A communications system through which users may access a digital repository or library

Video Skim (n): A brief capture of moving images

Visual Vocabulary (n): The terms used to describe and search for imagery from a digital repository

Section 4
Guiding Values in Digital Imagery

Chapter 12
Designing Informational Graphics for a Global Multi-Cultural Context

ABSTRACT

With many e-learning courses, modules, and artifacts being created for global delivery, those who design informational graphics need to be aware of the global environment for which they are building. They need to be more aware of the diverse cultural milieu and learning needs of the global learners. Visual imagery contains embedded meanings that may have different cultural implications in different milieu. This chapter will explore strategies to create digital images that are culturally neutral or at least culturally non-offensive. Building a layer of self-explanatory depth will also be helpful—for digital imagery with higher transferability and global utility.

CHAPTER OBJECTIVES

- Define cultural influences on human identity
- Explain how digital imagery may have cultural meanings and differing interpretations in its packaging
- Address the importance of cultural sensitivities in the building of learning artifacts for potential global deployment and use
- Investigate some universal cultural models
- Describe the Internet and WWW culture
- Explore ethical considerations in cultural aspects of digital imagery
- Discuss how to enhance the transferability of digital imagery to global contexts
- Introduce digital imagery use in e-learning in India as an exemplary case

DOI: 10.4018/978-1-60566-972-4.ch012

INTRODUCTION

Going global with digital imagery involves sharing materials in a variety of cultural, political, economic and social contexts. By default, anything posted on a website has the potential of going anywhere in the world based on the reach of the Internet and World Wide Web (WWW). Trainings and courses that are offered to all comers at universities often attract learners from various nations, people groups, demographics, and political persuasions. Research collaborations span institutions and often national boundaries as well. Too often, those who design such e-learning and related digital imagery go global as a default, without any conscious planning. Geopolitical strategies involve the reduction of local risk and the increase of local potential in terms of learning with the digital imagery.

Human identities are formed around social, national, historical, racial / ethnic, cultural, economical, religious / ethical, political, language – linguistic groups, educational factors, and gender identity, among others (see Figure 1). Added to this are the individual lived experiences which inform the respective interpretations of the world. Visual information is not value-neutral; rather, it is individually meaningful, context-dependent and perceptual. The audience changes how information is interpreted and accepted or not. In a presentation, a geopolitical strategist for a global corporation spoke of content as "the primary trust differentiator between international locales" (Edwards, 2004, n.p.). He went on to suggest that users of digital contents may assume intentionality in the distribution of offensive messages and depictions.

Conflicts may arise for a number of reasons with digital imagery. There may be misunderstandings of the image's meaning. There may be disagreements in interpretations. There may be differences in points of view, political stances, and value systems. There may be contentious ideas about whether particular images should have been captured at all. The aesthetics of imagery may carry meanings that are offensive. There may be ambiguous gestures with differing meanings and implications across social and cultural boundaries.

The importance of gestural depictions has informed the design of anatomically based human hands in animations:

Stretching from spiritual significance (e.g. blessing, palm reading), over idiomatic expressions (e.g. .to put one's life in someone's hands.), to the act of shaking hands, not only for greeting but also for ex-

Figure 1. Some cultural influences on human identity

Language / Linguistic Group	Education		Gender Identity
Racial / Ethnic	?		Political
Social	Historical		Cultural
Economic / Class	National		Religious / Ethical

pressing feelings like gratefulness or sympathy, the central importance of hands is mirrored in a broad spectrum of symbolism (Albrecht, Haber & Seidel, 2003, p. 99).

Indeed, imagery is polysemic or multi-meaninged, informed in part by the backgrounds and capacities of the viewers. People will look at images and find "things in them that were never consciously put down" (Krukowski, 2002, p. 184). Images have both denotative and connotative meanings—the formal surface meanings vs. the culturally interpreted ones.

The packaging of the imagery may offer grounds for conflict, too, depending on the larger context, the features of the imagery, and the graphical accoutrement. Deconstructing an image's many meanings may be quite tedious, but it may be more practical to put into place some basic cautions that may head off potential cultural misunderstandings, where possible. Figure 2 "The Packaging of Imagery" explores how imagery may be parsed for different levels of meanings, with the ambition of having small or non-existent blind spots.

Figure 2. The packaging of imagery

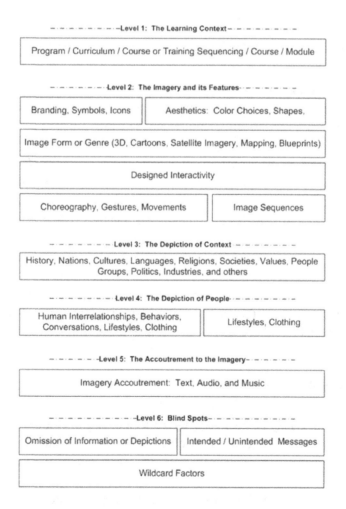

An added challenge comes from the many downstream uses of imagery and with how quickly and permanently materials on the Internet and WWW are deployed. In other words, once an image is published, it may spark a reaction and make its way around the globe in very short order.

CULTURAL SENSITIVITIES FOR GLOBAL DEPLOYMENT

The impact of culture may exist on a number of levels for digital imagery. Meanings may be interpreted at the top level of what is observed and depicted. Then, there are the deeper levels of culture, with rules of behavior and understandings that those from outside may not learn too quickly or easily. Such understandings may require a longer exposure to a particular region and a deeper knowledge of its languages, histories, peoples, religious ideologies and practices, and beliefs. Culture and politics are dynamic forces, so that suggests constant learning. Repeated uses of offensive imagery may jeopardize long-term instructional efficacy and learner trust. Transparency in this modern age means getting ahead of the negative message with crisis management: clarification of the message, retraction of the imagery, a timely apology, and improved digital imagery creation practices—if that's what's called for. Or it may well be possible that the proper response is a clarification of the message and maintenance of the *status quo.*

What is Culture?

There are a number of differing definitions of culture. For some, it is cumulative social knowledge and beliefs which guide people's behaviors; for others, it is partial knowledge gleaned from the past, from generation to generation. In other concepts, culture may be either constant or evolving.

One definition describes culture as a constant entity that includes shared beliefs, attitudes, values, and assumptions. Another definition considers culture as a variable entity dependent upon and evolving with the context. In this view, the cultural values and attitudes are seen as fragmented, variable, and 'in-the-making' (Convertino, Rosson, Asti, Mohammed & Zhang, 2006, p. 659).

One fairly comprehensive definition by Samovar and Porter defines culture as the "deposit of knowledge, experience, beliefs, values, attitudes, meanings, hierarchies, religion, notions of time, roles, spatial relations, concepts of the universe, and material objects and possessions acquired by a group of people in the course of generations through individual and group striving" (Olson & Olson, 2003 – 2004, p. 53). Many agree that an individual's culture may be invisible to those within it in part because it is acquired incrementally through acculturation.

Some Cultural Models Approaches

A number of cultural models may be applied to the understanding of culture in digital imagery design and use. One of the most well known theories involves G. Hofstede's Framework for Assessing Culture (2001). His model uses five bases for comparing cultures. They include the following:

- **power distance:** The amount of social acceptance for the unequal distribution of power (status) in society

- **individualism and collectivism:** The orientation of people towards independence and self vs. dependence and collective society
- **masculinity and femininity:** The expectations of role rigidity and differentiation based on gender
- **uncertainty avoidance:** The amount of discomfort or comfort with risk-taking or uncertainty
- **long-term or short-term orientation:** The perspective of long or short-term in planning for the future (Wikipedia, 2008)

Trompenaars and Hampden-Turner model ranks countries in terms of the following factors:

- **universalism and particularism:** Whether people in a society are oriented by rules or relationships with others
- **individualism and communitarianism:** A concept of the right balance between individual needs vs. group needs
- **specific vs. diffuse relationships:** Whether work cooperation may be conducted based on a narrowly defined relationship (like a contractual one) or requires strong personal relationships in the background
- **neutral vs. affective communication styles:** Whether emotions are restrained or expressed during an argument (or situations where there might be heightened tensions)

Other aspects of culture in this model include how status is accorded and distributed based on demographic features, education and work life; time orientation, such as "whether the past, present, or future is more important when considering action," or nature orientation ("whether people try to master nature, live in harmony with it, or let nature control them. A mastery orientation leads to a strong directive management ethic while the other two orientations lead to collaboration or passivity") (as cited in Gould, Zakaria, & Mohd, 2000, p. 163).

People hailing from different cultures have a shared sense of privacy, conceptualized as the opposite of public, with this definition "found this to be the most fundamental and broadly cross-cultural conceptualization of privacy" (Boyle & Greenberg, 2005, pp. 339 – 340). It is seen as a personal right that may be violated by others' intrusions or prying. "Thus, it is a privacy violation when the actions of others prevent one from obtaining the privacy he needs, he normally enjoys, and society deems that he ought to enjoy. The normalized definition of violation is important. For example, Schwartz [1968] calls surveillance an institutionalized form of privacy violation." Privacy violations may result in particular harms to the individual (Boyle & Greenberg, 2005, p. 343).

Hall's theory contrasts cultures based on approaches to time and communications patterns. A monochronic culture approaches time as a linear chronology, with discrete start and end times to events. A polychronic culture looks at time as a more malleable and flexible phenomena, where multi-tasking and interruptions are common (MacGregor, Hsieh, & Kruchten, 2005, p. 2). A "multiple time frame" (Hall, 1976, as cited in Bass, 1990, p. 772) makes coordination and decentralization difficult among people (Ronen, 1986, as cited in Bass, 1990, p. 772). Communications may exist in a high or a low context. A low-context culture results in speakers having to share precise and explicit meanings in their messages, whereas a high-context culture encourages more ambiguity because the assumption is that the others are already aware of the context and need less information (MacGregor, Hsieh, & Kruchten, 2005, p. 2).

Various types of cultural artifacts may carry meanings that may be politically or socially incendiary. Some authors suggest that symbols are superficial carriers of culture at one end of a continuum, and values contain deep manifestations of culture. In between are culturally defined heroes and rituals. Symbols are "words, gestures, pictures or objects" that embody particular meanings; these may develop easily and disappear easily. Heroes may be real or fictitious; they possess ideal features that are emulated by others. Rituals are collective activities that are "socially essential."

Values comprise the core of a culture, and these capture broad societal tendencies; these are so embedded into a culture that there's rare transfer of core values between cultures and peoples (Hofstede & Hofstede, 2005, as cited in Mazadi, Ghasem-Aghaee, & Ören, 2008, p. 136). Values are critical to understand because they are "linked inextricably to affect," and they may guide people's actions (Mazadi, Ghasem-Aghaee, & Ören, 2008, p. 136).

Kluckhohn & Strodtbeck have identified values orientations around which cultural groups differ. These theorists identify three relative positions where a culture may stand within each of these five orientations.

- **Human Nature:** People are born good, evil, or a mixture of both.
- **Person vs. Nature:** People value their subjugation to nature, mastery over nature, or harmony with nature.
- **Time Sense:** Priority is given to traditional customs, future plans, or present events.
- **Social Relations:** Society is organized around a lineal hierarchy of authority, collateral interests, or individual goals.
- **Space:** Business and life is conducted publicly or privately, or a mix of the two (MacGregor, Hsieh, & Kruchten, 2005, p. 1).

Yet another model, the Schwartz model, involves 10 discrete factors:

- *Power* (PO): Social status and prestige, control or dominance over people and resources.
- *Achievement* (AC): Personal success through demonstrating competence according to social standards.
- *Hedonism* (HE): Pleasure and sensuous gratification for oneself.
- *Stimulation* (ST): Excitement, novelty, and challenge in life.
- *Self-Direction* (SD): Independent thought and action, choosing, creating, exploring.
- *Universalism* (UN): Understanding, appreciation, tolerance and protection for the welfare of all people and for nature.
- *Benevolence* (BE): Preservation and enhancement of the welfare of people with whom one is in frequent personal contact.
- *Tradition* (TR): Respect, commitment and acceptance of the customs and ideas that traditional culture or religion provide the self.
- *Conformity* (CO): Restraint of actions, inclinations, and impulses likely to upset or harm others and violate social expectations or norms.
- *Security* (SE): Safety, harmony and stability of society, of relationships, and of self [Schwartz et al. 2001, as cited in Mazadi, Ghasem-Aghaee, & Ören, 2008, p. 138).

Similarities in these models refer to focuses on different aspects of culture and the values surrounding those in a particular culture. An underlying assumption may also be that culture may also be constantly changing. "Culture changes through the actions of individuals in the cultural context. Beliefs, claims, communicative moves that have one meaning before an intervention may begin to shift in their meaning as a result of other moves, made by other participants in the same cultural milieu" (Benkler, 2006, pp. 283 – 284).

The Internet and WWW Culture

Some researchers suggest that Website design may be informed better by a range of cross-cultural communications theories. Yusof and Zakaria make the point that the substructure of the Internet is a Western construct, with immersive worlds that encourage the expression of male-female avatar relationships that are culturally hostile to some cultural traditions. These authors suggest that immersive spaces should encourage religious values more in virtual spaces; support collectivist values; and offer a stronger cultural fit to non-Western cultures (2007).

The Internet was created in the United States of America, a Western country. As such, the design of its interface, IT applications, and usability is a total reflection of the Western cultural values. Since virtual world is a Western phenomenon, the cultural values are different from the non-Western cultures such as the Eastern or Islamic cultures. The fundamental issue to explore here thus relates to the compatibility between technological fit vs. cultural fit (Zakaria, Stanton, & Sarkar-Barney, 2004, as cited in Yusof & Zakaria, 2007, p. 101).

The low or high context may affect live interactive mediated conferencing:

High-context cultures convey much of their message through tone and gesture. For them, the video channel is important. If people are from different cultures, however, there are two effects: (1) the gestural signals could be misread; and (2) if most of the message is in the gesture and intonation, high-context people are differentially hindered if they are without video. Low-context people have the habit of explaining context and being detailed and explicit. They might be as well off in conveying their message in audio as video; high-context people are likely to be hindered without video (Olson & Olson, 2003 – 2004, p. 56)

Will the WWW simply evolve as unique discrete spaces for different cultural groups based on preferences, effectively creating large silos rather than shared spaces or common ground? H. Clark suggested that communications draw on common ground between people or their shared "knowledge, beliefs and suppositions" (Clark, as cited in Convertino, Rosson, Asti, Mohammed & Zhang, 2006, p. 659). Others argue for a "communal" common ground, which is inclusive of "people's cultural background such as historical facts, beliefs, norms, values, and skills" (Convertino, Rosson, Asti, Mohammed, & Zhang, 2006, p. 659). These researchers observe that there must be agreement on goals and means, in order to complete shared work successfully, and that concept applies well to global e-learning.

The Balance: Ethical Considerations

In light of the cultural considerations, it would seem wise to continually gather relevant cultural information from multiple trusted sources for a deeper understanding. Going on verified information makes more sense than assuming knowledge. Using information strategically mitigates risks in imagery, but it doesn't totally omit the risks of misunderstandings or conflicts.

While lessening potential for cultural strife is important, there may be greater considerations than getting along. If those creating the digital imagery are sure of their facts, then it would be incumbent upon them to represent the visual as realistically and accurately as possible, without manipulation.

Some Assumptions of Universals

Underlying the culturally unique approaches, there are some universals. Some that have been addressed in Chapter 1 deal with how people see physically and cognitively. There is some basis to believe that primary colors are consistent across cultures. Anthropologists Berlin and Kay (1969) published a study of more than 100 languages from diverse cultures:

In languages with only two basic color words, these are always black and white; if a third color is present, it is always red; the fourth and fifth are either yellow and then green, or green and then yellow; the sixth is always blue; the seventh is brown, followed by pink, purple, orange, and gray in no particular order. The key point here is that the first six terms define the primary axes of an opponent color model. This provides strong evidence that the neural base for these names is innate. Otherwise, we might expect to find cultures where lime green or turquoise is a basic color term. The cross-cultural evidence strongly supports the idea that certain colors, specifically, red, green, yellow, and blue, are far more valuable in coding data than others (Ware, 2004, p. 112).

C. Ware suggests that sensory codes will generally "be understood across cultural boundaries" except in instances where "some group has dictated that a sensory code be used arbitrarily in contradiction to the natural interpretation" (2004, p. 14).

A further idea is that of the "transnational tribe" (Rheingold, 2003, p. 12) enabled by the Internet and WWW. These are individuals with a digitally-enabled shared common knowledge and heritage. Those understandings may offer a kind of common ground for relationship-building. These are individuals who participate in open systems creation and sharing of digital imagery resources and information. The idealism of this system may appeal to many: "In an open system we compete with our imagination, not with a lock and key. The result is not only a large number of successful companies but a wider variety of choice for the consumer and an ever more nimble commercial sector, one capable of rapid change and growth. A truly open system is in the public domain and thoroughly available as a foundation on which everybody can build" (Negroponte, 1995, p. 47). A global culture then may be co-built between the participants of this open interchange.

There may be a visual language or grammar that people attain through their humanity and less so by socialization or acculturation. There may be visual grammars that are learned through culture. And then, there may also be learned imagery grammars from a global technologically enabled culture.

Examples of Multi-Meaninged Imagery

A publication is widely criticized for a cover artwork featuring a famous man accused of murdering his wife and her friend; the image was digitally darkened, causing a broad outcry of potential racism. A student criticizes an overseas instructor for using a flat 2D map that cut his country in half, instead of showing it as the center. An image of Mars shows what looks like a human face in the terrain. A national leader is reportedly ailing, but images of him doing official duties in the country suddenly emerge. Satellite imageries show sensitive locations of another country that may involve defense secrets; these may be justification for state action. Visual images have many implications for people's perceptions and behaviors. They lead to actions. And yet, the same image may have different meanings or interpretations depending on worldview and understandings and interpretations.

One study examined cross cultural differences between Chinese and Japanese participants in the interpretation of emotions on the faces of expressive digital avatars. "Those "misinterpreted" expressions are "sweat-on-the-face," "wide-eyed," and "closed-eyes." For example, the "wide-eyed" expression was interpreted as "surprised" by the Japanese subjects, while the Chinese subjects interpreted it as "intelligent" and used it when presenting a novel idea or asking questions" (Koda & Ishida, 2006, n.p.). These researchers found communications gaps, but similarities in other facial expression interpretations. Are the differences only at the margins, or are there fundamental differences?

ENHANCING TRANSFERABILITY TO GLOBAL CONTEXTS

The distributed consumption of digital imagery in e-learning means that the image contents may be interpreted through an individual's framework at the local level foremost, even if the imagery is used in group projects synchronously. The tendency to read images in a micro-second and to interpret that contributes to this greater need for cultural awareness and caution in imagery creation and design.

What then are the implications of the cultural awareness in terms of digital imagery capture, design and use? Should the originating culture of the image creator serve as the standard for the work? Should the image creator immerse in different cultures and then "version" imagery for "target cultures" (Bourges-Waldegg, Lafrenière, Tscheligi, Boy, & Prates, 2001, pp. 223 – 224) via cultural sensitivity? Should he or she integrate multiple points of view in self-explanatory images to accommodate a wider audience? Should the image creators strive for cultural neutrality by softening any possible hard edges to the visuals? Should he or she use purposive ambiguity, the opacity, or abstraction, that may make an image more palatable across many cultural uses?

These four approaches may be summarized as the following:

1. Local as All Reality
2. Versioning for Cultural Sensitivity
3. Integrated Multiple Points-of-View (Self-Explanatory Images)
4. Cultural Neutrality

Table 1 "Levels of Cultural Adjustment in Digital Imagery" addresses some possible high-level strategies in creating an image.

The Pros and Cons of Each "Cultural Adjustment" Approach

The cultural adjustments above have respective strengths and weaknesses.

Table 1. Levels of cultural adjustment in digital imagery (Hai-Jew, 2009)

Levels of Cultural Adjustment	Stance	Digital Imagery Strategy
1. Local as all Reality	My own culture is predominant, and my "local" is the global reality.	• No changes to the digital imagery
2. Versioning for Cultural Sensitivity	Different unique cultures have different points-of-view, and those views may need to be accommodated (to a degree). Specific and unique locales and audiences should get some of the visual messages, with which they may be comfortable.	• Versioning for specific different locales and audiences • Differentiating audiences • Localized languages • Close-in design • In-culture informants • Focusing on specific realities
3. Integrated Multiple Points-of-View (Self-Explanatory Images)	Different viewpoints about a particular topic should be integrated and directly addressed.	• Explanatory versions • Comprehensive image with multi—use • Clear caveats • Shimmering interpretations • Multi-lingual • Multi-interpretive • Adding multiple meanings
4. Cultural Neutrality	Different viewpoints about a particular topic should be ignored and over-simplified. Cultural issues may be finessed with delicate avoidance or purposive "lossiness" or ambiguity.	• Stripping out of cultural nuances • Application of neutral language • Over-simplification • Cautions in depictions and design choices • Avoidance of controversy • Using purposive ambiguity

1. Local as All Reality

People, of necessity, tend to incorporate local realities and parochialisms. Without regular global travel and interactivity with those from other countries, it may be quite difficult to gain a sense of what would have resonance for various global audiences and other localities' audiences. Having a voice for the local though is important and valuable for the world.

There may also be concerns about cultural hegemony, with some worldviews more dominant and other concerns and voices on the margins.

Technicity can thus be understood as a site of cultural hegemony in the twenty-first century; here we take our lead from interpreters of Gramsci, who used his work to understand the processes of struggle over meaning. 'Cultures are both shared and conflicting networks of meanings. Cultures are arenas in which different ways of articulating the world come into conflict and alliance'" (Storey 2000: x) (Dovey & Kennedy, 2006, p. 64).

What is put out into the world is seen as part of a larger debate and understandings that are competing for a kind of predominance. Selective information is projected into the world as a kind of "soft power".

2. Versioning for Cultural Sensitivity

Versioning for cultural sensitivity means creating images in a way for different receiving audiences. If each nation or people groups or other demographic niches of peoples have certain perspectives that they maintain, then it's possible that their interpretive lens may signal particular affinity with certain messages, images, and ideas; they may have preferences for depictions in visual imagery. In a sense, designers of imagery are building to an installed base of consumers of the images, with their preferred understandings and worldviews.

Those who would conceptualize and create graphics must understand the societal taboos and the subtleties and nuances of visual grammars. They should be immersed in multiple cultures as a cross-cultural traveler, not just a native of a defined place alone. They should have access to informants inside the target cultures for the best effects. Given the constant changing of cultures, the knowledge base has to be continually refreshed.

Versioning requires a fairly large skill set for photographers, who must put into the frame the palatable truths that are accepted by a particular group. There must be empathy and understanding of other views. There must be the ability to hold conflicting complexities. There may be a shading of imagery for ambiguity or neutrality. And yet, these approaches must be combined with a need to depict and pursue truth, even uncomfortable ones.

"Purposive ambiguity" refers to a strategic lack of clarity about a particular issue. Masterful communicators may deflect particular questions or lines of thought. In terms of imagery, degrees of abstraction may be a strategy—offering a high level view that may encompass multiple ones without going into controversial details. In some ways, articulating specifics may be too limiting or risky. The down side of such ambiguity is the avoidance that results in visual communicators avoiding actual issues which may be relevant.

3. Integrated Multiple Points-of-View (Self-Explanatory Images)

Another strategy is to incorporate multiple and contradictory points-of-view in one image. This is about transparency in the provenance of the image and the various interpretations. There may be overlays of information to add value and understanding about the different senses of realities. Where do the borders lie? Well, some say that the borders belong here, and others say here. This assumes that non-offense may be unavoidable. In this case, the tact is to offer the different versions of realities without taking sides. This is about full disclosures. This is about being crystal clear with information and intentions.

4. Cultural Neutrality

The cultural neutrality position suggests that non-offense is possible by created and building digital imagery to the lowest common denominator, or to the broad middle. This is about skirting controversy and focusing on shared understandings among many peoples. This is about creating harmony without compromising essential facts, which is a difficult balance.

Standards for Content Acceptance

The cultural adjustment strategies conceivably would have effects on every stage of the digital image pipeline. How visual information is collected, handled, edited, distributed, integrated into e-learning, and archived, may be affected by the general strategies. That awareness of what is considered valid and important visual information and the implications of the image on worldviews are critical.

No matter what the approach, practitioners in digital imagery would do well to practice a clear-eyed view of the visual realities they're engaging. It is important to articulate clear strategies for the handling of such imageries. One practice from mass media involves the floating of a particular "trial balloon" to test public acceptance. In a sense, digital visuals should test the boundaries of new ideas, even if some are discomfiting. There is a range of acceptable quality that must be decided by the visuals development team co-evolving resources for e-learning.

A larger skill set is expected of those working in this field. The up-side would involve greater transferability in terms of the uses of the imageries and optimally wider learning uses.

Technological Versioning

One other angle of consideration involves the technological versioning of digital imageries. With the pervasiveness of portable computing devices and ambient intelligence into real spaces (Buszko, Lee, & Helal, 2001), augmented reality, and augmented virtuality, images may play somewhat differently on the various devices—whether they're handhelds, laptops, head-mounted displays, computing accessories, or other elements.

CONCLUSION

This chapter does not take a prescriptive approach in terms of specifics. A conscious avoidance of stereotyping was used given the many complexities and sensitivities of this issue. Imageries are many-meaninged, and some have sparked violence and other unintended effects. For learning to work effectively, provoking high emotion tends to suppress the learning. To enhance learning, it may help to handle sensitive issues respectfully and in a balanced way. This chapter does not argue for inaccurate portrayals or soft-pedaling hard realities but for a greater awareness of cultural sensitivities and some strategies used for addressing these in digital imagery creation and use.

REFERENCES

Albrecht, I., Haber, J., & Seidel, H.-P. (2003). Construction and animation of anatomically based human hand models. In *Proceedings of the 2003 ACM SIGGRAPH/Eurographics symposium on Computer animation* (pp. 98-103). Aire-la-Ville, Switzerland: Eurographics Association.

Bass, B. M. (1990). *Bass & Stogdill's handbook of leadership: Theory, research & managerial applications (3rd ed.)*. New York: The Free Press.

Benkler, Y. (2006). *The wealth of networks*. New Haven, CT: Yale University Press.

Bhartiya Vidya Bhavan school in Kozhikode district, Kerala has replaced traditional blackboards (chalkboards) with digital boards through a partnership with Educomp Solutions. This experiment lets the teachers use graphics, animation and video clippings, diagrams and 3D images for teaching learning process.

Bourges-Waldegg, P., Lafrenière, D., Tscheligi, M., Boy, G., & Prates, R. O. (2001). Identifying 'target cultures': To what extent is that possible? In *CHI 2001* (pp. 223-224). New York: ACM.

Boyle, M., & Greenberg, S. (2005). The language of privacy: Learning from video media space analysis and design. *ACM Transactions on Computer-Human Interaction, 12*(2), 328–370. doi:10.1145/1067860.1067868

Buszko, D., Lee, W.-H., & Helal, A. (2001). Decentralized ad-hoc groupware API and framework for mobile collaboration. In *Proceedings of the 2001 International ACM SIGGROUP Conference on Supporting Group Work,* Boulder, Colorado, USA.

Convertino, G., Rosson, M. B., Asti, B., Mohammed, S., & Zhang, Y. (2006). Board-based collaboration in cross-cultural pairs. In *CHI '06 extended abstracts on Human factors in computing systems,* Montreal, Quebec, Canada (pp. 658-663). New York: ACM.

Dovey, J., & Kennedy, H. W. (2006). *Game cultures: Computer games as new media.* New York: Open University Press.

Edwards, T. (2004). *Senior geopolitical strategies at Microsoft Corporation.* Presentation at Shoreline Community College, Shoreline, WA.

eTechnology Group@IMRB (n.d.). *Vernacular Content Market in India.* Retrieved February 21, 2009, from http://www.iamai.in/Upload/Research/Vernacular%20Content%20Report_29.pdf

GOI. (1999). *National task force on information technology and software development: IT action plan Part III – long term national IT policy.* Retrieved February 25, 2009, from http://it-taskforce.nic.in/actplan3/

Gould, E. W., Zakaria, N., & Mohd, S. A. (2000). Applying culture to website design: A comparison of Malaysian and US websites. In *Proceedings of IEEE professional communication society international professional communication conference and Proceedings of the 18th annual ACM international conference on Computer documentation: technology & teamwork* (pp. 161). Piscataway, NJ: IEEE.

Kamlaskar, C. H. (2009). Assessing effectiveness of interactive electronics lab simulation: Learner's perspective. *Turkish Online Journal of Distance Education, 10*(1), 193–209.

Koda, T., & Ishida, T. (2006). Cross-cultural study of avatar expression interpretations. In *Proceedings of the 2005 Symposium on Applications and the Internet (SAINT '06).* Washington, DC: IEEE.

Krukowski, S. (2002). Folded: Negotiating the space between real and virtual worlds. In *ACM SIGGRAPH 2002* (pp. 184). New York: ACM.

MacGregor, E., Hsieh, Y., & Kruchten, P. (2005). Cultural patterns in software process mishaps: Incidents in global projects. In *Proceedings of Human and Social Factors of Software Engineering (HSSE '05),* St. Louis, Missouri (pp. 1-5).

Mazadi, Z., Ghasem-Aghaee, N., & Ören, T. I. (2008). Prelude to cultural software agents: Cultural backgrounds in agent simulation. In *Proceedings of the 2008 Spring Simulation Multiconference* (pp. 135-142).

Mukhopadhyay, M. (2000). Indian open and distance education prospect. In V.V. Reddy & S. Manjulika (Eds.), *The World of Open and Distance Learning* (pp. 490). New Delhi, India: Viva.

Negroponte, N. (1995). *Being digital.* New York: Alfred A. Knopf.

Olson, J. S., & Olson, G. M. (2003). Culture surprises in remote software development teams. *QUEUE Focus, 1*(9), 53–59.

Rangachar, B. (2008). e-Patashale initiative. *Digital Learning, 4*(12), 15.

Rheingold, H. (2003). *Smart mobs: The next social revolution.* New York: Perseus Books Group.

Srikanth, R. P. (2004 May 17). Kodak India eyes digital imaging revolution. *Express Computer*.

eTechnology Group@IMRB. (2007). *Online gaming India- 2007: The baseline report.* Retrieved February 21, 2009, from http://www.iamai.in/Upload/Research/OnlineGaminginIndia-March2007.pdf

Thorat, S. (2007 October 22). Strategy for Higher Education Expansion. *Press Information Bureau, Government of India.* Retrieved February 25, 2009, from http://pib.nic.in/release/rel_print_page1.asp?relid=32106

Ware, C. (2004). Foundation for a science of data visualization. In *Information Visualization: Perception for Design (2nd ed.).* San Francisco: Morgan Kaufmann Publishers.

Wikipedia. (2008). *Geert Hofstede.* Retrieved December 10, 2008, from http://en.wikipedia.org/wiki/Geert_Hofstede.

Yusof, S. A. M., & Zakaria, N. (2007). Islamic perspective: Virtual worlds as a Western-centric technology. *ACM SIGMIS Database, 38*(4), 100–103. doi:10.1145/1314234.1314253

KEY TERMS AND DEFINITIONS

Culture: Socially transmitted values, beliefs, and understandings

Cultural Sensitivity: An awareness of and responsiveness to cultural differences

Geopolitical: The intersection of political and economic realities on foreign policy and politics

Global: Related to the world, worldwide, universal

Localization: Focusing on the local or proxemic space, the individual experience

Multicultural: Related to a number of different cultures or value systems

Neutrality: A state of not taking sides; non-participation in a dispute

Subconscious: Below conscious awareness

SIDEBAR

Digital Imagery in E-Learning in India (An Exemplary Case)

Ramesh C. Sharma
Institute of Distance and Continuing Education, Guyana

Introduction

Indian higher education has witnessed phenomenal growth during the past six decades. At the time of attaining independence in 1947, there were only 20 universities and 500 colleges. By 2007, India had 378 universities and more than 18000 colleges (Thorat, 2007). India is most populated country in the world (second only to China). There is a large segment of population needing education. To serve such large masses, and the fact that formal educational institutions were not able to provide education to all, correspondence education was started in 1962 by establishing School of Correspondence Courses under Delhi University. That was the first step towards empowering masses with education. The scheme got much popularity and many other institutions started offering such courses. But quality became an issue later on and then first state open university was established in 1982 at Hyderabad and first national open university in New Delhi in 1985. Currently (till February 2009) there are 15 open universities in India.

An analysis of the trends indicates that the Indian open and distance education has passed through various generations (Mukhopadhyay, 2000): beginning with first generation in the form of classical correspondence print material mode. Second generation was marked by introducing personal contact programmes alongwith correspondence print material mode. The Third generation saw the introduction of electronic media (like radio, television, audio and video cassettes) as instructional delivery mechanisms. Internet has been the main instrument during next generation. The current generation is characterised by web based education delivery.

E-Learning in India

Main impetus was provided through the constitution of the National Task Force on Information Technology and Software Development in 1998. The IT Task Force recommended (GOI, 1999) that "Institutes of national importance such as IITs and IIITs will be encouraged to establish Virtual Institutes, particularly in the area of advanced Post Graduate and Continuing Education programs in IT, to support IT education and Research at other institutions in the country." It further recommended that "Government in association with IT HRD companies will aim to achieve 100% IT literacy at senior secondary level (10 + 2) in 5 years and at secondary level in 10 years."

Due to increase in telephone density, lowering the call charges, introduction of broadband connectivity, availability of PC on cheaper rates etc are some of the reasons for e-learning gaining momentum as a medium of instructions in India. Under the National Education Mission the Indian Government intends through ICT, to inter connect through broadband, all institutions of national importance/excellence, over 375 universities and about 18,600 colleges. Some of the important educational institutions, which initiated online education in India, are given in table 2.

Table 2. Some institutions providing online education in India

- Birla Institute of Technology and Sciences (http://vu.bits-pilani.ac.in)
- Indian Institute of Technology, Delhi (http://www.iitd.ac.in/courses)
- Indian Institute of Technology, Mumbai (http://www.dep.iitb.ac.in)
- Indira Gandhi National Open University (http://www.ignou.ac.in)
- Institute of Management Technology (http://www.imtonline.org)
- MedVarsity (http://www.medvarsity.com)
- Media Lab Asia, Department of Information technology, MCIT, Govt. of India (http://medialabasia.in/)
- National Programme on Technology Enhanced Learning (http://nptel.iitm.ac.in)
- Netvarsity (http://www.netvarsity.com)
- Punjab Technical University (http://www.ptuonline.com)
- The Sikkim Manipal University of Health, Medical and Technological Sciences http://www.smu.edu.in/smu_home.aspx
- Symbiosis Centre for Distance Learning (http://www.scdl.net)
- Tamil Virtual University (http://www.tamilvu.org)
- Yashwantrao Chavan Maharastra Open University (http://www.ycmou.com)

Digital Imagery and Lifestyle in India

The impact of digital imagery is noticed in India on our day-to-day lifestyles like entertainment, business, health or education. The country has progressed from analog to digital in all areas. The news, views, music, video, or data are all digitally manipulated. Entertainment industry has been most benefitted by the implications of digital imagery in terms of its impact on general masses. The news, sports, business, education, health, and religious channels all are using digital content. Major film studios be in Mumbai, Chennai, or Hyderabad have gone digital. The design, development, distribution and delivery of content all are digital. Banking sector and telecom sector have redefined their operations.

Digital imagery has been a boon for bridging digital divide in India in terms of providing educational opportunities. Applications have also been developed to preserve the culture and local traditions. Digital images and multimedia are being used in text based reading. Libraries and laboratories in India are giving real-life like experiences to the learners. Informedia project of the Carnegie Mellon University is helping creation of digital libraries.

MSR School of Advanced Studies (Bangalore, India) has also done pioneering work in Digital Image Processing.

Kamlaskar (2009) explained an experiment conducted at Yashwantrao Chavan Maharashtra Open University, Nashik (India) whereby the theory of Wien bridge oscillator {which is taught as a part of Basic Electronics' course of _Electronics Engineering Programme} was presented with use of text and animated graphics. An animation was developed as a step by step procedure to show how to mount the test circuit on the breadboard. Wien bridge oscillator lab activity was designed and created with the computer program Macromedia Flash Mx 2004.

Software Used in India for Digital Image Processing

Digital photography is the fastest growing sector in India. Latest and powerful camera enable the photographer to shoot high quality photographs but currently there is a gap between photographic labs and studios (Srikanth, 2004). Srikanth (2004) reported that on an average one lab serves 30 to 40 studios. The task is further increased in collecting films, processing, improving the quality of images, adding fancy borders, taking printouts and delivering them to the clients. Kodak India has worked on to this problem and developed a digital imaging solution having two components: Kodak wedding club software and a Virtual Private Network. There are two verions of wedding club software: studio version and a lab version. This software enables compression and encryption of digital files for faster transmission over networks. This software also enables image editing, multiple lab interconnection and multiple levels of compression. This has enabled the Indian photography segment to bring out personalised wedding cards and personalized calendars.

Most commonly used authoring tools being used are: ToolBook™, Flash™, Director™, Macromedia™, DreamWeaver™,etc. In addition Photoshop™, SoundForge™, Premiere™, Media100™, Illustrator™, CorelDraw™ and 3D Studio Max™are also used by the content developers.

The content creators create digital imagery to be used in Web Games, Mobile Games, E-Learning, Multimedia Presentations, Animation, Video and also Print for Corporate communication.

Digital Imagery for Computer and Online Gaming

Traditionally the game development sector in India has been developing content for overseas market. Due to the increasing interest (one of the reason is availability of high bandwidth broadband and reduced tariff plans) of users in India, several Indian companies have started customizing content for Indian market by using local themes, icons and games, for example, Kreeda.com and Games2win.com. To generate interest and traffic to the sites, Zapak.com takes advantage of mainstream advertising. Other initiatives include "low-order labour-intensive development work like porting (for mobile games) and part game development (cut scene animation for game cinematic, single level design, or a specific sequence of a game), which does not account for more than 10-15 per in the total volume of the entire game development cycle" (e Technology Group@IMRB, 2007).

Digital Imagery for Vernacular Content

In India there are 22 constitutionally approved spoken languages and over 1600 regional dialects. These languages have their own script. As per the report entitled, "Vernacular Content Market in India" of the eTechnology Group@IMRB (n.d.), Indian populace prefers print, audio and visual communication which is regional and local (figure 3). Therefore to provide boost to digital localisation, predictive translation initiatives such as context-specific literal translation as well as advanced solutions such as Optical Character Recognition (OCR) and Text-to-Speech are being put in place.

Rangachar (2008) during her presentation on e-Patashale Initiative revealed that in a computer class, the e-contents are used mostly as fillers. She recommends the need to identify what the learners want before offering them the e-contents. She also found that content, images and the delivery are not localised. She further recommends that through localization and customization of the e-content, ICT tools can be integrated effectively with traditional classroom teaching.

The Learn Indian Language through Artificial Intelligence (LILA) is an Intelligent Tutoring System [http://lilappp.cdac.in] uses language scripts, images, audio and video for enabling persons to learn Hindi.

Courses of Study in Digital Image Processing in India

There are private firms, for example, Dimension India Networks (P) Ltd (http://www.dimensioni.net/portfolio/image-processing.html) and Pentasoft Technologies Limited (http://www.pentasoftech.com/

Figure 3. Source: eTechnology Group@IMRB (n.d.)

default.aspx) undertaking work in and image processing an online learning. The courses in digital image processing are also offered by well established and government- sponsored universities also. Table 3 lists a few of them:

Table 3.

Project Indigeo Government Of India, Ministry of Mines http://gsiti.ap.nic.in/indigo.html	Project Indigeo of the GSI Training Institute, is a collaborative project between the Geological Survey of India, ITC (The Netherlands), Maastricht School of Management (The Netherlands) and Association of Exploration Geophysicists (India). The project is aimed at strengthening the application of digital techniques in geoscientific studies in GSI and other premier Earth Science Institutes in India. The Application software used are ArcGIS (ArcInfo/ArcView with ArcScan, Spatial Analyst (ArcGrid) and 3D Analyst (ArcTin) and Geostatistics extensions) for GIS, ILWIS for raster GIS, ERDAS Imagine for digital image processing, and AutoCAD Map Series and FreeHand with Map Publisher plug-in for digital map processing, Oracle 8i for DBMS, ArcSDE and ArcIMS for distributed GIS in the Intranet etc.
CS 661 Advanced Computer Graphics CS 663: Fundamentals of Digital Image Processing (DIP) The Indian Institute of Technology Bombay (IIT Bombay) http://www.iitb.ac.in/	Established in 1958, the Indian Institute of Technology Bombay (IIT Bombay) is one of the best higher Institutes of Technology in India provides facilities for higher education, research and training in various fields of Science and Technology. The Department of Computer Science and Engineering offers courses in Computer Graphics, Computer Vision and Image Understanding with a special focus on Computer-aided graphics design; Multimedia; High Performance computing; Visualization; Rendering; Graphics design and Animation; Computer vision; and Image retrieval.
Sri Venkateswara College Of Engineering, Sriperumbudur - Tamilnadu, India http://www.svce.ac.in/	The Department of Electronics and Communication Engineering offers a course in Digital Image Processing.

DOEACC Department of Information Technology, Ministry of Communications & Information Technology, Government of India, New Delhi. http://www.doeacc.edu.in/jsp/corporate_profile.jsp	DOEACC offers courses ranging from Entry Level to M.Tech Degree level: • Certificate Course on Computer Concepts (CCC) • Foundation (O) level • Advanced Diploma (A) level • MCA Degree equivalent (B) level and, • M.Tech Degree (C) level. http://www.doeacc.edu.in/jsp/syllabus/be8.htm BE8:-Digital Image Processing 1 Introduction to Digital Image processing 2 Image Sensing and Representation 3 Image Enhancement 4 Transform Domain Representation and Processing 5 Image Restoration 6 Binary Image Analysis 7 Color Image processing 8 Texture Analysis 9 Compression 10 Introduction to Image Understanding (Computer Vision) and Application
C-DAC, Kolkata http://www.kolkatacdac.in/html/imagepr.htm	Medical Image Processing Face Recognition National Resource Center on Steganography Small Target Tracking by Image Processing Techniques
Refresher Course on Advances in Digital Image Processing and LIDAR was held from 17-Nov-2008 to 06-Dec-2008, sponsored by University Grants Commission and coordinated by Centre for Spatial Information Technology, IST, Jawaharlal Nehru Technological University Hyderabad.	Main area of refresher course were: · Remote Sensing Data Acquisition · Digital Image Processing · Image enhancement · Image classification and change detection · LIDARPhysical principal of LiDAR · LiDAR sensor and data characterstics · Application of LiDAR and Advantages of LiDAR Technology
Center for Visual Information Technology (CVIT) International Institute of Information Technology, Hyderabad http://cvit.iiit.ac.in/index.php?page=home	The Centre for Visual Information Technology (CVIT) is a research centre at International Institute of Information Technology at Hyderabad. The centre is conducts research and advanced training in the fields of Computer Vision, Image Processing, Computer Graphics, Pattern Recognition and Machine Learning.

Digital Imagery Preservation

Digital preservation is one of the important aspects of digital imagery. Digital preservation is attained through error-free storage of digital information (be it a text, screenshots, interactive maps, screencasts, photo montages, fractals, genetic artworks, video stills, animated agents, rich skin designs, satellite imagery, live data-feed imagery, holography, 3D imaging, live webcam imagery, digital clay sculpting, acoustical imaging, and immersive spaces. Safe retrieval and accurate interpretation of saved information is crucial to digital preservation. Since e-content is the backbone of e-learning, therefore its preservation needs certain agreements, treaties, trademark issues and conventions to be observed in accordance with the Laws. Patent protection in India is ensured through the Indian Patents Act, 1970 which is in agreement within the framework of TRIPS Agreement [for more details refer to http://www.ipfrontline.com/depts/article.asp?id=11882&deptid=6]. In terms of Intellectual Property Rights, Digital Protection Measures and Security issues, there are various technical and legal difficulties in India. Most prominent is the absence of adequate and qualified "Techno-Legal Expertise". In addition to weak copyright laws, non-availability of funding and technical tools for digital preservation are other limitations.

Figure 4. Projects undertaken at Centre for Visual Information Technology http://cvit.iiit.ac.in/index.php?page=projects

Retinal Image Analysis
http://cvit.iiit.ac.in/projects/retina

Terrain Rendering and Information System
http://cvit.iiit.ac.in/projects/terrain

Data Generation Tool kit
http://cvit.iiit.ac.in/projects/DGTk

Recognition of Indian Language Documents
http://cvit.iiit.ac.in/projects/ildocumentRecognition

Retrieval of Document Images
http://cvit.iiit.ac.in/projects/documentRetrieval/

Retrieval from Video Databases
http://cvit.iiit.ac.in/projects/videoprocessing/

Content Based Image Retrieval : CBIR
http://cvit.iiit.ac.in/projects/cbir

Contours, Textures, Homography and Fourier Domain
http://cvit.iiit.ac.in/projects/homography

Biometrics
http://cvit.iiit.ac.in/projects/biometrics

Depth-Image Representations
http://cvit.iiit.ac.in/projects/dir

Endnote

As discussed above, the field of digital imagery is very promising in India. It is being used to a great extent in school education for example as a memory devices like imagery for information such as rules or principles. As also could be seen from the list of institution and companies offering courses or services in the area of image processing, this is coming up as a core course for research in Computer Science and Electronics Engineering in various Indian universities. As per the ancient Chinese coined the now popular proverb, "A picture speaks a thousand words" visual images form the most important part used across e-learning applications. Digital image processing has great scope in India in following application areas: document and medical imaging, computer vision & industrial applications, remote sensing & space applications, and military applications.

Imaging solutions and processes have been implemented for Forms Processing in admissions, examinations etc in Indian Universities in the form of Optical Mark Recognition, Optical Character Recognition, Intelligent Character Recognition, Barcode Recognition, etc. The field of digital imagery has great potential in India as various businesses like education, banking, financial institutions, hospitals, insurance, customer care, e-governance, manufacturing and telecom etc deal greatly with image compression, enhancement and data extraction from paper based data using technologies like Optical Mark Recognition, Optical Character Recognition, Intelligent Character Recognition, and Barcode Recognition. Developing suitable expertise and making relevant tools available is the need of hour.

Chapter 13
Applied Ethics for Digital Imagery

ABSTRACT

Graphical images have much power to evoke and represent realities, convey experiences, and share information. They may be used to share history. They may be used to discover realities and truths. In terms of the social uses of images, they may persuade individuals or whole populaces of people to take courses of action. With the growing technological affordances of image capture and creation, those who would build e-learning with imagery need to be aware of ethical guidelines in capturing, creating, handling and using digital imagery in a learning environment. The sources of these ethical guidelines include cultural values, laws, professional educational practices, professional journalistic practices, and personal ethics.

CHAPTER OBJECTIVES

- Demonstrate the need for foundational ethical considerations in the capturing, creation, handling, use and storage of digital imagery in an e-learning environment
- Describe the roles of faculty as creators, consumers and distributors of digital visual contents
- Explore a range of ethical guidelines from universal principles, social and cultural values, relevant laws, professional journalistic practices, professional educational practices, Net and Web ethics, and personal ethics
- Explain different paths for acquiring digital imagery for e-learning

DOI: 10.4018/978-1-60566-972-4.ch013

INTRODUCTION

Digital imagery plays a major role in creating lived senses of reality, particularly in an educational context. Images provide evidentiary proofs of particular historical events and scientific phenomena. Digital captures of artworks and cultural artifacts serve as protection of *realia*. Graphics help learners visualize abstract or heavily theoretical points. They express plans—in diagrams and blueprints. They reflect live terrain—whether it be in outer space, under the ocean, deep in the earth, or the Earth's surface. They express the original creativity of various artists. They convey heavy loads of information for analysis.

Why Ethical Concerns?

The nature of digital imagery raises ethical concerns. Digital imagery is highly malleable and changeable. An image may go through many iterations without the users along the way being aware of that. It's highly portable and may be distributed widely with a few simple button pushes. It may communicate information that is inaccurate or misleading. Used in a particular way, it can affect viewers on a subconscious level, beyond conscious awareness. Imagery is often used in a stand-alone way, without context, and without more than a brief glance, and yet people walk away with impressions and meanings. Mass media research has shown the primacy of the visual over the audio in audio-visuals in terms of human perceptions. Some of the information in an image may be intentional, but other aspects may be unintentional.

Following ethics in the capturing, creation, handling, use and storage of digital imagery in a learning environment involves plenty of vigilance and effort. To define what standards should be followed in a particular situation may depend on plenty of reflection and professional discussions. This chapter offers a generalized approach to this issue rather than a proscriptive approach.

Creators, Consumers and Distributors of Digital Visual Contents

To set the context, those who work in creating digital imagery for higher education work as creators, consumers and distributors of this content. As creators, they use their knowledge and expressive capabilities to express models, images, diagrams, blueprints, and simulations. As consumers, they use materials that are legally released (like royalty-free images) or those in the public domain. As distributors, they launch digital materials on websites, learning / course management systems (L/CMSes), digital repositories, and other venues. In a sense, they're also protectors of sensitive information that they may handle in their line of work, which requires secure handling. Considering each of these roles is critical for a 360-degree view of the applicable ethics.

The ethics of digital imagery in e-learning stem from context-based sources: cultural values, laws, professional journalistic practices, professional education practices, and personal ethics. These factors will differ depending on the particular context. In addition, e-learning involves several other core ethical impetuses. One involves wide accessibility, as defined by the Americans with Disabilities Act (ADA) and an in-field value of the interchangeability and portability of digital learning objects.

Figure 1, "Some Sources of Ethics in Applied Digital Imagery," shows how the seven main influences on ethics in applied digital imagery for e-learning are arrayed: universal principles, social and cultural values, relevant laws, professional journalistic practices, professional educational practices, net and Web ethics, and personal ethics. This figure addresses how these distill into principles, which lead

Figure 1. Some sources of ethics in applied digital imagery (Hai-Jew, 2009)

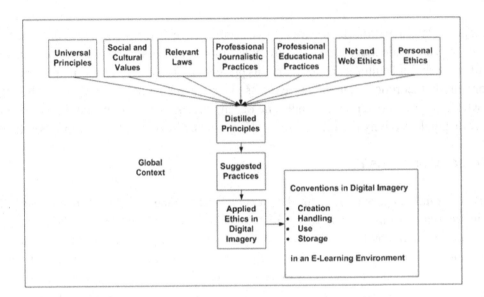

to applied practices, which translate into applied ethics and conventions in handling digital imagery in e-learning.

This uses a multi-paradigm approach. The ethic of justice focuses on rights and laws, and this approaches focuses on reasoned approaches to decision-making, not necessarily outcomes. The ethic of critique offers a politicized pedagogy that looks to rectify social inequities. The ethic of care is about putting the learner at the center of decisions, with "caring, concern, and connection" (Martin, 1993, as cited in Shapiro & Stefkovich, 2001, pp. 14 – 17). The ethic of the profession refers to the values-based principles within a particular field. In e-learning, that is currently being threshed out by drawing on a number of factors.

UNIVERSAL PRINCIPLES

It may be argued that some universal principles of applied digital imagery in e-learning could be some of the values touted globally: service to humanity, mutual understandings across cultures and people groups, peaceable co-existence, sharing of resources, and the sustainability of shared and constructive endeavors.

The closest things that there are to universal principles are findings of objective research of how people perceive visually. This research involves the physical structure of the human eyes and how they interact with the brain in a hard-wired way that may be resistant to change (Ware, 2004).

This research examines how people perceive colors, light and shade; objects and shapes; recognize faces; perceive surface textures, and perceive space. This research addresses depth perception and distance and track movements. Even more complex research delves into the interactions between imagery and verbals (text and speech), and how image memories are made both in the short-term working memory and the long-term memory. Summarizing this information is beyond the purview of this text. However, it is advisable to pursue reading the research to enhance imagery and visualization design for visual efficacy.

Some visual designs build on the physical realities. One example is how illusion is used for 2D to mimic 3D. Another involves the illusion of movement from a still image.

Contemporary optical art relies on moiré effects, in which the design interacts with the physiological tremor of the eye to produce the distracting appearance of vibration and movement (Tufte, 2001, p. 107).

The power of color and its effects have been studied at length, and various types of design schools address color theory in terms of aesthetics. Much effort has gone into the study of color and how it is perceived.

Color appearance, which is influenced by size, surrounding colors, and the adaptive ability of the human visual system, is complex, but progress is being made to create models that can accurately predict color appearance. Color appearance models (CAMs) begin with perceptual models and add the effect of the viewing environment, including local illumination and the surrounding colors (Stone, 2004, p. 7).

The concept of a "universal" learner has had some undesirable effects, particularly in terms of the assumption of the accessibility of a transparent Internet.

There appears to be a notion of a "generic" or "universal" user (learner) behind the notion of a transparent medium. Similarly, the notion of a generic or universal user has led to the creation of both public and private facilities and services that have proven inaccessible to individuals with disabilities who do not fit the "mold (Bricout, 2001, p. 268).

In recent years, there has also been research on how to design visualizations that are effective for human use, and authoring tools and image capture devices have been created with such design awareness.

Designing for Proper Visual Clarity

Some simple principles may be extracted here. Perception may be ambiguous. Those who would design imagery for e-learning need to ensure proper clarity. For example, the complexity of the visual image needs to fit the contents.

The use of two (or three) varying dimensions to show one-dimensional data is a weak and inefficient technique, capable of handling only very small data sets, often with error in design and ambiguity in perception. These designs cause so many problems that they should be avoided: The number of information-carrying (variable) dimensions depicted should not exceed the number of dimensions in the data (Tufte, 2001, p. 71).

Metaphors that are used for comparisons will need to be fitting. When information is an approximation or a projection, that should be made clear to the users. Distracting visual elements should be eliminated, to avoid visual overload. Redundancy may be used strategically and sparingly: "Redundancy, upon occasion, has its uses: giving a context and order to complexity, facilitating comparisons over various parts of the data, perhaps creating an aesthetic balance" (Tufte, 2001, p. 98).

Designing for Context

Because of the potential for misconstrual of an image without context, data should not be quoted out of context (Tufte, 2001). Decontextualization involves the risks of people building understandings of imagery through interpretations and assumptions. There should be sufficient context for fair representation of the information. This includes a clear sense of provenance, so users may track where the image came from in order to judge its veracity and usefulness.

Designing for Live Users

In this context, digital imagery is used for communications and learning. In light of that, user input is critical in the lead-up to a digital imagery build; user testing is a critical part of design in the alpha and beta-testing phases. Creating a valid feedback loop to capture user feedback and ideas will also be important. Getting feedback from those from various cultures will also enhance the global dexterity of the images.

This aspect of designing for live users also brings up distributive justice, the equal access to visual information by a global body of potential users. Ways to lower barriers to the use of digital imagery for e-learning has implications for the technological builds (building for standard computing platforms and using more universal languages), the intellectual property rights releases, cultural design of imagery, and user supports.

Understanding "Viewing Depths"

Digital imagery is polysemic. They convey information with multiple valid interpretations or meanings. One way to conceptualize this is through the following observation of "viewing depths":

Graphics can be designed to have at least three viewing depths: (1) what is seen from a distance, an overall structure usually aggregated from an underlying microstructure; (2) what is seen up close and in detail, the fine structure of the data; and (3) what is seen implicitly, underlying the graphic—that which is behind the graphic (Tufte, 2001, p. 155).

Aligning the multiple views will enhance the visual imagery. Games may maintain ranges of interpretations and are tested for these. Especially for political and sensitive games, these have to be tested for the polysemic, many-meaninged aspects (Aldrich, *Learning by Doing,*, 2005).

Excessive complexity in visualizations may be misleading and so should be designed with care.

The problem, however, is that abuse of such powerful visual representations may make people misinterpret the information or obscure the focus of the information. It is important to understand when, and how we should use complex visualization to help people understand and explore the information space more easily, and more accurately (Nakakoji, Takashima & Yamamoto, 2001, p. 77).

One of the first premises in is *primum non nocere,* or "first, do no harm," which suggests that digital visual imagery captured, created, handled, used and stored should not cause damage to others. It should convey truth. It should offer value to its viewers. It should have a clear provenance or history. It should not accidentally convey harmful meanings.

A universal approach would involve an ethic of neutrality and non-provocation, so informational value may be conveyed in ways that are not off-putting. Connotative symbols may be avoided, and only denotative ones used. The less "noise" there is in a digital image, the more effectively it may carry information.

SOCIAL AND CULTURAL VALUES

A social and cultural milieu affects the sense of shared values and common understandings about images and their roles. In a Western context, to over-generalize, one defining value may be that of democracy and egalitarianism. This may mean a more open approach to the creation of digital imagery, by experts and also by non-experts. Any individual with the abilities and access to the technologies may get in the game of digital image creation and the marketing and publishing of these. The originality of vision is much vaunted in the West, with images that are more rare and unusual as more valuable.

Images all involve some leeway for interpretation. There's a degree of ambiguity. People are preconditioned to consider images in a particular way based on their cultural backgrounds and prior learning. Minsky writes:

The point is that what we 'see' does not depend only on what reaches our eyes from the outside world. The manner in which we interpret those stimuli depends to a large extent on what is already taking place inside our agencies (1987, p. 209).

A culture offers a kind of authorizing environment for the creation, revision and use of particular digital images. This context is important to consider, in order to understand the boundaries of the allowable.

Freedom of Speech

The freedom of speech and the protections of the free press foster a divergence of viewpoints and voices; this results in a rich variety of viewpoints. Another shared value is the importance of factual and researched information. This suggests a hierarchy of images, with those that have a clear sourcing as more critical. The speed of information dissemination (as a form of technological determinism) means a much faster vetting and publishing cycle than in the more recent past.

Commercial Expression

There are social conventions around commercial expression, which has created expectations of image development and styling. There are expectations of in-depth editing and air-brushing of particular types of images. Photo enhancements are very common in mass media—in movies and in print. In news, the practice of adjusting digital colors for better production is common-place because such adjustments help bring the images to better accuracy to the original raw view. (The digital image captures may result in some color distortions, and the printing process with ink on paper also adds other skews.)

The Depiction of Human Relationships

Different regional and national value systems will inform how people and their interrelationships are depicted. They will inform what colors convey what information. They will define taboos in the environment—what may not be depicted for religious or political or cultural identity reasons. Each society defines how it views its citizens and depicts them with dignity, and without stereotyping. Designing images with a kind of cultural neutrality or a cultural sensitivity will be an important part of creating useful global e-learning.

Having cultural awareness must involve understandings of the various cultures and milieus that the images will be used in. There must be a balance of competing cultural concerns in making choices in creating and using digital imagery.

RELEVANT LAWS

A range of laws have implications for the use of digital imagery. In broad categories, there are those that protect the intellectual property of the images, those that establish the evidentiary validity for a court of law, those that promote their accessibility, and those that engage applicable contracts and agreements for the uses of interactive and immersive spaces. Being aware of these various applicable laws may enhance the work of those using e-learning imagery. "Building clean" means adhering to all extant laws, and these also vary between different regions and countries. While the social and cultural milieu informs connotative values for image design and use, laws offer more denotative or stated values.

Intellectual Property

All current laws regarding intellectual property apply to the online environment. Nothing is suspended simply because this is online. These laws include (1) copyright / intellectual property protections, (2) trademark protection and (3) patent laws (4) trade secrets.

The basic tenets of copyright follow: A work has de facto copyright at the moment of its creation. A © symbol is not required to establish the copyright. A work has copyright the moment it is fixed in tangible form. Owners of a work have rights to copy, distribute and gain reward from their works. Works created after 2002 are protected for 70 years after the death of the author or 95 years from date of publication if a work of "corporate authorship". Then, without copyright renewal, these often move into the public domain.

Plenty of digital imagery may be copyrighted: drawings, diagrams, tables, charts, maps, photos, videos, paintings, games, digital characters, and simulations. Copyright involves seven categories:

1) literary works; 2) musical works, including words; 3) dramatic works, including music; 4) panto-mimes and choreographic works; 5) pictorial, graphic and sculptural works; 6) motion pictures and audiovisual works; and 7) sound recordings (Rutherfoord, 2003, p. 189).

These may be stored on websites, tangible devices, mobile devices, repositories or libraries, and housed in any number of other ways. Works that were created a long time ago may be in the public domain. Government websites often host material with a release into the public domain. Works may be released by the copyright holder using Creative Commons™ releases. The assumption though is that if there is no clear release of copyright, someone likely holds copyright to a work.

Intellectual property rights refer to the ownership of creative works that are fixed in tangible form based on the Berne Convention globally and the US copyright laws (1976 onwards).

In the digital realm, the Digital Millennium Copyright Act (DMCA) of 1998 reaffirmed copyright into the digital domain and disallowed hacking or breaking systems to illegally use others copyrighted materials. Digital rights management endeavors involve various efforts to protect images in repositories and learning / course management systems; this also involves the watermarking of digital contents to check for "downstream" misuses of digital contents, such as illegally hosting copyrighted material on one's servers.

Many continuing endeavors strive to protect digital information.

The computing industry has experimented with a number of techniques for preventing unauthorized use of digital data, including physical dongles, software access keys, node-locked licensing schemes, copy-prevention software, obfuscation, and encryption with embedded keys. Most are either broken or bypassed by determined attackers, causing undue inconvenience and expense for nonmalicious users. High-profile data and software are particularly susceptible to attackers (Koller & Levoy, June 2005, p. 76)

Special protections go into protecting 3D image captures against so-called "reconstruction attacks".

To deter image-harvesting attacks, we perform automatic analysis of the server logs, detecting suspicious sequences or frequencies of image requests. We employ obfuscation to create hurdles for attackers by encrypting the rendering request messages sent from the client programs, as well as by encrypting the low-resolution client-side 3D models. The server imposes constraints on rendering requests, disallowing extremely close-up views of models and requiring a fixed field of view (Koller & Levoy, June 2005, p. 79).

There are endeavors to make some works streamable only, without downloading multimedia for it to play. Some sites use non-print, non-copy and non-downloadable protections to prevent the mis-use of copyrighted works.

The widespread use of mash-ups; the ease of publication on social networking, image sharing, and professional sites; the easy downloadability of a range of digital images, all complicate this issue of ownership. The download of podcasts onto mobile devices through RSS feeds has also made it more difficult to control the downstream uses of contents.

Instructors who work for accredited institutions of higher education have some protections. Section 107 of the Copyright Act (1976) includes fair use exceptions for teaching, scholarship and research … but this covers only some educational uses. Fair use depends on the following four points:

1. The purpose and character of the use (whether commercial or non-profit educational)
2. The nature of the copyrighted work
3. The amount and substantiality of the portion in relation to the copyrighted work as a whole
4. The effect of the use on the potential market or value of the copyrighted work

The Technology, Education and Copyright Harmonization Act (the TEACH Act) (2002) was inspired by the face-to-face teaching exception in copyright law that allows educators to "display and perform any copyrighted work—movies, videos, poems—in the classroom without the permission of the copyright holder" (Ashley, June 22, 2004, "The TEACH Act: Higher Education Challenges for Compliance," Educause Center for Applied Research, p. 2). The TEACH Act, originally recommended by the US Copyright Office of the Library of Congress, offers a separate set of rights, independent of fair use. This law allows for in-class performances and displays of copyrighted contents to a degree.

The TEACH Act requires that the institution be accredited, non-profit and educational; it also requires that the institution have a policy regarding the use of copyrighted materials, with proper notification of learners about copyright ownership. The TEACH Act allows limited use of copyrighted materials in online learning with a series of caveats. The digital work has to be educational and to be an integral part of the course session and learning; it has to have been lawfully made and acquired. Only reasonable portions of the work may be used. The work may only be transmitted to the students in the course, and there should be downstream controls to prevent the retention of the works for longer than the course session (such as through IP tracking, copy-disabling, print disabling, paste-disabling, content time-outs, and other endeavors).

Section 110 (2)'s expanded rights of The TEACH Act allows the transmitting of performances of all of a non-dramatic literary or musical work (as in a poetry or short story read, and all music besides opera, music videos and musicals). This also allows faculty to transmit "reasonable and limited portions" of any other performance, such as films, videos and any dramatic musical works. Third, it allows the transmittal of displays of any work "in amounts comparable to face-to-face displays". This Act does not apply to e-reserves, coursepacks, interlibrary loan materials, or the digital delivery of supplemental reading materials. Commercial documents are not included in the provisions of the TEACH Act, and nor are textbooks or digital contents provided under license or contract. This also does not apply to the conversation of materials from analog to digital formats "except when the converted material is sued solely for authorized transmissions and when a digital version of a work is unavailable or protected by technological measures," according to the Copyright Clearance Center.

Intellectual property also applies to trademarks, service marks, certification marks (like endorsements), or membership marks. A trademark or service mark identifies the source of products or services; distinguishes the trademark owner's products or services; helps consumers identify goods and services; protects consumers from confusion or fraud, and protects the trademark owner's investment in the trademark (Rony & Rony, 1998). Trademarks that are used in visual images should be captioned with the requisite ® for a registered mark or the ™ for a trademark, to prevent their dilution. Websites should have disclaimers in reference to trademarks. Trademarks should not be used into generic language (like "thermos," "yo-yo," and "dumpster"), as that will speed the disappearance of the brand value.

Patents protect formulas, patterns, compilations, programs, devices, methods, techniques or processes that may have economic value. These should be protected in visual imagery with proper labeling and non-shareability. Trade secrets, which are protected under the Uniform Trade Secrets Act and various state laws, should also be protected from distribution.

At the time of publication, there were endeavors to push through "orphaned works" legislation to protect those pursuing copyright on works with "lazy owners" who do not respond to queries. This legislation would also free up the use of works that have been abandoned and do not have identifiable owners. If this legislation passes, it may offer some protections to those who use due diligence in pursuing possible rights releases.

Designing for Truth: Evidentiary Validity

Humans can capture visual information and draw a sense of meaning in milliseconds.

It is reported that humans can get the gist of an image in 110 ms or less [Coltheart1999], while in this same period of time, humans can only read less than 1 word or skim 2 words. (The average English reader can read about 4.2 words/s, and can skim or scan at roughly 17 words/s [Chapman 1993, as cited in Xue, Zhou, & Zhang, 2008, p. 21:2).

While that speed is often seen as strength, this rapidity may also lead to incorrect inferences and ideas. This challenge is compounded by visual manipulations. Any number of manipulations may be done to particular images. Objects may be moved; lighting may be changed, features may be deleted, and false impressions may be created. Imagery may appeal to emotions and not to the logical mind. The conveyance of truth means that the information must be accurate. There may be a value to putting the raw image next to the processed (Tufte, 1997, *Visual Explanations,* p. 25), for a sense of contrast, a reality check.

Practitioners in the field have identified many methods for creating mischief.

Enthusiasts, partisans, and liars have long tinkered with graphical evidence by dequantifying images, selecting and hyping advantageous visual effects, distorting data. Recently, inexpensive computing and ingenious techniques for image processing have provided endless new opportunities for mischief. Arbitrary, transient, one-sided, fractured, undocumented materials have become the great predicament of image making and processing (Tufte, 1997, *Visual Explanations,* p. 25).

Various academic fields as well as different courts have legally defined standards for the validity of digital information. To use an aerial image to establish land boundaries, to use an image of a crime scene as evidence, to use an image to document a transmissible disease in a crop all involve different sets of requirements for validity.

Some simple fundamentals suggest that there be clear proportionality of the image to the actual measures (Tufte, 2001). And there needs to be correct color balance, so the lighting doesn't distort the image.

If digital technologies are used to create "forensic animations," those have to be created in a way that is non-biasing. Re-enactments and dramatizations are by nature difficult to create with objectivity. Virtual reality supports "the collation, interrogation, analysis and presentation of complex forensic data across a wide spectrum of crime-scene and accident scenarios. VR reconstructions of incidents have allowed the incidents to be visualised from multiple relevant positions within the virtual environment, something which can be beneficial within the dynamic, adversarial environment of the courtroom" (Burton, Schofield, & Goodwin, 2005, pp. 104 - 105). The potentials of this technology in the courtroom must be balanced against the potential for the introduction of prejudice and subconscious bias. This means that an audit trail for the information is critical, and the objective reconstruction of the incident must be done without "the lowering of critical faculties through the "mesmerizing effect" of multimedia (Burton, Schofield, & Goodwin, 2005, p. 105). Visual aids are often used to raise juror attention, increase their comprehension, present complex information more efficiently, and to persuade them.

Burton, Schofield and Goodwin (2005) elaborate on the use of technologies to gather, analyze and present evidence:

Better collection and analysis of evidence from a wide range of multimedia technologies can be achieved by the use of data from the devices of witnesses, and those involved in incidents. The devices which may provide additional evidence include mobile phones, PDAs, digital cameras, and closed-circuit TV. An example of such evidence would be photographs taken on a digital camera by a witness at the scene of a crime (pp. 103 - 104).

Accessibility

The use of visual multimedia enhances learning and may enhance accessibility of content "for those with low levels of literacy and with learning disabilities and other cognitive impairments. Unfortunately multimedia content frequently presents access barriers to many others, including blind, visually impaired, hearing impaired, and physically impaired users" (Sloan, Gibson, Milne & Gregor, 2003, p. 378). While new channels are opened for learning with multimedia, not all have equal access unless accessibility mitigations are put into place.

Accessibility is multi-faceted in terms of functions. However, the Web will not be equally accessible, allowing people with disabilities to access and contribute to the Web, until:

- Authoring tools and development environments (including content managements systems such as blogging applications) produce accessible Web content and have accessible interfaces;
- Browsers, multimedia players and assistive technologies provide a completely usable and accessible experience;
- Content is designed to be accessible (Chisholm & Henry, 2005, p. 31).

Section 508 (1998), an amendment to the Rehabilitation Act, of the Americans with Disabilities Act, stipulates that federal agencies must ensure that information technology must be accessible to individuals with disabilities. Institutions of higher education, which fall under the ADA and which also receive federal funds, are generally understood to have to abide by these guidelines. Universities must provide equal access to educational opportunities for "otherwise qualified" students. An otherwise qualified student is one who meets the academic and technical standards requisite for admission or participation. The course-taking experience for students with disabilities must be equivalent to that of other students. Accommodations should be planned at the beginning of online course development rather than on an ad hoc basis once a student enrolls in the course.

Disabilities affect a sixth of the U.S. population at any time. As the population ages, this percentage is likely to rise. "The nature of disabilities affecting Web access may be temporary or long-term, degenerative or fluctuating, and may affect any user at any time" (Sloan, Gibson, Milne & Gregor, 2003, p. 373). An estimated 10% of males have abnormal color vision. One author notes that it is quite easy to use color badly in terms of accessibility design (Stone, 2004).

There are formal endeavors to "work with the ageing community to obtain more direct input and contribution into the development of solutions and strategies for Web accessibility; revise existing and develop new educational materials to better reflect the accessibility needs of the ageing community on the Web; and to pursue standards coordination and harmonisation to promote the adoption and implementation of a common set of Web accessibility guidelines" (Abou-Zahra, Brewer, & Arch, 2008, p. 83).

Accessibility is viewed as a subgroup of usability, which is based on the user experience (Bergman & Johnson, 2001, as cited in Arion & Tutuianu, 2003, p. 389). Not only does learning have to be accessible, but it should also be intuitive and usable. This means that the visual interface has to be text reader-readable and logically structured. The disabilities of main concern are (1) visual acuity challenges (color blindness, low vision), (2) hearing or auditory challenges, (3) mobility challenges, and (4) mental processing.

Visual acuity challenges are addressed in several ways. First, all still images are labeled with "alt text," which describes the image contents for the learning value. Audio and video are transcribed into "timed text," live captioning or a transcript, in order to make them readable by a computerized text reader. This way, the video will not need to be "viewed" to convey its informational value. Motion and action also need annotation. These requirements pose special challenges in digital learning games, but various countries around the world have accessibility requirements for those as well (Pitts & Ashwin, 2005, p. 12). Audio games have been created for the blind for some time (Poluck, 2007, n.p.). Some of these audio-only games have been evolved for use by those with visual acuity issues to the broader public (Roden & Parberry, 2005).

Describing an image or a series of actions with text may be much more difficult than one first may assume. These should be normed among professional educators for the sufficient amount of information. The text descriptions should offer full descriptors for learning relevance and aesthetics.

To help blind users understand the visual layout of a document and the relationships between groups of objects or objects, parts of the document are labeled (Ishihara, Takagi, Itoh, & Asakawa, 2006, pp. 165 – 172). Tables need to be presented in a way so that their contents make sense, and the numbers in each cell are contextualized. This may mean a helpful textual description to introduce the table, the proper coding to make sure the labeling and cells render properly, and then textual analysis about the relevance of the table contents afterwards.

Second, if color is used to convey information, that is not the only mode through which data is communicated. For those with color blindness, they may need texture or text descriptors or other elements to highlight spatial information that is communicated (in part) by color. Colors should have proper contrasts for those with some visual acuity issues.

Third, users with vision challenges should have the ability to control the speed of automated simulation experiences; they should be able to conduct replays and to repeat the experience for learning value. There are other interventions, such as graphic user interface systems for those with severely impaired vision in mathematics class (Sribunruangrit, Marque, Lenay & Gapenne, 2004).

Those interacting with digital visuals for learning that have hearing or auditory challenges may do well to have text captioning that describes the sounds that are occurring. This also would involve transcripts of spoken words.

People with mobility issues may use a range of tools to engage with digital visuals. These include different input devices like eye-tracking hardware (video boards, digital cameras and CPUs) and gaze typing systems (Hansen & Hansen, Mar. 2006). There are Braille displays to convert digital text into touchable text. Other haptics devices may convey sound through vibrations.

In terms of mental processing challenges that may affect visual learning, dyslexia refers to deficits in visual, auditory or motor processes that cause challenges in reading comprehension and the reading of symbols. Cognitive disabilities affect some 7% of the general population of the U.S. (Carmien, DePaula, Gorman & Kintsch, 2003). Some interventions with these individuals include the use of intelligent computational agents deployed over mobile devices to provide distributed support systems and information ecologies.

Auditory perceptual deficits refer to the inability to fully capture information from a lecture, and this is often mitigated by instructional notes. Likewise, with visual-perceptual deficit, students "may have difficulty receiving or processing accurate information from their sense of sight. They may have problems picking out an object from a background, or they may not see things in the correct order. Strobe effects should be avoided because these may sicken or cause seizures for some people. Cybersickness or "simulator sickness" may affect some who immerse through virtual reality experiences (Knight & Arns, 2006, p. 162). For e-learning, defining the context of the use of the Web resource will enhance accessibility (Sloan, Heath, Hamilton, Kelly, Petrie & Phipps, 2006) and accessibility design.

Web 2.0 with its user-generated contents requires a holistic accessibility approach not addressed by the current published accessibility standards (Kelly, Nevile, Draffan & Fanou, 2008). New immersive technologies also require a greater complexity in building accessibility, because of volumetric depth, physical movement and temporality. Others suggest creating a social computing service, which also is very Web 2.0, to help those with Web accessibility needs:

Social Accessibility is an approach to drastically reduce the burden on site owners and to shorten the time to provide accessible Web content by allowing volunteers worldwide to 'renovate' any webpage on the Internet. Users encountering Web access problems anywhere at any time will be able to immediately report the problems to a social computing service. Volunteers can be quickly notified, and they can easily respond by creating and publishing the requested accessibility metadata—also helping any other users who encounter the same problems (Takagi, Itoh, Kawanaka, Kobayashi, & Asakawa, 2008, p. 193).

Still others argue for a mix of Web 2.0 with the usability of a Semantic Web with labeled resources.

Accessibility in Immersive Worlds

Accessibility in virtual worlds involves particular challenges for users with disabilities because these are almost exclusively visual environments (White, Fitzpatrick & McAllister, 2008). Trewin, Laff, Cavendar, and Hanson observe:

All of these simultaneous visual, audio, cognitive and motor demands represent potential barriers to users, especially to those with a disability. Because an avatar's behavior in the world is visible to others, the fear of looking clumsy or behaving inappropriately may also constitute a significant barrier to participation (2008, p. 2728).

Accessible games involve those designed for different "disability groups" and those general public games that have been adapted for greater accessibility. Work in this area includes natural language descriptions (in audio) of 3D environments, conducting environmental searches, and navigation (Trewin, Laff, Cavendar, & Hanson, 2008, p. 2728).

Audio cues and sound mapping, however, are not so accurate in depicting locations as compared to visual cues (White, Fitzpatrick & McAllister, 2008). In augmented reality spaces, an "enactive torch" using ultrasonics may indicate the presence of objects (White, Fitzpatrick & McAllister, 2008, p. 139). Devices that use force feedback (through vibrations) may also help visually impaired users to perceive virtual objects in the immersive environment (White, Fitzpatrick & McAllister, 2008).

Universal Design

The approach of universal design is seen as one way to ensure accessibility. This refers to the designing of products and environments that would be usable by all people to the greatest extent possible without the need for adaptation or specialized design. This concept is described by seven principles: equitable use, flexibility in use, simple and intuitive, perceptible information, tolerance for error, low physical effort, and size and space for approach and use.

These apply to the design of digital imagery in that the images are designed for use for people with diverse abilities. The alt-texting or captioning that is part of the workflow ensures this to a degree, and this value-added information supports people without visual acuity issues as well in their studies and memory retention. Designing immersive spaces to accommodate a wide range of individual preferences and abilities allows for personalizing experiences and makes the build work more efficient in the long run because of the greater number of people who may use these contents. Ensuring that digital visuals are simple and intuitive, regardless of the user's experience or prior knowledge or language skills, enhances the shelf life and usability of the visual. Information should be perceptible, no matter what the ambient conditions are or the user's general sensory abilities. The "tolerance for error" in a digital system means that the learner may avoid hazards or adverse consequences of accidental or unintended actions. The ability to "undo" an action is one example of resilience. Low physical effort requirements make it so that those with mobility challenges may most easily access the system, and with as little discomfort or fatigue as possible. The "size and space for approach and use" may be achieved with designing virtual online interfaces or immersive spaces with sufficient ease of reach for the various controls.

Technological Affordances

Most learning / course management systems (L/CMSes) on the market today are designed in accessible HTML. These were designed for easy screen enlargement. Text-to-speech readers may engage the contents. The main accessibility concerns in e-learning come from the authored images, interactivity, simulations and immersive spaces that are accessed for learning.

There are a number of those in technology design that have been working towards accessibility mitigations—to very positive effect. Rowland (2000) shows the roles of the following six stakeholders in online learning accessibility: the makers of browsers; assistive technology; Web authoring tools; courseware; resource providers, and resource users (as cited in Sloan, Gibson, Milne & Gregor, 2003, p. 379).

Additional accessibility challenges occur with multimodal deliveries of visual imagery and information. Many mobile devices do not have accessibility accommodations:

New browsing technologies such as TV-based Web browsers, Internet-enabled mobile phones and personal digital assistants (PDAs) bring with them restrictions in terms of display capabilities, input devices and rate of delivery of information. Such mobile devices are also more likely to be used outdoors, perhaps in adverse weather or excessively noisy conditions. Likewise, users of legacy browsing technologies and users with restricted Internet access or low-bandwidth Internet connections may encounter similar accessibility problems (Sloan, Gibson, Milne & Gregor, 2003, pp. 373 – 374).

Applicable Contracts to Interactive and Immersive Spaces

Those working with digital imagery in e-learning may build avatars and objects and spaces in 3D realms. They may create machine cinema (*machinima)* based on interactions in immersive spaces. They may upload imagery from a photo shoot into a shared image site.

What happens to their creations depends on the end user license agreements (EULAs) that define what happens to the materials once they're created or uploaded. A second factor for consideration is the portability of what has been built in immersive spaces: some 3D creations and objects may be ported off while others may only work in-microworld.

Other contracts that may be relevant include commercial ones for third-party contents. Whatever is purchased then involves an implied contract for the use of that content, which virtually never involves the making of extra copies.

There may be contracts that faculty and staff sign with a university that controls the intellectual property of materials created by them. Copyright may be shared by a group that has worked on a project, and individual group members may not have any rights to unilaterally publish or use that image without the permission of the others. The safest way to approach this is to have clear and legally written understandings that the team abides by.

PROFESSIONAL JOURNALISTIC ETHICS

The practices of journalism have ethical implications on the handling of digital imagery in e-learning. This is because so many digital images are "published" in the electronic and print realms.

First is the concept of sufficient facts for a "package." Simply expressed, this involves the 5Ws and 1H—the who, what, when, where, why and how, the full context. This suggests that digital imagery should be part of a full learning experience and not only a piece. And the sourcing of the imagery should be the closest to reality. The fact-checking in journalism may be extended to digital imagery, to ensure proper provenance. If part of a scene is a re-enactment, that should be identified as such. If a piece of video or information comes from a press release, that should also be identified—for clear chain of custody of the information.

Second, the information-gathering methodologies suggest the need for legal acquisition of the images—without trespassing, without misrepresentation, and without privacy infringements.

Third, the images should not be untrue, defamatory or libelous. There should be no changing of the substantive facts of the images in the visual captures. There should not be any obscenity.

Fourth, based on the proper crediting of news stories, all who've contributed to the creation of digital imagery should be professionally credited.

Fifth, the efforts to be non-biased and open to a variety of voices may carry over to the digital imagery captures and creations in e-learning. For example, a variety of possible interpretations may be built into a visualization, or a variety of images may be captured showing different perspectives.

PROFESSIONAL EDUCATIONAL PRACTICES

Professional educational practices may be applied squarely to the applied ethics in digital imagery. Curriculums are vetted for meanings and messages, with the merits of a curriculum "many-valued, multifaceted, context-dependent, and relative to larger social, philosophical, and educational viewpoints" (Walker & Soltis, 1997, p. 9). A curriculum may be seen as acculturating new generations, training for work and survival, developing the whole person, supporting a political system or challenging the existing one for social improvements (Joseph, Bravmann, Windschitl, Mikel & Green, 2000). Underpinning an educational approach and curriculum may be understood to be a range of philosophical foundations about the role of education and how humans think and develop; these include understandings of ultimate reality, normative approaches to teaching and learning, and moral imperatives (Ozmon & Craver, 2003).

While different domains have different educational practices, one is likely the value of the learning domain's history ("connecting to the canon"), its guiding principles, its standards for truth, and its worldview. Those elements may be supported in the capturing of images. Then, alternate voices and perspectives may also be brought into play.

Another academic principle may be that of professional camaraderie and sharing, to a degree. That may mean the sharing of information and shared imagery in repositories and digital libraries.

Yet another value is the centrality of learners and a respect for what they may bring to a field. This suggests the importance of developing digital imagery that has high learning value, and is user-manipulable and viewable. The value of user-created imagery may enhance the collections in repositories and may enhance the richness of sample student works in a department or a course.

The importance of credits in the creation of different course materials also carries over to the creation of digital imagery for e-learning, with a need for clear provenance and clear byline crediting. A corollary involves the high credentialing needed for respect in a particular field.

NET AND WEB ETHICS

When Tim Berners-Lee founded the WWW with his creation of HTML (hypertext markup) protocols, he expressed an interest in having the WWW a tool which would help people share knowledge. He has continued this push, most recently saying: "Individual creativity is very special, but group creativity -- when we do things together, which is what we actually have to do to solve all these big problems -- is even more interesting. And one of the reasons I wanted to make the Web a big sandbox is that I wanted it to be a tool for group creativity" (Wayne, 2007, n.p.).

Open-Source Sharing

The recent advancements in Web 2.0 have led to a culture of sharing: with new online communities, an explosion in knowledge-sharing, and new ways of releasing information to be used by the public for educational purposes. Wikis, blogs, social networking spaces, video databases, immersive metaworlds, digital content repositories, constant "twitters," and shared Web-based documents have encouraged unprecedented digital sharing.

Open educational resources and free courseware enable ever richer ways of learning with high quality digital contents. Open archives initiatives make the contents of numerous repositories much more accessible and usable. The advent of the so-called Semantic Web has started, with greater interoperability and clearer metadata labeling of digital contents. Popular referatories point to digital simulations and learning objects that are housed on other sites that may be used for higher learning.

The ethics of this sharing are first to abide by the rules of play, which means that reading the fine print and abiding by the agreements is important. Also, users need to give credit where it's due for the resources they use. And most important, they should not just free-ride on those who are creating and sharing the contents, but users should also contribute to the store of knowledge. If freeware is used, the users need to contribute financially to the health of the host organization, and if they have coding talents, they need to contribute to the intellectual heart of the endeavor—by modding the code or adding to it effectively.

Building for Interchangeability and Interoperability

To contribute means building in a way that others may use the digital visuals. This means that digital images need to be in common technological languages that others may access. This means that the images must be portable, movable on and off various repositories, learning / course management systems, and libraries.

The learning objects must be interoperable and interchangeable, so the visuals may be integrated with other learning systems for learning value. The objects must be labeled with proper metadata, so they may be identifiable and perused for possible usage.

The immersive imagery should be synchronously shareability as a design principle and as an ethic. The idea: "Shareability is a design principle that refers to how a system, interface, or device engages a group of collocated, co-present users in shared interactions around the same content (or the same object)" (Hornecker, Marshall & Rogers, 2007, p. 328).

PERSONAL ETHICS

Personal ethics may seem less critical in light of these various guidelines for applied ethics in dealing with digital imagery in e-learning. However, a very practical point is that individuals on the front lines are those that execute on these various endeavors. They are the ones who capture images in the field or studios or labs. They're the ones who create and edit images. They're the ones who handle and use imagery. They're the ones who upload the digital imagery for others' use in repositories. The individuals on the front lines need the greater awareness of the ethical principles and also their own ethics and principles, for the sake of self-regulation.

Capture

- In a live photo op situation, what images should be used, and which ones shouldn't?
- In situations where an image has to "go to press" online quickly, what are ways to vet images to make sure that nothing untoward is distributed and published?
- How may stereotypes of people not be conveyed in the images that are taken of them?

Creation

- What production values should be applied to an image capture, based on the limitations of technologies, time, funding, and techniques?
- How may all contributors to digital imagery get credit?

Handling and Use

- How may emotional manipulation be avoided in an image?
- How may users of digital images vet them for accuracy and non-manipulation?
- Are there misconceptions in an image that need to be addressed?
- Are there ways to sequence imagery for learning, but without subconscious "priming" or manipulations?
- How may the provenance of visual information be established? And if these cannot be established satisfactorily, should the images be used? And if so, in what situations?
- Should commercial stock images of a certain type of plant be used even if the image is illustrative and doesn't represent the complexity of the actual plant?
- What are the unspoken conventions of what images should or should not be used? And are those fair conventions? If not, what should be changed, and how?
- How does one feel about the coloration of traditionally b/w images?

Table 1. Going self-created, open source / free or purchased (Hai-Jew, 2009)

	1. Self-Created	2. Open-Source / Free	3. Purchased
Intellectual Property (IP) Grounds for Use	Own copyright Shared copyright Byline credits	Copyright release Public domain Source crediting	Contract Source crediting (often with embedded branding)
Investment	Research Design Execution Testing Deployment (time, energy and cost)	Search Vetting Download Integration (time, energy and cost)	Search Vetting Purchase Download Integration (time, energy and cost)
Techno Considerations	Authoring tools Universal files types for output Learner connectivity Browser plug-ins / players Digital Rights Management (DRM)	Compatibility with platforms, LMS, and other systems for storage and deployment Digital Rights Management (DRM)	Compatibility with platforms, LMS, and other systems for storage and deployment Digital Rights Management (DRM)
Pedagogical Considerations	Pedagogical fit for learners Editability and updatability Creation of activities, interactivity or assignments around the digital contents	Inheritance and adjustment considerations Editability and updatability Creation of activities, interactivity or assignments around the digital contents	Inheritance and adjustment considerations Editability and updatability Creation of activities, interactivity or assignments around the digital contents
Accessibility Standards	Fit with federal and state accessibility standards?	Fit with federal and state accessibility standards?	Fit with federal and state accessibility standards?
Course Policy regarding the Use of Digital Materials	Course policy regarding use of the digital materials	Course policy regarding use of the digital materials	Course policy regarding use of the digital materials
Possible Other Concerns	Distribution of copyrighted digital materials Aging out of materials / need for update or replacement	The use of widely available contents, less originality Aging out of materials / need for update or replacement	Continuing need for payments or subscriptions Aging out of materials / need for update or replacement

Storage and Publishing Out

- How broadly should an image created for the classroom be shared on the WWW?
- How should student-created images be legally acquired for later use in academics?
- How much metadata is needed?
- What level of copyrights release should be used, or should it be "all rights reserved"?

These are a few of the potential issues that those handling e-learning visual graphics may face. What are some strategies for a person to define his or her personal values? It may help to consider a range of possible professional issues, such as the above. Considering the questions that follow would also be practical.

- What are your foundational understandings of the applied ethical values in the use of digital imagery in e-learning?

- What are the relevant ethical considerations and practical steps in the capturing, creation, handling, use, and storage of digital imagery in a learning environment? Why?

DIGITAL IMAGERY FOR E-LEARNING: GOING SELF-CREATED, OPEN-SOURCE / FREE OR PURCHASED?

There are ethical ramifications in the acquisition of digital imagery for processing or direct use in e-learning. Those working with digital imagery may consider whether to self-create the images, go with open-source and royalty-free images, or to purchase contents from a third-party content provider by considering some of the following points (Table 1).

Learners need clear understandings of where digital imagery has come from and their rights to use (and sometimes distribute) the imagery. They also need explanations of the meanings behind the imagery, for accurate learning.

CONCLUSION

Ethical considerations for the capture, creation, storage, deployment and use of digital images will vary based on the context. Cultural values, laws, professional journalistic practices, professional education practices, and personal ethics all have insights to contribute. There are many universal concepts and here, however. The time spent reflecting on applied ethical values and designing these into work processes will benefit the work with higher quality outputs. Designing values into the digital imagery pipeline may create higher professional standards in the field and optimally result in more usable digital imagery resources for e-learning for all. Accessibility is a critical quality element in the building of e-learning artifacts, learning objects and immersive experiences. Also, the portability and interchangeability of digital learning objects supports key values of the World Wide Web and the ethos of Web 2.0.

REFERENCES

Abou-Zahra, S., Brewer, J., & Arch, A. (2008). Towards bridging the accessibility needs of people with disabilities and the ageing community. In *Proceedings of the 17th International World Wide Web Conference,* Beijing, China (pp. 83 – 86).

Aldrich, C. (2005). *Learning by doing: A comprehensive guide to simulations, computer games, and pedagogy in e-learning and other educational experiences.* San Francisco, CA: Pfeiffer.

Arion, M., & Tutuianu, M. I. (2003). Online learning for the visually impaired. In C. Ghaoui (Ed.), *Usability Evaluation of Online Learning Programs* (pp. 389). Hershey, PA: Information Science Publishing.

Bricout, J. C. (2001). Making computer-mediated education responsive to the accommodation needs of students with disabilities. *Journal of Social Work Education, 37*(2), 268.

Burton, A. M., Schofield, D., & Goodwin, L. M. (2005). Gates of global perception: Forensic graphics for evidence presentation. In *Proceedings of the 13th annual ACM International Conference on Multimedia (MM'05)* (pp. 103 – 104). New York: ACM.

Carmien, S., DePaula, R., Gorman, A., & Kintsch, A. (2003). Increasing workplace independence for people with cognitive disabilities by leveraging distributed cognition among caregivers and clients. In *Conference on Supporting Group Work* (pp. 95-104). New York: ACM.

Chisholm, W. A., & Henry, S. L. (2005). Interdependent components of Web accessibility. In *Proceedings of the 2005 International Cross-Disciplinary Workshop on Web Accessibility (W4A)*, Chiba, Japan (pp. 31). New York: ACM.

Hansen, D. W., & Hansen, J. P. (2006). Eye typing with common cameras. In *Proceedings of the 2006 Symposium on Eye Tracking Research & Applications* (pp. 55). New York: ACM.

Hornecker, E., Marshall, P., & Rogers, Y. (2007). From entry to access - how shareability comes about. In *Proceedings of Designing Pleasurable Products and Interfaces (DPPI '07)*, Helsinki, Finland (pp. 328).

Ishihara, T., Takagi, H. Y., Itoh, T., & Asakawa, C. (2006). Analyzing visual layout for a non-visual presentation-document interface. In *Proceedings of the 8th International ACM SIGACCESS Conference on Computers and Accessibility* (pp. 165-172). New York: ACM.

Joseph, P. B., Bravmann, S. L., Windschitl, M. A., Mikel, E. R., & Green, N. S. (2000). *Cultures of curriculum*. Mahwah, NJ: Lawrence Erlbaum Associates.

Kelly, B., Nevile, L., Draffan, E., & Fanou, S. (2008). One world, one Web… but great diversity. In *Proceedings of the 17th International World Wide Web Conference,* Beijing, China (pp. 141-147). New York: ACM.

Knight, M. M., & Arns, L. L. (2006). The relationship among age and other factors on incidence of cybersickness in immersive environment users. In *Proceedings of the 3rd symposium on Applied perception in graphics and visualization*, Boston, Massachusetts (pp. 162). New York: ACM.

Koller, D., & Levoy, M. (2005). Protecting 3D graphics content. *Communications of the ACM, 48*(6), 74. doi:10.1145/1064830.1064861

Minsky, M. (1987). *The society of mind*. New York: Simon & Schuster.

Nakakoji, K., Takashima, A., & Yamamoto, Y. (2001). Cognitive effects of animated visualization in exploratory visual data analysis. In *Fifth International Conference on Information Visualisation (IV'01) (pp. 77)*. Washington, DC: IEEE.

Ozmon, H. A., & Craver, S. M. (2003). *Philosophical foundations of education (7th ed.)*. Upper Saddle River, NJ: Prentice Hall.

Pitts, K., & Ashwin, A. (2005). Online games and simulations as aids to learning ethos, challenges and evaluation. *Interact, 31*, 12–13.

Poluck, M. (2007). Sticky by name, sticky by nature. Technology news for people with visual impairment. ++*E-ACCESS BULLETIN, 85*. Retrieved from http://www.headstar.com/eab/

Roden, T., & Parberry, I. (2005). Designing a narrative-based audio only 3D game engine. In *Proceedings of the 2005 ACM SIGCHI International Conference on Advances in computer entertainment technology* (pp. 274-277). New York: ACM.

Rutherfoord, R. H. (2004). Copyright, law and ethics on the Web: Issues for the computing educator. *Journal of the Consortium for Computing Sciences in Colleges, 19*(3), 189.

Shapiro, J. P., & Stefkovich, J. A. (2001). *Ethical leadership and decision-making in education: Applying theoretical perspectives to complex dilemmas.* Mahwah, NJ: Lawrence Erlbaum Associates.

Sloan, D., Gibson, L., Milne, S., & Gregor, P. (2003). Ensuring optimal accessibility of online learning resources. In C. Ghaoui (Ed.), *Usability Evaluation of Online Learning Programs* (pp. 373). Hershey, PA: Information Science Publishing.

Sloan, D., Heath, A., Hamilton, F., Kelly, B., Petrie, H., & Phipps, L. (2006). Contextual Web accessibility - Maximizing the benefit of accessibility guidelines. In *Proceedings of the 2006 international cross-disciplinary workshop on Web accessibility (W4A)*, Edinburgh, UK (pp. 121).

Sribunruangrit, N., Marque, C., Lenay, C., & Gapenne, O. (2004). Graphic-user-interface system for people with severely impaired vision in mathematics class. In *Proceedings of the 26th Annual International Conference of the IEEE EMBS* (pp. 5145- 5148). Washington, DC: IEEE.

Stone, M. C. (2004). Color in information display: Principles, perception, and models. In *ACM SIGGRAPH 2004* (pp. 1-8).

Takagi, H., Itoh, T., Kawanaka, S., Kobayashi, M., & Asakawa, C. (2008). Social accessibility: Achieving accessibility through collaborative metadata authoring. In *Proceedings of the 10th international ACM SIGACCESS conference on Computers and accessibility*, Halifax, Nova Scotia, Canada (pp. 193-200). New York: ACM.

Trewin, S. M., Laff, M. R., Cavender, A. C., & Hanson, V. L. (2008). Accessibility in virtual worlds. In *Proceedings of CHI 2008*, Florence, Italy (pp. 2727 – 2732). New York: ACM.

Tufte, E. R. (1997). *Visual explanations: Images and quantities, evidence and narrative.* Cheshire, CT: Graphics Press LLC.

Tufte, E. R. (2001). *The visual display of quantitative information (2nd ed.).* Cheshire, CT: Graphics Press.

Walker, D. F., & Soltis, J. F. (1997). *Curriculum and aims (3rd ed.).* New York: Teachers College Press.

Ware, C. (2004). Foundation for a science of data visualization. In *Information Visualization: Perception for Design (2nd ed)* (pp. 14). San Francisco, CA: Morgan Kaufmann Publishers.

Wayne, J. (2007). Tim Berners-Lee's Web of people. *OJR: Focusing on the Future of Digital Journalism.* Retrieved November 9, 2008, from http://www.ojr.org/ojr/stories/071204wayne/

White, G. R., Fitzpatrick, G., & McAllister, G. (2008). Toward accessible 3D virtual environments for the blind and visually impaired. In *3rd International Conference on Digital Interactive Media in Entertainment and the Arts*, Athens, Greece (pp. 134-141). New York: ACM.

Xue, X.-B., Zhou, Z.-H., & Zhang, Z.-F. (2008). Improving Web search using image snippets. *ACM Transactions on Internet Technology, 8*(4), 21–22. doi:10.1145/1391949.1391955

KEY TERMS AND DEFINITIONS

Accessibility: The field of ensuring that the widest number of people are able to obtain information from the WWW and to use this tool to its full capacities

Accessible: Usable by a wide spectrum of people with different abilities; not denying access to those with disabilities (mental, physical, or perceptual)

Adaptive Animation: A motion-based experiential learning that is accessible to a wide range of possible users

Adaptive Devices: A tool used to enhance the perceptive powers of people who may have various sensory disabilities

ALT Text: Alternative text used to describe images and their informational value

Auditory: Related to the sense of hearing

Browser: A software program that enables the reading of encoded documents in a suitable display via the WWW

Captioning: Words that correlate with an audio recording or video to enhance use by those with hearing impairments or who need foreign-language translation

Cognition: Mental processing; the awareness from perception, learning and reasoning

Color Appearance Model (CAM): Color science conceptualizations related to digital imagery

Culture: The cumulative creation of a peoples in a time of beliefs, values and expectations; excellent creations in artwork, literature, technologies and scholarly pursuits; unique beliefs and values of subgroups

Cybersickness (Also "Simulator Sickness"): Nausea and other symptoms that may result from a virtual reality situation

Defamation: Harming a person's reputation in an undeserved way

Digital Rights Management (DRM): Laws that protect the intellectual property of creators of digital works, technology used to limit rights access to various digital files

Download: The object taken off of a server or website

Encryption: The encoding of an image or digital information to limit access

Ethics: Moral principles that guide conduct

Freeware: Software distributed without cost

GNU: A recursive acronym that means "GNU's Not Unix!"

Hard-Wiring: An biological and structural pre-setting of human ability

Intellectual Property (IP): The concept and practice of ownership and benefitting from an individual's original creative thought (usually involving patents, copyrighted materials, and trademarks)

Libel: Malicious or damaging harm to another's reputation expressed in published words or pictures

Obscenity: Indecent or lewd

Open Source: A description of software that has public source code that may be modified by users; also known as "free software" but "free" of distribution restrictions (not necessarily cost-free)

Realia: Artifacts that are based on real things or are real, used as illustrations

Reflection: Careful thought or consideration

Screen Reader: A text-to-speech translator for use by blind or low-vision users

Slander: The spreading of negative rumors via speech

Spider: An automated software robot that is sent to search the WWW for particular pages or files

Timed Text: Words that are timed to coincide with oral speech or audio or video; words superimposed on the bottom of a video for use by the hearing-impaired or those who do not understand foreign dialogue

Transcript: A written reproduction of an aural recording or video object; a written or textual record

Universal Design: A concept of building objects and environments for the widest possible use among potential users (with diverse abilities and preferences)

Usability: A key principle of human-computer interaction focused around making systems easy to use and remember, error-tolerant and resilient

Visual Acuity: The keenness or sharpness of vision

Watermarking: A computer code (visible or invisible) that identifies a particular digital work's ownership and the provenance

Section 5
Looking Ahead to a Shimmering Digital Future

Chapter 14
Future Digital Imagery

ABSTRACT

The use of digital imagery in e-learning will likely become more widespread and pedagogically sophisticated, both in the near-term and far-term. The technologies for image capture and manipulation will allow more graphical affordances, including uses in 3D, 4D, ambient spaces, augmented realities and augmented virtualities. Visualizations will likely offer a greater variety of functionalities: more aid for real-time decision-making, more complex information streams, and synchronous real-world mitigations of crises and actions. The pedagogical strategies used around images may also grow more supportive of learning, with more shared research and teaching-and-learning experiences. More accurate labeling and storage of e-learning visuals will continue, with additions on both the privately held collections and the publicly shared resources. There may well be greater diversification of the applications of digital imagery capture, authoring, use, and sharing in different learning domains. Ideally, more professional creators of digital imagery will come online from various parts of the world to enhance the shared repository of learning for a global community.

CHAPTER OBJECTIVES

- Project changes in the pedagogical uses of digital imagery
- Consider how visual literacy may evolve
- Discuss the broadening roles of digital imagery in e-learning
- Explore the future of image capture and authoring
- Consider new procedures for quality imagery creation

DOI: 10.4018/978-1-60566-972-4.ch014

- Discuss the future labeling and storage of e-learning visuals
- Reflect on possible global multicultural trends in digital imagery for e-learning
- Mull the changing ethics, laws and practices related to digital imagery in e-learning
- Explore future digital image sharing

INTRODUCTION

Digital Imagery and Informational Graphics in E-Learning: Maximizing Visual Technologies has provided a basic overview of the varied uses of digital imagery in e-learning and offered some strategies to maximize their capture, creation, use and integration in learning contexts. This text has also looked at some pedagogical theories underlying the use of digital imagery, with the intention of broadening the roles of digital imagery in e-learning. This book has highlighted some features of digital image repositories and the progress in making them more searchable. There has also been reflection on multicultural global uses of imagery, for the greatest usability in the highest variety of situations.

This last short chapter explores where this issue may progress in the next few years, with a simple extension of trend lines from the present although this approach does not offer much in the way of true predictability. After all, disruptive technologies will emerge to revolutionize various fields. New applications of extant technologies help people see with new eyes. Research and development (R&D) continues to push the edges of the possible. The speed of changes in digital imagery capture, analysis, authoring, editing, delivery, and storage has been remarkable. The "socio" aspects of socio-technical collaborations should not be short-changed, as people are endlessly inventive and collaborative. The research on human visual perception and memory will also likely surface new ideas. What may be considered "visual literacy" today likely will change as this area of digital imagery in e-learning evolves.

This chapter will consider some basic questions:

- **Pedagogical Research:** What are some areas of pedagogical research that may offer value in considering the role of digital imagery in e-learning? How may pedagogical uses of digital images apply across the virtuality continuum (real environment, augmented reality, augmented virtuality and virtual environment)?
- **Visual Literacy:** What will visual literacy of the future potential look like? What knowledge and skills will need to be known?
- **Applied Roles for Digital Imagery:** What are some innovative applied roles in graphics in e-learning for the near-future? In ambient spaces? Augmented reality? Augmented virtuality? Haptics? Interfaces? What other types of synthesized and new types of digital graphics may be used in e-learning? How may imagery be used further for information extraction? Further information creation? Where is interactive and immersive imagery headed?
- **Capturing Tools:** What cutting-edge capturing and authoring tools may be on the horizon? What types of new devices may appear? Will there be further moves towards ubiquity of capture and sharing?
- **New Procedures for Quality Imagery:** What new procedures may be developed for creating quality imagery?
- **Collaborative Image Creation:** What new ways of collaborative image creation may be forthcoming?

- **Changing Strategies for Digital Imagery Integration into E-Learning:** What are some other near-future ways to integrate graphics into e-learning?
- **Digital Visual Storage and Distribution:** How may e-learning visuals be stored, accessed, and distributed in the future? What additional functions may be added to such repositories to enhance their value? What sorts of digital rights management may exist for digital imagery? Will there be more sophisticated downstream tracking of information?
- **Designing for a Global Audience:** What new ways may exist for designing informational graphics for a global audience?
- **Changing Ethics:** How will ethics be applied to digital imagery in the near future? Will digital imagery have clearer provenance and lineage? Will the main public have better abilities (like machine intelligence) to vet images and their origins? Will there be greater accessibility accommodations to ensure accessible access? Will there be greater interoperability and interchangeability of images between various digital systems for learning? Will there be splits in the definition of digital imagery ethics along regional blocks? Group identities?
- **Future Sharing:** Will there continue to be a great outpouring of user-created imagery for public use? Will there be further sharing through Creative Commons copyright and open source methods?

The learning curve for creating and using digital imagery in e-learning is quite high. One could speculate that it's the early adopters in e-learning who may be growing in sophistication regarding digital imagery. A perusal of the research literature in computing and information sciences differs greatly from the research in the educational literature, with the first advanced in applications and innovations, and the latter straggling in adoption of techniques and technologies. One can look at the current research and begin to see some traces of a very promising future of digital image capture, creation, and use.

This chapter explores a "shimmering" future that is not yet clear but is fast arriving with technological advances and evolving techniques (see Figure 1). The future is being written moment-by-moment, by every participant. The use of digital imagery in e-learning is a very large field, and no one really has a full handle on the various applications, so this chapter is offered in a general sense.

THE PEDAGOGICAL USES OF DIGITAL IMAGERY

Broadly applied, technological affordances in Internet and Web connectivity, memory devices, and digital visual file types will likely enable more faculty members in higher education (and K-12, for that matter) to integrate digital visuals into the learning. The endeavors to improve the informational value of imagery will continue. The pushes towards clearer accessibility and metadata use will evolve. Digital imagery in all their various dimensions (one-dimensional to four-dimensional ones, and even others) may improve in terms of portability between e-learning management systems, digital libraries, and other devices. There may be improved intermixing of image types for improved informational value.

The devices on which digital imagery may be used may become more rugged, particularly for in-environment uses in wifi-enabled augmented reality spaces. The learning may be more applicable over wider physical areas. And there may be larger scale endeavors to use context-aware learning in larger and more distributed "digital enclosures," like whole cities. The projection of such images may well move beyond installations and designed rooms and be more common in shared physical spaces. If the

Figure 1. The shimmering immersive digital future in Second Life™?

idea of wearable computing and smart accessories becomes more popular, computing with digital imagery as a mainstay will proliferate beyond current common uses and mainstream conceptualizations. These may include items like watches that control a range of devices, for example (Kim, He, Lyons & Starner, 2007).

In particular domains where visuals are a central part of the learning (such as those focused on weather systems, healthcare, the biological sciences, geography, geology, anthropology, art, architecture, industrial design, history, oceanography, and others), there will continue to be inroads made in terms of digital image captures and uses for learning.

There may be a wider use of faculty and learner-created otherworldly creations, without any equivalencies in nature. Synthetic sophistication of different forms of parallel universes, pseudo-natural phenomena, digital flora and fauna, intelligent AI-driven beings, and building structures may be imagined and shared visually. People may share collective digital hallucinations through the augmentation of visuals.

The modeling of various realities will improve with closer capturing of materials and textures, difficult image captures under extreme conditions (through ice, in space, under the oceans, through solid structures, and in difficult weather conditions), whole complex environments, and sensor-informed contexts will be more accurate and realistic and immersive. Larger data sets may be able to be handled for analysis and output visually for consumption, manipulation and potential reproduction; ideally, they would be available for direct location-independent access and decision-making.

The relationship between pedagogical purposes and hedonic ones may become closer, with some shared endeavors and overlapping purposes. Surely, academic interests and business ones have overlapped with shared endeavors through grant-funded research and researcher interchanges. Many thinkers in the field have been arguing for more entertainment pleasure in learning and more challenge in fun.

VISUAL LITERACY

The current definition of "visual literacy" is a tenuous and ambiguous one. Changes in technologies, methodologies, global ethics, and practices in the uses of digital imagery will affect the definitions of this term. The knowledge and skills needed to be a "digital inhabitant" in this evolving field will likely require a sharp learning curve and constant learning and practice.

Subject matter experts (SMEs) in their various fields may have to take on ever larger roles in the creation if digital visuals to refresh the visual stores of information in their fields. With such complex high-level learning and the nuances in digital imagery capture, those various skill sets would optimally be acquired in-field for the most competent responses. The uses of undergraduate and graduate student help will also be critical in this regard. Automated captures may also stand-in for human-achieved ones. Visual literacy will have to translate into both human and machine understandings.

BROADENING ROLES OF DIGITAL IMAGERY IN E-LEARNING

Many academic fields use digital imagery in creative and value-added ways. Digital imageries are created in various dimensions and with high levels of fidelity. They are realistic and synthetic. They are ortho-rectified for accuracy. They are delivered as stand-alone images or as part of sequences or integrated simulations or immersive experiences. They are used in various ambient spaces, and they augment both reality and virtuality. They may be captured statically or in motion; they may be pre-captured or live. The types of interfaces used to interact with imagery has involved various devices—some mobile, some desktop; some haptic (touch-based); some wearable, and some built into household furniture and devices.

Research into ways to more effectively use imagery in a range of learning domains would enhance the integration and deployment of visual imagery. For example, very little is addressed in the research about imagery in ubiquitous computing: through head-mounted displays, mobile devices, computer accessories, augmented reality and augmented virtuality.

Live information streams used in "situational awareness" also lacks sufficient research in the public domain. Ways to synthesize various visual data streams also would enhance the ability to use information well for learners in particular synchronous learning situations, which may involve live decision-making and coordination. Strategies to draw out richer information extraction using computer tools would be helpful, particularly in the areas of forensic analysis, to judge the context of an information capture and maybe its validity. More needs to be examined in terms of immersive visuals and that creation of interactive, perceptual and experiential realities. More sophisticated collaborative spaces around the creation and sharing of digital visuals may enhance the capture and sharing of such resources. Wearable computers and more creative types of human-computer interfaces may mean greater channels for visual image delivery, including retinal displays for direct visual input (Beckhaus & Kruijff, 2004).

The wider publics may have increased access to the computing power needed to handle larger image datasets than can be done on desktop machines.

Some of the above endeavors are more near-future ones than others. One can hope for synergies that may stem from advances in instructional, design, technological and user strategies. It's possible that many of these endeavors are in process, with little yet that has seeped into the public research literature. Some of the information above may be currently embargoed or simply not in the open-source, public domain. Still, advances seem to come in "punctuated equilibrium" innovations when "tipping points" are reached.

THE FUTURE OF DIGITAL IMAGERY CAPTURE AND AUTHORING

The devices for the capture of imagery may allow for more complex visual information-gathering and analysis. The difficulty of image captures in traditionally difficult venues for non-experts—such as at night, under water, or in a context of variable speed of the camera-person—will improve. The various configurations and arrays of image capture devices, cameras, sensors, and data loggers may offer more immersive and live situational awareness, and it may provide digital treasure troves of synchronized data. Automated, scripted image captures may lead to even more rich information. Ideally, these devices will lower in cost while still improving in capabilities—with price points at attainable levels for those working in e-learning globally.

NEW PROCEDURES FOR QUALITY IMAGERY CREATION

A key factor in improving quality image creation revolves around education and training in regards to the various technologies involved. Photo-editing programs have improved in terms of adding value to a poor initial image capture, which in the past was a serious barrier to a usable image. One example is the ability to change lighting in a synthetic immersive scene to "accommodate the dramatic, aesthetic, and communicative functions described by traditional lighting design theories, while taking artistic constraints on style, visual continuity, and aesthetic function into account" (El-Nasr & Horswill, 2004, p. 1).

The editing and processing technologies for imagery (which involves the "encapsulation" strategy of hiding complex functionalities from non-expert users) may be more accessible to a wider audience. This may mean an increased base of individuals who may create contents. Some editing devices involve two-handed interfaces for more effective and fuller design, such as one that mimics work at a light table (which sounds quite retro but high-tech). Computational photography hasn't yet found its way to wider publics because of related costs and complexities but could result in valuable imagery.

THE STORAGE AND DISTRIBUTION OF E-LEARNING VISUALS

Digital repositories of e-learning visuals (and related multimedia) have been in development for years, with evolving methodologies for more effective ingestion, protection and storage, search, and download. In all likelihood, there will have to be improved digital rights management endeavors to govern "downstream" uses.

More informal prosumers will create contents for broader sharing. The currently dismal state of provenancing of information may be improved with automatic capturing of location-sensitive data at the point of image capture, and there may be growing sophistication about metadata captures for the various digital works put online.

GLOBAL MULTICULTURAL TRENDS IN DIGITAL IMAGERY FOR E-LEARNING

As digital imagery becomes more widespread in e-learning, with global learners, practitioners in e-learning may achieve deeper understandings of what works in capturing and creating images that may be more culture-neutral or culture-sensitive to a particular context. It is hoped that while there may be greater nuanced understandings that stereotyping may be avoided. And it's important that difficult contradictions in world views may be addressed as well without unnecessary reformatting of some of that.

CHANGING ETHICS, LAWS AND PRACTICES

The ethical considerations around digital imagery will evolve with various occurrences and debates. What happens when imagery captured on the public streets of most Western natures get used for e-learning analysis? What happens to privacy rights with ubiquitous visual captures in public spaces? Who owns his or her own image? What sort of metadata capture and provenancing will stand up in a court of law when captured through image capture devices? What sorts of standards of image forensics will be used to settle disagreements over the realities depicted in the imagery? How will accessibility to the rich imagery in e-learning be improved? Will there be greater interoperability and interchangeability of images between various digital systems for learning for greater access and less disparity between the "haves" and the "have-nots"? Will there be endeavors to enable more people in the world to create, access and use digital imagery for e-learning?

Will mash-ups loosen intellectual property understandings, or will there be more enforcement of copyright through the various court systems?

Will there be competitions between academics with different datasets of images in the same way that there is competition between them for publications, public accolades and research grants? Who owns and can use co-created imagery between faculty and learners?

Will there be splits in the definition of digital imagery ethics along regional blocks? Group identities? Institutions? Or will there be global organizations to set some standards or understandings?

FUTURE DIGITAL IMAGE SHARING

With the trends towards lower costs of digital imagery development and the proliferation of open-source and free software for image editing and authoring, many more non-expert users may offer their imagery to a wider audience, under generous copyright releases. It's possible that ad hoc "crowd-sourcing" networks might create valuable repositories of publicly accessible images. Digital repositories work as distribution points for both free and for-pay images created by users. Some sites serve as go-betweens and infomediaries between those who want digital imagery and those willing to capture those images for pay. And the power of human networks to add value to existing sets of digital images may be magnified by the intercommunications and sharing. Ideally, contributors would create a stronger sense of the importance of provenance and quality image captures.

CONCLUSION

The technological and pedagogical potentials in this area are myriad. Even currently, the use of digital imagery in e-learning has not begun to reach saturation. Too often, many of those who teach in higher education have not the time to fully integrate images. There are numerous untapped resources that haven't been shared because of the unwieldiness of incorporating human-created metadata with the images, or the challenging work of rendering the images to standards. It is hoped that digital imagery may be used more broadly for the sake of more efficacious learning and data analysis. Also, given lowered costs of entry, many from around the world should be able to engage the use and creation of digital imagery in e-learning.

Many opportunities for research also exist. A cross-domain and within-domain meta-analyses of the uses of digital imagery in e-learning would the field. Longitudinal studies of digital imagery evolution in specific fields would also offer informational value. More research on ways to enhance digital imagery capture, editing, and deployment for enhanced research and learning would improve practices.

This concluding chapter is purposefully brief, in part, because this is a nascent field. *Digital Imagery and Informational Graphics in E-Learning: Maximizing Visual Technologies* has touched on some of the activities in the use of digital imagery in e-learning. Surely, where the future goes depends really on the many faculty and content creators now and into the future. Where this field goes will depend on practitioner voices, thoughts, hands, and creative contributions to digital imagery in e-learning.

REFERENCES

Beckhaus, S., & Kruijff, E. (2004). Unconventional human computer interfaces. In *Proceedings of the SIGGRAPH 2004*.

El-Nasr, M. S., & Horswill, I. (2004). Automating lighting design for interactive entertainment. *ACM Computers in Entertainment, 2*(2), 1–19. doi:10.1145/1008213.1008214

Kim, J., He, J., Lyons, K., & Starner, T. (2007). *The gesture watch: A wireless contact-free gesture based wrist interface*. Retrieved January 24, 2009, from http://ieeexplore.ieee.org/stamp/stamp.jsp?arnumber=04373770

KEY TERMS AND DEFINITIONS

Ambient Intelligence: Electronic environments that are responsive to people

Crowd Sourcing: The use of diverse groups of collaborators to solve shared issues

Data Logger: A device that is connected to a computer and that collects information as an integrated, stand-alone unit

Digital Enclosure: An immersive digital environment that tracks users' movements and behaviors

Immersiveness: The sense of a 3D full-surround digital environment, whether virtual, augmented reality, or a combination

Infomediary: An entity that gathers information and distributes it

Metadata: Data about information

Metadata Harvester: A software program that collects metadata automatically

Pervasive: Ever-present, surrounding fully

Sensor: A device that captures information either as a stand-alone device or part of a larger interconnected array

Ubiquitous (Ubi) Computing: Pervasive computing, anytime and anywhere; also mobile computing

Wearable Computing: The integration of computers and computing functionalities into clothing and accessories

APPENDIX

ACRONYM AND TECH SHORTHAND GLOSSARY

These are some acronyms commonly used in e-learning (Table 1). These may enhance functioning in this wide and complex field of digital imagery used in e-learning.

Table 1.

ADA	Americans with Disabilities Act
API	application programming interface
AR	augmented reality
ASR	automatic speech recognition
AV	augmented virtuality
AVR	augmented virtual reality
CAD	computer aided design
CAM	color appearance model
CAM	color management system
CATIA	computer-aided three-dimensional interactive application
CBIR	content-based image retrieval (from multimedia repositories)
CC	closed captioning
CDE	collaborative development environments
CFD	computational fluid dynamics
CFT	cross functional team
CG	computer graphics
CGI	computer generated imagery
CID	culture and image design
CLC	collaboration life cycle
CLE	continuous learning environment
CMC	computer mediated communications
CMYK	cyan, magenta, yellow and black
COPPA	Children's Online Privacy Protection Act
CSCW	computer supported collaborative work
CT	computer tomography
CVE	collaborative virtual environment
DEM	digital elevation model
DICOM	Digital Imaging and Communications in Medicine
DIS	distributed interactive simulation
DRM	Digital Rights Management
DTED	digital terrain elevation data
EEG	electroencephalogram
FACS	facial action coding system

FERPA	Family Education Rights and Privacy Act
GI	geographic information
GIS	geographic information systems
GUI	graphical user interface
GVT	global virtual team
HDR	high dynamic range
HMD	head-mounted display
I/O	input / output
IP	intellectual property
IPT	image perspective transformation ; (also) immersive projection technology
IR	information retrieval
IT	information technology
IVE	immersive virtual environments
JPEG, JPG	joint photographic experts group graphics file type / extension
LDR	low dynamic range
LIDAR	light detection and ranging
LO	learning object
LSCOM	Large-Scale Concept Ontology of Multimedia
MIR	multimedia information retrieval
MOA	memorandum of agreement
MOO	Multiple User Domains Object Oriented
MP3	Moving Picture Experts Group Layer-3 Audio
MP4	MPEG Layer-4 Audio
MRI	magnetic resonance imaging
MUVE	multi user virtual environments
MVE	modular visualization environment
NDK	near-duplicate keyframes
nm	nanometer
NPR	non-photorealistic rendering
OCR	optical character recognition
P2P	peer-to-peer
PROFI	perceptually-relevant retrieval of figurative images
PSE	problem solving environment
QBE	query by one example
QBH	query by humming
RF	relevance feedback
RGB	red, green, blue
ROI	region of interest
SH	spatial hypermedia
SVW	social virtual world
VC	virtual community
VE	virtual environment

VI	visually impaired
VLE	virtual learning environment
VMS	video media spaces
VQ	vector quantization
VR	virtual reality
VRML	Virtual Reality Markup Language
VT	virtual teaming
wi-fi	wireless fidelity
WISM	wireless image sensor networks

About the Contributors

Shalin Hai-Jew works as an instructional designer at Kansas State University and teaches for WashingtonOnline (WAOL). She has BAs in English and psychology, an MA in English (from the University of Washington) and an Ed.D. in Educational Leadership (2005) with a focus on Public Administration (from Seattle University, where she was a Morford Scholar). In the People's Republic of China, she taught at Jiangxi Normal University (1988 – 1990) and Northeast Agriculture University (1992 – 1994), the latter two years with the United Nations Development Programme (UNDP)/ United Nations Volunteers Programme (UNVP). She was a tenured faculty member in English / Communications, at Shoreline Community College. She writes as Eruditio Loginquitas in the blog she founded named Instructional Design Open Studio (IDOS). She is currently a reviewer for *Educause Quarterly* and MERLOT's *Journal of Online Learning and Teaching (JOLT)*, both by invitation. She was born in Huntsville, Alabama. She may be reached at haijes@gmail.com. She worked for an aerospace company as a faculty fellow to support their distance learning endeavors for two summers.

* * *

Brent A. Anders works as an Electronic Media Coordinator for the Office of Mediated Education at Kansas State University. His job duties include: educational media consulting, web accessibility/ usability, and videography (directing, capturing, editing and final production). Mr. Anders has a Bachelor's degree in Psychology, human computer interaction focus, and a Master's degree in Education, instructional technology focus. He also serves in the National Guard as a senior instructor for the Basic Non-commissioned Officers Course. Mr. Anders has been in the education field for over 10 years dealing with military training, distance education, educational media and higher education in general.

Jason Caudill is an Assistant Professor of Business at Carson-Newman College where he works in the Department of Management Information Systems and teaches courses including business information systems, networking, and general business courses such as introduction to management and entrepreneurship. Caudill has extensive experience in information systems, ranging from front-line technical support to system administration and technical documentation and training. Caudill's research interests include technology management and open source software. His doctoral work was done at the University of Tennessee, Knoxville, in Instructional Technology.

Diana Marrs has an MA in teaching and an MSIS degree. For eight years, she has managed the development and support of distance courses at the University of Kansas Edwards Campus. She also manages classroom technology including video conferencing and conducts faculty trainings for blackboard, video conferencing, and educational technology. She is currently working on her Ph.D. in Curriculum and Teaching at the University of Kansas (KU).

Ramesh C. Sharma holds a PhD in Education in the area of Educational Technology. He has been a teacher trainer and has taught Educational Technology, Educational Research and Statistics, Educational Measurement and Evaluation, Special Education, Psychodynamics of Mental Health Courses. He specializes in Web 2.0 technologies and on-line learning. He is the co-Editor of 'Asian Journal of Distance Education' ISSN 1347-9008, (www.ASIANJDE.org). He has co-authored a book on *Distance Education Research*, co-edited a book entitled *"Interactive Multimedia in Education and Training"* and *"Cases on Global E-Learning Practices: Successes and Pitfalls"* (Co-Editor Dr Sanjaya Mishra, both from Idea Group, USA). He is also an Advisory Board Member and author for the *"Encyclopedia of Distance Learning"* (four-volume set) released by Idea Group Publishing. He has also co-edited *"Ethical Practices and Implications in Distance Learning"* (2008) published from IGI-Global, USA.

Jason Maseberg-Tomlinson, M.S., is the Disability / Technology Specialist for Disability Support Services at Kansas State University. He has worked extensively with web accessibility, Braille, Music Braille, and adaptive technology. He currently focuses his work on distance education and learning management system accessibility. He is pursuing a doctorate at Kansas State University.

Index

photomosaic 235

photorealism 116

photo-realistic 153, 159, 160, 167

Piagetian model 184

pixellation 87

plenoptic 91, 113, 116

polychromatic 213

power distance 213

pre-attentive processing 27

present state 145

problem-solving environments (PSE) 50

process loss 220

proprioceptor 200

proscriptive 100

prosumers 57

prototype 158, 167, 210, 220

psychomotor skills 7

puzzle solving 72

R

raw files 220

raw image capture 150, 156, 165

recommender systems 149

redundancy principle 8, 105

referatory 264

reference photography 200

reflective interactivity 172

region of interest (ROI) 102, 116

relevance feedback 247, 264

remote gesturing technology 220

repository system 149

reusable learning object (RLO) 235

S

saccades 4, 26

satellite imagery 144

scaling algorithms 73

scanpaths 26

selective fidelity 191

semantic gap 247, 265

semiotics 91

semi-transparency 91

sensory channels 5

sensory-motor 6

sentient chips 54

shape grammars 213

short-wavelength 3

similarity retrieval 102, 113

single-lens reflex (SLR) 119

situated cognition 146, 160, 170, 177, 185

situational awareness 182

skill development 170

social liberation 8

social presence 200, 208

sociomedia 187

soft controlling 175

spatial contiguity principle 8

spatial hypermedia 87, 104, 111, 116, 182, 219

spatial matching 72

spectral 87, 103, 121, 122, 129

spectroscopes 119

speech recognition 71

spherical imagery 120

spherical motion imagery 120

static media theory 185

stereoscopic imaging 120

stereoscopic vision 181

stimulated recall 41

striate cortex 6

student retention 235

subconscious priming 9

subject matter expert (SME) 203

surface computing 81, 87

syllogisms 107

synaesthesia 235

synaptic paths 5

synchronous video 130

synthetic images 87

synthetic overlays 68

T

tangible interface 200

task efficiency 179, 200

team opacity 209, 220

telepresence 40, 41, 146, 147, 197

temporal bridge 209

temporal contiguity principle 8

temporal lobe 6

tensor field 87, 117

tessellation 87

textual narratives 159

texture gradients 23